450

American English Rhetoric

A Two-Track Writing Program
for Intermediate and
Advanced Students of English
as a Second Language

SECOND EDITION

Robert G. Bander

Holt, Rinehart and Winston

New York   Chicago   San Francisco   Atlanta   Dallas
Montreal   Toronto   London   Sydney

Library of Congress Cataloging in Publication Data

Bander, Robert G.
   American English rhetoric.

   Includes index.
   1. English language—Textbooks for foreigners.
I. Title.
PE1128.B297   1978   808'.0427   77-8654
ISBN 0-03-089979-6

ACKNOWLEDGMENTS

The author and publisher have made every effort to trace the ownership of all selections found in this book and to make full acknowledgment for their use. Thematic titles (within quotation marks) have been supplied by this author for the assistance of students.

Grateful acknowledgment is made to the following authors, publishers, agents, and individuals for their permission to reprint copyrighted materials.

ASSOCIATED BOOK PUBLISHERS LTD., for *The English Language* by C. L. Wrenn. Published by Methuen & Company, Ltd., London.

BRANDT & BRANDT. Excerpt from "Latinos vs. Gringos" by Carlos Fuentes. *Holiday* Magazine (October 1962). Reprint from *Holiday Magazine* © 1962 The Curtis Publishing Company. Also reprinted by permission of Brandt & Brandt.

BROADCAST MUSIC, INC., for "Grant and Lee: A Study in Contrasts" by Bruce Catton. Copyright © 1956 by Broadcast Music, Inc. Reprinted by permission.

COLUMBIA UNIVERSITY PRESS from Robert W. Smuts, *Women and Work in America*, pp. 36, 64. Copyright © 1959.

W. H. FREEMAN AND COMPANY PUBLISHERS from "The Ice Fish" by Johan T. Ruud, *Scientific American* (November 1965), "The Arrow of Time" by David Layzer (December 1975), "The Photographic Lens" by William H. Price (August 1976), "Science and the Citizen" (June 1976), "The Purple Membrane of Salt-Loving Bacteria" by Walter Stoeckenius (June 1976), "Joey: A 'Mechanical Boy'" by Bruno Bettelheim (March 1959), "Mars" by James B. Pollack (September 1975), "An Electron-Hole Liquid" by Gordon A. Thomas (June 1976).

THOMAS C. GRIFFITH extracts from "The Pacific Northwest" by Thomas C. Griffith from *The Atlantic Monthly* (April 1976). Copyright © 1976 by the Atlantic Monthly Company, Boston, Mass. Reprinted with permission.

HAMISH HAMILTON LTD. and MRS. JAMES THURBER. "The Fairly Intelligent Fly," "The Lion Who Wanted to Zoon;" "The Crow and the Oriole." Corp. © 1940 James Thurber. Copr. © 1968 Helen Thurber. From *Fables for Our Time*, published by Harper & Row, New York. Originally printed in *The New Yorker*. "Courtship Through the Ages." Copr. © 1945 James Thurber. Copr. © 1973 Helen W. Thurber and Rosemary Thurber Sauers. From *My World—and Welcome to It*, published by Harcourt Brace Jovanovich. Originally printed in *The New Yorker*.

HARCOURT BRACE JOVANOVICH, INC. and EDWARD ARNOLD (PUBLISHERS) LTD., for "What I Believe," Copyright © 1939, 1967 by E. M. Forster. Reprinted from his volume, *Two Cheers for Democracy* by permission of Harcourt Brace Jovanovich, Inc. and Edward Arnold (Publishers) Ltd.

HARPER & ROW PUBLISHERS, INC. Excerpts from pp. 17–18 and 24–25 in *Here Is New York* by E. B. White. Copyright 1949 by E. B. White. Reprinted by permission of Harper & Row, Publishers, Inc. Adaptation of "Survey Q4R Method of Studying" from *Effective Study*, 4th ed., by Francis P. Robinson. Copyright 1941, 1946 by Harper & Row, Publishers, Inc. Copyright © 1961, 1970 by Francis P. Robinson. From pp. 99–101 in *Science and Human Life* by J. B. S. Haldane. Copyright 1933 by Harper & Brothers. Renewed 1961 by J. B. S. Haldane. All by permission of Harper & Row, Publishers. Appendix 4, pp. 351–354. Adapted from pp. 439–445, after Merle Fifield, *The English Verb*. Muncie, Ind.: Ball State University, unpublished manuscript. Appendix 6, pp. 362–365. Adapted from pp. 468–469 in *Language and Life in the U.S.A.*, 2nd ed., by Gladys G. Doty and Janet Ross. Copyright © 1960, 1968 by Gladys G. Doty and Janet Ross. By permission of Harper & Row, Publishers, Inc.

Preface

The unique feature of this text for students of English as a second language is that it joins an intensive expository composition program with a handbook approach to essentials of grammar, punctuation, and vocabulary. The two-books-in-one concept of this second edition of *American English Rhetoric* makes it possible for an instructor to use the book at either the Intermediate or Advanced level.

Composition: A Two-Track Program

The usefulness of the text for both Intermediate and Advanced students is increased by the two-track composition sections at the close of Chapters 2–10. Each chapter's composition assignment offers two distinctly different sets of topics and writing approaches. Group I topics, in addition to being more basic than those of Group II, are also more highly structured; the Group I track provides practice in the same method of expository development studied elsewhere in a chapter. In contrast, Group II topics supply a creative alternative to Group I subjects for students who are especially imaginative or advanced. Here writing assignments are drawn from James Thurber fables and Woody Allen fantasies; "Doonesbury," "Peanuts," and *New Yorker* cartoons; a cryonics advertisement and the composition of a French schoolgirl; the fanciful novel *Alice's Adventures in Wonderland* and the rock music publication *Rolling Stone*. As students move through the book, composition topics become increasingly more complex.

Concluding the writing program, Chapter 11 contains four challenging composition units on the subjects of censorship, social protest, women's liberation, and love. An instructor may use these topics for special purposes throughout the course or save them for an end-of-course evaluation of student learning. Students will find seventy-four practice exercises to sharpen their writing, punctuation, and grammar skills. An especially useful reference source is the ten-part Appendix.

Since most chapters contain a wider selection of composition topics and writing approaches than are likely to be selected each week, an instructor can assign unused topics from earlier chapters as the course progresses.

Using the Model Selections

Each chapter from 2 through 10 opens with a model paragraph or composition that has its expository techniques annotated in the left margin.

These annotations suggest points for discussion and, consequently, models are seldom analyzed at length in the chapter itself. The models also provide material for dictation and in-class analysis.

Dictation has been found to be effective in teaching writing to students of English as a second language. If an instructor favors this approach, part or all of the model selections at the beginnings of Chapters 2 to 10 may be dictated as the first learning step. Dictation may be staged in two ways: "live" during a class session, or voice and energy may be conserved by recording the dictation on a cassette tape that is later played in class. If an instructor is not a native speaker of English, the dictation might be recorded by one who is.

Instructors who do not wish to teach composition by dictation may use the model selections solely as a basis for class discussion. They may utilize discussion of the annotated models to discover whether students have understood the annotated points. If any expository techniques seem unclear, other examples should be chosen from the text, or from other texts students are using.

How the Second Edition Has Been Changed

Although the format of the Second Edition is essentially the same as that of the First, the book incorporates some important changes that reflect the perceptive comments of both instructors and students. First, it is condensed from fifteen to eleven chapters. These chapters are reorganized to place basic material early in the text: subordination in Chapter 1, definite and indefinite articles in Chapter 2, modal auxiliaries in Chapter 3. Second, a clearcut division now occurs in Chapter 5 between earlier concentration on the paragraph in Chapters 1–4 to later focus on the longer expository composition in Chapters 5–10. This shift from paragraph to composition writing allows an instructor to adjust the use of the book to the students' demonstrated abilities and potentials. Third, copying as a composition approach is replaced by writing about varied topics supplied in each chapter. The topics are sometimes controversial, often innovative, hopefully always provocative. Fourth, an inner consistency of gradually increasing proficiency has been provided in vocabulary study; in writing, punctuation, and grammar exercises; and in composition assignments.

Some successful sections of the First Edition have been further developed. Outlining receives a fuller treatment in Chapter 5. Transitions, vital to expository writing, are presented with exercises in every chapter. More questions appear in the Questions for Discussion and Review sections of Chapters 2–10. The text contains seventy-four practice exercises and reviews; most have been lengthened with items gradated toward a gradually higher learning level. Four new model paragraphs and compositions with interest-generating topics replace earlier model selections. The Appendix contains four new parts: 5, Definite and Indefinite Articles; 8, Glossary of

Standard Usage; 9, Glossary of Grammatical Terms; and 10, Using Principles of Phonics to Recognize and Pronounce English Words.

Some less useful sections of the earlier edition, among them American English Idiom Study, have been eliminated. Vocabulary study, formerly geared to defining words in sentences, is changed to emphasize cloze procedure and context analysis. Readings and exercises on scientific and technical subjects now take the place of many of the First Edition's literary readings.

Some missing items have been added. The increase in composition topics has been noted above. Expanded, more concentrated coverage is given to definite and indefinite articles. Students gain much more practice in using modal auxiliaries through additional exercises. Complementing the First Edition's section on Writing an Introduction is a new section, Writing a Conclusion. Instructors who have requested more review exercises in writing, punctuation, and grammar will find them beginning in Chapter 5 and continuing to the end of the book.

The Second Edition's more intensive focus on contemporary life in the U.S.A., the text's increased range of humorous selections, and the illustrations appearing in each chapter give both the look and substance of a new book that still retains the fiber of the old.

The idea for this text grew from my reading of two scholarly articles. One was a monograph by Jean Praninskas. The second was the article "Cultural Thought Patterns in Intercultural Education" (*Language Learning*, XVI, nos. 1–2, 1–20), written by Professor Robert B. Kaplan of the English Communication Program for Foreign Students at the University of Southern California. Dr. Kaplan has graciously consented to the reprinting of his article in the *Instructor's Manual* to this text.

Experience in teaching European, Asian, and Arab students in their own countries has guided me in developing this book. From classes at Liceo Scientifico Vittorio Veneto in Milan and at the University of Pisa; from students at the University of Petroleum and Minerals in Dhahran, Saudi Arabia; from colleagues at the A.U.A. Language Center in Bangkok; and from East-West Center students at the University of Hawaii, I have learned the techniques that are offered here.

The single most important influence on this text has come from Professor Kaplan; consulting with him in Los Angeles gave me valuable direction in shaping the Second Edition. I am grateful as well to the students I have taught, both at home and abroad. Whatever they may have learned, I know that I have been the chief beneficiary of our collaborations.

The patient and supportive Holt, Rinehart and Winston staff—especially Harriett Prentiss, Ruth Chapman, Anita Baskin, and Susan Katz—and my alert and persevering wife Margaret have been vital forces in allowing me to add new wine to old bottles. I want to thank Professor Louis Trimble of the University of Washington for helping to identify material on scientific and technical writing to add to the text. And the others will know who they are: friends—both lay and professional—who, though unnamed, are far from unvalued.

R.G.B.

Palo Alto, California
October, 1977

Contents

Acknowledgments   ii
Preface   v

Chapter 1: The English Paragraph   1
UNITY   2
COHERENCE   3
THE TOPIC SENTENCE   5
THE PARAGRAPH OUTLINE   17
TWO KEYS—AND A QUESTION   18
The First Key: Transitions   19
The Second Key: Subordination   21
The Question   26

VOCABULARY GROWTH   27
Paragraph Puzzle   27
Word Clues   28

COMPOSITION: SHOW WHAT YOU HAVE
    LEARNED   30
Group I: Topics for the Humanities Student   30
Group II: Topics for the Science Student   30

Chapter 2: The Chronological Paragraph   31
WRITING ANALYSIS   32
Pronouns as Transitions   32
Chronological Paragraph Development   34
Variety in Sentence Openings   38
Variety in Sentence Structure and Length   40
Using Strong Active Verbs   43

PUNCTUATION POINTS   43
Two Uses of the Comma   43
Punctuating a Series   48

GRAMMAR SKILLS   50
Definite and Indefinite Articles   50
Choosing Correct Prepositions   51
Controlled Use of the Passive Voice   53
The Compound Predicate   55

QUESTIONS FOR DISCUSSION AND REVIEW   57
VOCABULARY GROWTH   57

Paragraph Puzzle   57
Word Clues   58

COMPOSITION: SHOW WHAT YOU HAVE
    LEARNED   60
Group I: Topics for Writing a Chronological Paragraph   60
Group II: Topics to Challenge Your Imagination   60

Chapter 3: The Spatial Paragraph   63

WRITING ANALYSIS   64

Transitions for Spatial Development   64
Spatial Paragraph Development   65
Review of the Controlling Idea   67
Writing in Specific Terms   69
Understanding Expletives   70

PUNCTUATION POINTS   72

The Comma Splice   72
The Run-on Sentence   74

GRAMMAR SKILLS   75

Modal Auxiliaries   75
Showing Possession   81
The Sentence Fragment   84

QUESTIONS FOR DISCUSSION AND REVIEW   86
VOCABULARY GROWTH   86

Paragraph Puzzle   86
Word Clues   87

COMPOSITION: SHOW WHAT YOU HAVE
    LEARNED   89
Group I: Topics for Writing a Spatial Paragraph   89
Group II: Topics to Challenge Your Imagination   89

Chapter 4: The Expository Paragraph (Developed by Examples)   92

WRITING ANALYSIS   93

Transitions for Expository Development   93
Expository Paragraph Development (by examples)   94
Variety in the Simple Sentence   98
Eliminating Unnecessary Words   100
The Periodic Sentence   102

PUNCTUATION POINTS   104

Understanding Restrictive and Nonrestrictive Elements   104

GRAMMAR SKILLS   106

Principles of Modification   106
Agreement of Pronoun and Antecedent   112

Agreement of Subject and Verb 114
Using Participles and Participial Phrases 116

QUESTIONS FOR DISCUSSION AND REVIEW 120
VOCABULARY GROWTH 120
Paragraph Puzzle 120
Word Clues 121

COMPOSITION: SHOW WHAT YOU HAVE
   LEARNED 123
Group I: Topics for Writing a Paragraph
   Developed by Examples 123
Group II: Topics to Challenge Your Imagination 124

Chapter 5: The Expository Composition (Developed by Examples) 126

WRITING ANALYSIS 128
Review of Transitions 128
Writing a Longer Composition 129
The Composition Outline 130
   What a Developed Outline Is 130
   Why It Is Fundamental to Writing 131
   How an Outline Is Thought Out 131
The Thesis Statement 134
Linking Paragraphs Together 135
Expository Development (by examples) 137

PUNCTUATION POINTS 142
The Semicolon 142
The Colon 144

GRAMMAR SKILLS 145
Parallelism 145
Correct Pronoun Reference 148
Review of Definite and Indefinite Articles 150

QUESTIONS FOR DISCUSSION AND REVIEW 151
VOCABULARY GROWTH 152
Paragraph Puzzle 152
Word Clues 152

COMPOSITION: SHOW WHAT YOU HAVE
   LEARNED 155
Group I: Topics for Writing a Composition
   Developed by Examples 155
Group II: Topics to Challenge Your Imagination 156

Chapter 6: The Expository Composition (Developed by Comparison and Contrast) 159

WRITING ANALYSIS 161
Transitions for Comparison and Contrast 161

Expository Development (by comparison and contrast)   162
Using Figurative Language   175
PUNCTUATION POINTS   177
Punctuating Parenthetical Elements   177
GRAMMAR SKILLS   180
The Elliptical Clause   180
Correlative Conjunctions   181
Review of Prepositions   183
QUESTIONS FOR DISCUSSION AND REVIEW   185
VOCABULARY GROWTH   185
Paragraph Puzzle   185
Word Clues   186
COMPOSITION: SHOW WHAT YOU HAVE
    LEARNED   189
Group I: Topics for Writing a Comparison or Contrast   189
Group II: Topics to Challenge Your Imagination   191

Chapter 7: The Expository Composition (Developed by Cause and Effect)   193

WRITING ANALYSIS   195
Synonyms as Transitions   195
Expository Development (by cause and effect)   196
Writing an Introduction   203
Review of Wordiness   211
PUNCTUATION POINTS   213
Using the Apostrophe   213
GRAMMAR SKILLS   215
Dangling Elements   215
Review of Subordination   217
QUESTIONS FOR DISCUSSION AND REVIEW   219
VOCABULARY GROWTH   220
Paragraph Puzzle   220
Word Clues   221
COMPOSITION: SHOW WHAT YOU HAVE
    LEARNED   224
Group I: Topics for Writing a Causal Analysis   224
Group II: Topics to Challenge Your Imagination   225

Chapter 8: The Expository Composition (Developed by Definition)   227

WRITING ANALYSIS   229
Coordinating Conjunctions as Transitions   229

Expository Development (by definition)   229
Force in Writing   237
Writing a Conclusion   239
Review of Varying Sentence Openings   244

PUNCTUATION POINTS   246

Punctuating Appositives   246

GRAMMAR SKILLS   247

Correct Agreement of Relative Pronouns   247
Review of Modal Auxiliaries   250
Review of Prepositions   251

QUESTIONS FOR DISCUSSION AND REVIEW   252
VOCABULARY GROWTH   253

Paragraph Puzzle   253
Word Clues   254

COMPOSITION: SHOW WHAT YOU HAVE
    LEARNED   257

Group I: Topics for Writing a Definition   257
Group II: Topics to Challenge Your Imagination   257

Chapter 9: The Expository Composition (Developed by Logical Division)   261

WRITING ANALYSIS   263

Repeating a Word for Coherence   263
Expository Development (by logical division)   265
Style in Writing   271
The Rhetorical Question   276
Review of Transitions within a Paragraph   277

PUNCTUATION POINTS   278

Miscellaneous Uses of the Comma   278

GRAMMAR SKILLS   279

Irregular Comparatives and Superlatives   279
Review of Definite and Indefinite Articles   281

QUESTIONS FOR DISCUSSION AND REVIEW   282
VOCABULARY GROWTH   283

Paragraph Puzzle   283
Word Clues   284

COMPOSITION: SHOW WHAT YOU HAVE
    LEARNED   286

Group I: Topics for Writing a Composition
    Developed by Logical Division   286
Group II: Topics to Challenge Your Imagination   288

Chapter 10: The Expository Composition (Developed by Logical Division)   291

WRITING ANALYSIS   293
Repeating a Structural Unit for Coherence   293
Expository Development (by logical division)   295
Tone in Writing   303
Two Matters of Word Arrangement   306
Review of Transitions between Paragraphs   308

PUNCTUATION POINTS   308
Punctuation Review   308

GRAMMAR SKILLS   311
Misplaced Modifiers   311
Review of Parallelism   313
Review of Prepositions   314

QUESTIONS FOR DISCUSSION AND REVIEW   315
VOCABULARY GROWTH   315
Paragraph Puzzle   315
Word Clues   316

COMPOSITION: SHOW WHAT YOU HAVE LEARNED   318
Group I: Topics for Writing a Composition Developed by Logical Division   318
Group II: Topics to Challenge Your Imagination   320

Chapter 11: Advanced Composition Topics   322

Topic 1: Censorship—a Burning Issue   322
Topic 2: Letting the Public Voice Be Heard   325
Topic 3: A Delicate Balance: Women's Liberation and Family Life   327
Topic 4: The Trials of Love   330

Appendix

1: Rules for Punctuation   333
2: Rules for Capitalization   343
3: Rules for Spelling   345
4: Principle Parts of Irregular Verbs   351
5: Definite and Indefinite Articles   355
6: Uses of Prepositions   362
7: Word Stems, Prefixes, and Suffixes   365
8: Glossary of Standard Usage   376
9: Glossary of Grammatical Terms   381
10: Using Principles of Phonics to Recognize and Pronounce English Words   390

Index   394

Chapter **1**

The
English
Paragraph

Drawing by W. Steig; © *1970, The New Yorker Magazine, Inc.*

A lonely clown in a drifting lifeboat has a special problem. All his life he has given pleasure to audiences with his antics and his painted-on smile. Floating on the sea, though, he turns his smile to a world that cannot understand it. Suddenly he can no longer communicate.

A student learning to write in a language that is not his own has a similar problem. Like the clown, he must learn to communicate in terms that his new world will understand. But every writer finds it hard to express in a new language the many ideas filling his mind. To release these bottled-up ideas, he must gain an understanding of the vocabulary and writing techniques of the new language. Only when he has done this will he be able to present himself to best advantage in writing.

This chapter offers the basic information needed for you to begin to write English well. To start with, you will examine the nature of the English paragraph. The Chinese have a saying, "A journey of 1,000 miles begins with the first step." Studying the material in this chapter is your first step toward mastery of written English.

Unity

For some international students, the concept of an English paragraph may be quite new. Just as a sentence is a group of words conveying a complete thought, so a paragraph is a group of sentences advancing the thought somewhat further. Each paragraph should leave a reader more informed at the end than he was at the beginning. A paragraph is normally identified by having its first sentence indented a few spaces. This indentation tells a reader that the material in the paragraph represents a separate unit of thought.

The fact that an English paragraph constitutes a separate unit of thought is its most important quality. In composing a paragraph, a writer discusses only one topic or one aspect of a topic. This characteristic of a paragraph is known as **unity**, or singleness of purpose. Because an English paragraph concentrates on a single idea, all the facts, examples, and reasons used to develop that idea must be relevant. A writer who introduces material that is not directly related to a paragraph's topic runs the risk of losing his reader.

Study the following short paragraph to help you better understand what unity is. The boldfaced words are transitions (see page 20). Notice that every sentence expands on the topic announced in the opening sentence: the beginnings of the sea. The writer even restates the subject in the fourth sentence to remind her reader (and perhaps herself) that all of the details toward the end of the paragraph should explain how the earth got its ocean —and *only* that topic.

Beginnings are apt to be shadowy, and so it is with the beginnings of that great mother of life, the sea. Many people have debated how and when the earth got its **ocean**, and it is not surprising that their explanations do not always agree. **For** the plain and inescapable truth is that no one was there to see, and in the absence of eyewitness accounts there is bound to be a certain amount of disagreement. **So** if I tell here a **story** of how the young planet Earth acquired an ocean, it must be a **story** pieced together from many sources and containing many whole chapters the details of which we can only imagine. The **story** is founded **on the testimony** of the earth's most ancient rocks, which were young when the earth was young; **on other evidence** written on the face of the earth's satellite, the moon; and **on hints** contained in the history of the sun and whole universe of star-filled space. **For** although no man was there to witness this cosmic birth, the stars and the moon and the rocks were there, and, **indeed**, had much to do with the fact that there is an ocean.

"Mother Sea: The Gray Beginnings," Rachel Carson, *The Sea Around Us*

Coherence

Writing in a foreign language at first may seem to be very like writing in your native language, but of course it isn't. The problem stems from more than a mere difference between words or symbols. It is also a matter of the arrangement of words together in a sentence. The words and word groups of one language don't fit together in the same way as the words of another language do. Perhaps even more important, ideas don't fit together in the same way from language to language. A Russian, an Egyptian, a Brazilian, and a Japanese tend to arrange their ideas on the same subject in quite different ways within a paragraph. These differences exist because each culture has its own special way of thinking. And how a person thinks largely determines how he writes. Thus, in order to write well in English, a foreign student should first understand how English speakers usually arrange their ideas. This arrangement of ideas can be called a **thought pattern**. And, even though English thought patterns are not native to you, once you understand them you can more easily imitate them. By doing this, you will succeed in writing more effective English.

A basic feature of the English paragraph is that it normally follows a straight line of development. This English thought pattern is important for a writer to understand. The paragraph often begins with a statement of its central idea, known as a **topic sentence**, followed by a series of subdivisions of the central idea. These subdivisions have the purpose of developing the topic sentence, preparing for the addition of other ideas in later paragraphs. In following a direct line of development, an English paragraph is very different, for instance, from an Oriental paragraph, which tends to follow a circular line of development. It also differs from a Semitic paragraph, which tends to follow parallel lines of development. A paragraph in Spanish, or in some other Romance language, differs in still another way: its line of thought is sometimes interrupted by rather complex digressions. Similarly, a paragraph in Russian often contains digressions. In different cultures, the various approaches to making a written statement are related to each culture's culturally influenced pat-

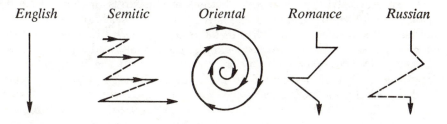

English   *Semitic*   *Oriental*   *Romance*   *Russian*

Diagram from Robert B. Kaplan, "Cultural Thought Patterns in Inter-Cultural Education," *Language Learning*, 16, nos. 1 and 2: 15.

terns of thinking, none of which is necessarily better than any other. For students of composition, however, an awareness that rhetorical patterns differ from one culture to another can help them become more quickly proficient in a writing pattern that is not native to them. The movement of paragraph development in various cultures is graphically represented on the preceding page (broken lines indicate largely irrelevant material introduced into a paragraph.

The typically straight line of development of an English paragraph is the basis of its particular type of **coherence.** An English paragraph is coherent when its ideas are clearly related to each other in orderly sequence. Each sentence in such a paragraph should naturally grow out of each previous sentence in developing the central idea. Ideally, there should be a sense of movement or flow, a going forward and building on what has been said before. You may hold your reader's interest if your paragraphs contain an occasional obscure, weak, or repetitious sentence, but too many such paragraphs could cause the reader to give up.

One way to achieve coherence is to arrange a paragraph's details in a systematic way that is appropriate for the subject matter. For example, many writers of English place their supporting detail in order of importance, often starting with the least important detail and ending with the most important one. Paragraph development by order of importance is an especially helpful way to gain coherence when you are writing an opinion or an argument. Paragraphs are also developed chronologically (mentioning events in the order they occur in time), spatially (moving from discussing one location to discussing another in some orderly sequence), from the general to the specific, or from the specific to the general. You can expect to use all of these systems of organizing ideas within a paragraph as you progress through the book, writing chronological and spatial paragraphs and both short and long expository compositions.

Another way to ensure a paragraph's coherence is to add various transitions to alert the reader to the direction the developing idea is taking. In the following paragraph, the writer gains coherence by leading the reader from one sentence to the next with transitional signals:

(1)Far more striking than any changes in the kinds of work done by women in the [U.S.A.] labor force is the shift of wives and mothers from household activities to the world of paid employment. (2)Emphasis on the new work of women, **however,** should not be allowed to obscure an equally important fact. (3)**Today,** as always, most of the time and effort of American wives is devoted to their responsibilities within the home and the family circle. (4)**This** is true even of those who are in the labor force. (5)**Since 1890** the demands of paid work have become much lighter. (6)The normal work week has decreased from sixty to forty hours; paid holidays and vacations have become universal; and most of the hard, physical labor that work once required has been eliminated. (7)Because of **these** developments, many women can work outside the home and still have time and energy left for home and family. [8]**Moreover**, most working mothers do not assume the burdens of a full schedule of paid work. [9]**Among** employed mothers of preschool children, four out of five worked only part time or less than half the year in 1956. [10]**Among** those whose children were in school, three out of five followed the same curtailed[1] work schedule. [11]And even **among** working wives who had no children at home, only a little more than half were year-round, full-time members of the labor force.

"Working Wives and Mothers," Robert W. Smuts, *Women and Work in America*

[1] *curtailed*: shortened

You can easily trace the devices that give this paragraph its coherence. The transition "however" connects the second sentence (2) to the first sentence (1); the adverb "today" links (3) to (2). The pronoun "this" joins (4) to (3), the phrase "since 1890" connects (5) to (4), and (6) contains examples of the point made in the previous sentence.

The pronoun "these" in (7) continues the forward movement of ideas listed in (6). The transition "moreover" links (8) to (7). And the repetition of the preposition "among" at the beginnings of sentences (9), (10), and (11) ties them together, forcefully ending the paragraph.

The Topic Sentence

To write a good paragraph, you first need to decide upon your purpose in writing. In other words, since each paragraph should be a separate unit of thought, you will need to decide in advance exactly what idea you are trying to communicate in each paragraph. Once you are sure of your idea, the next step is to make it clear to your reader. You can do this by stating your idea in a **topic sentence.** The topic sentence expresses your paragraph's central purpose. As you write a composition, you are responsible for keeping your purpose firmly in mind and continually signaling it to your reader. Notice that both the earlier model paragraphs that are cited as examples of unity and coherence have clearly stated topic sentences. In the Carson paragraph illustrating unity, the topic sentence is the first one; in the Smuts selection illustrating coherence, the topic sentence is the third.

Seeing your topic sentence written out will help you to focus on your subject. But if a topic sentence is expressed in terms that are too general, it will be less likely to help you achieve unity. To prevent yourself from introducing unrelated material, you will want to try in most of your topic sentences to use a word or group of words to express the chief point of a paragraph: its **controlling idea.** Occasionally the entire topic sentence will be needed to state this idea, but often it will appear in only a word or phrase. Study the following examples of broad, general topic sentences and the revisions of them. Each revision makes the original sentence more specific by emphasizing a controlling idea (boldfaced):

TOO GENERAL	CONTROLLING IDEA ADDED
2000: A Space Odyssey is an interesting movie.	*2001: A Space Odyssey* describes some of the **problems** of space travel.
The Olympic Games are exciting.	In the Olympic Games the athletes of many nations **compete intensely.**
Mahatma Ghandi was an inspiring leader.	Mahatma Ghandi used **passive resistance** to reach his political goals.
Music is enjoyable.	Music arouses many **different emotions** in listeners.

Here is a paragraph that illustrates how a topic sentence and controlling idea work to a writer's advantage. The short first sentence announces the paragraph's subject; the controlling idea is contained in the word "miracle":

It is a miracle that New York works at all. The whole thing is implausible.[1] Every time the residents brush their teeth, millions of gallons of water must be drawn from the Catskills and the hills of Westchester. When a young man in Manhattan writes a letter to his girl in Brooklyn, the love message gets blown to her through a pneumatic[2] tube—pfft— just like that. The subterranean[3] system of telephone cables, power lines, steam pipes, gas mains, and sewer pipes is reason enough to abandon the island to the gods and the weevils[4]. Every time an incision[5] is made in the pavement, the noisy surgeons expose ganglia[6] that are tangled beyond belief. By rights New York should have destroyed itself long ago, from panic or fire or rioting or failure of some vital supply line in its circulatory system or from some deep labyrinthine[7] short circuit. Long ago the city should have experienced an insoluble[8] traffic snarl at some impossible bottleneck.[9] It should have perished of hunger when food lines failed for a few days. It should have been wiped out by a plague starting in its slums or carried in by ships' rats. It should have been overwhelmed by the sea that licks at it on every side. The workers in its myriad cells should have succumbed[10] to nerves, from the fearful pall[11] of smoke-fog that drifts over every few days from Jersey, blotting out all light at noon and leaving the high offices suspended, men groping and depressed, and the sense of world's end. It should have been touched in the head by the August heat and gone off its rocker.[12]

"The Miracle of New York," E. B. White, *Here Is New York*

[1]*implausible:* lacking the appearance of truth. [2]*pneumatic:* operated by compressed air. [3]*subterranean:* underground. [4]*weevils:* small beetles, often pests. [5]*incision:* cut, gash. [6]*ganglia:* centers of energy, activity, or strength; nerve cells. [7]*labyrinthine:* intricate; perplexing. [8]*insoluble:* incapable of being solved. [9]*bottleneck:* narrow or congested passageway. [10]*succumbed:* given in to. [11]*pall:* gloomy atmosphere or effect. [12]*gone off its rocker:* gone mad.

E. B. White's paragraph is unified because every detail in each sentence relates back to the controlling idea that New York's survival is miraculous. Coherence comes from arranging details in an increasing order of magnitude, starting with discomfort and ending with madness.

Although the topic sentence is often placed at the beginning of a paragraph, it may appear in other places: sometimes it is found at the end; sometimes it appears in the middle; sometimes it does not appear at all, but is understood. But no matter where it is placed, the topic sentence governs paragraph development. By stating your controlling idea in each paragraph, you make clear your purpose in writing. This helps you to develop the paper and your reader to understand it.

Now let's examine further English paragraphs that illustrate the points we have been considering. Analyze each by asking yourself three questions:
1. Is it unified?
2. Does it have a topic sentence expressing a controlling idea?
3. Is it coherent?

I. Japanese women have changed since the war. They have become prettier, brighter, more decisive,[1] more outspoken.[2] The young people certainly are far more logical and and far less sentimental[3] than the prewar[4] generations. Some regret this. They think women, in gaining their freedom, have lost their femininity[5]—their modesty, their warmth, their shy grace. They accuse women of being drawn to superficial[6] things. A modern Japanese woman, they say, instead of trying to enrich her inner self, is in a mad scramble [7] to ape[8] anything that is new and foreign—fashions, cosmetics,[9] hairdos,[10] rock-and-roll.[11] And there are many Japanese who say that a caricature[12] of an up-to-date[13] wife is one who sits beside a washing machine in a house that has no hot running water.

"Japanese Women," Reiko Hatsumi, *The Mercurial Women*

[1]*decisive:* firm in making decisions. [2]*outspoken:* likely to express their views. [3]*sentimental:* weakly emotional. [4]*prewar:* before a war; as used here, before World War II. [5]*femininity:* womanly quality. [6]*superficial:* shallow, unimportant. [7]*mad scramble:* wild rush. [8]*ape:* imitate. [9]*cosmetics:* beauty aids. [10]*hairdos:* ways of arranging hair. [11]*rock-and-roll:* noisy music popular among young people. [12]*caricature:* humorous exaggeration. [13]*up-to-date:* modern.

Is the first paragraph unified? Because it deals only with the subject of Japanese women, we can say that it is. If the writer had added information about Japanese manufacturing or Japanese transportation, though, the paragraph would not have been unified. **Where are its topic sentence and controlling idea?** The topic sentence is the first one; the words "Japanese women have changed" express the controlling idea. **Is it coherent?** Its second and third sentence develop the topic sentence through examples. The fourth sentence, "Some regret this," allows the writer to narrow down his discussion from the main idea about Japanese women (they have changed) to a subdivision of that idea (they have acquired some undesirable traits). Thus, the paragraph is developed in a direct line from a topic sentence through a subdivision of the main idea to several concrete examples of the subdivision (fashion, cosmetics, rock-and-roll, washing machines). It is coherent.

II. The vegetable and fruit and flower merchants are surrounded by baskets of purple eggplant,[1] green peppers, strings of tiny silvery onions, heads[2] of bitter Indian spinach, and a dozen Indian vegetables for which I don't even know the English names. I had forgotten about the profusion[3] of fruit in India—it is only during the brief, intense summer that you see much variety of fruit in Moscow. In Russia, as winter approaches, all vegetables except for potatoes and the pervasive[4] cabbage in soup seem to disappear from the menus.

"An Indian Bazaar," Santha Rama Rau, *Gifts of Passage*

[1]*eggplant:* a vegetable. [2]*heads:* single, whole units; often used with vegetables. [3]*profusion:* abundant variety, great many. [4]*pervasive:* spread throughout.

Is the second paragraph unified? This brief paragraph presents a contrast. That is, it points out the differences in the availability of fruits and vegetables in India and in Russia. It has unity because it speaks only of fruits and vegetables, not of jewelry or automobiles, and it limits its discussion of countries to India and Russia. **Where are its topic sentence and controlling idea?** The topic sentence is placed in the middle of the paragraph. It announces the controlling idea, a contrast between India and Russia: "I had forgotten about the profusion of fruit in India—it is only during the brief, intense summer that you see much variety of fruit in Moscow." **Is it coherent?** The thought development is divided into three parts. Each part is directly related to the others, and all three parts are placed in a logical order. The first sentence describes the profusion of fruits and vegetables in India. The second topic sentence proposes a contrast between India and Russia. The third sentence completes the contrast, illustrating the scarcity of vegetables in Russia. Therefore the paragraph has a direct line of thought development. It has coherence.

III. In some of the Quechua [language] of Peru and Bolivia one speaks of the future as "behind oneself" and the past as "ahead." Such interpretations[1] of time have given rise to remarks by foreigners that the Quechuas have "a perverted[2] philosophical instinct." However, the Quechuas argue, "If you try to see the past and future with your mind's eye,[3] which can you see?" The obvious answer is that we can "see" the past and not the future, to which the Quechua replies, "Then, if you can see the past, it must be ahead of you; and the future, which you cannot see, is behind you." Such an explanation does not mean that the Quechuas worked out a philosophical interpretation of the past and future before talking about it, but it does suggest that there may be equally valid[4] but opposite ways of describing the same thing.

"How the Quechuas Think," Eugene Nida, *Customs and Cultures*

[1]*interpretations:* explanations. [2]*perverted:* twisted, distorted. [3]*mind's eye:* imagination. [4]*valid:* acceptable, convincing.

Is the third paragraph unified? The subject matter here deals with an interpretation of time that is different from the usual one. In discussing a Latin American way of looking at the past and the future, the writer does not add unrelated material. His paragraph has unity. **Where are its topic sentence and controlling idea?** Not until the very end of this paragraph does the topic sentence emerge. The main part of the controlling idea is stated at the close of the final sentence: "Such an explanation . . . does suggest that there may be equally valid but opposite ways of describing the same thing." The controlling idea is expressed in the words "equally valid but opposite." **Is it coherent?** This paragraph is based on **inductive** reasoning. Inductive reasoning begins with facts or examples used to prove the truth of a concluding general statement. (In contrast, **deductive** reasoning opens with a general statement, followed by supporting facts or examples.) By first explaining the Quechuas' unusual approach to the question of time, the writer has supplied convincing support for his conclusion that "there may be equally valid but opposite ways of describing the same thing." The paragraph is coherent because of the direct logical connection between the examples given in the beginning sentences and the generalization drawn from it in the final sentence.

IV. In all the Arab states the military officer corps has provided an important contribution to the new elite.[1] The armies and air forces, even to a greater extent than government departments organized along European lines, have provided effective training and experience in organization and command and have developed a sense of responsibility. The first generation of officers in the Egyptian and Iraqi armies to be drawn from all levels of society, rather than exclusively from the upper classes, produced the leaders of the revolutions of the 1950s. Many of them coming from the middle or lower middle classes brought with them political ideas opposed to those of the established order[2] and to its dependence upon the association with Great Britain and the West. The military life gave them education, special technical skills, the habit of organization, and awareness of the political uses of military power. It was natural, therefore, that these officers should take an important place among the new elite.

"The Military Officer Corps," Charles D. Creamans, *The Arabs and the World*

[1]*elite:* highest class. [2]*established order:* existing government.

Is the fourth paragraph unified? All six sentences give facts about the same subject: the Arab military officer corps. This results in a firmly unified paragraph. **Where are its topic sentence and controlling idea?** The controlling idea—"important contribution"—is stated in the opening sentence and repeated in slightly different terms in the final sentence. By placing his topic sentence both at the beginning and end of his paragraph, the writer gains two advantages. First, he creates a strong organizational frame. Second, through repetition he further emphasizes his controlling idea. **Is it coherent?** This is a coherent paragraph because the four ideas that support the controlling idea are arranged in order of increasing importance. Beginning with the officers' training, continuing with their service in the revolutions of the 1950s, adding their political break with the established order, and concluding with their awareness of the political uses of military power, the paragraph builds to a natural climax, or peak of importance. In explaining the source of the officers' present power, the the fourth sentence is a vital one. By placing it toward the close of his paragraph, the writer gains coherence.

V. A level consists of a high-powered telescope (20 to 40 diameters) with a spirit level attached to it in such a manner that, when its bubble is centered, the line of sight is horizontal. The purposes of the telescope are to fix the direction of the line of sight and to magnify the apparent sizes of objects observed. In Colonial times telescopes were too large for practical surveying, and they were not used on surveying instruments until the end of the nineteenth century. Their use tremendously increases the speed and precision with which measurements can be taken. These telescopes have a vertical cross hair for lining up the telescope on points and a horizontal cross hair with which readings are made on level rods. . . . (Black widow spider webs are commonly used to make cross hairs for surveying instruments.)

"Levels for Surveying," Jack C. McCormac, *Surveying*

Is the fifth paragraph unified? The purpose of this selection is to explain what a surveyor's level is and how it operates. All of the sentences are related to this purpose. **Where are its topic sentence and controlling idea?** The first sentence clearly announces the topic as the level; then the paragraph is developed from the controlling idea of "telescope." **Is it coherent?** Moving from definition through historical background to present-day use and appearance of levels, the paragraph reveals a planned coherence.

EXERCISE 1
Unity

Write out the sentence in each paragraph that is unrelated to the controlling idea. Think about why it is unrelated and why the author, without meaning to, may have inserted the unnecessary sentence.

1. Pearls are gathered by men known as pearl divers. Actually, these men do not dive. They are lowered by a rope to the bottom of the sea.

Many tourists to Japan enjoy shopping for cultured pearls. Pearl gatherers work in pairs, with one remaining at the surface to help the other return from his dive. An experienced pearl diver can stay down about a minute and a half and can often make as many as thirty dives in one day.

2. For hundreds of years, man has made use of the talents of monkeys. Egyptian paintings of 2000 B.C. show baboons gathering fruit for their masters. Even in 1879, in Abyssinia, monkeys were still being used as torchbearers at feasts. The monkeys would sit in a row on a bench and hold the lights until the guests went home. Then the monkeys would eat. Most of the world's zoos contain a variety of monkeys for people to watch.

3. Except for some bare spots and a few mountain peaks, Antarctica is covered with an icy frosting perhaps 2,000 feet deep. Along the coast, the frosting spills off into the Ross and Weddell Seas, forming a great ice barrier. This ice is not ice as we know it. It is névé, or glacial snow that has been pressed together. A refrigerator permits people to keep food fresh for long periods of time. Long ago, during the Ice Age, névé covered other areas of the world. Today, Antarctica still remains in the Ice Age.

4. Not all chance discoveries are made in laboratories. Some occur in the most unlikely places. While walking through a Paris street, Dr. René Laennec observed some children at play. He noticed one child cupping his ear on an old wooden plank. Another child at the other end of the plank was tapping a message to him on the wood. Laennec had had trouble that very morning trying to hear the heartbeat of one of his fat patients. In the children's game he at once recognized the principle of the stethoscope. The discovery of the X ray has also contributed greatly to the advance of modern medicine. Laennec rushed home and built the first crude stethoscope from a slender, hollow wooden tube. Then he hurried back to the hospital to try it on his patient. It worked. He was able to listen to his heartbeat.

5. The Olympic Games are a display of international goodwill. The ceremonies, with their emphasis upon both nationalism and internationalism, are a thrilling sight to see. World Fairs, such as those held in Montreal in 1967 and in Tokyo in 1970, attract visitors from all parts of the world. At the start, the king or president of the country in which the Olympic Games are being held is presented. The national anthem of his country is sung. Then follows a parade of all the contestants, each bearing his country's flag and shield. This march is accompanied by a fanfare of trumpets. When the Olympic flag is raised, guns fire a salute. Doves, symbols of peace, are released. Finally the sacred fire is lit. The Olympic flame is set alight by a torch that has been carried by relay runners all the way from Olympia, Greece. The sacred fire then burns throughout the entire Olympic Games.

6. Growing dwarfed, or miniature, trees is not only a challenging craft but also a decorative art form. This hobby has been practiced for centuries in the Orient. A popular word for this attractive nature hobby is the Japanese term *bonsai*, although the Chinese have had an equally notable history in dwarfing trees. The chrysanthemum is a traditional Japanese flower.

7. At a time when only two or three million Indians lived in what is now the United States, nearly thirty million Indians lived in Mexico and Central America. Today, Mexico City is one of the most cosmopolitan cities in the Western Hemisphere. The Mayan civilization was extremely widespread. So far, only a hundred or so of the cities built by the Mayas and related tribes have been unearthed. But stone figures, pottery, and other objects left by the Mayas have been found at more than 15,000 sites in Mexico, Guatemala, and elsewhere in Central America. Undoubtedly, hundreds of these places conceal the ruins of Mayan cities.

8. Parrots and mynah birds are famous for their ability to reproduce human speech. Mynah birds can imitate human vowel sounds better than parrots, but parrots can remember a larger vocabulary. The record is 100 words. The parrot, with it vivid green and red feathers, is more brightly colored than the black mynah bird. Many parrots learn to associate particular words with specific actions. They may say "goodbye" when someone leaves the room or "hello" when the telephone rings. It is difficult, however, to show that such words have a real meaning for the parrot. They certainly do not serve among parrots for communication, which, after all, is the function of language.

9. Millions of years ago, Australia was linked to Asia by a land bridge. Then an earthquake caused the land bridge to buckle in deep folds. The sea rushed in, and Australia became an island. When the Christmas holidays arrive, the climate in Australia is sunny and warm. Many animals that once wandered back and forth across the land bridge were stranded in Australia. The gentle marsupials (animals with pouches) were among the stranded. Though fierce beasts killed them off elsewhere, they were able to survive in Australia.

10. One of the most striking and recent observations of researchers has suggested the very strong possibility that some persons may be able to see with their fingertips. The first word of this strange observation came from a Russian scientist. He reported the case of a remarkable twenty-two-year-old girl. She could detect color by her sense of touch and read a newspaper by running her fingers over the print. American scientists received the news with some doubts. However, their doubts soon turned to wonder when an American scientist reported an American woman who could identify colors by touch alone. American and Russian space scientists have been working intensely on programs to

explore the moon and other planets. Meanwhile, the Russians claim to have turned up two more cases of fingertip seeing. Such cases seem to indicate strongly that certain human beings may indeed possess this sixth sense.

EXERCISE 2
Coherence

Revise these paragraphs for greater coherence by arranging the sentences in a logical order.

1. Fifth, place logs and larger pieces of wood over the branches. Second, twist newspaper into small knots. You will be rewarded with a roaring blaze. Fourth, cover this pile with a few small branches. You should follow several steps if you want to build a campfire. Third, make a pile on the ground of several paper knots. Lay the larger pieces of wood on the campfire from different directions. First collect a good supply of wood, both small branches and larger logs. Finally, strike a match and ignite the paper at the bottom of the campfire, lighting it in several places.

2. George always shaves and dresses before eating. Sometimes he falls asleep again. Then he brushes his teeth, puts on his coat, and says good-bye before he leaves for the office. When the alarm clock rings, George wakes up and shuts it off. If this happens, his mother wakes him up so that he won't be late for work. After he finishes breakfast, he usually reads the morning newspaper.

3. Pine trees grew down to the lake's edge, so we had to walk through a small pine forest to reach the water. We drove as close as we could to the lake, parked the car, and got out. John was the first one to dive into the lake. As we drove down the road, the lake came into view. He laughed at us for being afraid to get our hair wet. We decided to stop and take a swim for an hour.

4. I didn't mind waiting for the seasons to change, though, for the best time of all is Paris in the spring. I used to watch the leaves falling from the trees in the public gardens. I first arrived in Paris in the summer, and I was surprised at how warm it is there in August. When the air is fresh, flower buds appear, and branches are covered with new green leaves. When autumn arrived, however, the climate became delightful. The winter months were wet and cold. But at least I could cool off by swimming in the Seine River.

5. Begin by breaking the eggs into a bowl, adding small amounts of salt, pepper, and milk. When the butter in the frying pan is melted, pour in the egg batter. To make a small omelet you need three eggs, a slice of cheese, salt, pepper, butter, milk, a frying pan, a bowl, and a spatula. Then heat the frying pan over a medium fire, melting a small amount

of butter in it. After the eggs are partially cooked, place a slice of cheese on them and fold one half of the omelet over the other half. Remove from the frying pan and serve.

EXERCISE 3
The Topic Sentence

A. *Write out the topic sentence in each of the following paragraphs.*

1. Those who have made thorough studies of the vocabularies of aboriginal languages have found that these languages have rich resources of available words. The Maya language of Yucatan has at least 20,000 words, the Aztec of central Mexico about 27,000, and the Zulu language of South Africa possesses more than 30,000. Some other languages may not have as many, but the vocabulary of any language, irrespective of how primitive the people may seem, must be reckoned in the thousands, not in hundreds of words.

2. In the small French town, the town clerk spends two hours or so talking in the café every day. The village doctor often drops in for an apéritif when he is between calls. People from outlying sections of the valley who come to the village only on official business at the town hall drop into the café and leave news of their neighborhood. Through the café owner the postman relays messages that he has been given on his route. With these and many other sources of information at his disposal, the café owner usually knows better than anyone else in the village the news of the community.

3. In the past it was possible to know in advance what occupations would exist when a boy became a man. Today the life span of occupations has also been compressed. The computer programmer, who was first heard of in the 1950s, will be as extinct as the blacksmith within a number of years. Individuals now train for a profession and look forward to remaining in that profession for the entire period of their working life. Yet within a generation the notion of serving in a single occupation for one's entire life may seem quaintly antique. Individuals may need to be trained to serve successively in three, four, or half a dozen different professions in the course of a career. The job will no longer serve as man's anchor and organizing principle.

4. The interpretation of words is a never-ending task for any citizen in a modern society. We now have, as a result of modern means of communication, hundreds of thousands of words flung at us daily. We are constantly being talked at, by teachers, preachers, salesmen, public officials, and motion-picture sound tracks. The cries of the hawkers of soft drinks, soap chips, and laxatives pursue us into our very homes, thanks to the radio—and in some houses the radio is never turned off from morning to night. Daily the newsboy brings us, in large cities, from

thirty to fifty enormous pages of print, and almost three times that amount on Sunday. The mailman brings magazine and direct-mail advertising. We go out and get more words at bookstores and libraries. Billboards confront us on the highways, and we even take portable radios with us to the seashore. Words fill our lives.

B. *The controlling idea of a topic sentence is the key word or group of words that expresses its basic idea. List the word or words containing the controlling idea in the following topic sentences.*

Example: Good study habits are **useful** *to a college student.*
Example: Holiday ocean cruises attract **four types** *of passengers.*
Example: Censorship of films, television, and printed matter is a **controversial issue** *in some countries.*

1. In ancient times, three types of calendars were used.
2. One of the busiest seasons for travel agents is the summer.
3. Some people see electronic computers as a threat to modern man.
4. Map-reading skills can be helpful in many school subjects.
5. Two most unusual things were found in the city apartments.
6. In 1930 marine biologists made a strange discovery off the coast of Africa.
7. The noise level in large factories has caused problems for many manufacturers.
8. Traveling by airplane has several advantages over traveling by train.
9. Many automobile drivers have the habit of taking risks.
10. The whooping crane is a very rare species of bird.

C. *Revise these topic sentences to narrow the focus by stressing a controlling idea.*

Example: ORIGINAL   The Porsche is a fine car.
         REVISION   **Superior engine performance** and **beautiful design** make the Porsche a fine automobile.
Example: ORIGINAL   Today many young people have developed a culture of their own.
         REVISION   **Long hair, colorful clothing,** and **new musical forms** are part of the new culture of many of today's young people.
Example: ORIGINAL   Good cameras are manufactured in many countries.
         REVISION   Good cameras are manufactured in **Germany, Japan,** and the **United States.**

1. Participation in college athletics is beneficial.
2. Motion pictures should be censored.

3. People could make better use of their leisure time.
4. Marriage for couples under twenty is foolish.
5. The United Nations should take a stronger role in world affairs.
6. Studying a foreign language is useful.
7. A college education is becoming more important every year.
8. Buddhism is popular.

D. *In the following paragraphs the beginning topic sentences have been omitted. After reading each paragraph carefully, construct a topic sentence that contains the main idea of the paragraph. Then write out the complete paragraph. If you do not feel a topic sentence is needed, explain why.*

1. A visitor to Athens in the early fourth century B.C. wrote: "It is illegal here to deal a slave a blow. In the street he won't step aside to let you pass. Indeed you can't tell a slave by his dress; he looks like all the rest. They can go to the theater too. Really, the Athenians have established a kind of equality between slaves and free men." They were never a possible source of danger to the state as they were in Rome. There were no terrible slave wars and uprisings in Athens. In Rome, crucifixion was called "the slave's punishment." The Athenians did not practice crucifixion and had no so-called slave's punishment. They were not afraid of their slaves.

2. A very common type is simple plagiarism. Unable or too lazy to formulate ideas in their own words, some students simply copy their papers from those of other students or from reports in books and magazines and then submit them as original work. To help them during examinations, students write notes and formulas on the cuffs of their shirts, on the covers of books, and on the palms of their hands. A common technique is for students to leave the examination room to reach a previously hidden bit of information. And, finally, there are the traditional code signals used during examinations when a well-prepared student transmits his information by means of hand signals to one or more students taking the same examination.

3. The idea may seem enticing, but unfortunately it is seldom true. All young people do not reach maturity at the same time in their lives. Nor can a youth be trained to grow up within a strict pattern from beginning, on his thirteenth birthday, to end, on his twenty-first. Each individual must form his own pattern. Each adolescent must be allowed to think for himself. He needs the opportunity to seek the answers to questions that trouble him, to develop his own individual ideas. He needs to develop the courage to help him admit willingly when he is wrong. The satisfaction of these needs cannot be taught; it must be learned slowly, at a person's own rate. Give the adolescent his chance. Do not force him into a familiar pattern. Let him build his own knowledge on his own experience. Let him learn patience; do not expect miracles. Let him seek, but do not find for him. And, most important of all, give him time.

4. Books can be found to fit almost every need, temper, or interest. Books can be read when you are in the mood; they do not have to be taken in periodic doses. Books are both more personal and more impersonal than professors. Books have an inner confidence which individuals seldom show; they rarely have to be on the defensive. Books can afford to be bold and courageous and exploratory; they do not have to be so careful of boards of trustees, colleagues, and community opinion. Books are infinitely diverse; they run the gamut of human activity. Books can be found to express every point of view; if you want a different point of view, you can read a different book. Even your professor is at his best when he writes books and articles; the teaching performance rarely equals the writing effort.

5. There are people who have argued that women are as good as men, but I do not recall anyone who has argued that women were better than or superior to men. How could one argue such a case in the face of all the evidence to the contrary? Is it not a fact that by far the largest number of geniuses, great painters, poets, philosophers, scientists, and musicians have been men, and that women have made, by comparison, a very poor showing? Clearly the superiority is with men. Where are the Leonardos, the Michelangelos, the Shakespeares, the Galileos, the Bachs of the feminine sex? In fields in which women have excelled, in poetry and the novel, how many poets and novelists of really first rank have there been? Haven't well-bred young women been educated for centuries in music? And how many among them have been great composers or instrumentalists? Composers—none of the first rank. Instrumentalists—well, in the recent period there have been such accomplished artists as Alicia de Larrocha and Erica Morini. Possibly there is a clue here to the question asked. May it not be that women are just about to emerge from the period of subjection during which they were the slaves of the masculine world? (*Suggestion to the student: phrase the topic sentence for this paragraph in the form of a question.*)

The Paragraph Outline

Most of the paragraphs you have read in Chapter 1 have been arranged according to a plan. Let's reconstruct the outline of two of these paragraphs:

Topic Sentence: Pearls are gathered by men known as pearl divers.
1. Divers are lowered by ropes to the bottom of the sea.
2. Divers work in pairs.
3. Divers can stay down a minute and a half and make thirty dives a day.

Topic Sentence: For hundreds of years, man has made use of the monkeys.
1. Baboons gathered fruit for the Egyptians in 2000 B.C.
2. Monkeys were used as torchbearers in 1879 in Abyssinia.

When you briefly outline paragraphs like this *before* you write, you can check quickly to see that they will be tightly unified and coherent. (You can quickly and efficiently outline paragraphs by jotting down topics expressed in a word or phrase, rather than in an entire sentence. This is called a "topic outline.")

Both of the preceding outlines ensure that the paragraphs written from them will be unified because no details unrelated to the controlling idea have been included. Moreover, both paragraphs will be coherent because their supporting details are arranged in order of time. In the first paragraph, pearl diving is described according to the sequence of steps in the diving process. In the second paragraph, the older example of working monkeys is used before the more recent example.

An outline can be helpful both when you are writing a paper outside of class and when you are writing a composition or examination under pressure of time in the classroom. If you first establish the basic framework of your paragraph, you can give more attention to clear and accurate expression of your ideas.

Examine this example of a brief paragraph outline, expressed in gramatically equal phrases for easy reference, on the subject of the advantages of a college education:

Topic Sentence: A college education has several advantages for young people.
1. Trains in professional skills
2. Develops powers of reasoning, analysis, and judgment
3. Expands cultural background

The order in which a writer first thinks of a paragraph's supporting detail is often not the most effective sequence for writing. Once the topics are written out, they can be rearranged to build a paragraph to a strong climax. This is the real reason for paragraph outlining. Imagine, for instance, the difference between a paragraph written from the above outline and a paragraph written from the following rearranged topics:

1. Expands cultural background
2. Develops powers of reasoning, analysis, and judgment
3. Trains in professional skills

Two Keys—and a Question

It is no easy matter, this learning to write—in one's native language or in a second language. No magic formula will guarantee instant success. As with all worthwhile goals, becoming a good writer takes time and effort.

But even though there is no magic formula, there *is* a kind of magic available to you in using this book. This magic depends on your ability to focus on two techniques of composition that, if practiced and mastered, will increase your skill in writing English more surely than almost any other techniques you might study. What are these two techniques? The first is the use of transitions; the second is subordination.

THE FIRST KEY: TRANSITIONS

Only you can make certain that your paragraphs have unity. If you train yourself, you can develop the habit of sifting your thoughts as you write, rejecting any unrelated ideas that may intrude. In the equally important matter of coherence, though, you don't stand alone; you have helpers. Transitions can assist you by connecting sentences in meaningful ways, clarifying relationships between ideas by indicating forward movement or shifts in the directions of your thinking.

The coherence of almost any paragraph will benefit from the presence of transitions, whether the paragraph is developing a single idea or several related ideas. If the relationship of ideas is not immediately clear, providing transitions becomes essential. Normally, the more ideas a paragraph contains, the more explicit and extensive transitions need to be.

Transitions can take several forms. First, you can use a group of transitional words (**thus, therefore, moreover, nevertheless, however**) or phrases (**in fact, to conclude, on the contrary, for instance**). Second, pronouns often serve as transitions by referring back to antecedents in an earlier sentence. Some adjectives can also act as effective transitions (**first, second**). So can coordinating conjunctions (**and, but, for, or nor**) when placed at the beginnings of sentences. Repeating a word or phrase from one sentence to another is a further transitional device. A rhetorical question also helps to move the thought forward (the rhetorical question is discussed in Chapter 9). See how another form of transition—synonyms—works through the simple words "sea" and "ocean" in the opening two sentences of Rachel Carson's paragraph earlier in this chapter. Even symbols can serve as transitional elements by creating numerical (1., 2., 3.) or alphabetical (a., b., c.) listings; these are particularly useful in technical writing.

In addition, the grammatical structures of subordination and parallelism work to add coherence to writing. (Subordination is discussed in the following section, and parallelism is explained in Chapter 5.)

In the following paragraph, the boldfaced transitions clarify the progression of ideas in a complex piece of technical writing:

The appearance of infrared[1] luminescence[2] at unusually long wavelengths[3] is a sure signal that some new substance with an energy lower

[1]*infrared:* having a wavelength greater than that of visible red light and shorter than that of a microwave. [2]*luminescence:* emission of light, such as fluorescence and phosphorescence, not directly attributable to the heat that produces incandescence. [3]*wavelengths:* distance, measured along the line of propagation, between two points representing similar phases of two consecutive waves.

than that of the excitons[4] is present in a semiconductor.[5] **How has the substance been identified as a liquid made of electrons[6] and holes? This is** an important question, which has been answered through three kinds of experiment. **First,** the scattering of infrared radiation[7] by the new substance indicates that it is segregated from the gas in regions of a separate phase. **This** information alone, **however,** cannot reveal whether the substance consists of crystallites[8] of a solid or droplets of a **liquid.** That it is actually a **liquid** is shown by observing the effects of heating the substance: its density[9] varies like that of a liquid and it apparently does not freeze. **Finally,** it must be determined how the charge carriers are associated in the liquid, and **that** can be ascertained from the luminescence spectrum.[10] The shape of the spectrum is what would be expected for a fluid made up of independent electrons and holes.

"An Electron-Hole Liquid," Gordon A. Thomas, *Scientific American* (June 1976)

[4]*excitons:* main energy source. [5]*semiconductor:* one of a class of substances (germanium, silicon, or lead sulfide, for example) whose electronic conductivity at ordinary temperatures is between that of a metal and that of an insulator. [6]*electrons:* atomic particles carrying a unit charge of negative electricity. [7]*radiation:* emission and propagation of radiant energy. [8]*crystallites:* minute bodies not truly crystalline but resulting from a crystallizing process; found in igneous (formed by volcanic action or intense heat) rocks. [9]*density:* mass of a substance per unit of its volume. [10]*spectrum:* image formed by radiant energy directed through a spectroscope; in this image each wavelength corresponds to a specific band or line in a progressive series characteristic of the emitting source.

Note the variety of transitions that appear here: (1) A rhetorical question; (2) The pronoun "this" used twice and the pronoun "that"; (3) The adjective "first'; (4) Repeating a word "liquid . . . liquid."; and (5) The transitional words "however" and "finally."

Because transitions are essential to clear writing, they receive a major emphasis in the text. You will find transition exercises in Chapters 2–10. In addition, transitions are annotated in the left margins of most model paragraphs and compositions, and transition use is discussed in connection with many sample writing selections.

Before you leave Chapter 1, review how effectively the boldfaced transitions have worked in the Carson paragraph on page 2 and in the Robert W. Smuts paragraph on pages 4–5.

Here is a partial list of transitions with their uses:

Explanation: now, thus, for, in this case
Emphasis: indeed, certainly, above all
Qualification: but, however, yet, unless, except for
Illustration: for example, for instance, thus
Comparison: like, similarly, likewise, in the same way
Contrast: in contrast, on the other hand, instead, unlike
Concession: admittedly, nevertheless, of course, although, after all

Consequence: therefore, as a result, consequently, thus, hence, so, accordingly

Summation: in conclusion, to sum up, all in all, finally

THE SECOND KEY: SUBORDINATION

Subordination is the technique of putting together ideas that are **unequal** in weight so that the relative importance of each will be quickly apparent to the reader. Through subordination, you can focus on the central, or controlling, idea of your sentence by placing it in the independent clause and placing the less important idea in a dependent clause or phrase. (For a discussion of clauses and phrases, consult "Two Uses of the Comma" page 43–44.) The explanation of subordination and the exercises in this chapter will help you to develop this skill. Notes in the margins of many model compositions direct you to frequent examples of subordination contained there. Subordination is reviewed in Chapter 7.

Here is a typical example, borrowed from a later model paragraph, of subordination by means of a dependent adverb clause:

Subordinated Clause (Italics) | *Even though you can buy the same brand of soap, toothpaste, and sugar-free carbonated drink in all 50*
Controlling Idea (Boldface) | *states,* **the U.S.A. reveals major regional differences.**

The controlling idea here, of course, is not the first one you read: that you can buy soap, toothpaste, or diet beverages anywhere in the United States. Instead, the controlling idea (that the U.S.A. displays many regional differences) appears in an independent clause at the end of the sentence.

Earlier paragraphs in Chapter 1 show evidence of writers putting subordination to good use:

Subordinated Clause (Italics) | 1. *Because of these developments,* many **women can still work** outside the home **and** still **have time and**
Controlling Idea (Boldface) | **energy left** for home and family. (From Smuts, *Women and Work in America*)

(This is an example of subordination by an introductory adverb clause. The controlling idea, that women can both work and maintain a home, is expressed in the independent clause.)

Subordinated Clause (Italics) | 2. *When a young man in Manhattan writes to his girl in Brooklyn,* the **love message gets blown** to her
Controlling Idea (Boldface) | through a pneumatic tube—pfft—just like that. (From White, *Here Is New York*)

(This is another example of subordination by an introductory adverb clause. The controlling idea, that letters travel underground between New York boroughs, appears in the independent clause.)

Subordinated Clause
(Italics)

Controlling Idea
(Boldface)

3. **A modern Japanese woman,** they say, *instead of trying to enrich her inner self, is* **in a mad scramble to** ape anything that is new and foreign—fashions, cosmetics, hairdos, rock-and-roll. (From Hatsumi, *The Mercurial Women*)

(This is an example of subordination by an internal adverb phrase. The controlling idea, that Japanese women are fascinated with new and foreign things, is located in the independent clause.)

Subordinated Clause
(Italics)

Controlling Idea
(Boldface)

4. In Russia, *as winter approaches,* **all vegetables** except for potatoes and the pervasive cabbage in soup **seem to disappear** from the menus. (From Rau, *Gifts of Passage*)

(This is an example of subordination by an internal adverb clause. The controlling idea, that most vegetables disappear from menus, is found in the independent clause.)

Although an idea is often subordinated by an adverb clause, it may also be subordinated in several different ways: by placing it in an adjective clause, a modifying phrase, or an appositive. Study all the ways to subordinate before practicing on the exercises that follow:

1. **By an adverb clause.** Identify the less important idea by placing a subordinate conjunction before it. Subordinate adverb clauses convey the ideas of time, place, cause or reason, purpose or result, and concession. The meanings are expressed in the subordinating conjunctions:

Time

Subordinating conjunctions include *before, after, when, whenever, while, until, since.*
John repaired the flat tire **while I made sandwiches.**
Before she could answer the telephone, it stopped ringing.

Place

Subordinating conjunctions include *where, wherever.*
They planted a cypress tree **where the poplar tree had been growing.**
Wherever you travel, think of me.

Cause or Reason

Subordinating conjunctions include *since, because, as, as if, as though, as long as, whereas.*
Because it is late, I have to leave.
He walked **as if he had sprained his ankle.**

Purpose or Result

Subordinating conjunctions include *that, so, so that, in order that.*
We went downtown **so that we could do some shopping.**
In order that he might better understand mathematics, Robert hired a tutor.

Concession or Contrast	Subordinating conjunctions include *although, though, even though, provided that, unless, if, than.* **Although she watered the lawn every day,** the grass turned brown. You will put on weight **if you eat too many pies and cakes.**

2. By an adjective clause. Introduce the less important idea in an adjective clause beginning with *who*, *which*, or *that*.

Weak	John comes from a large, lower-class family, and he enrolled in college this fall.
Improved	John, **who comes from a large, lower-class family,** enrolled in college this fall.
Weak	The dean issued a bulletin, and it said the library would remain open on weekends.
Improved	The dean issued a bulletin **that said the library would remain open on weekends.**

3. By a modifying phrase. Use a prepositional phrase as an adjective or adverb modifier, or use a participial phrase.

Weak	The house is at the end of the street, and it was designed by Palladio.
Prepositional Phrase	The house **at the end of the street** was designed by Palladio.
Weak	The guards were fully armed, and they expected trouble.
Participial Phrase	**Expecting trouble,** the guards were fully armed.

4. By an appositive. An appositive can appear at the beginning, in the middle, or at the end of a sentence.

Weak	Knut Hamsun was a Norwegian novelist, and he won a Nobel Prize.
Improved	**A Nobel Prize winner,** Knut Hamsun was a Norwegian novelist.
Weak	Mr. Edwards is the manager of the store, and he is a city councilman.
Improved	Mr. Edwards, **the manager of the store,** is a city councilman.
Weak	My uncle brought me a gift, and it was a wristwatch.
Improved	My uncle brought me a gift, **a wristwatch.**

Subordination does not take place in isolated sentences. It is a matter directly related to the context of a paragraph. Whether or not you should subordinate within a sentence depends on at least two things: first, the ideas you are dealing with; and second, the kinds of sentences surrounding the sentence that you are devising. A writer normally distinguishes between ideas that are roughly equal, and therefore better expressed through parallelism, and those that are unequal, and therefore better expressed through subordination. But it would be a mistake to write a composition in which most or all of the sentences contained subordinated ideas. A writer works toward sentence variety by expanding, contracting, and rearranging his ideas to allow him to express himself in a number of different sentence patterns. He combines simple, compound, and complex sentences in order to avoid a monotonous style. Aware that subordination is one of the most important characteristics of modern English prose, he uses it whenever it will help him to communicate his ideas more clearly.

EXERCISE 4
Subordination

A. *In the following sentences, identify the independent clauses that contain the controlling ideas.*

1. When the workers stopped for lunch, people were allowed to enter the building.
2. If you are careful about what you eat, you will enjoy your trip to Mexico more.
3. Since our animals needed to be fed and rested, we stopped driving between sunset and sunrise.
4. We hurried to the airport when we learned that our uncle was arriving at noon.
5. Although the end of the term was nearly at hand, Jerry has not completed all of the projects he had hoped to finish.
6. They drove to the village where the Balinese dance was to take place.
7. Because the average life of a honey bee during the working season is only six weeks, new bees are continually needed to replace old ones.
8. In order to make it easier to pedal uphill, the bicyclist shifted gears.
9. Carlos decided to renew the lease on his New York apartment even though he was growing tired of city life.
10. Don't open the door of the darkroom until the red light has been turned off.

B. *Subordinate an idea in each of the following sentences in the way indicated.*

By an adverb clause
1. He wanted to go to medical school, and he studied diligently during his senior year of college.

2. We waited at the airport for an hour, and the helicopter never arrived.
3. You want me to help you with your homework, but you must help me clean the apartment first.
4. The invitation came, and I decided to go to the seminar at Lausanne for the weekend.

By an adjective clause

5. Mr. Symonds was a high school teacher for many years, and now he is teaching at the university.
6. I am driving to the railroad station to meet a businessman, and he is coming from Nairobi.
7. Frank Lloyd Wright was a famous architect, and he designed the Guggenheim Museum in New York.
8. Helen is studying the history of art, and she will go to the Sorbonne next year.

By a prepositional phrase

9. The car had red wheels, and it won the first race.
10. He told me to look in the unabridged dictionary, and it was on his desk.
11. Professor Blake found his car, and it was in the garage.
12. I had a ticket for the concert in London, and I gave it to Jeffrey.

By a participial phrase

13. The boys were caught in a sudden rainstorm, and they took refuge in a haystack.
14. Mr. Carruthers was named vice-president of the company last year, and he was promoted to president yesterday.
15. His sister was calling for help, and she sounded hysterical.
16. The ambassador delivered a speech first, and then he flew to Brazil.

By an appositive

17. Mr. Chang is the executive manager of our firm, and he came to this country only three years ago.
18. His new book is a volume of short plays, and it received favorable reviews from most critics.
19. Montreal was the site of the 1967 Expo, and it is one of the world's liveliest cities.
20. The kennel is a home for lost dogs, and that is where we found our boxer puppy.

C. *Rewrite the following paragraph, combining the numbered groups of sentences into single complex sentences containing both an independent and a dependent clause. Label them as adjective or adverb clauses.*

Example   I was in college. I had a roommate. He was studying to be a lawyer.

    (Adv. cl.)   (Adj. cl.)

When I was in college, I had a roommate **who was studying to be a lawyer.**

(1) I was twenty years old. I had a friend, Paul Desmond. He liked motorcycles. (2) Paul heard about a store. This store was having a sale of motorcycles. (3) The store owner would let Paul try out a new motorcycle for three days. He had to give the owner a fifty-dollar deposit. (4) Paul couldn't afford to part with fifty dollars. He gave the money to the owner anyway. (5) He drove the motorcycle around the city that afternoon. He decided that he liked it very much. (6) I told him that I would like to see how the motorcycle performed. He asked me to ride with him the next day. (7) We were ready to leave. My mother gave us a picnic lunch. I packed it on the motorcycle. (8) Our friends told us to have a good time. This was what we intended to do. We decided to drive far out into the country to find a stream to swim in. (9) But on the road leading out of the city we collided with an automobile. It was crossing an intersection. (10) The motorcycle was damaged. Paul lost his fifty-dollar deposit. He had borrowed it from his father. (11) We were both slightly injured, receiving scratches and bruises. Paul's interest in motorcycles remained strong.

THE QUESTION

"What kind of audience is my writing directed to?"

At first glance this question may seem to you to have an obvious answer. But the question does have both present and future importance. At the present time, you are writing for the general literate public, which also includes your teacher. Ask yourself whether this audience expects of you writing that is formal or informal, serious or humorous, statistical or philosophical, conventional or experimental. The answer should help you to create compositions that successfully communicate your ideas.

For the future, the question of what kind of audience your writing is directed to will also be relevant. Whenever you write in English, you should adjust your manner of composition to suit the reader just as you refocus your camera each time you take a new photograph. The kinds of writing done in preparing a medical report, an engineering prospectus, a literary thesis, or a legal brief differ widely.

To help you understand how English prose can be modulated, sections on style and tone appear later in this book—style in Chapter 9, tone in Chapter 10. These are included to help you appreciate more fully the subtle variations on which really fluent English written communication depends.

Vocabulary Growth

Vocabulary study at the end of each chapter consists of two exercises that ask you to discover the meanings of words through analyzing the context surrounding them. In the first exercise, Paragraph Puzzle, you will fill in the blanks that have been left out of a paragraph at regular intervals. You will often need to refer to the context to make the right choices. The second exercise, Word Clues, is a re-creation of what really happens when you read a passage. When an unfamiliar word turns up, you don't always look it up in a dictionary. You can often successfully deduce its meaning from finding a nearby word or word group—often a synonym—that will suggest the meaning of the unfamiliar word.

To gain further help in building your English vocabulary, study the material in Appendix 10, Using Principles of Phonics to Recognize and Pronounce English Words.

PARAGRAPH PUZZLE

Complete the paragraph by choosing the right word to fill in each blank. When choice is difficult, refer to neighboring words or sentences for help.

How do we know that dogs............color-blind? This has been
(have, show, are, is)

tested in............same way that it has been............what dogs
(that, a, their, the)   (discovered, heard, told, said)

can hear. The attempt............been made to train dogs to...........
(have, has, shall, is)   (whine, cry, bark, salivate)

when they are shown certain different............, just as they were
(colors, odors, cards, tastes)

trained so.............their mouths watered when definite musical
(this, those, that, this)

............were sounded. Such experiments have turned...........
(comedies, notes, cries, cheers)   (in, out, around, about)

failures: it has been found impossible............make dogs distinguish
(for, if, not, to)

colors from one............as signals for their dinner . . . Monkeys,
(other, another, over, under)

...........the other hand, are able to............colors. They have
(in, an, on, for)   (try, paint, call, distinguish)

been trained successfully............go for their meal to a............,
(to, have, has, for)   (corner, cupboard, castle, kennel)

the door of which was painted............a certain color, and to ignore
(about, of, in, up)

..........available cupboards with differently colored doors,..........
(other, another, if, for)   (under, over, on, in)

which there was no food. Apart...........monkeys and apes, however,
(for, from, by, in)

most mammals............to be color-blind, at any rate............
(seem, show, try, tell)   (that, thus, these, those)

which have been scientifically tested. Even............have been shown
(bears, bulls, calves, colts)

not to see............as a color. In spite of............belief, they
(red, blue, yellow, green)   (proud, holy, regular, popular)

are not excited by............, and they cannot distinguish red from
(red, blue, yellow, green)

............gray. No doubt any bright waving............excites a
(light, dark, cold, hot)   (flag, cap, cloth, hand)

high-spirited bull.

"The Colors That Animals Can See," H. Munro Fox, *The Personality of Animals*

WORD CLUES

A. *In the following paragraphs, the boldfaced word is the vocabulary word; the italicized word is the "Context Clue" to the meaning of the vocabulary word. Take three steps in this exercise: (1) Write out the vocabulary word and context clue in the blanks below each paragraph; (2) Enter your best guess as to the meaning of the vocabulary word in the "Probable Meaning" blank; (3) Look up the word's dictionary definition and write it out concisely in the proper blank.*

Example:

In order to understand how to **administer** the test, the professor first read the directions on the front of the sealed envelope. Then he *gave the tests* to the students, telling them to place the tests face down on their desks.

Vocabulary Word.......................................

Context Clue.......................................

Probable Meaning.......................................

Dictionary Definition.......................................

1. When John approached the edge of the cliff, he *guessed* that the edge would be strong enough to walk on. But when the ground collapsed beneath his feet, he learned that his **assumption** had been wrong.

    Vocabulary Word...

    Context Clue...

    Probable Meaning...

    Dictionary Definition..

2. The doctor explained the **distinction** between influenza and pneumonia by outlining the *different symptoms* of each disease.

    Vocabulary Word...

    Context Clue...

    Probable Meaning...

    Dictionary Definition..

3. To **analyze** the contents of the drink, Alan *examined* drops of the liquid under a microscope. This *study* convinced him that no toxic matter was present.

    Vocabulary Word...

    Context Clue...

    Probable Meaning...

    Dictionary Definition..

4. After Brian had finished cutting the second piece of lumber for the patio roof, he found that it did not **correspond** with the first piece: the second was too long. To make the second piece *match* the first piece, he trimmed off half an inch.

    Vocabulary Word...

    Context Clue...

    Probable Meaning...

    Dictionary Definition..

5. Marie wanted *to move* into her new apartment next week, but her landlady told her it would not be possible to **occupy** the premises until the first of the month.

    Vocabulary Word...

    Context Clue...

    Probable Meaning...

    Dictionary Definition..

B. *A list of various forms of each vocabulary word follows. For each number, choose a form different from the vocabulary word and use it meaningfully in a sentence. For example, in 2., use any form except the noun* **distinction.** *Write a total of five sentences.*

Verbs	Nouns	Adjectives	Adverbs
1. to assume	assumption	assumptive	
2.	distinction distinctiveness	distinct distinctive	distinctly distinctively
3. to analyze	analysis analyst	analytic	analytically
4. to correspond	correspondent correspondence	corresponding	correspondingly
5. to occupy	occupant occupation occupier occupancy	occupational	occupationally

Composition: Show What You Have Learned

Use one of the topic sentences below as the beginning of a paragraph. Make sure that your paragraph demonstrates the principles of unity and coherence.

Choose a composition topic from either Group I or Group II.

GROUP I: TOPICS FOR THE HUMANITIES STUDENT

1. Television exerts a strong influence on present-day life.
2. The revolutions that took place in France, the United States, and Russia resulted in major changes in those countries.
3. My favorite musical instrument is the . . . .
4. Of the books I have read, the one that seems most valuable to me is . . . .
5. Much can be learned about a culture by studying its funeral practices.
6. . . . is the most fascinating museum (or art gallery) that I have visited.

GROUP II: TOPICS FOR THE SCIENCE STUDENT

1. Bacteria are often confused with viruses.
2. The importance of oxygen to mankind cannot be overstated.
3. Mathematics is called a universal language—and for good reason.
4. The computer has changed the science of accounting.
5. Mechanics is the oldest of all the physical sciences.
6. In engineering, one of the most important concepts is that of measurement.

Chapter **2**

The
Chronological
Paragraph

How to Enlarge a Photograph

Topic sentence
at beginning of
paragraph

Subordination by
participial phrase

Compound predicate

Opening with
infinitive phrase

Opening with
prepositional phrase

Making a photographic enlargement is a process that can be done in a series of simple steps. A smaller photograph is made larger through a series of mechanical and chemical actions. The room in which an enlargement is made, **called a "darkroom," need not be** totally dark but **may be lighted** by special lamps that produce a kind of light to which enlarging paper is not sensitive. Supplies needed for enlargement include an enlarger (a machine with lamp and lens), three different liquid solutions with a tray for each, and a stock of enlarging paper. Enlarging paper comes in different grades. In determining the correct grade to choose, first study the range of contrast in your negative. If the negative has sharp contrasts, a "soft" paper will reduce them. If the negative has little contrast, though, a "hard" paper will heighten contrasts. **To begin work,** place a photographic negative in the machine's negative carrier. Then turn on the lamp to check the lens adjustment. **In the printing process,** this lamp passes light through the negative to the lens to focus rays on the enlarging paper. The light reaching the paper then produces a latent[1] image that is later made visible by

[1]*latent:* not visible but capable of being developed or expressed.

31

Transition

chemical action. How light or dark the final enlargement will be depends on the amount of light striking the paper. Once you are satisfied that the enlarger lens is properly focused, turn off the light. **Now** you are ready for the next step: making a test strip on which you will try several different timed exposures to determine the best one for your negative. Select a narrow piece of enlarging paper as your test strip. Place it on the enlarger easel and, for your first exposure, cover most of the paper with a piece of cardboard to block out light. In steps lasting a few seconds each, move the cardboard across the test strip a few seconds at a time,

Subordination by participial phrase

exposing additional segments of the paper. Five or six segments should be enough. Drop the test strip into the tray containing the developing chemical; development normally takes about two minutes. **Then** transfer

Transition

the test strip for a few seconds to another tray containing "stop bath," a solution that halts further development of the image. Finally, move the paper to a third

Comma for appositive

tray for a "fixing bath," in which the image is made permanent. Although this complete final chemical action takes about five minutes, you may remove the test strip after only a few seconds of soaking to examine it under a bright light. The developed test strip will contain examples of five or six different exposure times.

Subordination by adverb clause

When you have selected the exposure that is most to your liking, place a fresh piece of enlarging paper on the easel, make the exposure you have selected, develop

Commas in series

the image, fix and wash the print, and dry it. All that remains is to properly mount your finished enlargement to show it off to full advantage.

Writing Analysis

PRONOUNS AS TRANSITIONS

In the first chapter you have studied lists of transitions that are helpful in giving coherence to your paragraph, making it easier for the reader to follow your line of thought from one sentence to the next. These transitions have included general expressions, such as **moreover** and **on the other hand,** as well as transitions particularly suited to chronological development. There are other words that will also help you to tie together your ideas. These words are pronouns.

In addition to substituting for nouns, pronouns function as linking words. They carry a thought forward either within a single sentence (We wondered what **this** meant.) or between two sentences (We looked at the fishing boats. **They** were tied up at the dock.). Pronouns commonly serving as transitions are **I, you, he, she, they, them, this, that, these, those, one, such,** and **it.**

In addition to creating paragraph coherence, pronouns help a writer in other ways. For one thing, they make it unnecessary to repeat words too often. Observe the awkward repetition in the first sentence below before a pronoun is substituted for the phrase "borrow money":

> Even to borrow money is wrong, according to Kant, because if everyone did borrow money, there would be no money left to borrow.

> Even to borrow money is wrong, according to Kant, because if every one did **this,** there would be no money left to borrow.

Using pronouns also frequently permits a writer to express an idea in fewer words. By substituting two pronouns in the sentence below, two words can be eliminated and needless repetition avoided:

> If a person feels that a law is unjust, the person should work to repeal the law.

> If a person feels that a law is unjust, he should work to repeal **it.**

Read this example of a short paragraph in which pronouns keep the thought moving smoothly from sentence to sentence with a minimum of words:

> Karl wrote a number of suggestions to the newspaper about low-cost housing. Although **they** were not all practical suggestions, **they** were original enough to be published, leading to a surprising response from the public. Hundreds of letters were written to the editor. Some of **them** favored Karl's plans; others criticized **them.** The editor chose five letters in favor of Karl's plans and five letters opposed to **them. These** were all published in the newspaper the following week.

EXERCISE 5
Pronouns as Transitions

Rewrite this paragraph, substituting appropriate pronouns for the bold-faced phrases.

> The college athletic director was disturbed by the poor attendance at college athletic events. **The athletic director** thought that both students and townspeople should support the college teams by attending games. **The games** seldom drew more than fifty spectators. Because of **the games' seldom drawing more than fifty spectators,** the teams needed new equipment and new uniforms. **The new equipment and new uniforms** cost more money than the athletic department could afford. To help

improve matters, the director wrote letters to several city businessmen, asking for their help. **Several city businessmen** all replied to the letters, promising to encourage their employees to attend the sports events. Three businessmen contributed money to help pay for the teams' expenses. **The money** was used to purchase new track shoes and new basketballs.

CHRONOLOGICAL PARAGRAPH DEVELOPMENT

The logical way to write about a process is in order of time, or chronologically. A writer begins with the first step in a process and describes the sequence in order until he reaches the last step. This kind of organization can be used in a single paragraph or in a much longer essay. Both factual writing and works of fiction, such as short stories and novels, are often developed chronologically.

The model paragraph on enlarging a photograph demonstrates the importance for process writing of a firm chronological organization, made evident to the reader by well-placed transitions. Notice that the writer virtually leads the reader by the hand through the steps of exposing and developing a test strip. The sequence opens with the phrase "to begin work." It continues with these signal words: "then," "in the printing process," "once you are satisfied," "now," "select," "place," "in steps lasting a few minutes each," "drop," and "then." At this point, the conclusion of the process is announced by the transition, "finally." The result of this painstaking effort on the writer's part is what every writer hopes for: absolute clarity.

College students find many uses for chronological development. In science courses, the time sequence is a natural form or organization for describing a process. Here is a short paragraph in which the writer, telling how to build a simple device for observing the sun, naturally presents the different steps in the order in which they should be taken:

> To build your own sunscope, get a carton and cut a hole in one side, big enough to poke your head through. Paste white paper on the inside surface that you will be facing. Then punch a pinhole into the opposite side high enough so that the little shaft of light will miss your head. For a sharper image you can make a better pinhole by cutting a one-inch-square hole in the carton, taping a piece of aluminum foil over this hole, and then making the pinhole in the foil. Finally, tape the box shut and cover all light leaks with black tape.
>
> "Building a Sunscope," *Life* (July 12, 1963)

Notice that each step in the process of building a sunscope is presented in order, from first to last. Furthermore, the two connectives "then" and "finally" add coherence to this brief process paragraph.

Sometimes several related processes are discussed in a short passage, each of them chronologically. This is often true in technical writing, as in the following selection from an electrical principles textbook that describes how a circuit breaker and reverse-current relay work:

One of the most widespread uses of the electromagnetic principle is in *relays*. These are nothing more than magnetically operated switches. Such switches could have one contact (single pole) or many contacts (double pole, triple pole, etc.). The contacts could be *normally open* and are closed by electromagnetic action, or, vice versa, the contacts could be *normally closed* and are opened by electromagnetic action. An example of this second type is the *circuit breaker* used to protect against overloads or short circuits. The circuit breaker is closed manually to apply power. Should the current in the circuit at any time exceed some preset limit, the electromagnetic action of the relay will cause the circuit breaker contacts to open. Another example of the normally-closed relay is the *reverse-current* relay used in the battery-charging circuits of aircraft and automobiles. When the engine is running at above some minimum speed, the generator charges the battery. If the engine is stopped (or running at too low a speed), the generator cannot supply power to the battery, but the battery could discharge—or even be short-circuited— through the generator. A reverse-current relay will open the circuit between generator and battery and prevent discharge of the battery. . . . This simple electromagnetic device is a major factor in our automated technology. In the home, relays are responsible for the clicks and clacks heard during operation of dishwashers, clothes washers, air conditioners, etc. In industry, relays are the "fingers" that control the sequence of operation in the myriad[1] of automated processes.

"Relays," J. J. DeFrance, *Electrical Fundamentals*

[1]*myriad:* vast number.

Explaining electrical fundamentals in writing is a tricky business, even for the scientifically minded student. The writer of the above paragraph succeeds, though, because he realizes that the more complex one's subject matter is, the greater is the need for transitions, relatively short sentences, and vocabulary that is simple and direct.

The care with which the writer has signaled his thought progression in the first four sentences with pronouns and repeated words is typical of his entire approach:

TRANSITION BETWEEN SENTENCES 1 and 2:	". . . in **relays. These** are . . ."
TRANSITION BETWEEN SENTENCES 2 and 3:	" . . . operated **switches. Such switches** could . . ."
TRANSITION BETWEEN SENTENCES 3 and 4:	". . . many **contacts** (double pole, triple pole, etc.). The **contacts** could . . ."

As the paragraph continues, two additional transitions play an important part: "An example . . ." and "Another example. . . ." And in the concluding two sentences, the writer uses parallelism to clarify his ideas: "In the home . . ." and "In industry . . . ."

Observe the use of the modal "should" in the middle of the first paragraph. This modal is correctly used here to express conditional probability. Modals are further explained in Chapter 3.

Another example of chronological development is found in the following passage telling of a new method of study. The process is known as the Survey Q3R Method for studying textbooks. In addition to illustrating chronological development, this selection may help you to improve your study habits:

The title for this new higher-level study skill is abbreviated[1] in the current fashion to make it easier to remember and to make reference to it more simple. The symbols [Q3R] stand for the steps which the student follows in using the method; a description of each of these steps is given below:

Survey
1. *Glance over the headings in the chapter to see the few big points which will be developed.* This survey should not take more than a minute and will show the three to six core[2] ideas around which the rest of the discussion will cluster.[3] If the chapter has a final summary paragraph, this will also list the ideas developed in the chapter. This orientation will help you organize the ideas as you read them later.

Question
2. Now begin to work. *Turn the first heading into a question.* This will arouse your curiosity and so increase comprehension. It will bring to mind information already known, thus helping you to understand that section more quickly. And the question will make important points stand out while explanatory detail is recognized as such. This turning the heading into a question can be done on the instant of reading the heading, but it demands a conscious effort on the part of the reader to make this query[4] for which he must read to find the answer.

Read
3. *Read to answer that question,* i.e., to the end of the first headed section. This is not a passive[5] plowing along each line but an active search for the answer.

[1]*abbreviated:* shortened, made brief. [2]*core:* central, essential. [3]*cluster:* gather,

Recite

4. Having read the first section, look away from the book and try briefly to *recite the answer to your question*. Use your own words and name an example. If you can do this, you know what is in the book; if you can't, glance over the section again. An excellent way to do this reciting from memory is to jot down cue[6] phrases in outline form on a sheet of paper. Make these notes very brief!

Now repeat steps 2, 3, and 4 on each succeeding headed section. That is, turn the next heading into a question, read to answer that question, and recite the answer by jotting down cue phrases in your outline. Read in this way until the entire lesson is complete.

Review

5. When the lesson has thus been read through, *look over your notes and get a bird's-eye view*[7] of the points and of their relationship and *check your memory* as to the content by reciting on the major subpoints under each heading. This checking of memory can be done by covering up the notes and trying to recall the main points. Then expose each major point and try to recall the subpoints listed under it.

These five steps of the Survey Q3R Method—Survey, Question, Read, Recite, and Review—when polished into a smooth and efficient method should result in the student reading faster, picking out the important points, and fixing them in memory. The student will find one other worthwhile outcome: quiz questions will seem happily familiar because the headings turned into questions are usually the points emphasized in quizzes. In predicting actual quiz questions and looking up the answers beforehand, the student feels that he is effectively studying what is important in a course.

"The Survey Q3R Study Method," Francis P. Robinson, *Effective Study*

group. [4]*query:* question. [5]*passive:* not working, inactive. [6]*cue:* hint, suggestion, reminder. [7]*bird's-eye view:* view from above, overall view.

This passage about the Q3R method of study sets up a sequence of steps for the student to follow. To emphasize the time order of these steps, the writer has included several connectives. Such words as "now" at points 2 and 4 and "then" at point 5 effectively mark off the chronological development. In addition, many introductory -*ing* phrases, such as "Having read the first section. . . ." at point 4, are useful transitional devices for time order So are introductory clauses beginning with adverbs expressing time ("when," "during," "before," "after," "while," "until," "since"). An example of this technique occurs at point 5: "When the lesson has thus been read through. . . ."

As you begin to write your process paragraph using chronological development, review the techniques used in the model paragraph and the three additional examples you have read. Notice how the writers begin their sentences. Observe how they link their sentences together. Note that when a rather complicated process is being described, sentences are kept short so that the reader will not become confused. Use patterns and techniques similar to those in these writings to create a stronger paragraph of your own.

VARIETY IN SENTENCE OPENINGS

Writers of English sometimes fall into the monotonous habit of starting every sentence with its subject. Of course, it is often desirable to place a subject at the beginning of a sentence. You will find many sentences in this chapter that begin with a subject; the first sentence in this paragraph is an example. But to achieve a varied and pleasing style, English writers often place words, phrases, or clauses before the subject of a sentence. By doing this, they avoid the monotony of a paragraph in which all the sentences begin in the same way.

The following examples will help you to learn how to vary your sentence openings:

1. Begin sentences with an appositive.

Subject first	The forest ranger, an expert in forest fire control, talked to the campers about safety in the woods.
Transposed appositive first	**An expert in forest fire control,** the forest ranger talked to the campers about safety in the woods.

2. Begin sentences with single-word modifiers.

Subject first	The time for decision had finally come.
Single-word modifier first	**Finally,** the time for decision had come.
Subject first	Cardinal Richelieu was shrewd and powerful and had enormous influence upon the king of France.
Single-word modifiers first	**Shrewd and powerful,** Cardinal Richelieu had enormous influence upon the king of France.

3. Begin sentences with phrase modifiers.

Subject first	Madame Curie was an industrious worker in the scientific laboratory.

Prepositional phrase first	**In the scientific laboratory,** Madame Curie was an industrious worker.
Subject first	The inspectors looked through several suitcases to find the hidden papers.
Infinitive phrase first	**To find the hidden papers,** the inspectors looked through several suitcases.
Subject first	Von Karajan conducted *Fidelio* without waiting for news of his revised contract.
Gerund phrase first	**Without waiting for news of his revised contract,** Von Karajan conducted *Fidelio.*
Subject first	Confucius studied people's actions and learned a great deal about human nature.
Participial phrase first	**Studying people's actions,** Confucius learned a great deal about human nature.

4. Begin sentences with clause modifiers.

Subject first	The gardeners had to plant roses when they ran out of carnations.
Adverb clause first	**When they ran out of carnations,** the gardeners had to plant roses.
Subject first	The young representative's fondest hope was that the legislature would pass the antismoking bill.
Noun clause first	**That the legislature would pass the antismoking bill** was the young legislator's fondest hope.

EXERCISE 6
Sentence Openings

Revise the following sentences so that they begin in the various ways mentioned in parentheses.

1. The pioneer was strong and healthy and lived to be 112 years old. (Begin with single-word modifiers.)
2. Mr. Boyd was angry and began to defend his reputation with strong arguments. (Begin with a single-word modifier.)
3. Richard Halliburton began his travels at a very early age and had many exotic adventures. (Begin with a present participial phrase.)
4. The university will open on September 19 unless circumstances force a postponement. (Begin with an adverb clause.)
5. The Carnegie Foundation president listed all the grants in his annual report. (Begin with a prepositional phrase.)
6. The sailors wandered into town and overstayed their leave during their night in port. (Begin with a prepositional phrase.)

7. Plato, the author of the Socratic dialogues, is read by many philosophy students. (Begin with an appositive.)
8. Tolstoy, completing *Anna Karenina*, won national recognition in Russia. (Begin with a past participial phrase.)
9. The mosaics at the University of Mexico, praised by art critics throughout the world, are one of the beautiful things to see in Mexico City. (Begin with a present participial phrase.)
10. Garibaldi, a national hero in Italy, brought about important political changes in that country. (Begin with an appositive.)
11. One of our greatest fears was that the car would be stolen. (Begin with a noun clause.)
12. An American television viewer can gain a liberal education by watching the Public Broadcasting System channels. (Begin with a gerund phrase.)
13. The American soprano took her vocal training in Milan to become a major opera star. (Begin with an infinitive phrase.)
14. They decided to plant oleander hedges around the property lines of their home site. (Begin with a prepositional phrase.)
15. You may regret in leisure what you impulsively do in haste. (Begin with a noun clause.)

VARIETY IN SENTENCE STRUCTURE AND LENGTH

Students usually will not pay close attention to a boring book. Yet few students realize that their own writing can also fail to hold a reader's attention. You can't always be sure that *what* you have to say will interest a reader. But you can be reasonably sure that *how* you say it will hold his attention. If you give close attention to composing sentences of different structures and different lengths, your prose style will become a more attractive setting for your thoughts.

Look first at a paragraph that has been written in a monotonous way. Most of its sentences are too similar in both structure and length. Then read the second paragraph to see how the same content can be presented in a more vital way through sentence variety:

Monotonous Style

Ludwig van Beethoven overcame many personal problems to achieve artistic greatness. He was a major composer of the nineteenth century. He was born in Bonn, Germany, in 1770 and first studied music with the court organist, Gilles van der Eeden. His father was excessively strict and given to heavy drinking. His mother died when Beethoven was a young man, and he was named guardian of his two younger brothers. He was appointed deputy court organist to Christian Gottlob Neefe at a surprisingly early age in 1782 He also played harpsichord and viola. He was sent to Vienna in 1792 by his patron, Count Ferdinand Waldstein, to study music under Haydn. Beethoven remained unmarried. He was troubled by financial worries throughout his adult life. His payments from publishers were irregular, and his patrons were erratic in supporting him. He was also continually plagued by ill health. An ear infection led to his tragic deafness in 1819. His writing of music continued, however, in spite of this handicap. He completed mature masterpieces of great musical depth: three piano sonatas, four string quartets, the *Missa Solemnis*, and the 9th Symphony. He died in 1827. During his life he was passionately dedicated to independence. He often flew into fits of rage. Goethe once said of him: "I am astonished by his talent but he is unfortunately an altogether untamed personality." His personality may have been untamed, but his music shows great discipline and control, and that is how we remember him best.

Varied Style

Ludwig van Beethoven, a major composer of the nineteenth century, overcame many personal problems to achieve artistic greatness. Born in Bonn, Germany, in 1770, he first studied music with the court organist, Gilles van der Eeden. His father was excessively strict and given to heavy drinking. When his mother died, Beethoven, then a young man, was named guardian of his two younger brothers. Appointed deputy court organist to Christian Gottlob Neefe at a surprisingly early age in 1782, Beethoven also played harpsichord and viola. In 1792 he was sent to Vienna by his patron, Count Ferdinand Waldstein, to study music under Haydn. Beethoven remained unmarried. Because of irregular payments from his publishers and erratic support from his patrons, he was troubled by financial worries throughout his adult life. Continually plagued by ill health, he developed an ear infection which led to his tragic deafness in 1819. In spite of this handicap, however, he continued to write music. He completed mature masterpieces of great musical depth: three piano sonatas, four string quartets, the *Missa Solemnis*, and the 9th Symphony. He died in 1827. His life was marked by a passionate dedication to independence. Noting that Beethoven often flew into fits of rage, Goethe once said of him, "I am astonished by his talent, but he is unfortunately an altogether untamed personality." Although Beethoven's personality may have been untamed, his music shows great discipline and control, and this is how we remember him best.

Note that the sentence structure of the second paragraph has been improved over that of the first paragraph by adding three types of sentence openings:

1. By introductory prepositional phrases
    In 1792 . . .
    In his later years . . .
2. By introductory participial phrases
    Appointed deputy court organist . . .
    Continually plagued by ill health . . .

3. By introductory adverb clauses
   When his mother died . . .
   Although Beethoven's personality may have been untamed . . .

Varied Length

Variety in sentence length has also been improved in the second paragraph. The shortest sentence has three words; the longest one contains twenty-eight words.

Study this analysis of the difference in sentence variety between the first and second paragraphs:

	1st Par.	2nd Par.
Sentences beginning with the subject	20	4
Sentences beginning with a modifier	0	10
Simple and compound sentences	19	11
Complex and compound-complex sentences	0	3
Average sentence length	13 wds.	17 wds.

These paragraphs have shown that variety in sentence structure and length can add interest to a piece of writing. Take into consideration these three important reasons for a writer purposefully to vary his sentence structure and sentence length:

1. To hold the reader's interest.
2. To create a more polished and mature prose style.
3. To give added emphasis to the ideas he is presenting.

EXERCISE 7
Sentence Structure and Length

Rewrite this paragraph, revising it to create differences in structure and length of sentences.

Learning a new language is best accomplished by living in a foreign country. Brief trips as a tourist barely afford the visitor the opportunities to master purely superficial phrases such as "How are you?" or "Where's the bank?" You should establish a residence for at least six months. Shorter stays are only prolonged vacations. The day-to-day living routines require you to learn vocabulary necessary to mail a letter or get your kitchen faucet repaired. This survival instinct forces you to face the language head-on rather than to be satisfied with flowery tourist formalities. You can immerse yourself among the chattering women buying plump tomatoes in an open-air market. You can ride along with workers on their way to a factory in a trolley. You can attend the plays, films, and lectures available in most foreign cities. You will find that each experience provides opportunities to hear a language spoken in the local idiom by expressive, colorful people. You can learn to read, speak, think—even *dream* in a language other than your own through such in-depth exposures.

USING STRONG ACTIVE VERBS

Writers often fail to realize the importance of the verb in an English sentence. In the preface to *Modern English Usage*, editor Jacques Barzun says, "This book deals specifically with American faults of language and style, such as the tendency to write by means of nouns instead of verbs." In addition to stressing nouns, many writers tend to use adjectives and adverbs too often, failing to realize that the heart of the sentence is the verb.

Not all verbs are equally strong, however. Strangely enough, the verb that most people learn first and continue to use repeatedly can be one of the weakest: the **be** verb. Any form of this verb, including *is, are, were,* and *has been,* may weaken a paragraph, especially a descriptive or narrative paragraph. Other frequently used verbs, such as *go, feel, have,* and *become,* can also be improved upon, in many cases. Most final compositions will be better if a writer goes over his first draft carefully, replacing many of the overworked verbs with more forceful ones.

Consider three examples in which strong verbs are substituted for weaker ones:

Weak	The voice from the control tower **sounded** in our earphones.
Strong	The voice from the control tower **crackled** in our earphones.
Weak	Black smoke **was coming** out of the rear of the engine.
Strong	Black smoke **belched** out of the rear of the engine.
Weak	Flames **were reaching** the gasoline tanks.
Strong	Flames **licked** over the gasoline tanks.

As you increase your English vocabulary, try to learn a variety of colorful verbs. A well-chosen verb will give surprising power to a sentence.

EXERCISE 8
Strong Active Verbs

Look through the reading selections in this text or in other books, in magazines, or in newspapers to find ten especially strong active verbs. Write out the ten sentences in which the verbs appear.

Punctuation Points

TWO USES OF THE COMMA

Knowing some basic facts about the structural patterns of English sentences will help you to understand more clearly the principles of English punctuation. Before looking at two uses of the comma, therefore, let's review the clause and the phrase.

A clause is a group of words containing a subject and a verb. A phrase consists of two or more words not including a subject and verb. A clause may be either **independent** (in which case it makes a single predication and is understood as a complete unit of thought) or **dependent** (in which case it is an incomplete unit of thought and needs to be attached to an independent clause). An independent clause, with or without modifiers, is considered a simple sentence if no other clauses are attached:

We like Christmas parties. *(Independent clause; simple sentence)*

Two independent clauses joined by a coordinating conjunction form a *compound sentence.* The chief coordinating conjunctions are *and, but, for, or,* and *nor:*

We began our study at eight, and we didn't finish until two. *(Two independent clauses; compound sentence)*

Other types of sentences are the complex sentence, made up of one independent clause and one or more dependent clauses, and the compound-complex sentence, containing two or more independent clauses and one or more dependent clauses. A dependent clause functions as either a noun clause or as an adjective or adverb modifier. (A modifier is a word or group of words that qualifies, limits, describes, or restricts another word or group of words.) Unlike an independent clause, a dependent clause is introduced by a subordinating word, sometimes not expressed, which signals that it cannot stand alone as a sentence:

We decided **that we would go** to a restaurant. *(Dependent noun clause introduced by the subordinating word* **that***; complex sentence)*
The man **who questioned us** was a detective. *(Dependent adjective clause introduced by the subordinating word* **who***; complex sentence)*
We invited many guests **because we wanted to have a large party.** *(Dependent adverb clause introduced by the subordinating word* **because***; complex sentence)*

Punctuating Compound Sentences   Now you are ready to examine two rules for using the comma. First, a comma is generally placed before the coordinating conjunction in a compound sentence. However, a comma should not be placed in a simple sentence to separate a **compound predicate** —two or more verbs connected by a conjunction and referring back to a single subject. Notice the difference in punctuation of these two types of sentences:

The committee *met* at three and *adjourned* at four o'clock.
    (Simple sentence with a compound predicate; no comma needed)
The *committee met* at three, and *it adjourned* at four o'clock.
    (Compound sentence with two independent clauses; comma needed)

He *bought* a red evening dress and *gave* it to his wife for her birthday.
   (*Simple sentence; compound predicate; no comma*)
He *bought* a red evening dress, and *he gave* it to his wife for her birthday.
   (*Compound sentence; two independent clauses; comma needed*)

A helpful rule to follow in punctuating these kinds of sentences is the following: if one sentence can be broken into two separate and complete sentences, a comma is necessary before the conjunction. If the sentence cannot be divided into two independent parts, a comma is not needed. Let's apply this rule to three sentences.

1. This decision is important, for each part of the production should be coordinated with every other part. *This decision is important. Each part of the production should be coordinated with every other part.* (Two separate, complete sentences; comma needed before the conjunction *for*)
2. Does the play require a realistic approach, or should it be staged as a fantasy? *Does the play require a realistic approach? Should it be staged as a fantasy?* (Two separate, complete sentences; comma needed before the conjunction *or*)
3. First, he thinks of the taste of his audience and chooses a play that they will both understand and enjoy. *First, he thinks of the tastes of his audience. And chooses a play that they will both understand and enjoy.* (One complete sentence, one sentence fragment; two unequal parts; no comma needed before the conjunction *and*)

When a compound sentence is very short, a comma before the conjunction is not essential:

The thunder roared and the lightning flashed.

EXERCISE 9
Punctuating Compound Sentences

A. *Write out the following sentences, adding commas where necessary.*

1. The chairman rapped on the table and waited for order.
2. The chairman rapped on the table and the audience quieted down.
3. You can lead a horse to water but you can't make him drink.
4. Sam decided to go to summer school but not to take courses for credit.
5. The dancers canceled their Tuesday performance but scheduled another concert for Sunday.
6. Hot air rises but cold air sinks.
7. A product must be advertised or the public will not be interested in buying it.
8. You will either drive to Paris or take the train to Lyon.
9. Paul pulled over to the side of the road and let the other car pass.

10. Lawrence has worked after school and on Saturdays and he has bought a car with his savings.
11. I have heard about the pianist and harpist and want to see them perform.
12. You will want to pick up a schedule for the football season will be exciting.
13. Sheila gave her sister a recipe for a delicious carrot cake.
14. Neither the time you have spent nor the money you have invested seems to have produced results.
15. They decided not to take a vacation this year nor did they plan for many long weekend trips.

B. *The following sentences are correct as they are written. Copy them, adding the words in parentheses at the points indicated by the caret (∧). If the additional words make a comma necessary, add it.*

1. I have decided to take your advice ∧ . (and enroll in college)
2. Kevin's mother approved of the plan ∧ . (but his father was doubtful)
3. The city will have to increase the bus fares ∧ . (or reduce the service)
4. How can Karl study and eat ∧ at the same time? (and listen to the radio)
5. Mr. Perez turned around and ∧ looked at us disapprovingly. (he)
6. They tried to telephone their parents ∧ . (but failed to get through).
7. You can decide whether to continue ∧ after you have taken five lessons. (or to stop)
8. Mother was washing clothes in the basement ∧ . (and didn't hear the doorbell)
9. The maid packed us a picnic lunch ∧ . (for our trip to the woods)
10. Nothing remains on the calendar ∧ . (for the semester has ended)

Punctuating Introductory Clauses and Phrases   A second rule for using the comma concerns words used at the beginning of sentences. Commas are often used to set off introductory dependent clauses and phrases preceding independent clauses. Examples of the comma used to set off an introductory clause and phrase follow:

While the crew scrambled out of the emergency exits, (introductory clause) I looked quickly at the burning engine.
Expecting an explosion at any moment, (introductory phrase) we plunged toward the airfield.

The general practice for placing or not placing a comma after an introductory clause or phrase is this:

1. Place a comma after an introductory adverb clause.

After he wrote the poem, he sent it to the magazine.

2. Place a comma after an introductory participle or a participial phrase.

   Waiting, he listened carefully. (*Participle*)
   Jumping across the river, he grabbed for the rope. (*Participial phrase*)

3. Place a comma after an introductory prepositional phrase if it is long and complicated. No comma is needed after a short introductory prepositional phrase.

   During the first half of the movie we saw last week, I found it hard to become interested in the plot.
   For her birthday she received a gold bracelet.

4. Place a comma after any other introductory clause or phrase if it contains two or more adjectives, if it is transitional, if there is a chance of misreading the sentence, or if it is an appositive. (An appositive is a substantive that explains another substantive.)

   Tired and dirty, they returned to the camp. (*Adjectives*)
   On the other hand, it may be wise to wait. (*Transitional phrase*)
   For only two, two pounds of steak is too much (*May be misread*)
   A famous opera singer, the visiting speaker told of his experiences working at La Scala Opera House. (*Appositive*)

EXERCISE 10
Punctuating Introductory Clauses and Phrases

Write out these sentences, adding commas where necessary.

1. A Nobel Prize winner the mathematician was offered a post at the university.
2. Surprised and happy they accepted the award.
3. Feeling a chill go down my spine I reached for the flashlight.
4. When we first met Stephen was a college student.
5. In the early days of the automobile industry cars were expensive because so few of them were produced.
6. Ever since the invention of printing man's educational level has steadily risen.
7. On the ship he felt seasick.
8. Although he shouted our name we did not hear him.
9. After the meeting was opened the minutes were read.
10. Running I caught up with them strolling ahead in the road.
11. During winter and spring the drought-stricken farmers in fourteen states received help from the Department of Agriculture.
12. When Seward negotiated the purchase of Alaska in 1867 most Americans thought of the region as a barren, desolate land of snow and ice.
13. In order to provide for the physical fitness of its students Switzerland's schools place much emphasis on calisthenics and physical education courses.

14. Because the water comes from artesian wells it is very pure.
15. Possessing unusual mechanical ability Claude is active in the construction business, building roads, docks, and bridges.

PUNCTUATING A SERIES

Writers of English differ in their approach to punctuating a series, such as **book, pencil, and paper.** Some writers place a comma before the conjunction "and" in a series; others do not. Many times the meaning of a series is perfectly clear without a comma before the conjunction, as in **book, pencil and paper.** But when there is more than one "and" in a series, it can result in confusion:

Confusing	Mr. Bruce ordered grapefruit, coffee with sugar and ham and eggs.
Clear	Mr. Bruce ordered grapefruit, coffee with sugar, and ham and eggs.

Because a missing comma before the conjunction in a series will sometimes confuse the reader, it is advisable to place a comma before the conjunction in all series constructions:

He visited Brazil, Argentina, and Paraguay.
They sent books for the son, records for the daughter, and a set of dishes for the parents.

Here are additional points to observe in punctuating series:

1. Do not place a comma before the first item or after the last item in a series.

Wrong	After the picnic they found three shoes, a blanket, and a tennis ball, on the beach.
Right	After the picnic they found three shoes, a blanket, and a tennis ball on the beach.

2. If all of the items in a series are connected by **and** or **or,** do not use commas:

They telephoned Ruth and Alice and Jane.
We could leave on Wednesday or Thursday or Friday of next week.

3. Words customarily used in pairs, such as **ham and eggs, bread and butter, and pen and ink,** are set off as one item in a series:

For a late supper we had roast beef, rolls and butter, asparagus, and ice cream and cake.

4. Do not use a comma before the final adjective in a series if the adjective is thought of as part of the noun:

Wrong   It was a hot, humid, bright, August day.
Right   It was a hot, humid, bright August day.
Right   She is a sweet, charming, obedient young child.

5. Short independent clauses in a series may be separated by commas:

We worked, we swam, we read, we slept, and we saw the summer pass by too quickly.

EXERCISE 11
Punctuating a Series

Write out these sentences, adding commas where they are needed.

1. The states you must visit include New York Massachusetts Colorado and California.
2. Mrs. Evans asked the waitress for coffee toast and ham and eggs.
3. In everyone's opinion, she was a very sweet generous and thoughtful lady.
4. The bus pulled away, leaving him on a country road without his hat coat luggage and lunch box.
5. Our ship shuddered as the waves battered it the rain beat on its deck and the wind tore its sail.
6. Sitting on the patio, we gazed at the large pale and yellow moon hanging low in the sky.
7. A man reveals his character by his actions by the things he says and by the people he associates with.
8. For their vacation the couple decided to go first to Yosemite National Park next to Lake Tahoe and finally to Big Sur.
9. The Navajo Indian reservation was parched flat and deserted.
10. The Siamese cat is sleek restless and temperamental; the Persian cat is furry and slow-moving and regal.
11. Among the creative arts that flourish in Bali are music dance painting and woodcarving.
12. Brazil Argentina Peru and Bolivia are four South American countries that experienced revolutions in the 1930s.
13. You will want to see the Library of Congress the Capitol and the National Gallery of Art when you are in Washington.
14. To cook clams, dip them in beaten egg roll them in flour and fry them in deep fat for three minutes.
15. The poppy from which morphine heroin and codeine are derived is grown mainly in China India Iran and Turkey.

Grammar Skills

DEFINITE AND INDEFINITE ARTICLES

The traditional American saying "First things first" certainly applies to definite and indefinite articles. Because these tiny noun modifiers—*the, a,* and *an*—are consistently troublesome for nonnative writers, let's turn to them early in the course.

Keep in mind three important differences between definite and indefinite articles:

1. Difference in number
   An indefinite article *can only refer* to singular nouns.

a message	**BUT NOT**	**a** messages
an island		**an** islands

   But the definite article *can refer to* either a singular or plural noun.

the message	**OR**	**the** messages
the island		**the** islands

2. Difference in degree of specificity
   An indefinite article *does not* make a noun more specific.

   > You need **a passport** for international travel. (A single item, not specific.)
   > The student ate **an apple.** (A single item, not specific.)

   But the definite article *does* make a noun more specific.

   > **The passport** is in his attache case. (A specific passport.)
   > The student ate **the apple.** (A specific apple, such as the apple from the bowl.)

3. Difference in relation to uncountable nouns
   An indefinite article *is not used* with an uncountable noun (a noun such as **beauty, goodness, coffee, history, business, or football** that does not signify a single item or unit).
   But the definite article *can be placed* before an uncountable noun to make it more specific or to restrict it.

   > **Milk** is a nutritious drink. (Uncountable noun, not restricted.)
   > **The milk** in the refrigerator is cold. (Uncountable noun, restricted.)
   > **Justice** has been done. (Uncountable noun, not restricted.)
   > The press questioned **the justice** of the verdict. (Uncountable noun, restricted.)

To learn more about article usage before beginning the review that follows in this chapter and in Chapters 5 and 9, read over the information on

Definite and Indefinite Articles that appears in Appendix 5. Then test your refreshed knowledge.

EXERCISE 12
Definite and Indefinite Articles

A. *Write out this paragraph, inserting the definite article* **the** *when necessary in the blank spaces.*

Despite......apparent similarities between......Japanese and British motorcycles, they reveal some very real differences. Both types of...... vehicles have......engines, seats, steering bars, and fenders. Both use mixtures of......gasoline and oil, and both operate on......internal combustion principle. However,......Japanese bikes are low-powered compared to......high-powered British bikes. Another difference is that ......Japanese bikes wear out quickly whereas......British bikes are very strongly built. ......most important difference, though, is that ......Japanese machine is much less expensive than its British counterpart. This accounts for......tremendous popularity of......Japanese product.

B. *Write out these sentences, placing the indefinite article* **a** *or* **an** *before a noun wherever it is needed.*

1. People who take trip on ship almost always have good time.
2. In the morning they take walk around the deck or read magazine or book.
3. There is outdoor swimming pool and indoor recreation area.
4. Deck steward serves cup of soup at 11 A.M.
5. There are deck chairs to rest in and library with desks if passenger wants to write letter.
6. Large lunch makes everyone feel like taking afternoon nap.
7. Number of shops are open in the afternoon if passenger wants to make purchase.
8. Seven-course dinner is followed by dance or game of cards.
9. Many passengers walk outside at night for view of the sea and stars.
10. Ocean trip is experience I would like to repeat every year.

CHOOSING CORRECT PREPOSITIONS

For many bilingual students, the smallest English words sometimes present the largest problems. This is particularly true of prepositions. A preposition may be defined as a connecting word showing the relation of a noun or substitute for a noun to some other word in the sentence. Some of the most common prepositions are **around, among, across, above, about, below, behind, by, beyond, before, beside, beneath, except, for, from, in,** into, of, on, out, over, to, toward, through, upon, until, under, with, without, during, and concerning.

Several words are sometimes prepositions and sometimes adverbs, depending on how they are used in a sentence. These include around, down, in, on, off, out, over, and up. Such words are prepositions if they are followed by expressed objects; they are adverbs if they are not followed by objects:

Preposition	He walked out the door.
Adverb	He walked out.
Preposition	He drove around the block.
Adverb	He looked around.

Frequently two or three words are combined to form a preposition: according to, as to, in regard to, in spite of, instead of, because of, on account of, out of.

Prepositions appear constantly in English speech and writing. They cause trouble because sometimes they can be used interchangeably (He sat on the chair.; He sat in the chair.), because a single preposition can be used to express several different ideas (He is tall for his age.; I swam for an hour.), and because prepositions are often combined with verbs to create phrasal verbs (to look after someone; to look down on someone).

Prepositions commonly begin phrases that are used either as adjectives, modifying substantives (The hat with the feather costs ten dollars.) or as adverbs, modifying verbs, adjectives, or other adverbs (They contributed to the Red Cross.). Over ninety percent of preposition usage involves these nine prepositions: with, to, from, at, in, of, by, for, and on.

In Appendix 6 you will find lists of the most common meanings of these nine prepositions. Your most efficient method of study is to read prepositional phrases aloud until you can automatically produce the correct preposition construction when needed. Note that, in speaking, prepositions normally receive weak stress. To give you further practice in choosing correct prepositions, exercises will follow in this and later chapters.

EXERCISE 13
Prepositions

Write out each sentence, placing the correct preposition in each blank. Refer to Appendix 6 if you need help in choosing prepositions.

1. We made an appointment......9 o'clock......their house, but...... my way to meet her, I drove......a tree.
2. ......the twentieth......June we sailed......San Francisco...... Tokyo, expecting to arrive......the Japanese capital......the middle......July.

3. When my father is . . . . . . work, he concentrates so intently . . . . . . what he is doing that he does not notice people who come . . . . . . his office.
4. The shirt that I bought . . . . . . Barry was placed . . . . . . a gift box and tied . . . . . . red ribbon.
5. I applied . . . . . . a scholarship to study . . . . . . the University . . . . . . Colorado.
6. Anthropologists write . . . . . . life . . . . . . other cultures and learn much . . . . . . field trips . . . . . . remote areas.
7. We laughed so loudly . . . . . . the English film that we spilled our cups . . . . . . Coca-Cola . . . . . . the floor.
8. Although I wanted to go . . . . . . the village alone, my brother insisted . . . . . . coming . . . . . . me.
9. . . . . . . the first day . . . . . . our trip we drove . . . . . . two hundred miles.
10. Awakened . . . . . . the barking dogs, Mike leaped out . . . . . . bed and threw one . . . . . . his shoes . . . . . . the noisy animals.
11. Would you please tell me how to get . . . . . . the football field?
12. Yes, you go down Elm Street . . . . . . two blocks and then turn right . . . . . . Baldwin Avenue.
13. Drive . . . . . . Baldwin Avenue . . . . . . about three miles until you go . . . . . . a bridge and . . . . . . a tunnel.
14. Five blocks after you leave the tunnel, turn right . . . . . . Pacific Street, and . . . . . . the middle . . . . . . the block you will see the main entrance . . . . . . the football field.
15. I would suggest that you park your car . . . . . . the parking lot . . . . . . the football stadium.

CONTROLLED USE OF THE PASSIVE VOICE

Although passive voice verbs fill a definite need in English prose, a writer who chooses a passive without a good reason and who uses passive verbs too often will find that his writing lacks force. The antidote? Check the voice of verbs before writing the final draft of a paper; substitute active verbs for passives wherever possible. Doing this will give your writing a decided lift.

The active voice forms this construction: Someone **did** something. The passive voice forms this one: Something **was done** by someone. In the active voice, the subject does the acting or is in the state expressed by the verb:

The dog **chased** the cat.
Jim **likes** ice cream.
The president **signed** the bill.

In the passive voice, the object in the sentence is shifted to the subject position. The active verb is replaced by some form of *be* plus a past participle:

The cat **was chased** by the dog.
Ice cream **is liked** by Jim.
The bill **was signed.**

The passive voice is used much more frequently in scientific and technical writing than it is in general expository writing. Research shows that certain verbs commonly used in scientific writing customarily appear in the passive voice 51-100 percent of the time; among these are **connect, convert, attribute, activate, conduct, deduce, examine, measure,** and **record.**

Sometimes choosing the passive voice will help you gain the proper emphasis. The sentence "The bill was signed" shows the passive voice being used for this purpose. By placing the word **bill** in the subject position, the writer stresses it. In this case the doer of the action is less important than the thing acted upon.

The passive voice is appropriate in the following instances:

1. When the doer of the action is unimportant or unknown.

    The newspaper **was left** at our door.
    The deadline **was extended** for two days.
    A storm warning **was broadcast** to all ships.
    The battle **had been** lost.

2. When you want to place a noun next to a clause that modifies it.

    The old man **was hit** by a truck, which then ran off the road.
    Jack **was appointed** to the council by the dean, who respected his leadership qualities.

3. When you want to eliminate a vague pronoun subject.

    Vague   At the party **they** served punch and cake.
    Improved   At the party punch and cake **were served.**

The passive voice can also help to add variety to writing. Passive voice verbs will permit you to reduce the number of sentences beginning with the expletives "there" and "it," neither of which is particularly strong:

Expletive   **There** are many ways to vary the basic English sentence pattern of subject-verb-object.

Passive voice   The basic English sentence pattern of subject-verb-object **can be varied** in many ways.

On a page full of active sentences, moreover, the passive voice can also create variety, although adding phrases and clauses accomplishes this more effectively.

Even though the passive voice presents advantages at times to a writer, you should not rely on it unnecessarily. If the following sentence had been written with a passive verb, it would have been weaker:

Active   Socrates **refused** the chance to escape from prison.
Passive   The chance to escape from prison **was refused** by Socrates.

However, the passive voice would have been appropriate if this idea had been expressed in another context:

> The chance to escape from prison **was refused** by Socrates but not by King Richard.

EXERCISE 14
Passive Voice Verbs

A. *Revise the sentences containing awkward uses of the passive by substituting active forms. Write out sentences in which passives are effective without making any changes.*

1. Your letter has been received and carefully read by me.
2. That was a crisis in my life which will never be forgotten.
3. He had for years professed himself to be a democrat, and his belief in the sovereignty of the people was frequently announced.
4. Our hostess took us to the movie, and afterwards a delicious dinner was served.
5. Many trees were blown down by the storm.
6. After a short stop for dinner, our journey was resumed.
7. This story was told to me by the host.
8. I went to Yellowstone Park last summer, and the geysers were greatly enjoyed.
9. Many old friends were seen at the picnic.
10. Her umbrella was forgotten by my wife.

B. *Revise each sentence by substituting the passive voice verb for the active form whenever it would improve the sentence. Write out sentences that are effective as they are without making any changes.*

1. In many regions they cut and thresh the wheat at one time with big machines called combines.
2. I have never seen a basketball game.
3. In college they expect a student to study at least two hours for each class.
4. The voters elected Theodore Roosevelt President of the United States in 1904.
5. One should not permit the oil in an engine to run low.

THE COMPOUND PREDICATE

At an early stage, learners of English usually begin by writing simple sentences:

> Students attend classes.

They progress to putting two independent clauses together to form a compound sentence:

Students attend classes, and they participate in sports.

If a student depends too heavily upon this sentence construction, however, his writing will become monotonous. To avoid using too many compound sentences in a composition, try forming sentences with **compound predicates.**

A compound predicate consists of two or more verbs having a single subject. By changing a compound sentence to a simple sentence with a compound predicate, you can reduce the number of words in a sentence. Let's make this change in the compound sentence in the previous paragraph:

Compound sentence	Students **attend** classes, and they **participate** in sports.
Simple sentence, compound predicate	Students **attend** classes and **participate** in sports.
Compound sentence	The company president **wrote** a letter, and he **gave** it to his secretary to type.
Simple sentence, compound predicate	The company president **wrote** a letter and **gave** it to his secretary to type.

Using compound predicates helps a writer in several ways. Not only is he able to reduce the number of words needed to express an idea but also he can gain clarity through the parallelism that is a characteristic of compound predicates. These effects are illustrated in two simple sentences containing compound predicates:

They are **seated** around drums or **playing** wind intruments.
Here I **can read** books, **listen** to music, and **relive** the adventures of the past through the familiar objects around me.

EXERCISE 15
The Compound Predicate

Write out the following sentences, revising them so that they contain compound predicates.

1. The council met at three, and they adjourned at four o'clock.
2. You should give me your telephone number, and you should wait for my call.
3. The ranger spotted smoke rising from the forest. He telephoned the fire department.
4. I will save my money, and I will invest it in buying land.
5. The architecture of Brasilia has attracted much attention, and it has won many architectural awards.
6. The ship took on passengers at noon, it cruised up the Bosphorus, and it stopped at sunset to allow tourists to eat dinner in a Turkish village.

7. Modern grammarians have found many weaknesses in traditional grammar. They follow an inductive approach in teaching linguistics.
8. The visiting dignitaries landed at the Nairobi Airport, and they were met by the prime minister.
9. Paul was offered scholarships to three colleges, and he spent three weeks deciding which one to accept.
10. I ate in a very good restaurant in Taiwan; later I explored the city.
11. The Western cities have not yet had to deal with this problem, and they do not recognize its seriousness.
12. He and his wife were married last spring. They expect to attend the University of Wisconsin next fall.
13. She walked slowly into the room, and she sat down.
14. The lifeboats can be uncovered quickly. They can be lowered by one man in a very short time.
15. France faces the Atlantic Ocean in the west, and she is bordered by five countries in the east—Belgium, Luxembourg, Germany, Switzerland, and Italy.

Questions for Discussion and Review

1. In the model paragraph, the writer has placed two consecutive sentences that open with the same adverb clause in order to clarify the process explanation. Locate these two sentences.
2. Find a sentence in the model paragraph that begins with a gerund phrase.
3. Identify the transitions used in "Building a Sunscope."
4. At what points does the writer of the paragraph on electromagnetic principles use clauses and phrases at the beginnings of sentences to vary his sentence openings?
5. Find examples of transitions used for coherence in the selection on the Survey Q3R study method.
6. Write out five compound sentences, using a different coordinating conjunction in each sentence.

Vocabulary Growth

PARAGRAPH PUZZLE

Complete the paragraph by choosing the right word to fill in each blank. When choice is difficult, refer to neighboring words or sentences for help.

A 1968 survey............California State University, Los Angeles,
        (at, around, under, over)

indicated............an estimated 2,300 black students (10.5 percent
        (which, that, of, in)

............total enrollment) and 1,800 Mexican-American............
(on, at, for, of)   (farmers, workers, students, professors)

(8.2 percent of the total) were enrolled............Cal State. Another
                                        (on, at, for, of)

study shows 1,400 students............Spanish surnames in attendance.
                        (with, by, if, on)

Including Asian-Americans............American Indians, nearly 30 per-
                        (if, and, but, nor)

cent of Cal State's 21,000 students............from ethnic minorities.
                        (was, were, is, are)

Comparison with earlier..............indicates that the proportion of
                        (hours, decades, years, centuries)

............students at the college has been increasing. The percentage
(athletic, studious, majority, minority)

............minority students, particularly black and Mexican-American,
(on, of, for, at)

at............college far exceeded the percentage for any............
(there, the, which, what)   (either, over, other, under)

major four-year college or university in California. ....state col-
                        (For, After, Over, Under)

leges as a whole, the enrollment............black students is 2.9 percent
                        (of, at, or, for)

and the............of Mexican-American students is............2.9
        (enlistment, entrapment, enlightment,   (either, neither, also, except)
                enrollment)
percent of the total.

WORD CLUES

A. *In the following paragraph, the boldfaced word is the vocabulary word; the italicized word is the "Context Clue" to the meaning of the vocabulary word.*

1. Although the young couple hoped to **maintain** both a home in the city and a vacation cabin at the lake, they found that *keeping two houses was too expensive.*

    Vocabulary Word...

    Context Clue..

    Probable Meaning..

    Dictionary Definition...................................

2. From Sally's original idea of having a simple breakfast for the new neighbors, a more ambitious plan began to **evolve.** In the end, the breakfast *had grown* into a festive luncheon of crepes, fruit salad, cheeses, and wine.

>   Vocabulary Word. . . . .
>
>   Context Clue. . . . .
>
>   Probable Meaning. . . . .
>
>   Dictionary Definition. . . . .

3. After her return from Europe, Lucia was asked which **element** of her trip had been most satisfactory. After thinking about her experiences, she decided that her introduction to new foods had been the most rewarding *part of her travel.*

>   Vocabulary Word. . . . .
>
>   Context Clue. . . . .
>
>   Probable Meaning. . . . .
>
>   Dictionary Definition. . . . .

4. By reading extensively on the subject of solar energy, Mark was able to **perceive** that the idea of using natural energy had not yet been widely accepted. This *insight* led him to write an article urging the government to give greater priority to the country's energy problems.

>   Vocabulary Word. . . . .
>
>   Context Clue. . . . .
>
>   Probable Meaning. . . . .
>
>   Dictionary Definition. . . . .

5. Most of the audience found the speaker's comments to be far too **abstract.** They would have preferred that he lectured in more *specific* terms.

>   Vocabulary Word. . . . .
>
>   Context Clue. . . . .
>
>   Probable Meaning. . . . .
>
>   Dictionary Definition. . . . .

   B. *A list of various forms of each vocabulary word follows. For each number, choose a form different from the vocabulary word and use it meaningfully in a sentence. For example, in 3., use any form except the noun* **element.** *Write a total of five sentences.*

Verbs	Nouns	Adjectives	Adverbs
1. to maintain	maintenance	maintained	
2. to evolve	evolution	evolved	
3.	element	elementary elemental	
4. to perceive	perception	perceptive	perceptively
5. to abstract	abstract abstraction abstractness abstractedness	abstract abstracted	abstractly abstractedly

Composition: Show What You Have Learned

Chose a composition topic from either Group I or Group II.

GROUP I: TOPICS FOR WRITING A CHRONOLOGICAL PARAGRAPH

This is the week that you will use chronological development to write a process paragraph. For this reason, a topic should not be hard to decide upon. You could simply write about the process of composing a paragraph. In case this does not appeal to you, though, here are other possibilities:

1. Write about a mechanical process, such as building a model airplane, taking apart an alarm clock, repairing a radio, or working on an automobile engine.
2. Write about a crafts process, such as making a quilt, sewing a dress, firing ceramics, doing needlepoint, or working with leather.
3. Write about a building process, such as building a chair, table, bookcase, cabinet, room divider, or trellis.
4. Write about a cooking process, such as following a recipe for an omelet, soup, stew, or dessert.
5. Write about a gardening process, such as planting seeds, growing a plant indoors, planting a tree, or pruning.

Place a topic sentence at the beginning of your paragraph.

GROUP II: TOPICS TO CHALLENGE YOUR IMAGINATION

The process of learning a new language is one of the most demanding—and most rewarding—processes a student can experience. The reward comes when the learner realizes that, along with acquiring a new language, he has gained a whole new set of cultural concepts.

At right you see an eye-catching magazine advertisement for a U.S.A. dictionary publisher. The advertisement is very American. For one thing,

cry·on·ics

Webster's New Collegiate Dictionary

**America's Best-Selling Dictionary.
It's where the words live.**

Webster's New Collegiate Dictionary doesn't just define words. It makes words come alive. It unlocks the secrets of such chillingly futuristic words as "cryonics," as well as over 22,000 new words from today's living language. With over 150,000 entries in all, it's the most vivid, up-to-date dictionary of the decade. Only $9.95, thumb-indexed.

From Merriam-Webster.
Springfield, Mass. 01101

*Advertisement reprinted by permission of G. & C. Merriam Co.,
Publishers of the Merriam-Webster dictionaries.*

it focuses on the future, something Americans are fond of doing. For another, it adds a humorous touch using the word "chillingly" in a double sense to mean both "frigidly" and "frighteningly." Many Americans appreciate such puns.

"Cryonics" is a word that is probably unfamiliar to most readers of English, both native and nonnative. It is a word of the future, describing that branch of physics dealing with preserving objects at very low temperatures. It is not inconceivable that, in the future, human beings may choose to be frozen at some period of their lives so they experience "rebirth" 100 or more years later.

As a basis for four composition topics, let's assume that indefinite human preservation is an accomplished fact. Choose one of these to write about. Begin your paragraph with a topic sentence.

1. Assume that you are the scientist who has perfected the technique of preserving human life indefinitely through cryonics. Explain what equipment is necessary and what process is followed in freezing, storing, and thawing out bodies.
2. Explain why you would, or would not, agree to be frozen so that you could take advantage of human cryonics.
3. If you *would* participate in a cryonics experiment, explain at what age you would want to be frozen and for how long you would want to remain in suspended animation.
4. Assume that cryonics has always been possible. Choose a historical person and explain the probable adjustments that person would need to make if he were thawed back into life at the present time.

Chapter **3**

The Spatial Paragraph

The U.S.A.—Many Countries in One

<table>
<tr>
<td>Subordination by introductory participial phrase</td>
<td rowspan="12">**Traveling across the U.S.A.,** you don't need a passport to move from state to state. But sometimes it seems as if you should have one. **Even though you can buy the same brand of soap, toothpaste, and sugar-free carbonated drink in all 50 states, the U.S.A. reveals major regional differences.** Variations in climate and geography account for many of these contrasts. Some Eastern seaboard[1] cities, **for example,** show a strong European influence. **Boston contains cobbled traces of London.** In Philadelphia and Washington, large boulevards reminiscent[2] of Paris fan out. New York is different: the skyscraper canyons and intense metropolitan life of Manhattan Island make this city uniquely[3] North American. The U.S.A.'s Southeast, **though,** has a very different look and feel. Florida offers tropical Miami Beach, with its man-made explosion of hotel cubes, and the fascinating natural wonder of the Everglades. New Orleans is a city steeped in the rich, almost overripe, atmosphere of France and Africa; it **simmers** with a baroque[4] sleepiness. Moving on to</td>
</tr>
<tr><td>Subordination by introductory adverb clause</td></tr>
<tr><td>Transition</td></tr>
<tr><td>Short sentence for variety</td></tr>
<tr><td>Colon introducing list</td></tr>
<tr><td>Transition</td></tr>
<tr><td>Strong active verb</td></tr>
</table>

[1]*seaboard:* land or region bordering the sea. [2]*reminiscent:* recalling the past.
[3]*uniquely:* unlike any other. [4]*baroque:* fanciful, fantastic architectural style.

Texas, you'll come upon a vast state that rings with superlatives.[5] One of its cities—Houston—has taken great strides in progressive city planning, and the world's most expansive airport stretches out between Dallas and Fort Worth. **North to the Great Plains states,** flatness of terrain[6] is the rule. Windy, lakeside Chicago and the heavy-winter cities of Minneapolis and Milwaukee are **as** different from New York **as** Frankfurt is. West from Chicago, Denver nestles at the base of the Rocky Mountain region, an area that **may** remind you of Switzerland's splendor. To travel south of the Rockies is to see one of the U.S.A.'s most colorful sections—the high, intermediate, and low deserts of the Southwest. New Mexico, **with its artists' village of Taos,** and Arizona, **with its stunning Painted Desert and Grand Canyon,** seems to form a separate country. On the West Coast, California, like Texas, stands apart from all the other states. California is an innovative[7] state **(its freeway network and system of higher education—both multilevel—are remarkable),** and its vistas delight the eye. In the U.S.A.'s northwest corner, Washington and Oregon comprise[8] the big timber land, **a rainy pocket** of the country. The newest of the states, **Alaska and Hawaii,** feature climate, terrain, and customs far different from any found in the conterminous[9] United States. Subtropical Hawaii has been molded by its Polynesian and Oriental population; Alaska takes its tone from its Arctic climate and Eskimo heritage. **Despite its attempts to become a homogeneous[10] country, the U.S.A. is as diverse[11] as the symbols of its many regions: surfboard and totem pole, ski slope and saguaro cactus, igloo and Empire State Building.**

Margin notes:
- Comma in compound sentence
- Transition
- Comparative form
- Modal
- Commas around nonrestrictive phrases
- Parenthetical statement
- Metaphor
- Commas around appositive
- Commas in series / Semicolon joining independent clauses
- Topic sentence at end of paragraph

[5]*superlatives:* expressing the highest degree of eminence or achievement. [6]*terrain:* a piece or plot of ground. [7]*innovative:* introducing new ideas and methods. [8]*compromise:* contain; include. [9]*conterminous:* having a common boundary line. [10]*homogeneous:* having the some composition, structure, or character throughout. [11]*diverse:* marked by distinct differences.

Writing Analysis

TRANSITIONS FOR SPATIAL DEVELOPMENT

The model paragraph contains a number of transitions that clarify the spatial development. One example will demonstrate how this is done.

Having moved from discussing the northeastern U.S.A. to discussing the South toward the beginning of the paper, the writer wants to signal his reader that still another shift is coming. So he begins a sentence with the transitional phrase "Moving on to Texas." This prepares readers to accept a new development in the topic, easing them into the move west from New Orleans to Texas. Notice that several transitional phrases indicating changes in direction are used to give this composition coherence.

Here is a list of transitions that you will find helpful in carrying the thought on from one sentence to the next. These are often used in spatial development:

above	before me	here	on the left
across from	below	in the distance	on the right
adjacent to	beyond	nearby	opposite
also	further	next to	on top of
up	down	close to	beneath
under	around	near to	over

EXERCISE 16
Spatial Transitions

Below is a topic sentence for a spatial paragraph, followed by supporting detail to develop the paragraph. On a sheet of paper, sketch out a map of a college campus, locating each building where you think it belongs in relation to the other buildings. Then write out a paragraph beginning with the topic sentence below. Add spatial transitions to introduce each of the eight buildings according to their order of location.

Topic sentence   On my first visit to the college campus, I saw many buildings.

Supporting detail   1. The administration building
2. The library
3. The classroom buildings
4. The faculty offices
5. The student center and cafeteria
6. The bookstore
7. The gymnasium and athletic fields
8. The student dormitories

SPATIAL PARAGRAPH DEVELOPMENT

If a writer follows a spatial development, details are arranged according to their location and their relationship to each other. Spatial development is especially suited to subject matter dealing with places or areas. Such a development would work well if you were describing a limited interior, such as a classroom or the inside of a submarine; a description might be developed spatially by following the order in which an observer's eye would travel around the room—from left to right, or from right to left. Spatial development would also be effective if you were writing about a very broad area, such as the continent of Latin America or the solar system.

A clearcut example of spatial development is Victor Hugo's description of the battle of Waterloo. In order to clarify the movement of the armies, Hugo first explains the shape of the battlefield. Then he fits the opposing troops on to this ground plan. Beginning by comparing the battlefield to a familiar figure—the capital letter "A"—he goes on, step by step, to place details on that basic figure:

> Those who would get a clear idea of the battle of Wateroo have only to lay down upon the ground in their mind a capital A. The left stroke of the A is the road from Nivelles; the right stroke is the road from Genappe; the cross of the A is the sunken road from Chain to Braine-l'Alleud. The top of the A is Mont St. Jean; Wellington is there. The left-hand lower point is Hougomont; Reille is there with Jerome Bonaparte. The right-hand lower point is La Belle Alliance; Napoleon is there. A little below the point where the cross of the A meets, and cuts the right stroke, is La Haie Sainte. At the middle of this cross is the precise[1] point where the final battle word was spoken. There the lion is placed, the involuntary[2] symbol of the supreme heroism[3] of the imperial guard.
>
> The triangle contained at the top of the A, between the two strokes and the cross, is the plateau[4] of Mont St. Jean. The struggle for this plateau was the whole of the battle.
>
> The wings of the two armies extended to the right and left of the two roads from Genappe and from Nivelles; D'Erlon being opposite Picton, Reille opposite Hill.
>
> Behind the point of the A, behind the plateau of Mont St. Jean, is the forest of the Soignes.
>
> As to the plain itself, we must imagine a vast, undulating[5] country; each wave commands the next, and these undulations, rising toward Mont St. Jean, are there bounded by the forest.
>
>   "The Battle of Waterloo," Victor Hugo, *Les Misérables*

[1]*precise:* exact. [2]*involuntary:* unintentional, occurring against one's consent or choice. [3]*heroism:* bravery. [4]*plateau:* wide expanse of elevated, level land. [5]*undulating:* having the appearance of waves.

Hugo relies upon a comparison to depict his scene. Transitions also play a part here in linking the details together. In this translation from French to English, Hugo's translator repeatedly uses the directional words "left," "right," "top," "lower," and "middle." What other connectives signal his spatial development?

The model paragraph for this chapter illustrates how a wide-range subject such as travel in the U.S.A. can be developed spatially. Yet spatial development can be applied equally well to a description of a very limited scene. Let's look at a nature description that is an example of spatial development on a small scale. The selection was written by the western United States author Jack London:

> It was the green heart of the canyon, where the walls swerved back from the rigid plan and relieved their harshness of line by making a little sheltered nook[1] and filling it to the brim with sweetness and roundness and softness. Here all things rested. Even the narrow stream ceased its turbulent[2] down-rush long enough to form a quiet pool. . . .
>
> On one side, beginning at the very lip of the pool, was a tiny meadow, a cool, resilient[3] surface of green that extended to the base of the frowning wall. Beyond the pool a gentle slope of earth ran up and up to meet the opposing wall. Fine grass covered the slope—grass that was spangled[4] with flowers, with here and there patches of color, orange and purple and golden. Below, the canyon was shut in. There was no view. The walls leaned together abruptly, and the canyon ended in a chaos[5] of rocks, moss-covered and hidden by a green screen of vines and creepers and boughs of trees. Up the canyon rose far hills and peaks, the big foothills, pine-covered and remote. And far beyond, like clouds upon the border of the sky, towered minarets[6] of white, where the Sierra's eternal[7] snows flashed austerely[8] the blazes of the sun.
>
> "All Gold Canyon," *Jack London*

[1]*nook:* narrow, concealed place. [2]*turbulent:* wild, agitated. [3]*resilient:* elastic, buoyant. [4]*spangled:* decorated. [5]*chaos:* great disorder and confusion. [6]*minarets:* towers. [7]*eternal:* everlasting, unending. [8]*austerely:* starkly, severely.

In this selection the canyon is described as it would be studied through the moving eyes of an onlooker. There is a natural movement from the smallest and nearest object—the quiet pool—to the largest and farthest one—the Sierra mountains. In the second paragraph, the spatial development is made clear by transitions: "on one side"; "beyond the pool"; "below"; "up the canyon"; "and far beyond."

REVIEW OF THE CONTROLLING IDEA

In "The U.S.A.—Many Countries in One," the writer has chosen to emphasize his controlling idea by stating it twice, once at the beginning and once at the end of his paragraph. The topic sentence is the third one of the paragraph; here the central idea (". . . the U.S.A. reveals many regional differences") appears. This idea is restated in different words in the concluding sentence: ". . . the U.S.A. is as diverse as the symbols of its many regions." By placing a topic sentence both at the beginning and end of this paragraph, the writer creates an effective frame for his passage.

There are other reasons for placing a topic sentence both at the beginning and end of a paragraph; by doing this, the writer can give added emphasis to a controlling idea. The following selection illustrates this. The subject here is the powerful effect that rock music has had upon the United

States ever since the Beatles introduced their sound to the world in the 1960s:

> If the [1960s] taught us all about the inadequacies of the old main-stream without solving them, the decade did send people marching to a new tune and, most of all, to a new beat. It became fashionable again to be different, to be distinct, ethnically, socially, and personally. We sang not about love and marriage, paper dolls, kissing at the garden gate, and the girl next door, but about society's child, Lucy in the sky with diamonds, and how I'd love to turn you on. The unvarnished[1] brutality and overt[2] sexuality of Elvis Presley and the hipsterism of the fifties was tamed. Margaret Mead calls ours a prefigurative[4] culture in which the children are natives and the adults immigrants. The beat of rock made Glenn Miller and Lawrence Welk sound pallid,[5] and its message rebuked[6] the plastic[7] world even more effectively than the official social critics. ("We gave her everything money could buy," goes the voice. "Fun money can't buy," comes the response. "She's leaving home after living alone.")
>
> "The Beatles and Their Beat," Peter Schrag, *The Decline of the WASP*

[1]*unvarnished:* raw. [2]*overt:* not hidden; open. [3]*transcended:* surpassed; became superior to. [4]*prefigurative:* to picture to oneself, or imagine, beforehand. [5]*pallid:* pale; faint in color. [6] *rebuked:* blamed or scolded in a harsh way. [7]*plastic:* hypocritically false or synthetic.

In the topic sentence, the first one in the paragraph, the controlling idea is expressed in the words ". . . the decade did send people marching . . . to a new **beat.**" In the third from last sentence, this idea is repeated and enlarged upon: "The **beat** of rock . . . rebuked the plastic world even more effectively than the official social critics." The fact that this is a rather dense passage, tightly packed with ideas, may have led the writer to repeat his topic sentence. He might justifiably have felt that, by the time the reader reached the last sentence, he could lose track of the paragraph's controlling idea. The repetition of the word "beat" keeps this idea alive.

Often it is enough to state a controlling idea only once within a paragraph. But by the time a reader reaches the end of many paragraphs, he may need a reminder of the central point that the writer began with. The American playwright Eugene O'Neill once said that whenever he wanted to be sure of communicating an idea in a play, he would include it in three separate scenes. Although a play is different from an essay in many ways, this principle of repetition has meaning for a student of composition. A sensible plan for organizing either a paragraph or a full-length composition is this:

1. Tell your reader what you are going to do.
2. Do it.
3. Tell your reader what you have just done.

WRITING IN SPECIFIC TERMS

Glance over the model paragraph to pick out examples of the most prominent specific detail. Probably the words "soap, toothpaste, and sugar-free carbonated drink" will first jump out at you. This is an instance of the writer using concrete terms to pinpoint his idea. Someone once said that a picture is worth 1,000 words. In some ways, concrete detail can be compared with a photograph. It helps a reader to move from the abstract level to the specific or concrete.

Other examples of specific detail from the model include Washington and Philadelphia's "large boulevards," New York's "skyscraper canyons," Miami Beach's "hotel cubes," the Dallas-Fort Worth airport, New Mexico's Taos, and California's freeways and higher education system. The composition concludes with a burst of illustrative detail: "surfboard and totem pole, ski slope and saguaro cactus, igloo and Empire State Building." Writing that contains such specific terms remains in the reader's mind long after he has put down your paper.

Look at three further examples of specifics adding important substance to paragraphs. By emphasizing concrete detail, the writer of the following paragraph produces a highly informative paragraph about the planet Mars:

> Even in the absence of samples from the surface of Mars, a good deal can be inferred about its bulk composition. Its density, for example, is only 70 percent the density of the earth. Presumably Mars was formed in a region of the solar nebula that was cool enough to allow the condensation of compounds incorporating a wide variety of elements. The planet is probably well supplied with minerals containing combinations of magnesium, iron, silicon and oxygen (ferromagnesian silicates), and combinations of iron and sulfur (troilite). There may also be some free iron. Because Mars formed in a cooler region of the solar nebula than the earth did, however, more of its iron combined with other elements and less is in the form of metallic iron. This difference may explain why Mars has a lower density than the earth. Temperature conditions also favored the formation of some water-bearing silicate materials. In addition to these more abundant materials, Mars contains compounds incorporating small amounts of the long-lived radioactive isotopes of uranium, thorium, and potassium.
>
> "Mars," James R. Pollack, *Scientific American* (September 1975)

Specifics crop up here in the description of Mars' mineral components—magnesium, iron, silicon, and others. In scientific writing, details such as these help to establish factual credibility.

Still another way to add specific detail to your writing is by using statistics. As the following selection shows, figures can give strong support in expository or argumentative writing:

> From 1970 to 1974, consumer prices rose in the U.S. at an overall annual rate of 6.5 percent. By 1974 the U.S. had reached double digit

inflation. . . . The price level increases were not smooth and steady but were instead subject to rather wide variations. A family earning $10,000 in 1967 would have been poorer in 1973 had its income not increased to at least $13,750. Many families did earn income increases from 1967 to 1973 which more than offset the increases in consumer prices, but many others did not. Thus, the increases in prices induced[1] a redistribution of income away from those individuals and families whose income tended to be relatively fixed. Also, families who had increases in their incomes may have been misled into thinking they had earned more substantial real purchasing power increases than they did. The effect of inflation, then, was to erode[2] fixed incomes and to deflate[3] increases in money incomes.

"What Inflation Means," Frank C. Wyckoff, *Macroeconomics*

[1]*induced:* caused; brought about. [2]*erode:* eat into; lessen. [3]*deflate:* make smaller or less important.

Here, dates, percentages, and dollar amounts are all cited to give a specific picture of the inflationary trend in the United States in the early 1970s.

Finally, notice the degree to which the writer of the following selection about the Swedish singer Jenny Lind relies on detail for his effect:

The quality and extent of Swedish-American cultural relations is dramatically illustrated by the account of Jenny Lind's American tour from 1850 to 1852. She gave 95 concerts under contract to Phineas T. Barnum and an additional 40 under her own management before returning to Europe. She enthralled American audiences. "Jenny Lind fever" swept the country, and the name of the "Swedish Nightingale" was heard everywhere: "There were Jenny Lind dolls and other toys for girls, Jenny Lind gloves, bonnets, shawls, and many other articles for the ladies, and even Jenny Lind cigars for the men. Pianos, sofas, and chairs, as well as sausages and pancakes, were also named for the singer from Sweden. Her portrait could be had on glassware, china, pottery, fans, and in numerous other forms. Baby girls were christened Jenny or Jenny Lind, and at least one boy was given the names Phineas Barnum."

"Jenny Lind," Frank R. DeFederico, *Smithsonian* (September 1976)

In mentioning the years of her American tour, the number of concerts given, and names of the many products that were inspired by the "Swedish Nightingale," the writer specifically conveys the impact that Jenny Lind had on North American audiences.

UNDERSTANDING EXPLETIVES

An expletive is a "filler" word (*it, there*) placed at the beginning of a sentence to allow the subject to appear later in the sentence; it often combines with some form of the **be** verb. Although an expletive can often work better than any other construction to express an idea, it tends to be overused by English writers. When relied upon unnecessarily, it contributes to wordiness.

Normally, expletives are most effectively used in short sentences. Here is an example of an expletive that works well:

Why should the government have fallen?

There were several reasons.

In contrast, here is an example of an unnecessary expletive. Notice that, when it is removed, the sentence contains two fewer words:

With expletive   **There are** several advantages to buying a Eurailpass.

Expletive removed   Buying a Eurailpass offers several advantages.

Consider two even more extreme examples of reducing the number of words in a sentence by eliminating expletives:

Wordy   **There are** numerous travel agencies that exist throughout the world.

(10 words)

Shortened   Numerous travel agencies exist throughout the world.

(7 words)

Wordy   **There are** going to be certain parts of your garden that are your favorites for summertime relaxing and entertaining.

(18 words)

Shortened   Certain parts of your garden will be your favorites for summertime relaxing and entertaining.

(14 words)

When it is possible to avoid using an expletive, you might be doing more than just achieving word economy. You may be eliminating a **be** verb— one of the least expressive verbs you can choose.

EXERCISE 17
Using Expletives

Revise any of the following sentences that would be improved by having expletives eliminated. Write out sentences in which expletives are desirable without making any change.

1. It was in Tahiti that I found some of the world's most beautiful plants.
2. There are many bears roaming the campgrounds in Yosemite Valley.
3. It was 50,000 years ago that 10 million tons of meteorites crashed into the earth, creating an immense crater.
4. There are times when it is wise to hesitate.
5. There were paintings of Goya, Valesquez, and Rubens in Madrid's Prado Museum.
6. It is the sweet fragrance of the eucalyptus tree that you are smelling.

7. There are mountain goats and big-horned sheep living among the mountain crags.
8. It is still possible to catch the plane.
9. It was to please the Indians that many of the Mission churches were painted in bold colors.
10. There is a warm ocean current, running south from Point Concepcion, that makes the water's temperature agreeably mild.
11. There was an explosion in the paint factory that caused extensive damage.
12. There are hundreds of American bald eagles lining the banks of the Chilkat River along Alaska's Haines Highway in the fall.
13. It is from Iran that some of the most handsome rugs are imported.
14. There are especially durable knitting yarns available today that are both mothproof and colorfast.
15. There were three blankets folded in the closet.
16. It was after winning the Olympic gold medal for the decathlon that the athlete was offered a movie contract.
17. It is possible to save money by hiring an architect to help you avoid costly building mistakes.
18. It was the coldest day of the year.
19. There is a permanent-magnet alternator instead of the usual brushes on this alternator-generator that is powered by a one-cylinder gas engine.
20. There was an unexpected three-hour delay.

Punctuation Points

THE COMMA SPLICE

We couldn't decide upon a new car, there were many attractive models.

In the above sentence, two independent clauses are connected by a comma. This results in the punctuation error known as the **comma splice**. You can test for a comma splice by substituting a period for the comma:

We couldn't decide upon a new car. There were many attractive models.

If the two clauses can stand alone as separate sentences, then a comma alone cannot correctly join them. If you use a comma to combine two independent clauses into a single compound sentence, the comma must be followed by a coordinating conjunction (**and, but, for, or, nor**):

We couldn't decide upon a new car, for there were so many attractive models.

A comma splice may be corrected in four ways: (1) Add a coordinating conjunction following the comma, (2) Add a subordinating adverb, making the second clause dependent on the first, (3) Add a semicolon, or (4) Add a period, separating the clauses into two sentences.

I learned to like poetry when I read Kipling, his strong rhythms appealed to me. (Comma splice)

Coordinating conjunction	I learned to like poetry when I read Kipling, **for** his strong rhythms appealed to me.
Subordinating adverb	I learned to like poetry when I read Kipling **because** his strong rhythms appealed to me.
Semicolon	I learned to like poetry when I read Kipling; his strong rhythms appealed to me.
Period	I learned to like poetry when I read Kipling. His strong rhythms appealed to me.

EXERCISE 18
The Comma Splice

A. *Write out these sentences, correcting the comma splices according to the directions in parentheses.*

(Add a subordinating adverb to 1. and 2.)
1. She brought him home, he was a lovable dog.
2. He would not do any manual labor, he was willing to do any type of office work.

(Add a coordinating conjunction to 3. and 4.)
3. I invited him to the party, he didn't come.
4. At a track meet the average spectator is not aware of the name of the front runner, his attention is on the grace and speed of the human body.

(Add a semicolon to 5. and 6.)
5. They don't want to travel, they'd rather stay home.
6. His scholastic ability is far above average, his personality is very engaging.

(Add a period to 7. and 8.)
7. We shopped all day, therefore we were very tired by evening.
8. In ancient India there was no caste system, the people were one united body.

B. *Write out these sentences, correcting any comma splices that you find.*

1. Collecting stamps can be more than a hobby, it can be a profitable business.
2. Since I want to be a doctor, I have to study biology.
3. Chess is an intellectual game, it requires careful thought.
4. First I bought a train ticket, then I telephoned home.

5. There are some advantages to military service, but basic training is **not** one of them.
6. Two letters arrived on Tuesday, a third one came on Wednesday.
7. Sight is the most perfect of our senses, one of the most delightful of them all.
8. Scott is the only surviving member of his family, his parents and sister perished in the sinking of the *Andrea Doria* years ago.
9. Your dress does not fit well, you should return to the store to exchange it.
10. Denmark maintains that all of Greenland is Danish, but Norway insists that eastern Greenland, north of Scoresby Sound, is Norwegian.

THE RUN-ON SENTENCE

The term "run-on sentence" (or "fused sentence") describes two independent clauses run together without any punctuation between them. Such a sentence is even more confusing to a reader than the related error, the comma splice. Because the run-on contains no clues as to how words group together, it can easily be misread. Run-on sentences can be corrected by joining the two clauses with a comma and a conjunction, by inserting a semicolon between the two clauses if they are closely related, or by breaking the sentence into two sentences:

Run-on	The fruit pickers walked out of the orchards a meeting had been called to discuss a possible strike.
Comma, conjunction inserted	The fruit pickers walked out of the orchards, for a meeting had been called to discuss a possible strike.
Run-on	Philip wrote steadily for an hour the results were good.
Semicolon inserted	Philip wrote steadily for an hour; the results were good.
Run-on	Our first stop in the Far East was Hong Kong there we spent two days shopping.
Two sentences	Our first stop in the Far East was Hong Kong. There we spent two days shopping.

EXERCISE 19
The Run-On Sentence

Correct the following run-on sentences.

1. The average wage was twenty-five dollars a week this was hardly enough for a family to live on.
2. Wagner was not always praised as a great composer his music was **at** first severely condemned by critics.
3. The labor leaders were not optimistic about settling the strike **in fact** they predicted it could last as long as three months.
4. Mexico City is colorfully decorated at Christmas large neon flowers are hung on the sides of tall buildings and lighted at night.

5. Skilled climbers can reach the mountain summit at least this is what experts in the field believe.
6. Fireworks, now legally banned, are used less in the United States than they used to be the main exception occurs during the great public displays on the Fourth of July.
7. Many of the Indian legends have been recorded for years others are still being heard and written down by white men for the first time.
8. Stradivari was not Italy's only great violin maker Amati and Da Solo were also impeccable craftsmen.
9. Ore deposits in Michigan are very rich the copper obtained is unparalleled in quality.
10. Foreign travelers who concentrate only on the U.S.A.'s East coast miss many scenic wonders Flagstaff is a captivating base from which to explore Arizona's Grand Canyon and Painted Desert.
11. The bicycle race was a highlight of the Olympics at Montreal the Czech rider narrowly beat the French rider to win the gold medal.
12. Tape recorders have become extremely useful in contemporary life they are handy both in businesses and in homes.
13. Las Vegas is an oasis of light on the desert instead of clusters of palm trees, though, a visitor finds clusters of slot machines.
14. Installment buying has become common in the U.S.A. many families furnish their homes by purchasing goods on credit.
15. Boxing in Thailand differs greatly from boxing in Western countries Thai boxers are allowed to use their feet to kick their opponent.

Grammar Skills

MODAL AUXILIARIES

Like prepositions, modal auxiliaries are chosen with almost instinctive correctness by native speakers of English. For international students, though, the case is very different. For them, both modals and prepositions are small but formidable words, and many students feel uncertain about using them correctly.

Let's identify the English modals, understand their function, and examine some of the different meanings they may have. By definition, modals are auxiliaries used with verbs to make statements, not of fact, but rather of **possibility, obligation,** or **necessity.** There are ten modals:

can	might	ought (to)	shall	should
may	must	could	will	would

Possibility	He **may** win a scholarship.
Obligation	You **should** invite her to the party.
Necessity	They **must** tell us when they are coming.

Modals differ from the other auxiliaries (**be, do, have**) in that they have no *s*-forms or participles. Nor does the form of the modal necessarily indicate the time reference of the sentence in which it is used. Modals are often found in independent clauses following introductory clauses beginning with **if**. Such **if** clauses, making a statement that is contrary to fact, create the need for a modal in the main clause:

> If I were a king, I **would** create more holidays.
> If I had the chance, I **might** try out for the soccer team.

In a declarative sentence, a modal is usually directly followed by a verb (He *can* win the race.). In a sentence responding to a question, however, the modal is often used alone (*Can* George *win* the race? Yes, he *can*.). Notice that when a modal is used in a question, it normally opens the senence and is separated from the verb by the subject (*Will* the committee *announce* its decision today?).

Some modals are frequently used interchangeably, especially in colloquial speech. For instance, *may* and *must* both signify necessity when they are used negatively:

> You **may** not enter.
> You **must** not enter.

Similarly, the modals *should*, *ought*, and *must* can all be used to express obligation (They *should* write for reservations before Tuesday. They *ought to*. . . . They *must*. . .).

Now study over the various meanings expressed by the English modals:

Can
Ability	Susan **can** bake a cake.
	Can you wait until I finish ironing?

May
Possibility	If we drive faster, we **may** reach Munich tonight.
Request	**May** I ask you a question?
Permission	Students **may** leave when they complete the test.
Necessity	"You **may** not go out tonight," he said.

Might
Possibility	The hurricane **might** pass over the city soon.
Courteous request	**Might** I telephone you tomorrow?

Must (**Have to** is an alternate form)
Logical conclusion	When the telephone rang, I knew it **must** be Jack. (. . . **had to** be Jack.)
Necessity	People **must** wash their clothes regularly. (People **have to** wash. . . .)
Obligation	Drivers **must** obey the traffic laws.

Ought (to)

Obligation	Citizens **ought to** vote in national elections.
Something that is advisable to do	You **ought to** learn better manners.
Something that is expected	The opera **ought to** start in a short while.

Shall

First-person questions requesting assent	**Shall** I close the door now?
Simple futurity, first person only (mostly British usage)	I **shall** wait to hear from you.

Will

Simple futurity, first, second, and third persons (general American usage)	The concert **will** begin at 8 P.M. I **will** meet you at noon today.
Promise (stressed)	He **will** answer her letter as soon as he can.
Determination, first, second, and third persons (stressed)	I **will** (**I'll**) study for that quiz until I know that I can surely pass it.
Inevitability	What **will** be, **will** be.

Could

Past ability	He **could** add and subtract when he was four.
Possibiliy	If you like, we **could** go away for the weekend.

Should

Obligation	Everyone **should** keep his promises.
Something that is advisable to do	Many children **should** eat less candy.
Something that is expected	We **should** be landing at the airport in fifteen minutes.
Conditional probability	**Should** that happen, he will be very disappointed.

Would

Customary past action	When we were children, we **would** play games every day.
Courteous request	**Would** you explain this problem to me, please?
Future uncertainty	I **would** plan to attend if I thought that I **would** be in town.
Wish	I **would** like to thank you for your help.
Refusal (with "not")	Her brother **would not** move.

Modal forms figure importantly in a few of the most common American English idioms:

1. **Can't help** (past time: *couldn't help*) is an idiom that expresses inability to avoid or prevent something. It is followed by an *ing*-form or by *it*.

The actor **can't help** his feeling of stagefright.
She **can't help** laughing when he tells a joke.
They **couldn't help** missing the boat yesterday.

2. **Would like** is a polite synonym for *want*. It is often followed by an infinitive.

    a. A statement with **would like** expresses an invitation.

His father asked Paul if he **would like** to eat.
The lawyer asked, "**Would** you **like** to cross-examine the witness?"

    b. A statement with **would like** expresses an order.

I **would like** a seat on the aisle.
I **would like** the check, please.

3. **Would rather** is an idiom that means *prefer*. It is followed by the simple form of the verb.

The doctor said that he **would rather** return tomorrow.
Would you **rather** wait inside the station for the bus?

4. **Had better** is an idiom that expresses advisability. It is followed by the simple verb form. (Even though *had* is a past form, it does not refer to the past in this idiom.) *Had* is often joined to a pronoun subject by means of a contraction.

You **had better** get your flu shot soon.
He'd better wake up when the alarm clock goes off.
They'd better be at the airport an hour ahead of time.

EXERCISE 20
Modals

A. *Listed below are some sports. Assuming that you have recently become proficient in them, write a sentence about each based on the example.*

Example: ski
    Last year I **couldn't** ski, but this year I **can.**

1. swim
2. play tennis
3. ice skate
4. ride a horse
5. play golf

B. *Listed below are some activities. Assuming you have lost the ability to perform them, write a sentence about each based on the example.*

Example: drive all day

Ten years ago I **could** drive all day, but now I **can't.**

1. run a mile
2. dance for hours
3. eat huge meals
4. sleep all night without waking up
5. read fine print

C. *Listed below are some things that may be advisable to do. Write a sentence about each based on the example, using* **should** *or* **ought.**

Example: study for examinations

You **ought** to study for examinations.

1. brush your teeth daily
2. eat a balanced diet
3. sleep seven to nine hours every night
4. rest occasionally
5. exercise each day
6. treat pets kindly
7. be considerate of neighbors
8. remember friends on their birthdays
9. be honest in business dealings
10. keep your living quarters clean

D. *Listed below are pairs of activities. Tell what is permitted and what is not permitted based on the example.*

Example: drive at age 16/exceed the speed limit

You **may** drive at age 16, but you **may not** exceed the speed limit.

1. study silently/fall asleep in class
2. take a holiday tomorrow/be late for class
3. use a book during your open book test/cheat during a test
4. ask the teacher a question/talk to other students during class
5. visit with friends after class/bring a friend to class
6. go to the movies/return home after midnight
7. try on a new dress / spend more than $30 for it
8. borrow the car/drive it out of town
9. go shopping/charge your purchases
10. play your records/turn up the volume too high

E. *Listed below are some things that didn't happen. Assuming that they should have happened, write a sentence about each based on the example.*

Example: George **didn't** *mail the letter.*
George **should have** mailed the letter.

1. Ruth didn't go to the dance.
2. Anne didn't apply for a passport.
3. Mrs. Wilson didn't turn off the stove.
4. Frank didn't close the door.
5. Jim failed to mow the lawn.
6. Ramon failed to renew his visa.
7. Alice failed to switch on the light.
8. They forgot to pay their taxes.
9. She forgot to telephone her mother.
10. Mr. Teilman forgot to wind his watch.

F. *Listed below are some things we may not know for certain about the past. Make a guess about each based on the example.*

Example: *The first fire*
The first fire **may** have been caused by lightning.

1. The first tree
2. The first flower
3. The first animal
4. The first bird
5. The first fish
6. The first school
7. The first shoe
8. The first clothing
9. The first wheeled vehicle
10. The first candy

G. *Listed below are statements followed by words in parentheses. Tell what you infer about each based on the example.*

Example: *The dog is barking.* (visitor)
The dog **must** have seen a visitor.

1. She goes everywhere with Jack. (like)
2. The professor is staying home today. (sick)
3. The key won't fit into the lock. (bent)
4. Fred won first prize in the diving competition. (good)
5. The night is cold. (snow)
6. The train didn't arrive. (late)
7. Gerald sold his car. (tired)
8. I hear the telephone ringing. (telephoning)

9. They didn't attend the concert. (too busy)
10. The student walks three miles to school every day. (energy)

H. *Make sentences of the combinations listed below based on the example.*

Example: be frank (can't help)
   He **can't help** being frank.

1. be honest (can't help)
2. feel happy (can't help)
3. travel more (would like)
4. lose weight (would like)
5. go out to dinner (would like)
6. come tomorrow (would rather)
7. read a novel (would rather)
8. answer his mail (had better)
9. make his bed (had better)
10. take my hand if the lights go out (had better)

SHOWING POSSESSION

To form the possessive case of a noun in a Romance language, such as French, you would write "the hat of the boy." In English, this type of phrase is also used in some cases to show possession: the president of the company. But a second way to express the possessive form of English nouns is to add an apostrophe and sometimes the letter "s" to the noun: the boy's hat; the company's president.

A phrase is often used to show possession in English when a writer wants to place the emphasis on the possessor. For example, in the phrase "the stories of Saroyan," the reader's attention is focused more strongly on the name Saroyan than it would have been if an apostrophe plus "s" had been used: Saroyan's stories. In many cases, though, using a phrase to show possession leads to awkwardness of expression. One would avoid writing "The pen of my aunt has been lost." An apostrophe plus "s" is perhaps more generally used and is preferred in forming possessive of indefinite pronouns (somebody's hat) or time (three weeks' vacation) and of number or amount (three dollars' worth). When an article precedes a proper name, the possessive is not used (the Maugham essay).

Study these rules for forming possessive in English:

1. To form the possessive case of a singular noun, add an apostrophe and an *s*.

Frank's opinion
my uncle's raincoat
the automobile's tires

In words of more than one syllable which end in an *s* sound, you generally form the singular possessive by adding the apostrophe without the *s*. However, some writers prefer to add the apostrophe plus *s* unless this results in an awkward pronunciation, as in the case of "Parnassus's heights."

Henry James' stories				Henry James's stories
the princess' crown	}	or	{	the princess's crown
Mr. Burgess' ring				Mr. Burgess's ring

2. To form the possessive case of a plural noun not ending in *s*, add **an** apostrophe and an *s*.

children's games
men's clubs
women's fashions

3. To form the possessive case of a plural noun ending in an *s*, add the apostrophe only.

boys' bicycles
stores' shopping hours
airlines' schedules

4. The indefinite pronouns—*one, everyone, everybody, somebody, nobody,* etc.—form their possessive case in the same way as nouns.

Nobody's number was called.
One's taste in music often changes.
Somebody's coat was left in the room.

When indefinite pronouns are used with *else*, the possessive is formed in this way: *everyone else's, nobody else's.*

5. Personal pronouns in the possessive case—*his, hers, its, ours, yours, theirs, whose*—do not require an apostrophe.

I thought the paper was **theirs.**
Do you know **whose** scarf this is?
In Switzerland you can find skiing at **its** best.

Notice the difference between the possessive pronoun *its* and the contraction of *it is: it's* (the letter *i* is omitted). Although their meanings are different, both *its* and *it's* have the same pronunciation.

6. In hyphenated words, names of business firms, and words showing joint possession, only the last word is made possessive.

Hyphenated words

commander-in-chief's visit (Singular possessive) chiefs' (Plural)
father-in-law's secretary

Names of business firms

Arden and Alpert's cosmetic firm
Dun and Bradstreet's publications

Joint possession

Cathy and Ruth's room
Tim and Jack's duty

7. When two or more persons possess something individually, each of their names is possessive in form.

Tim's and Jack's cars

8. The words *minute, hour, day, week, month, year,* and so on require an apostrophe when they are used as possessive adjectives. Words telling amounts in cents or dollars, when used as possessive adjectives, also require apostrophes.

a minute's rest, ten minutes' rest
a day's work, five days' work
one cent's worth, ten cents' worth
one dollar's worth, twenty dollars' worth

EXERCISE 21
Possessives

A. *Copy the italicized words in the following list in two columns. Label the first column "Singular Possessive," and write the singular possessive form of each word in this column. Label the second column "Plural Possessive," and write the plural possessive form of each word in this column.*

Example:

	Singular Possessive	*Plural Possessive*
GIRL SHOES	GIRL'S SHOES	GIRLS' SHOES

1. citizen rights
2. boy suits
3. brother books
4. movie scenes
5. worker wages

6. dog bones
7. elephant tusks
8. friend opinions
9. parent responsibilities
10. club dues

11. child coats
12. woman scarves
13. shelf contents
14. tooth roots
15. sheep wool

B. *In the following list the possessive relationship is shown by means of a phrase. Change each so that the possessive case of the noun or pronoun is used to express the same relationship.*

Example: a semester of fifteen weeks
a fifteen weeks' semester

1. personality of a person
2. novels of Leo Tolstoy

3. vacation of two weeks
4. home of the mother-in-law
5. school of David and Peter
6. poetry of Dylan Thomas
7. testimony of the witness
8. products of Johnson & Johnson
9. worth of one dollar
10. delay of two years
11. events of the day
12. top of it
13. ring of the actress
14. report of the sergeant-at-arms
15. the sweater of Andrew and the sweater of Howard

THE SENTENCE FRAGMENT

To be complete a sentence must have a subject and a predicate expressed or implied. And the predicate must contain a finite form of the verb. (A finite form is one that can assert action or existence, ask a question, or give a command.) A sentence lacking any of these elements is called a **sentence fragment.**

Student writers are usually asked to form complete sentences in their compositions, for it is difficult to use sentence fragments well until one has gained complete control over written English. But for the experienced writer, fragments are a legitimate stylistic device. Look below at the paragraphs of a professional writer who has made an unusually extensive use of sentence fragments. Discussing the perils that can befall a bachelor, George F. Gilder inserts four verbless sentences in each of his essay's two opening paragraphs:

> The single man. An image of freedom and power. A man on horseback, riding into the sunset with his gun. The town and its women would never forget, never be the same. But the man would never change, just move on. To other women, other towns. As he rides away, the sunset gives him a romantic glow.
>
> The single man. The naked nomad in the bedrooms of the land. The celebrity at the party, combed by eyes of envy and desire. The hero of the film and television drama: cool, violent, sensuous, fugitive, *free.*
>
> "Naked Nomads," George F. Gilder, *Boston Globe*, February 9, 1975

Professional writers purposely use sentence fragments for several reasons. Fragments can effectively emphasize an idea, add force to an emotion, or help build to a climax, or high point. In contrast, student writers often write sentence fragments by mistake. For this reason, it is wise to postpone using sentence fragments until your instructor is sure that you can differentiate between a complete sentence and a fragmentary one.

Here are three ways to eliminate sentence fragments:

1. By changing a participle to a verb requiring a subject.

Sentence fragment	The result **being** that she lost the election.
Complete sentence	The result **was** that she lost the election.

2. By connecting a fragment to the preceding sentence with a comma

Sentence fragment	They guided us to the edge of the village. **Leaving us to find our way home alone.**
Complete sentence	They guided us to the edge of the village, leaving us to find our way home alone.

3. By building the fragment into a complete separate sentence

Sentence fragment	They planned for a trip to Peru. **A trip to give them many new experiences.**
Two sentences	They planned for a trip to Peru. It would be a trip to give them many new experiences.

EXERCISE 22
The Sentence Fragment

Revise each of the following passages that is fragmentary so that it reads logically and smoothly. If you find one that is correct, write a "C" instead of a corrected passage.

Example: On the school steps I saw Jim. Waiting for a ride home.
    On the school steps I saw Jim, waiting for a ride home.

1. I have always wanted a roommate who would be a close friend. One that I could take home with me for the holidays.
2. I appreciated their financial assistance. Which made it possible for me to attend college.
3. We left the boys at the beach. Uncertain as to whether or not they should swim for another hour.
4. She was startled by a faint noise. Somebody was walking outside in the garden.
5. The lack of telephone service being one of the greatest drawbacks.
6. It seemed that our behavior was never satisfactory. Whether we asked questions or remained silent.
7. His training gave him a good background for pursuing research. First at the university and later at the Rockefeller Institute.
8. I was called into the office first. My name being at the head of the list.
9. Conflicts at home should be settled in the same way that conflicts among nations are. By talking the problem through.
10. We were finally taken to a room full of mattresses. Large mattresses, small mattresses, circular mattresses, hard mattresses, but despite an earnest search, I could find no soft mattresses.

11. It was a beautiful specimen of rainbow trout. One that anyone would be proud of catching.
12. Finally he discarded his old ideas and developed new ideas. Ideas more realistic.
13. This method of hypnotism produces varying degrees of hysterics. Eventually sleep comes.
14. We find it a very interesting subject. So really fascinating that we want to tell you about it.
15. The bicycle, starting on the top of the hill, gained speed as it reached the bottom.

Questions for Discussion and Review

1. Point out examples of specific detail in the model paragraph.
2. Explain how the writer of the model paragraph has varied his sentence openings.
3. One strong, active verb has been identified in the model paragraph. Can you find others?
4. Identify the transitions in the model paragraph that are particularly related to the spatial development.
5. What modal auxiliaries appear in Hugo's "The Battle of Waterloo"?
6. Can you think of another approach Hugo might have chosen to describe the battlefield of Waterloo if he had not used the device of the capital "A"?
7. Count the number of words in each sentence in the first paragraph of London's "All Gold Canyon." How many words does the longest sentence contain? The shortest sentence? Why is his shortest sentence placed where it is?
8. Is Pollack justified in using an expletive halfway through his selection "Mars"?

Vocabulary Growth

PARAGRAPH PUZZLE

Complete the paragraph by choosing the right word to fill in each blank. When choice is difficult, refer to neighboring words or sentences for help.

Everybody dances. If you have . . . . swerved to avoid stepping
                    (ever, never, before, after)

on a crack . . . . the sidewalk, you have danced. If you . . . .
        (over, under, in, on)   (has, have, shall, should)

ever kneeled to pray, you have . . . . For these actions have fig-
                    (sung, swum, skipped, danced)

ured importantly...........the history of dance. Dance goes...........
      (about, for, in, around)   (forward, back, up, down)

to the beginnings of civilization—............the tribe—where natives
         (at, for, of, to)

danced to get...........they wanted. Primitive dance was...........
    (when, why, which, what)   (about, above, under, over)

all practical, not the social dancing...........know today. Natives ap-
       (we, us, their, them)

proached dance with..........seriousness as a way to help...........
      (little, great, less, least)   (a, an, that, the)

tribe in the crucial process............survival. Dance was believed to
        (to, over, of, at)

be the.............direct way to repel locusts, to.............rain to
  (most, least, first, last)   (cause, happen, try, take)

fall, to insure that...........male heir would be born, and...........
      (the, this, a, an)   (for, of, to, at)

guarantee victory in a forthcoming battle.

   Primitive...........was generally done by many...........mov-
  (food, dance, spells, harvest)   (people, cattle, monkeys, birds)

ing in the same manner and direction. ....all dances had lead-
      (Since, Despite, Thus, Although)

ers, solo dances............rare. Much use was made of............
     (are, was, were, is)   (only, every, some, all)

part of the body. And so............were these tribal dances that, if
     (comic, boring, solemn, tiring)

............African native should miss a single step, ...could
(a, an, the, this)   (he, they, she, her)

be put to death..........the spot. Fortunately, the same rigid..........
    (in, at, on, around)   (sticks, messages, reviews, rules)

that governed the lives of Bushmen...........Hottentots do not apply
       (or, for, with, in)

in the...........relaxed settings of today's discotheques.
(less, more, least, most)

WORD CLUES

A. *In the following paragraphs, the boldfaced word is the vocabulary word; the italicized word is the "Context Clue" to the meaning of the vocabulary word.*

1. After failing to get much response by telephoning the personnel offices of many business firms, Walter decided to try a new **approach** to looking for a job. This time, he *started* by writing many letters of application.

> Vocabulary Word...
>
> Context Clue..
>
> Probable Meaning..
>
> Dictionary Definition.......................................

2. Since the trigonometry problem was too **complex** for Ruth to understand, she made an appointment with her professor to help work out the *difficulties.*

> Vocabulary Word...
>
> Context Clue..
>
> Probable Meaning..
>
> Dictionary Definition.......................................

3. Tim and Mike enjoyed all of the circus acts, but their favorite performers—the trained elephants—appeared at *the end of the show.* The children told all of their friends about this exciting **conclusion.**

> Vocabulary Word...
>
> Context Clue..
>
> Probable Meaning..
>
> Dictionary Definition.......................................

4. Noticing Mr. Adams arriving at work any time between 8 and 10 A.M., his supervisor asked him to change his *irregular* work habits. The boss wanted Mr. Adams to perform in a more **consistent** way.

> Vocabulary Word...
>
> Context Clue..
>
> Probable Meaning..
>
> Dictionary Definition.......................................

5. If you want to **concentrate** on listening to music, you will have to stop daydreaming and *focus on* the composer's line of musical development.

> Vocabulary Word...
>
> Context Clue..
>
> Probable Meaning..
>
> Dictionary Definition.......................................

B. *A list of various forms of each vocabulary word follows. For each number, choose a form different from the vocabulary word and use it meaningfully in a sentence. For example, in 5, use any form except the verb* **concentrate***. Write a total of five sentences.*

Verbs	Nouns	Adjectives	Adverbs
1. to approach	approach	approachable	
2.	complex complexity	complex	
3. to conclude	conclusion	conclusive inconclusive	conclusively
4. to consist	consistency inconsistency	consistent inconsistent	consistently
5. to concentrate to concenter	concentration concentrator concentrativeness	concentrated concentrative concentric	concentratively

Composition: Show What You Have Learned

Choose a composition topic from either Group I or Group II.

GROUP I: TOPICS FOR WRITING A SPATIAL PARAGRAPH

Having experimented with chronological organization in the last chapter, you are ready to advance to a new way of building a paragraph. Using spatial development, write a paragraph on one of the following subjects:

1. The home you grew up in.
2. Your favorite city.
3. A country you have traveled in or would like to travel in.

In this paragraph place topic sentences at both the beginning and end.

GROUP II: TOPICS TO CHALLENGE YOUR IMAGINATION

The Scots poet Robert Burns once wrote that people would indeed be lucky if they had the power to see themselves as others see them. Sometimes, as in the case of the handwritten essay on the following page, such insight is possible. This composition was written by Anne, a twelve-year-old student at a bilingual school in Paris.

Of course, the reader of this short essay should take two points into account in reacting to it. First, Anne is writing from secondhand, not firsthand, experience; she has not yet visited the U.S.A. Second, Anne is relatively young. Her vision is necessarily limited because of her age.

What does America mean to me?

I never went to America, so I can't really say something on it, but I know many people who have been there and I have seen many American films. in all of them, there is a gun..

I think that American people are "always" fighting themselves for something or an other. This vast country is populated by beautiful and rich ladies and thieves, like in Chicago... America is a very rich country: it is the Americans, who first went on the moon, American TV has 13 channels. The Americans are very intelligent but not very organized; the president is always killed or kicked out....

I can describe America like this The men, who have their little brief-cases and their hat. The rich women, The cinema, the big cars, all the gadjets, the big towns, the thieves, the hot-dogs and the base-ball...

"Anne's" essay originally appeared in L'Express, Paris. *Reprinted by permission of* Atlas, July 1976.

Since you are a student who is older and who possibly has traveled more widely than Anne, use her composition as a basis for writing a paragraph on the same subject, "What Does America Mean to Me?" Approach this assignment in either of the following ways:

1. If you find that, despite her youth and inexperience, Anne's ideas about the U.S.A. are accurate, rewrite her composition. Retaining most or all of her thoughts, condense the essay into a single paragraph. Improve its coherence by using these techniques:

    a. Add transitions

    b. Subordinate some sentences by adding adverb clauses and participial phrases.

    c. Use parallelism.

2. If you disagree with most or all of the ideas in Anne's essay, state your own ideas on the same subject in a unified, coherent paragraph.

Chapter 4

The Expository Paragraph
(Developed by Examples)

A Man to Remember

	Perhaps the most vital person I have ever met is an Italian professor of philosophy who teaches at the University of Pisa. Although I last met this man eight years
Present perfect verb	ago, I **have not forgotten** his special qualities. **First of**
Transition	**all**, I was impressed by his devotion[1] to teaching. **Be-**
Subordination by introductory adverb clause	**cause his lectures were always well-prepared and clearly delivered**, students swarmed[2] into his classroom.
Parallelism	His followers appreciated the fact **that he believed in** what he taught and **that he was** intellectually stimulating. Furthermore, he could be counted on to explain his
Concrete detail	ideas in an imaginative way, introducing such aids to understanding as **paintings, recordings, pieces of sculpture, and guest lecturers.** Once he even sang a song in
Transition	class to illustrate a point. **Second,** I admired the fact that he would confer with students outside of the class-
Subordination by introductory participial phrase	room or talk with them on the telephone. **Drinking coffee in the snack bar,**[3] he would easily make friends with students. Sometimes he would challenge a student to a game of chess. At other times, he would join groups
Specific detail	to discuss subjects ranging from **astronomy to scuba**

[1]*devotion:* strong affection. [2]*swarmed:* came in great numbers. [3]*snack bar:*

Semicolon joining
independent
clauses

Transition

Subordination by
introductory adverb
clause

Punctuating an
appositive

diving.[4] Many young people visited him in his office for academic advice; others came to his home for social evenings. **Finally,** I was attracted by his lively wit.[5] He believed that no class hour is a success unless the students and the professor share several chuckles and at least one loud laugh. Through his sense of humor, he made learning more enjoyable and more lasting. **If it is true that life makes a wise man smile and a foolish man cry,** then my friend is truly a wise man. Probably the best example of his wit is this bit of wisdom with which he once ended a lecture: "It is as dangerous for man to model himself upon his invention, the machine, as it would be for God to model Himself upon His invention."

restaurant serving light meals. [4]*scuba diving:* underwater swimming with a compressed-air breathing apparatus. [5]*wit:* intelligent humor.

Writing Analysis

TRANSITIONS FOR EXPOSITORY DEVELOPMENT

The model paragraph has three main divisions, each developing one aspect of the Italian professor's nature: his devotion to teaching, his friendliness, and his wit. Each time a new division is introduced, the reader is alerted to the shift in thought by a transition. These three chief linking elements are "first of all," "second," and "finally."

Other transitions also appear in the paragraph. The very first word, "perhaps," serves to lead the reader to the opening controlling idea. Two additional transitions are "furthermore" and "once." Toward the middle of the paragraph, two sentences that are parallel in structure are begun by similar transitions: "sometimes" and "at other times." Placing paired phrases like these in consecutive parallel sentences is a good way to add coherence to your writing.

Even though transitions are often necessary, learn to use them in moderation. Sometimes a series of sentences with parallel clauses or phrases can focus a reader's attention on the developing idea more gracefully than a series of transitions. Too many transitions in a composition can slow down the forward movement and make the sentences appear overloaded. On the other hand, you can be sure that you will want to include some transitions in almost any college paper that you write.

Here are some transitions that are often used in expository writing. Consult this list for ideas in linking together the sentences you will write in this week's paragraph, as well as the paragraphs you will write in connection with later chapters:

first, second (and so on)	as a result	for this purpose
but	at last	furthermore
finally	consequently	moreover
also	for example	likewise
another	for instance	next
yet	in addition	on the contrary
once	in this case	in summary
such	otherwise	on the other hand
then	in closing	in conclusion
thus	now	therefore

EXERCISE 23
Expository Transitions

Write out the sentences, placing appropriate transitions in the blanks. Underline the words you add.

People in many countries have learned to enjoy watching television. The programs they see are of three general types. ...., they may watch entertainment shows. This type of program draws from many creative fields. ...., concerts, opera, cartoons, popular musical and variety shows, dramatic series, movies, and interview shows all appear on the television screen. The............type of television program is the sports show. Before television became popular, a person interested in sports might never expect to attend the Olympic Games, held in a different country every four years. ...., people in almost any part of the world may watch the Olympic Games as they happen. The............type of television program is the news program. ...., newspapers used to be the chief source of news for many people. ....television brings world events in pictures and sound into people's living rooms. In some countries, such as England and Italy, the state owns and operates one or more television stations. ...., no revenue-producing advertising appears on these channels. ...., advertising is an essential part of the commercial television industry in the United States. This is not true, ..., of American educational television. Early television sets produced a black-and-white picture. .... sets receive pictures in color. Further advances are being made in television technology. Scientists are adapting television so that people having a telephone conversation will be able to see each other on a small television screen. ...., it seems probable that we will watch television more often in the future than we do at the present time.

EXPOSITORY PARAGRAPH DEVELOPMENT (by examples)

In previous chapters, you have written papers of two different types: a process paragraph and a descriptive one. Your paragraphs have been organized by chronological and spatial methods. Beginning with this chapter, though, you will concentrate on writing exposition. The purpose of expository writing is to present facts or ideas by using various techniques of development that are discussed in this and the following chapters.

Expository writing is the type most frequently used in college courses. English compositions, physics laboratory reports, history research papers, essay tests in any subject—all of these call for logical analysis. Among the various ways to develop an analysis are examples, comparison, contrast, definition, cause and effect, and logical division. You will study each of these methods, beginning in this chapter with development by examples.

Most composition instructors would probably agree that students use too few examples in their writing. Perhaps because of a lack of background in a subject, a student may rely on broad, general statements that are neither interesting nor convincing. If a student were always able to draw from his personal experience in writing, the tendency to generalize might be more easily overcome. But this is not always possible. When working with an unfamiliar subject, though, a resourceful student will explore the library to find background material and supporting examples for his paper.

Using examples in a composition can be compared to presenting evidence in a courtroom. Evidence serves to make a legal case more specific; it helps to convince the jurors. Examples make a composition more specific; they add substance to the writer's controlling idea. For example, if you are writing an expository paper about progress in the railroad industry, your examples might include the luxurious Italian train, the Settebello, connecting Milan and Rome; the 125-mile-per-hour Japanese train running on the Hokkaido Line from Tokyo to Osaka; and the extensive Trans-European Express trains which span the Continent. Examples such as these would lend force to your writing. To take another case, suppose that you were asked to write an argumentative paper based on the proposal that capital punishment should be abolished. If you filled your composition only with personal opinion, the resulting paper would probably not convince your reader. If, on the other hand, you did some library research and were able to include examples of lower crime rates in countries that have abolished capital punishment, your paper would probably have more persuasive force.

The number of examples needed to develop a paper depends on the difficulty of your subject, the length of your paper, and your own ingenuity. In some cases, a single example, fully explored, is enough. At other times, you may think it desirable to include three, six, or a dozen examples in writing a composition. Choose only those examples that forcefully and logically illustrate your thesis. An example can be an effective piece of evidence. Your chief measurement of its probable effectiveness is the degree to which it supports the point being developed. Ask yourself this question: "Is this example really relevant to what I am trying to say?" Try to select examples that are unusual, ones that will catch and hold your reader's attention. Finally, arrange your examples in order of increasing importance, so that the strongest example is saved for last. By doing this, you will be placing your best material in the most emphatic part of your paragraph or composition, the conclusion.

Sometimes, in developing with examples, one particularly significant or dramatic example can suggest the organization of the entire paper. It can be saved for last and other examples selected to build up to it. This has been the case in the model paragraph. The Italian professor's wit has been discussed last because the writer felt that the direct quotation would make a good climax to the paragraph.

At other times, a writer may feel that several examples will be needed to supply evidence for the point he is making. In the following short paragraph on the subject of primitive languages, the writer has chosen a broad range of examples to support his thesis:

> Those who have made thorough studies of the vocabularies of aboriginal[1] languages have found that these languages have rich resources of available words. The Maya language of Yucatan has at least 20,000 words, the Aztec of central Mexico about 27,000, and the Zulu language of South Africa possesses more than 30,000. Some other languages may not have as many, but the vocabulary of any language, irrespective of[2] how primitive the people may seem, must be reckoned in thousands, not in hundreds of words.
>
> "Vocabularies of Aboriginal Languages," Eugene A. Nida, *Customs and Cultures*

[1]*aboriginal:* primitive. [2]*irrespective of:* without regard to.

To prove that native languages contain larger vocabularies than is commonly believed, the author selects two examples from the American continent and a third example from the continent of Africa. These examples are particularly good ones because they are specific: they include the approximate number of words found in each language. In expanding the main point, the writer arranges the three languages according to the sizes of their respective vocabularies, from the fewest words to most words. The Zulu language, containing the largest vocabulary, is mentioned last.

A second paragraph demonstrating the use of statistics is this passage concerning Latin American education:

> With the exception of universities controlled by church, municipal,[1] or private corporations,[2] Latin American universities are national schools regulated by federal laws and statutes.[3] The measure of autonomy[4] granted to many universities, however, makes for considerable variation in requirements even within a given[5] country. A few of the national universities are large, with enrollments of some[6] 20,000 or more students, as, for example, the National University of Mexico and the National University of Buenos Aires. The National University of La Plata in Argentina

[1]*municipal:* city. [2]*corporations:* organized groups. [3]*statutes:* regulations. [4]*autonomy:* independence. [5]*given:* specific, particular. [6]*some:* about, nearly.

and the University of Havana each has an enrollment of over 15,000. Brazil, in addition to its 11 universities, has more than 100 single-faculty professional schools, with enrollments ranging from 50 to 200 students.

"Latin American Universities," Marjorie C. Johnston, *The Encyclopedia Americana*

The principle of reserving the most impressive example for last is illustrated in this selection. The earlier examples are not strictly arranged in order of size, although the paragraph might be improved if they were. But the writer has ended with the most forceful example. The fact that Brazil has eleven universities and over 100 professional schools is the most impressive evidence of the scope of higher education in Latin America.

Generally a few well-chosen examples, arranged in order of increasing importance, will serve an author's purpose better than a great number of examples. However, there are exceptions to this principle. Perhaps to suggest the excitement of its subject—unusual ways that some Americans celebrated their 1976 Bicentennial—the following paragraph is chock full of examples:

Most Americans began their [1976 Bicentennial] celebration in traditional ways—barbecues in Texas, clambakes in Maryland, ox-roasts in West Virginia, an old-fashioned bonfire in Litchfield, N.H., and in Philadelphia 635 block parties, probably a record. But on the Fourth of July weekend, it seemed, the uncommon was commonplace. Boston and Hawaii, for example, teamed up a nation-spanning ceremony blending the nation's newest science and its oldest history. A telescope at Mauna Kea Observatory in Hawaii captured the light emitted by a star 200 light years ago, which tripped a sensor, which flipped a switch—lighting a lamp in Boston's Old North Church, Paul Revere's storied beacon of 1775. A Californian who thinks big raised a 67 by 102 foot flag over his Mojave Desert ranch, an operation for which he has laid out $10,000 in poles and cables. In Salt Lake City, a family had a dip in their swimming pool, the bottom of which they painted as a flag. In Miramar, Fla., a mother and her children gift-wrapped their house in red, white, and blue bunting.

"The U.S.A.'s Bicentennial," adapted from the *San Francisco Examiner*, 4 July 1976

Note that the writer here begins by briefly mentioning traditional ways of celebrating the Bicentennial before presenting his main thesis—that "the uncommon was commonplace." By doing this, he heightens the effect of the examples of unusual activities that form the main body of the paragraph.

Your choice of subject for this week's composition will depend on the number and quality of the examples you can find. Once you have collected your examples, decide which is the strongest one and save it for the end of your paragraph. Arrange the other examples so that they build up to the final one in order of increasing importance. Make an effort to obtain a broad range of examples.

VARIETY IN THE SIMPLE SENTENCE

Much of your writing practice in this course will be centered upon choosing particular sentence types to fit the ideas you are expressing. In Chapter 1 you practiced subordinating a less important idea to a more important one. In Chapter 5 you will learn how to place ideas of equal weight in parallel structures. When you use these techniques of subordination and parallelism, the sentences you write may often be compound or complex ones.

As you come to use these advanced types of sentences, however, you will want to vary them with simpler forms. The simple sentence, made up of a single independent clause, can be helpful to a writer. It states an idea clearly and directly. It can effectively emphasize an important idea. When used sparingly and in combination with other types of sentences, a simple sentence provides a needed change of stylistic pace. The shortest possible sentences are a verb with an understood subject ("Listen.") and a subject-verb without modifiers ("Dogs bark."). Both are simple sentences. Notice that not all short sentences are simple ones, however; the sentence "I listen when he speaks" is a complex sentence, consisting of two clauses, one independent and one dependent.

Examples from model paragraphs and other writings show varieties of the simple sentence, some of them containing modifying elements:

I was stunned.
Once he even sang a song in class to illustrate a point.
Boston contains cobbled traces of London.
I flipped a switch, releasing a flow of fire extinguisher fluid inside the
    third engine.

The first sentence, containing only a subject and a verb, is dramatically short. The second sentence opens with an adverb (once); a prepositional phrase (in class) and an infinitive phrase (to illustrate a point) follow the main clause. The third sentence contains a colorful adjective (cobbled) modifying "traces" and a concluding prepositional phrase (of London). The fourth sentence ends with a fairly long participial phrase containing two prepositional phrases (releasing a flow of fire extinguisher fluid inside the third engine). These are only a few of the grammatical elements that can give the simple sentence many different appearances.

The following simple sentence illustrate two common but important ways to achieve sentence variety: the adverb and the appositive.

Simple sentences with adverbs	The story ended **unhappily.** He **finally** decided to study Chinese. **Slowly** he walked toward the door.

When an adverb is modifying a verb, it can appear in various positions in a sentence. For instance, in the third example above, the adverb "slowly" modifies the verb "walked." The sentence could also have been written in other ways: He **slowly** walked toward the door; He walked **slowly** toward the door; or He walked toward the door **slowly.** When an adverb is modifying an adjective or another adverb, however, it cannot be shifted around so readily within a sentence. It must remain next to the word modified:

> (Adv.)
> He can play ping pong **fairly** well.
> (Adj.)
> The hurricane was **extremely** destructive.
> (Adj.)
> **Only** one narrow road leads to the lighthouse.

Sometimes changing the position of an adverb will alter the meaning of a sentence. For example, "The story ended unhappily." means that the story ended sadly, whereas "Unhappily the story ended." means that the listener is sorry that the story has ended. By taking advantage of the flexibility of many adverbs, though, a writer can add considerable variety to simple sentences. From time to time you will probably find it helpful to stress an adverb by placing it at the beginning or end of a sentence.

Simple sentences with appositives

> **A noted undersea explorer,** Jacques Costeau has filmed some remarkable scenes of sharks.
> My sister, **an accomplished pianist,** will give a concert soon.
> They visited La Scala, **one of the world's most attractive opera houses.**

These simple sentences have been varied by the appositives placed at the beginning, in the middle, and at the end. Many appositives are actually shortened forms of dependent adjective clauses: "My sister, **who is an accomplished pianist,** will give a concert soon." By placing this idea in an appositive, you eliminate **who is,** gaining the advantage of economy of words. To rely too heavily on either the appositive or the adjective clause would lead to a monotonous style, however. In writing a paragraph, you will want to include both simple sentences with appositives and complex sentences with dependent adjective clauses.

EXERCISE 24
Varying Simple Sentences

A. *Combine each pair of simple sentences into one simple sentence containing an appositive. Place some appositives at the beginning of sentences, some within sentences, and some at the end of sentences.*

1. Khamphone was a young man from Laos. He wanted to become an electrical engineer.
2. He mailed a scholarship application to the East-West Center. It is an educational and cultural institution for Asian and American students.

3. The Center is located in Honolulu. It is a branch of the University of Hawaii.
4. Three months later, Khamphone received a reply. It was a letter of acceptance to the East-West Center.
5. He had been awarded a four-year scholarship. It was a total sum of four thousand dollars.

B. *Write out the following sentences, adding the adverbs in parentheses. Place some adverbs at the beginning of sentences, some within sentences, and some at the end of sentences.*

1. He will leave on vacation. (soon)
2. The comedian's performance was entertaining. (genuinely)
3. Her appetite began to disappear. (slowly)
4. The radio will be repaired. (eventually)
5. Popular music has a strong rhythm. (often)
6. They go swimming in the rain. (never)
7. The drummer practiced all afternoon. (noisily)
8. She was eager to visit the Prado Museum in Madrid. (very)
9. He bandaged his injured arm. (carefully)
10. The campers left cans, bottles, and paper on the picnic grounds. (thoughtlessly)

ELIMINATING UNNECESSARY WORDS

When you are writing or revising a composition, you will want to give some attention to eliminating useless words. This is one of the surest ways to improve the quality of your writing. If the writer of the model paragraph had included all of the words that appear in the following version, he could justifiably be considered wordy or verbose (using a wearisome and unnecessary number of words). Notice how much better this paragraph is when these unnecessary words are canceled out:

Perhaps the most interesting person I have ever met is an ~~interesting~~ Italian professor of philosophy who teaches ~~courses~~ at the University of Pisa ~~in Italy~~. Although I last met this man eight years ago, I have not forgotten ~~over the long years~~ his special qualities. First of all, I was impressed ~~from the beginning~~ by his ~~complete~~ devotion to teaching ~~his students~~. Because his lectures were always well-prepared and ~~invariably~~ clearly delivered, ~~a great~~ many students ~~always~~ swarmed into his classroom, ~~filling the classroom to capacity~~. His ~~many~~ followers ~~also~~ appreciated the fact that he ~~thoroughly~~ believed in what he taught ~~to students~~ and that he was ~~always~~ intellectually stimulating ~~to hear~~. Furthermore, he could be counted on ~~in every class session~~ to explain his ideas in an imaginative way, introducing such ~~various~~ aids to ~~student~~ understanding as oil paintings, phonograph records, pieces of sculpture, and guest lecturers ~~who were invited to speak to the class~~. Once he even sang a song in class ~~before the students' eyes~~ in order to illustrate a ~~philosophical~~ point. Second, I admired the fact that he would confer with students ~~at almost any time~~ outside of the classroom or talk with them on the telephone. Drinking coffee in the snack bar ~~after having taught a class,~~ he would easily make friends with students ~~with great ease.~~ Sometimes he would ~~issue a~~ challenge ~~to~~ a student to ~~join with him in~~ a game of chess. At other times, he would ~~quite readily~~ join groups ~~of students~~ to discuss subjects ranging ~~broadly~~ from astronomy to scuba diving. Many young people visited him ~~at one time or another~~ in his office for academic advice; others came to his home for ~~the purpose of~~ social evenings. Finally, I was ~~favorably impressed and~~ attracted by his lively wit. He believed that no class hour is a success unless, during it, the students and the professor ~~have a reason to join together to~~ share several chuckles and at least one loud laugh. Through his ~~inimitable and captivating~~ sense of humor, he made learning ~~much~~ more enjoyable and ~~much~~ more lasting. If it is true, ~~as it seems to be,~~ that life makes a wise man smile and a foolish man cry, then my friend is ~~without question~~ truly a wise man. Probably the best example ~~he could possibly have given to us~~ of his wit is this ~~interesting~~ idea with which he once ended a lecture: "It is as dangerous for man to model himself upon his invention, the machine, as it would be for God to model Himself upon His invention."

If all of the unneeded words had been left in this paragraph, it would have been a glaring example of **wordiness.** Wordiness occurs when a writer needlessly repeats a word or when he lapses into redundancy, using more words than he needs to express an idea.

1. <u>**Unnecessary repetition of a word:**</u> By repeating the word "interesting" in the first sentence, the writer slows down the movement of thought and adds no additional information. In the same sentence, the word "Italy" in the phrase "in Italy" repeats a word that has been used earlier: "an **Italian** professor of philosophy." Following the statement "the students swarmed into his classroom," the word "classroom" in the phrase "filling the classroom to capacity" is repetitive. So is the word "ease" in the phrase "with great ease" that follows the word "easily." In the phrase "impressed and attracted," the word "impressed" has been used earlier in the third sentence and is not needed in any case. Can you find other crossed-out examples of word repetition?

2. <u>**Redundancy:**</u> In the second sentence, the phrase "over the long years" is redundant. The reader already knows that eight years have passed. The phrase "issue a challenge to" can be reduced to the single word, "challenge," without changing the idea. In the clause "others came to his home for the purpose of social evenings," the words "the purpose of" add nothing to the idea. The phrase "before the students' eyes" is unnecessary in the sentence telling of the professor's singing. A number of superfluous adjectives and adverbs—"complete," "invariably," "a great many," "quite

readily," "broadly," "inimitable and captivating"—can be effectively cut out. What other examples of crossed-out redundant words and phrases do you notice?

EXERCISE 25
Wordiness

Rewrite the following paragraph, eliminating all words that are repetitive or superfluous. Do not eliminate any facts, and do not change the meaning of any of the sentences.

It is surprising to find how many different kinds of clothing are worn in many various and different parts of the world we live in. In the city of London or on the streets of New York, most of the men wear the usual outfits of coats and trousers, called suits, along with a shirt and a necktie, which is worn around the neck. Some women in these particular cities also wear trousers and jackets that have much in common with what men wear and that are known to most people as pants suits. On the several islands of Hawaii, men wear brightly colored, patterned shirts called *aloha* shirts. Women, at least many women, wear very much the same color and pattern in long dresses which have come to be called *muumuus*. In Japan, most men wear business suits such as the kind you see in New York or London, as we have mentioned earlier. But most especially in the outlying country that lies outside of Tokyo, a great many Japanese women wear the long-sleeved, traditional dress, known as the *kimono*, with its wide belt, called the *obi*. Moving around in Southeast Asia, you are certain to see a mixture of Eastern and Western dress on both men and women alike. Sometimes, members of both sexes in Southeast Asia wear a piece of colorful cotton material wrapped around the human being's body. This is the *sarong*. Surely one of the loveliest and most beautiful of women's dresses is found in Vietnam. This dress really consists of long trousers of a light material, with transparent panels hanging from the woman's waist to her feet at front and back. The dress has long sleeves and a high neck. Another beautiful woman's dress is worn in India. Popularly called the *sari*, this dress is made of filmy sheer material in intense colors, sometimes with metallic threads. It is wrapped and folded around the woman's body and draped over her head. The most exciting and distinctive man's dress or garment is found even farther around the world, however, in the desert kingdom of Saudi Arabia, where there is a lot of sand. Here the full white robe, which goes by the name of the *thobe*, topped with a flowing white headdress, makes every man on the desert of Arabia look like a desert chieftain.

The Periodic Sentence

A periodic sentence is one in which the main thought is not completed until the very end of the sentence. Often this type of sentence is more effective than one in which the main thought is given first, followed by one or more modifying clauses or phrases. This is so because, by withholding the key word or words of the sentence until the end, a sense of anticipation is created in the reader. Therefore a periodic sentence is likely to be more emphatic than a sentence with a looser construction.

Notice the difference between the loose and periodic construction in the following examples. In each periodic sentence, the main idea falls at the end.

Loose construction	The history of English words is the history of our civilization in many ways.
Periodic sentence	In many ways, the history of English words **is the history of our civilization.**
Loose construction	She was offered a professional contract after winning the Olympic gold medal for figure skating, according to newspaper reports.
Periodic sentence	According to newspaper reports, after winning the Olympic gold medal for figure skating, she was offered **a professional contract.**
Loose construction	There have been many great discoveries made by scientists in the twentieth century.
Periodic sentence	Scientists in the twentieth century have made **many great discoveries.**

EXERCISE 26
The Periodic Sentence

Revise the following sentences so that the final emphasis falls on the idea in the clause presently at the beginning of each sentence.

1. The course was not very difficult, although I didn't receive a high grade.
2. He felt that the world had come to an end when he wasn't chosen for the football team.
3. It requires steady nerves to do the job safely.
4. The plane began to shudder noticeably as soon as it lifted off the runway.
5. She filled a bucket with water to put out the fire.
6. Jane walked out of his life, bursting into tears as she left the room.
7. William Butler Yeats is one of my favorite poets.
8. There are many exercises to do if you want to build a muscular body.
9. Summer is the most enjoyable season for many people.
10. He played the violin well because he had been trained in it from an early age.
11. A textbook helps to organize a course; supplementary readings help to enrich a course.

12. The automobile is the greatest economic factor in modern American life, as economists have pointed out.
13. "You can't have your cake and eat it, too" is a familiar saying in the U.S.A.
14. Some voting systems are better than others in certain situations.
15. The basic economic foundation of the classical Greek civilization has been revealed by excavations at a site in the Peloponnesus.

Punctuation Points

UNDERSTANDING RESTRICTIVE AND NONRESTRICTIVE ELEMENTS

A restrictive element is one that is so important to the idea of the sentence that it could not be removed without seriously disturbing clarity. Since it firmly restricts, or limits, the meaning, it cannot be dropped.

One test of a restrictive element is that it is read without pausing before it or without raising or lowering the voice. Because it is essential to the meaning of the sentence, a restrictive element is not set off by commas:

Restrictive phrase	The dog **with the leather collar** belongs to our neighbor. (There are several dogs on the street, but only the one with a leather collar belongs to our neighbor.)
Restrictive clause	The cheese **that I like best** comes from Italy. (There are many cheeses from many countries, but the one I like best comes from Italy.)

In contrast, a nonrestrictive element may add interesting or useful information to a sentence, but it does not so firmly restrict the meaning that it cannot be removed. A nonrestrictive element does not contain information that is essential to the understanding of the sentence. If it were removed, the central idea of the sentence would still be intact. When reading or speaking, we separate a nonrestrictive element from the rest of the sentence by a pause, a change in voice, or both. When writing, we set it off by commas:

Nonrestrictive phrase	Milk, **containing calcium,** is recommended for children's diets.
Nonrestrictive clause	My mother, **who was eating a sandwich,** asked if I was ready for lunch.

Notice that there are three distinctions between restrictive and nonrestrictive elements:

1. In pronunciation

A restrictive element is generally joined to the rest of the sentence in speech; a nonrestrictive one is separated by pauses before and after it and by a change in voice.

2. **In form**

A restrictive element is joined without punctuation to the rest of the sentence; a nonrestrictive one is separated by commas before and after it.

3. **In meaning**

A restrictive element narrows a reference to include only part of a whole; a nonrestrictive one includes the whole:

Restrictive	Students **who ask questions** increase their understanding of a topic. (*Some* students)
Nonrestrictive	Mr. Fuller's students, **who ask questions,** increase their understanding of a topic. (*All* students)

It may further help you to recognize differences between restrictive and nonrestrictive elements if you notice that proper nouns, the names of persons, places, or things (*the Taj Mahal, the Eiffel Tower, John F. Kennedy, my uncle Howard*), are generally followed by nonrestrictive elements. Common nouns (milk, dog, cheese) may be followed by either restrictive or nonrestrictive elements, depending upon how specifically they are identified in the sentence:

Restrictive	The old mosque **which you told us about** was very nice. (That certain mosque, not the other two old ones)
Nonrestrictive	The Blue Mosque, **which you told us about,** was larger than I had expected it to be. (Proper noun, telling which mosque)
Restrictive	The problem **which we will study today** is on page eight. (Which problem?)
Nonrestrictive	The fifth problem, **which you have already worked on,** may be omitted. (The problem is specifically identified.)
Restrictive	A man **who was wearing a yellow shirt** asked me for a cigarette. (Which man?)
Nonrestrictive	Mr. Thomas, **who was wearing a yellow shirt,** asked me for a cigarette. (Proper noun, telling who asked)

See Punctuating Appositives in Chapter 8 for additional information about restrictive and nonrestrictive elements.

EXERCISE 27
Punctuating Nonrestrictive Elements

Write out the following sentences, adding commas to set off nonrestrictive elements whenever necessary.

1. The next exercise which you have already done may be left out.
2. There are people I am sure who will say that the water is too cold.

3. The house with the green shutters is the one we will buy.
4. The Smith's house with its broken shutters stood by the road.
5. Lee De Forest the inventor of the three-element vacuum tube patented more than 300 other inventions.
6. Every young wife who lives in an apartment dreams of someday owning a house.
7. Our next-door neighbor who has been a good friend to us promised to take care of our garden while we were away.
8. The old gas stove which was stained in many places was kept in service because it has six burners.
9. A person who visits Kuala Lumpur can see many handsome new buildings.
10. The boy who was throwing stones was scolded by the teacher.
11. My brother Philip who builds model airplanes has won many contests.
12. The poet dedicated his book to my mother who died last year.
13. Who would have thought that the Pulitzer Prize for reporting which is normally given annually would not have been awarded this year?
14. Students who choose to write a term paper will not have to take the final examination.
15. My father who is very fond of sports often takes us to the ice skating rink at Rockefeller Plaza.

Grammar Skills

PRINCIPLES OF MODIFICATION

Understanding how modifiers function in English sentences will help you to build better sentences. For a sentence often contains words, phrases, and clauses that make more specific the meaning of other parts of the sentence. These modifiers tend to stand as near as possible to the elements they modify.

Modifiers are divided, according to the way in which they function, into three classes: adjectives, adverbs, and nouns.

Adjective Modifiers   Adjective modifiers serve to describe, limit, or qualify nouns. An adjective modifier may be placed either immediately before a substantive (*The* **red** *coat is mine.*) or after a linking verb, such as *is, become, appear,* or *feel* (*He was* **tired** *after a long day's work.*). Adjectives tell what a substantive is like, what state it is in, or which one it is.

Adjectives are numerous—*green, ambitious, sincere, intelligent, loving, cold, worried*—and they make both regular changes (*strong, stronger, strongest*) and irregular changes (*good, better, best*) for comparison.

An adjective modifier may be a single word, a phrase, or a clause. Single-word adjectives usually *precede* the substantive or follow a linking verb. (An adjective following a linking verb is called a *predicate adjective.*) Adjective phrases and clauses, however, normally *follow* the substantive. In the following sentences, notice the position of the adjectives in relation to the substantives they modify:

Small farms seem **peaceful** to travelers **who pass by.**

Our new house has **a tin roof** and **an acre of pasture.**

Note that the articles *a, an,* and *the* are adjectives that serve to designate or limit a noun.

Adverb Modifiers   Unlike adjectives, adverbs have more than a single function as modifiers. They can modify verbs, adjectives, and other adverbs.

Modifying a verb	She dressed **neatly.**
Modifying an adjective	The sun is **very** hot.
Modifying an adverb	She is **not** very careful.

The function of adverb modifiers can be listed in an easily memorized series of key words:

when (time)
where (place)
how (manner, condition, or reason)
how much (extent or number; relationship in a series)
why (cause or reason)

Many adverbs are formed by adding the suffix *-ly* to adjectives: soft*ly,* final*ly,* eager*ly.* When *-ly* is added to nouns, however, it produces adjectives, as in man*ly* (His rescue of the drowning boy was a *manly* act).

Many adverbs are compared by using *more* or *most,* or *less* and *least,* with the positive degree: *perfectly, more perfectly, most perfectly; eagerly, more eagerly, most eagerly.* A few adverbs are compared by adding *-er* and *-est* to the positive forms: soon, soon*er,* soon*est;* fast, fast*er,* fast*est.* Some adverbs have an irregular comparison:

POSITIVE	COMPARATIVE	SUPERLATIVE
badly, ill	worse	worst
good, well	better	best
little	less	least
much	more	most
far	farther, further	farthest, furthest
near	nearer	nearest, next

In placing single-word adverbs, you will find that they usually precede adjectives and other adverbs. When they modify verbs, they often follow them or come between a verb and its auxiliary. Adverbs normally follow the nouns they are modifying. Generally speaking, adverb modifiers are capable of being shifted about within a sentence much more than adjective modifiers.

The following sentence contains (1) an introductory adverb clause, (2) prepositional phrases used as adverb modifiers, and (3) a single adverb:

(1)   (2)
When Raymond found his briefcase, he lifted it **from the table** and **care-**
(3)   (2)
fully examined the book that had been autographed **by Albert Schweitzer.**

The introductory adverb clause (1) conveys the idea of time (when). It does not modify another word in the sentence but instead modifies the verbal idea in the independent clause: it identifies the time when Raymond *lifted* the briefcase from the table. The two prepositional phrases (2) show, respectively, the place (where) that the briefcase was found and the manner (how) in which it had been autographed. The single adverb (3) indicates the manner (how) in which Raymond opened the briefcase.

Noun Modifiers   Nouns may be modified by adjectives; they may also be modified by other nouns. Both types of modification are extremely common in English, as the following partial list suggests:

ADJECTIVE MODIFIERS	NOUN MODIFIERS
a *successful* attorney	a *corporation* attorney
a *deadly* poison	a *rat* poison
a *fast* track	a *race* track
a *broken* hose	a *garden* hose
an *ambitious* salesman	a *book* salesman
a *gentle* pat	a *love* pat
a *friendly* partner	a *business* partner

An adjective and noun modifier may come from the same root. Usually there is some difference in meaning:

a *stony* road (rough)	a *stone* road
a *nervous* specialist	a *nerve* specialist
a *seedy* salesman (unkempt)	a *seed* salesman
a *beautiful* shop	a *beauty* shop

Sometimes the meaning is the same:

a *golden* chain	a *gold* chain
a *promotional* bulletin	a *promotion* bulletin

You can usually decide whether the modifier of a noun is an adjective or another noun by the fact that you can often place an intensifier, such as *very* or *rather*, before an adjective modifier but not before a noun modifier. For example, consider the modified noun *college president*. You could say "a very *wise* president" (adjective) but **not** "a very *college* president" (noun). Or take the modified noun *city hall*. You could say "a rather *new* hall" (adjective) but **not** "a rather *city* hall" (noun). Another test is to change the phrase into a sentence with a *be* verb. An adjective modifying a noun will fit meaningfully into such a sentence pattern: "The president is *wise*." But a noun modifying a noun will **not**: "The president is *college*."

Noun modifiers are an important feature of English grammar. They appear in some of the most commonly used phrases: *paper towel; beach ball; shoe shine; kitchen door; marriage counselor; evening newspaper; garage key; living room.*

When a noun is modified by both an adjective and another noun, the adjective always comes first. We say, an old cow barn, **not** a cow old barn; a rich eye doctor, **not** an eye rich doctor.

Noun Compounds in Scientific and Technical English   Noun compounds are often used in scientific and technical English writing. They usually represent "shorthand" versions of these longer grammatical elements:

1. Prepositional phrases: A **differential time domain** equation is the time domain of a differential equation.
2. Strings of prepositional phrases: **Momentum transfer experiments** are experiments of the transfer of momentum.
3. Nouns modified by relative clauses: **Automatic controller action** is controller action that is automatic.
4. Nouns modified by gerund phrases: A **fluid bed reactor** is a reactor containing a fluid bed.
5. Combinations of these: An **air pressure signal device** is a device that signals the pressure of air.
   A **quiescent state fluid bed reactor** is a reactor containing a fluid bed in a quiescent state. [Or: in a state of quiescence]

Note that although most of the elements of compounds are nouns, adjectives can also be elements in noun compounds. At times these adjective elements remain adjectives in the longer form (see 3. above); at other times, they become nouns in the full form (see 5. above).

If the compound contains noun groups (or noun-adjective groups), these groups are not normally broken up when the compound is translated to the longer form: A **fluid bed reactor** is not a reactor containing a bed that is fluid.

If any of the nouns in the long form are plural, they become singular in the compound—except for the last noun of the compound, which is the general class being described by the nouns preceding it: Reactors containing fluid beds become *not* **fluid beds reactors** but **fluid bed reactors.**

Usually a full form is translated into a noun compound by reversing the order of the elements:

   (1)   (2)   (3)

Experiments in the transfer of momentum becomes

   (3)   (2)   (1)

momentum transfer experiments.

Some compounds are easily translated back into relative clauses:

a book binder = a person who binds books (or a machine that binds books)

a shoe store = a store in which shoes are sold

Some compounds are not easily translatable:

a telephone book = a book that contains the numbers of the telephones in a given place

a department store = a store containing several different departments for selling different types of things

symphony music = music of the type called "symphonic"

EXERCISE 28
Adjective, Adverb, and Noun Modifiers

 A. *Write out each boldfaced word or group of words. Identify each item as an adjective, adverb, or noun modifier, and tell which word in the sentence it modifies.*

1. **For hours** she worked **at the sewing machine,** and the **beautiful** dress was **ready** for **her** daughter **that** evening.
2. The **camping** trip began **on Monday** and ended **three** days **later.**
3. A car **which was coming toward us** veered **suddenly** into **our** lane.
4. Mary, **who is the prettiest girl in the class,** was invited to the **graduation** party **at the Hilton Hotel.**
5. **Many of your longer** sentences seemed **awkward to me when I first read your paper.**

 B. *Write out these sentences, supplying modifiers for each blank according to instructions.*

1. There were . . . . people in the railroad station.
      (adv.)

2. My brother's bicycle had a . . . . time.
        (adj.)

3. We found the cat . . . .
      (adv. phrase)

4. The flowers . . . . added a touch of color to the room.
     (adj. phrase)

5. The boy, ... , ate his dinner in a hurry.
     (adj. clause)

6. . . . ., we were happy.
   (adv. clause)

C. *Make compounds of the following phrases.*

1. a collar for a dog. . . . .
2. a closet for clothes. . . . .
3. a faucet from which hot water comes. . . . .
4. a plan for building a school. . . . .
5. a ticket for an airplane trip. . . . .
6. a company that mines gold. . . . .
7. a stove that burns oil. . . . .
8. a machine that automatically grades papers (examinations). . . . .
   . . . .
9. a machine that is used to grade (make smooth) roads. . . . .
   . . . .
10. a machine that grades roads and is made of steel. . . . .
    . . . .

D. *Make compounds of the following technical word groups.*

Example: A reactor containing a fluid bed is a **fluid bed reactor.**

1. A pump whose speed is variable is. . . . .
2. Computations of drops in pressure is . . . .
3. A vessel for the storage of liquid is. . . . .
4. A signal for the output of pressure is. . . . .
5. A subtraction operator that is symbolic is. . . . .
6. An analysis of the size of particle is. . . . .
7. Conditions for laminar flow is. . . . .
8. A reference change that has been prearranged is. . . . .
9. The mixing diffusivities of solids is. . . . .
10. The transfer function for the transducer is. . . . .

E. *Translate the following technical noun compounds into their longer forms.*

Example: Air fluidized beds are **beds fluidized with air.**

1. A single particle heat transfer model is. . . . .
2. Different diameter lead glass particles are. . . . .

3. A gamma-ray absorption technique is...........................

4. A fluidized bed solids inventory is............................

5. A high-frequency current penetration welding process is...........
....

6. A new-type prestressed concrete pressure vessel is..............
....

7. A solid-state variable motor-speed control is....................

8. A symbolic subtraction operator is.............................

9. An image intensifier screen is.................................

10. Individual heater heat transfer coefficients is.....................

AGREEMENT OF PRONOUN AND ANTECEDENT

The antecedent of a pronoun is the word to which the pronoun refers. In the sentence "Mr. Harris washed his car," "Mr. Harris" is the antecedent of the pronoun "his." A pronoun always agrees with its antecedent in both number and gender. Thus in the sentence above, "his," like "Mr. Harris," is both singular and masculine. A plural pronoun is used when the antecedent is plural: "The *voters* cast *their* ballots." In regard to gender, the pronoun is masculine *(he, his, him)* when the antecedent is masculine, feminine when the antecedent is feminine *(she, her, hers)*, and neuter *(it, its)* when the antecedent is neither masculine nor feminine *(water, book, automobile)*. Study these examples of pronouns agreeing with their antecedents:

The **student** turned in **his** book.
The **girls** learned that **their** applications had been accepted.
She expressed **her** opinion on the voting issue.
The **committee members** will give **their** report in March.
Every **nation** is proud of **its** heroes.

Two or more singular antecedents joined by *or* or *nor* are referred to by a singular pronoun:

If **Jane or Mary** asks for **her** coat, tell her it is in the next room.

Two antecedents joined by "and" are referred to by a plural pronoun:

George and Paul telephoned **their** wives.

Such words as *one, everyone, everybody, no one, nobody, each, either, neither, anyone, anybody, someone,* and *somebody* are generally referred to by a singular pronoun in formal usage and by a plural pronoun in colloquial usage. Even though such compound pronouns as "everyone" and "somebody" often cause agreement problems, you can remember the correct formal rule by separating them into two parts and adding the word

"single" between the parts "*Everyone* (every *single* one) forgot *his* money."
Even though a phrase containing a plural noun appears after the antecedent,
the pronoun remains singular in formal usage to agree with its antecedent:
"*Neither* of the men remembered *his* telephone number." However, plural
agreement of the pronoun with such singular antecedents as *everybody* is
becoming increasingly common in both English speech and writing.

Here are additional examples of singular agreement:

Everyone at the meeting expressed **his** opinion. (Colloquial: **their**)
If **somebody** asks for me, tell **him** I've gone to the country. (Colloquial:
   them)
Has **either** of the candidates offered to deliver **his** speech tomorrow?
(Colloquial: **their**)
Nobody voiced **his** disapproval of the measure (Colloquial: **their**)

A relative pronoun (*who, which, that*) agrees in number with the antecedent immediately preceding it, not with a noun or pronoun located earlier
in the sentence:

We visited one of the **airplanes which were** on display. **(Which** is plural
   because it agrees with **airplanes,** not with **one.**
They are members of the **team that is** expected to win the championship.
(That is singular because it agrees with **team,** not with **members.**

EXERCISE 29
Agreement of Pronoun and Antecedent

Write out the sentences, choosing the correct pronoun for formal usage.

1. The students voted for (his, their) representative.
2. Everyone has (his, their) job to do.
3. All the boys mailed (his, their) letters home.
4. Neither of the girls remembered to pack (her, their) gloves.
5. Nobody raised (his, their) hand to answer the question.
6. Each of the countries sent (its, their) representative to Paris.
7. If a person intends to go to college, (he, they) should concentrate on
   getting a high scholastic average.
8. No one on the camping trip brought (his, their) flashlight.
9. Someone telephoned but declined to leave (her, their) name.
10. They bought two of the books which (was, were) on sale.
11. Has either of the boys lost (his, their) tennis racket?
12. If anyone phones for me, tell (him, them) I've gone out.
13. Ruth and Helen decided to share (her, their) dessert.
14. Someone has left (his, their) sweater on the bench.
15. If Mark or Larry wants to go to graduate school, (he, they) should
    apply early.

AGREEMENT OF SUBJECT AND VERB

A number of structural patterns in English may cause a writer to puzzle over the proper subject–verb agreement. The following rules, based on current writing practice, will help to answer many of your questions about whether to choose a singular or plural verb.

1. A compound subject (two or more elements joined by "and") is plural and requires a plural verb form.

   A letter and a telegram **have** arrived for Mrs. Thompson. (The subject "a letter and a telegram" is plural, so you need a plural verb.)

2. Subjects that are compound in appearance but which function as singular units may take singular verbs.

   Your screeching and shouting **is** making her nervous.
   When a man reaches forty years of age, his vigor and creativity **is** at its peak.

3. A verb phrase used as a subject always takes a singular verb form.

   Asking your employer for special favors **is** not a wise thing to do.
   To send food and clothing to the flood victims **was** his first thought.

4. A phrase placed between a subject and a verb (such as "along with," "together with," "in addition to," or "as well as") does not affect the verb form.

   A box of groceries **was** left by the door. ("Box" is the subject, not "groceries.")
   The captain, along with three crew members, **was** decorated for bravery. ("Captain" is the subject, not "members.")

5. When a form of the verb "be" connects a subject of one number with a predicate nominative of another number, the verb agrees in number with the subject.

   The planets **were** the object of my study.
   The object of my study **was** the planets.

   Cameras **are** the country's leading export.
   The country's leading export **is** cameras.

6. In inverted sentence order, the verb agrees in number with the subject, which follows the verb.

   Resting on the boat's deck **were** two briefcases. ("Briefcases" is the subject, not "deck.")
   Under these blankets **sleeps** my brother. ("Brother" is the subject, not "blankets.")

7. Collective nouns (nouns naming a group of persons or things), such as *family, team, committee, crowd, group, number, crew,* and *series,* may take either singular or plural verbs, depending on which sounds more natural to the user. A singular verb is always correct with collective nouns unless a plural form is needed to keep the sentence from sounding nonsensical.

A group of students **has** (or **have**) left on vacation.
A number of spectators **was** (or **were**) hurt when the racing car drove into the grandstand.
My family **is** living in Argentina.
My family **are** taking separate vacations.
The team **is** on its way to the playing field.

8. Nouns that are plural in form but singular in meaning, such as *physics, mathematics, politics, athletics, checkers, mechanics, economics,* and *acoustics,* normally take singular verbs. The noun *data,* which is plural in both form and meaning, is also generally followed by a singular verb.

Mathematics **is** difficult for many students.
The data **has** proved helpful in his research

9. A plural noun that establishes a weight, measurement, period of time, or amount of money normally takes a singular verb when it is being used as a single unit. When such a noun clearly indicates a plurality of units, however, it takes a plural verb.

Two dollars **is** (or **are**) missing from my wallet.
Three dollar bills **are** (not **is**) on the table.
During the Middle Ages, thirty-eight years **was** considered a long life span.
A hundred and fifty pounds **is** (not **are**) what I used to weigh.

10. In the constructions *either (neither) . . . or (nor)* and *not only . . . but also,* the verb agrees with the element of the subject nearer to the verb. (The conjunction *or* alone sometimes functions as *either . . . or.*)

Either the college president or the college trustees **are** responsible for setting the policy. (Plural subject "trustees" takes a plural verb.)
Either the college trustees or the college president **is** responsible for setting the policy. (Singular subject "president" takes a singular verb.)
Not only the mayor but also the city council members **oppose** the new zoning law. (Plural subject "members" takes a plural verb.)
Not only the city council members but also the mayor **opposes** the new zoning law. (Singular subject "mayor" takes a singular verb.)
The butler or the maids **are** working today. (Plural subject "maids" takes a plural verb).
The maids or the butler **is** working today. (Singular subject "butler" takes a singular verb.)

EXERCISE 30
Agreement of Subject and Verb

Write out the following sentences, choosing and underlining the correct verb from the two in parentheses.

1. Visiting an airport to watch incoming planes (is, are) a pleasure to many people.
2. A pen and a pencil (was, were) lying on the desk.
3. Sitting on the window ledge (was, were) three colored bottles.
4. The boxes of candy (was, were) given to Patricia on her birthday.
5. The committee (was, were) unanimous in its decision.
6. The committee (has, have) divided opinions about the issue.
7. Not only the mother but also the brothers (favors, favor) selling the family home.
8. Two gallons of gasoline (is, are) all I can afford.
9. Either the two colonels or the commanding general (is, are) going to make the inspection trip.
10. A bouquet of roses (was, were) ordered for the table's centerpiece.
11. The sputtering and coughing of the engine (makes, make) me want to junk that car.
12. One of the hotel guests (needs, need) a telephone directory and a bottle of champagne.
13. Waiting for a bus for two hours (is, are) not my idea of a stimulating experience.
14. Politics (is, are) a fascinating study.
15. The roller skating rink or the twin cinemas (is, are) open until midnight.

USING PARTICIPLES AND PARTICIPIAL PHRASES

Because you are trying to polish your skill in writing English, you will benefit from using participles and participial phrases. After understanding the functions of participles, you should try to include them in every paper you write. Participles are popular in much current English writing because they are an efficient means of expression. They allow a writer to compress his ideas into fewer words, and they add an active, vivid quality to compositions. For these reasons, participle use is one of the most prominent features of modern English prose.

Identifying Participles   Participles are found in the form of adjectives, parts of finite verbs, and absolute constructions (see Appendix 9 for an explanation of finite verbs, absolute constructions, and other grammatical terms):

1. *As adjectives*

He threw the ball from a **sitting** position. (Participle modifying **position**)
A small boy, **sobbing bitterly,** ran toward me. (Participial phrase modifying **boy**)

2. *As parts of finite verbs*

They are **looking** for a new house.
We have been **waiting** for an hour.

3. *In absolute constructions*

The dishes **washed,** she could at last relax.
The boat **sinking,** we swam to shore.

Participles can express present time, habitual/nonpast time, or past time:

Present Participle   **Singing** happily, he works from morning until night.
Past Participle   Having **sung** the first song, the soprano left the stage.

Participles can be used in many positions in a sentence. In the following sentences, participial phrases appear in three positions:

Beginning   **Expecting an explosion at any moment,** I glanced out again at the right wing.
Middle   Fire trucks, **their sirens screaming,** raced up to us as we squealed to a stop.
End   I throttled forward, and we lumbered ahead, **slowly lifting off the ground.**

Effective Use of Participles   A composition can be weakened if the writer uses more words than are needed to express an idea (wordiness) or if he strings together several independent clauses with *so's* and *and's* (stringy sentence). You can avoid both of these flaws by adding participles and participial phrases to your sentences. Look at these examples showing how participles can reduce the number of words in sentences:

Wordy   The fact that the mothers were working gave them little time to take care of their children.
Improved   **Working,** the mothers had little time to take care of their children.

Wordy   After we were frightened by the explosion, we telephoned the fire station.
Improved   **Frightened by the explosion,** we telephoned the fire station.

Often two sentences can be combined into one by means of a participial phrase:

Audrey was greatly surprised by the news. She immediately telephoned her parents.
Greatly surprised by the news, Audrey immediately telephoned her parents.

Karl was eager to leave the city. He threw his clothes into a suitcase.
Eager to leave the city, Karl threw his clothes into a suitcase.

The student was tired of studying. He took a rest.
Tired of studying, the student took a rest.

Second, consider how participles help to tighten up stringy sentences:

Stringy sentence	Raymond was living in Rome, and he found it expensive there, so he took a part-time job.
Improved	**Finding that living in Rome was expensive,** Raymond took a part-time job.
Stringy sentence	Roger entered into the spirit of the party, and he forgot his usual shyness, so he enjoyed himself very much.
Improved	**Entering into the spirit of the party and forgetting his usual shyness,** Roger enjoyed himself very much.

EXERCISE 31
Participles and Participial Phrases

A. *Combine each pair of sentences into a single sentence beginning with a present participle.*

Example: They leave India in May. They will go to Beirut.
Leaving India in May, they will go to Beirut.

1. We walk to the store. We get our daily exercise.
2. Jane was disturbed by the noise. She turned off the radio.
3. I overheard his remark. I burst out laughing.
4. Gary was tired. He decided to go to bed.
5. She was afraid of the snake. She ran into the house.

B. *Combine each pair of sentences into a single sentence beginning with a past participle.*

Example: He read the article. He gave me his opinion.
Having read the article, he gave me his opinion.

1. The boys lost their way. They shouted for their friends.
2. We had a flat tire. We were an hour late in arriving.
3. The palace guards were warned of a plot against the government. They were fully armed.
4. The deer saw us. It leaped gracefully over the wall.
5. I called him. I went on to the stadium.

C. *Improve these wordy and stringy sentences by adding participles and dropping any unnecessary words.*

Example: He was thinking about his family, and he was wondering why he hadn't heard from them for so long, so he decided to write a letter home.
Thinking about his family and wondering why he hadn't heard from them for so long, he decided to write a letter home.

1. Evelyn was eating a piece of cake, and she was listening to what Tony was saying, so she paid no attention to the television program.
2. The river overflowed its banks, and it flooded the city streets, and it overturned automobiles, so much property was destroyed.
3. There are small cabins and open shelters along the trail, and we felt sure about sleeping quarters, so we didn't take many blankets on our hiking trip.
4. The men began their search for the lost child at once, but they had no clues to follow, so they sent for more help.
5. The story begins with the family's trip to Peru, and it tells how they worked in the fields, and goes on to explain how they saved money and finally bought a farm.

D. *Combine each pair of sentences into a single sentence, reducing one of the sentences to a participial phrase.*

Example: Elizabeth was expecting to graduate in June. She studied hard.
Expecting to graduate in June, Elizabeth studied hard.

1. The boy was happy with his new dog. He spent every possible moment training him.
2. John was interested in going to South America. He visited a travel agent.
3. Savita became anxious about her scholastic standing. She talked with her professor.
4. They were strongly in favor of another election. They campaigned for it.
5. The fire was hotter than an inferno. It burned for two days.
6. Ellen was afraid of breaking the glass top. She was careful in moving the table.
7. The people of the world were fascinated with the first landing on the moon. They watched the event on television.
8. The animals were unfamiliar with their new life in the zoo. They became restless and ill-tempered.
9. The astronomer was pleased with his new telescope. He found that it gave him a much better view of the constellations.
10. The musicians from Australia were extremely popular in Europe. They performed at several clubs in Paris.
11. This ancient tree has long been famous in Idaho legend. It is linked to the history of the trappers and fur traders.
12. The church was built in 1829. It is the oldest European structure still in use in the South Pacific.
13. One of the most unusual desert water sports is artificial surfing on machine-generated waves in a large tank. It is popular near Phoenix.
14. Outdoor furniture generally takes up more space than indoor furniture. It reduces the amount of space available for container plants.

15. This alternator-generator is powered by a one-cylinder gas engine. It has a permanent-magnet alternator instead of the usual generator with brushes.

Questions for Discussion and Review

1. Find a compound predicate in the model paragraph.
2. In the model paragraph, point out an example (not the one boldfaced) of subordination by a participial phrase.
3. List the examples that have been used to develop the model paragraph.
4. Revise the following sentence from the model paragraph so that a comma is correctly used in place of the semicolon: "Many young people visited him in his office for academic advice; others came to his home for social evenings."
5. Identify the transitions that appear in the paragraphs about Latin American universities and the U.S.A.'s Bicentennial.
6. Locate the topic sentences in both the model paragraph and in the paragraph about the U.S.A.'s Bicentennial.
7. In the paragraph about Latin American universities, the topic sentence does not appear but is implied. Paragraphs are sometimes written with implied topic sentences, but if the writer has maintained control, his reader should be able to deduce from the paragraph's development what the unstated topic sentence and controlling idea are. Write out an appropriate topic sentence for this paragraph. Underline the controlling idea.
8. This chapter contains at least one example of a sentence beginning with an expletive. By quickly skimming over the model paragraph, example paragraphs, text, and exercises, can you find this expletive? Is its use justified?

Vocabulary Growth

PARAGRAPH PUZZLE

Complete the paragraph by choosing the right word to fill in each blank. When choice is difficult, refer to neighboring words or sentences for help.

One of the most remarkable developments in . . . . electronic
(a, an, the, such)

age has been the televising . . . . college-level courses. Now stu-
(at, for, in, of)

dents may sit . . . . their homes and watch lectures and . . . .
(in, on, over, under)   (supplies, exposures, displays, demonstrations)

on their television sets. This development . . . . been particularly
(have, has, should, shall)

well received in California. ...., a group of twenty two-year
          (Where, However, Therefore, Here)

community............in the San Francisco area has............such
(high schools, libraries, colleges, dairies) (sponsored, settled, spoken, taken)

courses as Environmental Study, Science............Civilization, and
             (but, for, nor, and)

Basic Clothing Construction. More............ten thousand Bay Area
          (there, then, these, than)

residents have ....in these courses, receiving instruction in
   (expected, entered, enrolled, exposed)

............homes. Students enroll in a college.............to their
(his, her, them, their)   (nearest, farthest, highest, tallest)

home; they pay a............registration fee, but there is no...........
    (cheap, small, slim, sharp)   (tuition, toll, tariff, tax)

charge. Students purchase books to read.............conjunction with
          (on, or, of, in)

each course. Colleges may............reports, projects, discussions, or
     (repeat, require, resort, repair)

examinations in.............with the course. Each cooperating college
(control, confusion, contrary, connection)

............the amount of academic credit it...........offer. Courses
(deduces, decides, adds, defers)   (may, might, will, would)

are televised on both............and public television stations. This is
    (control, kitchen, corporate, commercial)

............of the most dramatic examples of............U.S.A.'s at-
(one, some, many, certain)   (a, an, this, the)

tempts to spread education to............people.
    (their, its, our, your)

WORD CLUES

A. *In the following paragraphs, the boldfaced word is the vocabulary word; the italicized word is the "Context Clue" to the meaning of the vocabulary word.*

1. Andy objected to the **constant** barking of the dogs next door. He complained to the police that the disturbing noise had been *continuing for a long time.*

     Vocabulary Word......................................

     Context Clue..

Probable Meaning. . . . .

Dictionary Definition. . . . .

2. The **construction** of the skyscraper began in 1976. If no labor disputes arise, *work* on the building was expected to be completed in 1978.

Vocabulary Word. . . . .

Context Clue. . . . .

Probable Meaning. . . . .

Dictionary Definition. . . . .

3. Since the **definition** of the picture on their old television set has become unclear, my parents have decided to buy a new color set with a picture that has greater *clarity of detail.*

Vocabulary Word. . . . .

Context Clue. . . . .

Probable Meaning. . . . .

Dictionary Definition. . . . .

4. Etymologists are concerned with finding the **derivation** of words. To do this, they trace a word back to its *original form and meaning.*

Vocabulary Word. . . . .

Context Clue. . . . .

Probable Meaning. . . . .

Dictionary Definition. . . . .

5. The department store representative will **demonstrate** the ease of cooking with our new frying pan by *preparing* scrambled eggs for Saturday's customers.

demonstrate

Vocabulary Word. . . . .

preparing

Context Clue. . . . .

Probable Meaning. . . . .

to explain or describe by use of experiments

Dictionary Definition. . . . .

or examples

. . . .

B. *A list of various forms of each vocabulary word follows. For each number, choose a form different from the vocabulary word and use it mean-*

ingfully in a sentence. For example, in 1., use any form except the adjective
constant. *Write a total of five sentences.*

Verbs	Nouns	Adjectives	Adverbs
1.	constant constancy	constant	constantly
2. to construct	construct construction constructionist	constructive constructible	constructively
3. to define to redefine	definition definiteness	definite definable undefined	definitely indefinitely definitively
4. to derive	deriver derivation	derivative derivable derivational	derivatively
5. to demonstrate	demonstrant demonstrator demonstration demonstrableness	demonstrable demonstrative	demonstrably demonstrability demonstratively

Composition: Show What You Have Learned

Choose a composition topic from either Group I or Group II

GROUP I: TOPICS FOR WRITING A PARAGRAPH DEVELOPED BY EXAMPLES

The three writing assignments that follow will let you practice developing an expository paragraph by examples in the way that is most appealing to you. Follow one of these approaches to arrive at a topic for this week's writing:

1. Choose any subject you are interested in to write about in a paragraph developed by examples.
2. Select a topic that you haven't written about from among the composition topics in Chapters 1, 2, and 3. Use this topic as the basis for developing a paragraph by examples.
3. Look again at the cartoon of the clown adrift in the lifeboat on page 1. His situation could best be described as a "poignant" one.

   If the meaning of "poignant" is unfamiliar to you, find the definition in your dictionary. Then, although you may never have been shipwrecked, try to put yourself in the clown's place—to feel what he is feeling. When you have succeeded in doing this, use examples as the basis of your analytical development to write an expository paragraph about a situation you have experienced (or that someone you know has experienced) that could also be termed "poignant."

GROUP II: TOPICS TO CHALLENGE YOUR IMAGINATION

Copr. © 1940 James Thurber. Copr. © 1968 Helen Thurber.
From Fables for Our Time, *published by Harper & Row, New York.*
Originally printed in The New Yorker.

THE FAIRLY INTELLIGENT FLY

A large spider in an old house built a beautiful web in which to catch flies. Every time a fly landed on the web and was entangled in it the spider devoured him, so that when another fly came along he would think the web was a safe and quiet place in which to rest. One day a fairly intelligent fly buzzed around above the web so long without lighting that the spider appeared and said, "Come on down." But the fly was too clever for him and said, "I never light where I don't see other flies, and I don't see any other flies in your house." So he flew away until he came to a place where there were a great many other flies. He was about to settle down among them when a bee buzzed up and said, "Hold it, stupid, that's flypaper. All those flies are trapped." "Don't be silly," said the fly, "they're dancing." So he settled down and became stuck to the flypaper with all the other flies.

Moral: There is no safety in numbers, or in anything else.

James Thurber, *Fables for Our Time*

If you'd like to strike out on a different writing track, here are two further possibilities. Above is a modern fable complete with a moral, "The Fairly Intelligent Fly," written by the American humorist James Thurber. A dictionary defines a "fable" as "A brief tale embodying a moral and using persons, animals, or inanimate things as characters." Although the characters in Thurber's fable are insects, they clearly represent people.

Based on your reading of the fable, choose either of these two writing projects:

1. All living creatures survive through their wits. But sometimes, as in the case of the fly, even the most carefully thought-out plans and precautions break down. Like the fly, human beings often misinterpret situations, bringing about their own downfall. If you have observed this happening to yourself, a relative, or a friend, tell about it.
2. Write a short fable like Thurber's, using animals or insects to represent humans to illustrate some aspect of danger. Conclude the fable with a moral.

Chapter **5**

The Expository Composition
(Developed by Examples)

New Lifestyles from Old Philosophies

The accumulated wisdom of religions and philosophies from around the globe offers much guidance to people who are shaping lifestyles appropriate to the last quarter of the twentieth century. **From the Orient, from the Arab World, and from the West** come ideas that have endured. **Here are some of them.**

Buddhism, Christianity, and many other beliefs recognize the value of the Golden Rule: "Do unto others as you would have others do unto you." The Greek philosopher Socrates illustrated the Golden Rule at the end of his life. Sentenced to death in the fifth century B.C. for his heretical[1] social and religious views, he refused the chance to escape from prison. **This was his reasoning.** When a person is born, **Socrates pointed out,** he enters into an implied contract with the state. Because of this, the individual has the right to expect protection from the state throughout his lifetime. **In turn,** the state has an equally strong claim on the citizen to obey its laws. If a person feels that a law is unjust, said Socrates, he has two courses of action. He can **either** work to influence the repeal[2] of the law **or** renounce[3]

Parallelism

Thesis statement

Colon introducing appositive

Short sentence for variety

Comma around parenthetical element

Transition

Correlative conjunctions

---

[1]*heretical:* contrary to established doctrine. [2]*repeal:* cancel, revoke. [3]*renounce:* give up. [4] *insight:* understanding of the inner nature or true character of a

126

<table>
<tr><td>Pronoun for
coherence</td><td>his citizenship. But he must not break the law. In **this,** he is no different from the state, which must not neglect its duty to the citizen. Socrates' experience speaks to</td></tr>
</table>

Pronoun for
coherence

Modal

his citizenship. But he must not break the law. In **this,** he is no different from the state, which must not neglect its duty to the citizen. Socrates' experience speaks to the modern man who sometimes **may** be tempted to use extreme means to upset the delicate balance existing between a citizen and his state.

Transition between
paragraphs

Subordination by
participial phrase

A second insight[4] stems from the "categorical imperative," **first formulated by the German philosopher Immanuel Kant in his 1785 work Metaphysic of Morals.** **Stated simply,** the "categorical imperative" holds that a person should act as if the example of his action were to become a general law for all men to follow. Following **this** premise,[5] one would find it difficult to justify theft or murder. Even to borrow money is wrong, according to Kant, because if everyone did this, there would be no money left to borrow.

Pronoun for
coherence

Transition between
paragraphs

Semicolon joining
independent clauses

Compound predicate

Further guidelines are found in the teachings of Mohammed, collected in the Koran. His Islamic contributions express a profound humanism;[6] Mohammed emphasized the dignity of man and viewed the whole of humanity as a single nation. He both **encouraged** the expansion of knowledge and **placed** great importance on the value of work, however humble it might be. Today's young crafts people, skillfully working to create woven goods or jewelry or candles, and the street musicians in many North American cities are all following the industrious[7] tradition of Mohammed.

Transition between
paragraphs

Still another precept,[8] this one from the Buddhist religion, is illustrated by the custom of buying a bird in a small wooden cage in order to open the cage's door and release the bird. The underlying ideas of gentleness and freedom have a timeless relevance.[9]

Transition between
paragraphs

Comma with
quotation

Finally, the two short sentences carved by the Greeks on the Temple of Delphi can give superb direction to human life regardless of time or place. "Know thyself," says one inscription, offering advice that is vital but not easy to follow. And "Nothing in excess"[10] reads the second, echoing the Golden Mean, or middle

thing. [5]*premise:* proposition serving as a ground for argument. [6]*humanism:* system of thought in which human ideals and the perfection of the human personality are made central. [7]*industrious:* hard-working; diligent. [8]*precept:* rule prescribing a particular kind of conduct or action. [9]*relevance:* fitting or

Pronoun for
coherence

way, stressed[11] by many religions. **This** rule of avoiding excess in actions can apply equally well to almost
every phase of life, including eating, drinking, sleeping, working, playing, thinking, and feeling.

appropriate to any given situation. [10]*excess:* over and above what is expected
or usual. [11]*stressed:* given special importance.

Writing Analysis

REVIEW OF TRANSITIONS

Now that you have learned the importance of transitions in expository
writing, see how adept you are at supplying transitions in the following
review exercise. (You may want to refer to lists of transitions on pages 20–
21 and 94.)

EXERCISE 32
Transition Review

A. *For numbers 1-7, combine each pair of simple sentences to form a
single sentence by adding a transitional word or phrase. Make sure that
you express the exact shade of meaning, that you use the proper punctuation before and after the transition, and that you change the capitalization
wherever necessary. Avoid using any transition more than once.*

1. The camellias are certainly beautiful. .... I have seen finer
   ones.
2. The camellias are certainly beautiful. .... I have never seen
   finer ones.
3. The barometer is falling rapidly. .... It will rain.
4. It did rain. .... There was no picnic.
5. We now began to realize the danger of taking the cliff road after a
   rain. .... We turned back.
6. He smiled in a sardonic, merciless way. .... He lifted his gun
   and fired.
7. The sheriff fully understood the danger of entering the undergrowth.
   .... He did it without hesitation.

B. *For numbers 8-15, leave two sentences but add appropriate transitions
at the beginnings of all second sentences.*

8. The manager expects too much work of me. .... He is gruff
   and unpleasant in giving instructions.
9. One must drive carefully in a city. .... He will have an
   accident.
10. He is not a disagreeable person. .... He is very courteous
    and obliging.

11. Louise will be away for three weeks. .... That is what her brother told me.
12. There are many half-sunken logs in the stream. .... It will be necessary to use much caution in paddling the raft.
13. I can't drive very well. .... I am willing to learn.
14. Their living room is imaginatively decorated. .... The frames of the chairs and the bases of the tables are made from animal horns.
15. Timothy is very quiet and reserved. .... He might be called shy.

WRITING A LONGER COMPOSITION

This week's writing model is, for the first time, longer than a single paragraph because in Chapters 5 through 11 you will advance to writing compositions of several paragraphs. "New Lifestyles from Old Philosophies" contains six paragraphs, each of them having a special purpose. The first paragraph is introductory; the next four paragraphs discuss in turn four different philosophies—the Golden Rule, the categorical imperative, ideas from the Koran, and a Buddhist idea. The sixth paragraph combines a discussion of Greek thought with a concluding statement.

As you begin writing compositions, you will need to develop additional composition skills. Perhaps most important is being able to recognize the point at which one paragraph ends and the next one begins. Reviewing the discussion of the English paragraph in Chapter 1 may help you here. Keep in mind that a paragraph constitutes a single unit of thought and that its purpose is to discuss only one topic or one aspect of a topic. In the model composition, each paragraph is limited to a single aspect of the subject of philosophy.

When writing about an abstract subject such as philosophy, you should carefully prepare your reader for shifts in thought. Notice how idea development has been indicated in the model by beginning each paragraph with a topic sentence. Such an opening topic sentence puts the controlling idea squarely before a reader, keeping his mind in tune with yours. The first paragraph's opening topic sentence explains further the composition's title. Then the next two sentences combine to express the thesis statement (see page 134), stating that the composition will focus on philosophical ideas that have endured.

The five paragraphs of the main development each begin with a topic sentence: "Buddhism, Christianity, and many other beliefs recognize the value of **the Golden Rule** . . ."; "A second insight stems from **the categorical imperative** . . ."; "Further guidelines are collected in **the teaching of Mohammed** . . ."; "Still another precept, this one from **the Buddhist religion** . . ."; and "Finally, **the two short sentences** carved by the Greeks on **the Temple of Delphi.** . . ." In each of these sentences, the boldfaced controlling idea can easily be identified. To be unified, of course, a paragraph should discuss only that material related to its controlling idea. When there is no more to say on a topic, it is time to begin a new paragraph.

Sometimes the decision to begin a new paragraph almost becomes a matter of instinct that might be compared with shifting gears on an automobile. Most experienced drivers develop an "ear" that tells them when it is necessary to shift gears. They listen to the sound of their engines and develop a sense about shifting gears after the automobile has reached a certain speed. Similarly, writers listen to the rhythm of their paragraph. They can hear it begin, gain momentum, and reach a peak. They develop a sense that tells them when it is necessary to shift into a new paragraph. In moving from one paragraph to the next, they try to make clear the connection in thought between the paragraph they are concluding and the new one they are beginning.

THE COMPOSITION OUTLINE

Since developing a full outline becomes more important as you write longer papers, the following discussion will prepare you for the weeks ahead. Let's examine what a full outline is, why it is fundamental to writing, and how a writer goes about constructing one.

What a Developed Outline Is

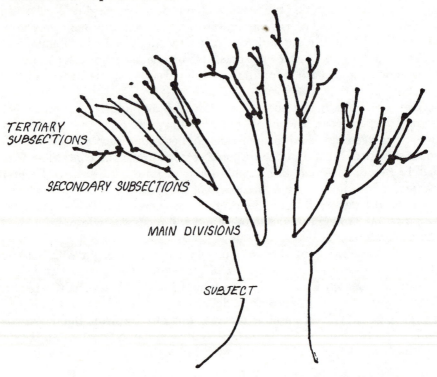

TERTIARY
SUBSECTIONS

SECONDARY SUBSECTIONS

MAIN DIVISIONS

SUBJECT

You might find it helpful to compare the form of a developed outline with the shape of a tree. Think of the subject of your composition as the main trunk of the tree. Two or three main branches spread out from the trunk: these are the two or three main divisions of your outline, listed in Roman numerals (I., II.). From each main branch, two or more smaller limbs angle off: these are your outline's secondary subsections, listed in capital letters (A., B.). And from each smaller limb, still smaller twigs grow: these are the tertiary subsections of your outline, listed in Arabic numerals (1., 2.).

Why It Is Fundamental to Writing

Outlining is valuable because it is the basic step toward producing a coherent composition. It causes you to do two necessary things. First, it makes you **identify your purpose** in writing. You must do this because, in order to begin to outline, you have to mentally "walk around" the subject you have selected, looking at it from all sides, until you decide upon the most workable "slice" to take. This is a pick-and-choose process. You try one approach to dividing the subject into main divisions, reject it, think of another, perhaps reject it, and continue until you have arrived at the smaller parts that best fit your needs.

Second, writing an outline makes you **arrange information in a logical way**, a way that will most forcefully express your ideas. As you will see, deciding on the purpose of your paper and working out the details of the outline go hand in hand.

How an Outline Is Thought Out

Suppose we are preparing to write a composition on the subject "Sports in the U.S.A." Our purpose is to present information on sports we have become familiar with. To construct an outline for this, as for any subject, we must break down the general topic into smaller divisions. (Remember that there are generally many different ways to break down any subject into parts.) We must decide upon the various possibilities for main divisions, sift through them, and select the main divisions that are most logical and workable.

So we begin to "walk around" the subject "Sports in the U.S.A." to decide on an appropriate breakdown into main divisions. We first think of organizing this subject by naming the sports themselves:

I. Baseball
II. Football
III. Basketball
IV. Swimming
V. Golf
VI. Tennis
VII. Soccer

We stop, though, before listing all the sports we know because we quickly see that this approach to the subject has more disadvantages than advantages. For one thing, the list of main divisions is far too long; these should usually be held to two or three. For another, a composition written from this kind of organization would probably be fairly dull, a kind of catalogue listing.

We think more deeply. Since it's important to narrow down the number of main divisions, we begin to consider *aspects* of sports. Several of these come to mind. First, what about **amateur** and **professional** sports? We soon discard this idea for two reasons: (1) The breakdown is not sharp enough since many sports can be both amateur and professional; (2) We don't want to make the materialistic aspect of sports the chief focus of our paper.

We move on to another possibility: **major** and **minor** sports. Here, though, another problem comes up. This kind of organization would require us to make value judgments that might lessen the credibility of our composition. Basketball, baseball, and football are certainly major sports, but what about tennis—is it major or minor? The divisions here, although sharper than those for amateur and professional sports, may produce arbitrary writing. But we seem to be drawing closer to an outline that will be workable and a focus that will be effective.

Finally, pressing ahead to a fourth choice, we think of **team** sports and **individual** sports. These main divisions seem to be more promising. Still, this breakdown is not without its flaws. Like amateur and professional sports, these main divisions overlap. Some sports, such as tennis, are played by both individuals and teams.

After balancing all four possibilities for main divisions of "Sports in the U.S.A.," though, we decide that the fourth, **team** and **individual** sports, is the best choice, focusing as it does on the *nature* of the sports. All that remains is to make the main divisions work logically by qualifying them a bit. We do this by extending the two divisions to three: the first will include sports that are always played with teams, the second those that are played either individually *or* with teams, and the third those that are always played individually. The names of the sports (or sports categories) become secondary subsections (A., B.); further information related to each sport or category becomes tertiary subsections (1., 2.). Here's what we come up with:

SPORTS IN THE U.S.A.
I. Team Sports
   A. Football
      1. Amateur
      2. Professional
   B. Basketball
      1. Amateur
      2. Professional

    C. Baseball
       1. Amateur
       2. Professional

II. Sports for Teams or Individuals
    A. Tennis
       1. Amateur
       2. Professional
    B. Swimming

III. Individual Sports
    A. Golf
       1. Amateur
       2. Professional
    B. Snow skiing
       1. Slope skiing
       2. Cross country skiing
    C. Water sports
       1. Water skiing
       2. Scuba diving
       3. Snorkeling
    D. Bicycling
    E. Jogging
    F. Mountain climbing

This completed outline raises several points about the process of outlining:

1. To create a working outline requires considerable thought; the first possibility you think of may not be the best one.
2. Most outlines work well with only two or three main divisions.
3. The main divisions and all subsections of an outline should each be respectively equal to each other in rank; that is, the five secondary subsections under the last main division (golf, snow sports, water sports, bicycling, jogging, and mountain climbing) are all of the same classification. Similarly, all of the items in the tertiary subsections in this section are equal to each other and to the items in all other tertiary groups (amateur and professional; slope skiing and cross country skiing; water skiing, scuba diving, and snorkeling).
4. All items within a main division or subsection are normally written in parallel form (slope skiing and cross country skiing).
5. Each main division and subsection should be arranged in an orderly sequence. For example, the team sports are arranged chronologically from an autumn sport (football) through a winter sport (basketball) to a spring sport (baseball). Under individual sports, the items have been arranged in order of decreasing popularity, from the most popular sport, golf, to the least popular one, mountain climbing.

6. Each subsection should contain at least two points; if it had only one, this would cover all the ground that its main point covers.

EXERCISE 33
Creating an Outline

Choose one topic from List I and one topic from List II. Write an outline for each. Include in your outlines two or three main divisions, secondary subsections, and tertiary subsections.

LIST I	LIST II
Countries I Would Like to Visit	Strength Means Many Things
Music That I Listen to	Why a Sense of Humor Is Important
Leisure Time Ideas	Politics Is Fascinating
Modes of Travel I Have Experienced	Health: Our Number One Concern
Foods That Please Me	Power Takes Many Forms
My Reading Habits	Budgeting One's Income
Personal Grooming	How Accidental Is Luck?

THE THESIS STATEMENT

Through studying paragraphs in the first four chapters, you have seen examples and read discussions of the various places where a topic sentence may appear: beginning or end of a paragraph, both beginning and end, and topic sentence implied. Now that you have the purpose and use of the topic sentence firmly in mind, it's time to extend your scope to the equivalent of the topic sentence in the longer composition: the thesis statement. Like the topic sentence, the thesis statement announces the writer's purpose—but in this case the purpose of the **entire** composition, not merely of a single paragraph.

Normally, the thesis statement appears in the first paragraph as a straightforward expression of the writer's intent. In order for writing to succeed, a reader needs this information. If a writer's purpose isn't stated, if a reader has to deduce it by backtracking through the composition one or more times, he may lose interest. The earlier you communicate your purpose in writing, the better prepared he will be to track the developing thought line in your paper.

Look at the model paragraph in this chapter for an example of the thesis statement working well. In the opening paragraph of "New Lifestyles from Old Philosophies," the final two sentences tell the reader in unmistakable terms exactly what the writer is going to do: "From the Orient, from the Arab World, and from the West come ideas that have endured. Here are some of them."

Note that beginning with a thesis statement is especially appropriate for a formal composition. It is useful in all types of analysis—definition, cause and effect, comparison and contrast, argumentation. Once you have mastered the art of placing the thesis statement at the opening of the composition, though, you may want to experiment with other possibilities for locating it. In Chapter 10's model composition, "Let's Go to the Movies . . . ," the thesis statement appears as the very last sentence of the composition: "Just as opera was the typical art form of the 18th century, so film seems likely to become the representative art form of the 20th century." In this composition, the opening paragraph, in addition to providing an introduction to the subject of movies, signals the reader that the primary line of development will be an analysis of some outstanding films.

LINKING PARAGRAPHS TOGETHER

Whenever you are writing a paper of more than one paragraph, you will be concerned with making clear to the reader the relation between paragraphs. Since a paragraph represents a unit of thought, a writer often needs to establish a connection between each paragraph unit in order to clarify his developing idea.

Review the four basic ways to create transitions between paragraphs by studying over the following examples. In each example below, think of the first sentence as the final sentence of a paragraph and the second sentence as the opening one of the following paragraph:

1. **Use a pronoun** that refers to a person, idea, or thing just mentioned in the preceding paragraph.

    Example: . . . *In addition, they carried a wireless radio set, warm clothing, and an extra three weeks' food supply.*

    Because of **these** *careful preparations, the expedition was ready when the unexpected emergency happened* . . .

    Example: . . . *Nor did they understand the need for keeping our plans completely secret.*

    Since **that** *was a necessary condition to the success of our undertaking, they had to be convinced* . . .

    (Other pronouns commonly used in this way are **he, they, this, those, them,** and **it.**)

2. **Repeat a key word** used in the preceding paragraph.

    Example: . . . *Third, the Board of Directors agreed to* **offer** *Mr. Gray the presidency of the air line.*

    When the **offer** *was made, it was not immediately accepted* . . .

    Example: . . . *But a child should be given training in* good **manners,** *for this will help him throughout his life.*

    Good **manners** *are not always easy to teach, however; in fact, many parents find this one of their most difficult tasks* . . .

3. **Repeat a phrase** referring directly to the preceding idea.

> *Example:*   *... And the entire world has felt the effect of the* **small,** *inexpensive* **transistor radio.**
>
> **Small transistor radios** *are found throughout the globe—on the beaches of Malaysia, on the farms of Denmark, and in Bedouin tents in Saudi Arabia ...*

> *Example:*   *... For several months the geologists lived in the caravan crossing* **the most dangerous part of the desert.**
>
> **The desert was most dangerous here** *because of the hostile natives, the extreme temperature change, and the lack of any water supply ...*

4. **Use transitions.**

    Most of the transitions that link sentences together can also serve as a bridge between paragraphs. The following are frequently used:

consequently	another	for example	moreover
finally	as a result	for instance	nevertheless
otherwise	at last	furthermore	on the other hand
similarly	at this time	in fact	such
accordingly	too	likewise	then
therefore	thus	also	

> *Example:*   *... A fourth possibility is travel by bus.*
>
> *Automobile, train, and bus travel are much slower than travel by air;* **however,** *each has certain advantages for the traveler whose main goal is not speed ...*

> *Example:*   *... From this I gathered that there was a restlessness among the population that could, in time, lead to rebellion.*
>
> **Another** *sign of discontent was the writing on the city's walls ...*

Notice how the six paragraphs in the model composition have been linked together. The final sentence of the first paragraph is a transitional signal: **Here are some of the beliefs.** This leads logically into the first sentence of the second paragraph, which begins with a listing of Buddhist, Christian, and other beliefs. The third paragraph opens with the phrase **A second insight;** the fourth with **Further guidelines;** the fifth with **Still another precept;** the sixth with **Finally.** In each new paragraph, these essential first words inform the reader that the train of thought of the previous paragraph has ended and that a new aspect of the subject is to be introduced.

You see that the process of linking paragraphs together requires, if not more planning, perhaps at least more imagination and ingenuity than that of placing transitions between and within sentences. But the result is worth the effort.

EXPOSITORY DEVELOPMENT (by examples)

In the previous chapter you read four selections that are developed chiefly by examples. All of the passages, those discussing the Italian professor, aboriginal languages, Latin American universities, and the U.S.A.'s Bicentennial celebration, are informative in nature. They are examples of expository writing. How well the authors presented their points depended largely upon the persuasiveness of their examples.

The model composition beginning this chapter is another expository passage. Its purpose is to explain some of the world's most fundamental philosophical ideas. The short essay is built on examples. Among them are the Golden Rule, the experiences of Socrates, the categorical imperative of Immanuel Kant, and the inscriptions on the Temple of Delphi. By its nature, philosophy is an abstract subject. Because of this, it can be confusing to someone who is untrained in the subject. Realizing that his composition would probably not communicate its ideas to the reader if it were written in wholly general terms, the writer has relied upon examples in order to be more specific and easily understandable.

A second instance of a writer making his explanation clearer through examples is this paragraph explaining Newton's principle of relativity. The concept of relativity is a complex one. To define it in terms that a general reader can understand, Barnett chooses familiar examples, a train and a ship:

Anyone who has ever ridden on a railroad train knows how rapidly another train flashes by when it is traveling in the opposite direction and conversely[1] how it may look almost motionless when it is moving in the same direction. A variation of this effect can be very deceptive[2] in an enclosed station like Grand Central Terminal in New York. Once in a while a train gets under way so gently that passengers feel no recoil[3] whatever. Then if they happened to look out the window and see another train slide past on the next track, they have no way of knowing which train is in motion and which is at rest; nor can they tell how fast either one is moving or in which direction. The only way they can judge their situation is by looking out the other side of the car for some fixed body of reference like the station platform or a signal light. Sir Isaac Newton was aware of these tricks of motion, only he thought in terms of ships. He knew that on a calm day at sea a sailor can shave himself or drink soup as comfortably as when his ship is lying motionless in harbor. The water in his basin, the soup in his bowl, will remain unruffled[4] whether the ship is making five knots,[5] 15 knots, or 25 knots. So unless he peers out at the sea it will be impossible for him to know how fast his ship is moving or indeed if it is moving at all. Of course, if the sea should get rough or the ship change course abruptly, then he will sense

[1]*conversely:* to the contrary. [2]*deceptive:* causing a false impression. [3]*recoil:* backward movement. [4]*unruffled:* without ripples, smooth. [5] *knots:* speed in

his state of motion. But granted the idealized[6] conditions of a glass-calm sea and a silent ship, nothing that happens below decks—no amount of observation or mechanical experiment performed *inside* the ship— will disclose[7] its velocity through the sea. The physical principle suggested by these considerations was formulated by Newton in 1687. "The motions of bodies included in a given space," he wrote, "are the same among themselves, whether that space is at rest or moves uniformly[8] forward in a straight line." This is known as the Newtonian or Galilean Relativity Principle. It can also be phrased in more general terms: mechanical laws which are valid[9] in one place are equally valid in any other place which moves uniformly relative[10] to the first.

"The Newtonian Relativity Principle," Lincoln Barnett, *The Universe and Dr. Einstein*

nautical miles per hour, one knot being equal to 1.1516 statute miles per hour. [6]*idealized:* perfect. [7]*disclose:* expose, reveal. [8]*uniformly:* at an unchanging rate. [9]*valid:* based on evidence that can be supported. [10]*relative:* in relation to.

In explaining relativity, Barnett might have decided to use only one example, that of the ship. This probably would have conveyed the idea quite well. But by adding a second example of the train, he makes relativity still more understandable to the reader, particularly the reader who is more familiar with train travel than with travel by ship. When you write, follow Barnett's practice of choosing examples that will be meaningful to your reader.

Notice that Barnett has organized his paragraph so that it moves from the specific to the general. He might have followed another plan, beginning with the generalizations about Newton's relativity principle and ending with the two specific examples. Instead, he chose to place his examples first, concluding with summary generalizations. This organization, in which specific facts or examples lead up to a general conclusion, is **inductive.** The opposite approach, in which an opening generalization is followed by specific facts or examples, is **deductive.** Do you think that a deductive organization would have better presented the concept of relativity in this paragraph?

Sometimes a writer will benefit from using a single, extended example rather than many brief examples. This happens in the next passage. Here the topic is how to use a computer effectively. To explain the process as clearly as possible, the writer brings in a personal experience as an illustrative example:

The user must have a firm idea of what he expects the computer to do for him before he can use the computer effectively. He needs to "know what he knows" and "what he doesn't know." In other words, in any given problem, certain information to be processed is available— mathematical formulas and data from experiments, a list of student names and grades, an airline schedule, and police records, to name some examples. The user wants to use the computer to modify the input information to obtain some output. He must decide what that output is to be. He must have a good idea of how the computer is to serve in the processing of his information.

He then must decide whether or not the use of the computer to solve his problem is worth the effort and expense involved. A personal experience of mine may serve to illustrate this point. I came upon a contest for which the prize was a trip to Hawaii. The rules of the contest were simple: the entrant who submitted the longest list of 4-letter words in the English language to be constructed from a given set of 14 letters would win first prize. A quick calculation shows that there are 14^4 or 38,416 possible 4-letter combinations of the 14 given letters. I then wrote and ran a program whose input was the 14 given letters and output was all the possible combinations of the letters, 2744 lines of printed output, each line consisting of 14 4-letter combinations.

What now? It was easy to eliminate "words" such as CCCC. But how about some more questionable ones such as PITH (or is it PYTH?). Do slang or vulgar words count? The next step was to sit down with the dictionary and go through the list of words, deciding which ones were real words and which ones were not. I belatedly[1] realized that this is exactly what I would have had to do even if I had not used the computer to generate the list of words; all the computer did was to supply a list of letters. Had a list of all valid 4-letter words been available for use by the computer, the computer could have completed the entire problem. However, this was not the case.

In other words, the example described above is an example of failure on my part to analyze the problem involved from start to finish. Had I done so, I would have realized that the cost in my and the computer's time would be really wasted. Millions of dollars and thousands of manhours are wasted every year for exactly the same reason. The user must determine if the use of the computer could help him and, if so, whether or not the benefits he could derive[2] from its use justify[3] the time and expense involved.

"Using a Computer," Walter G. Rudd, *Assembly Language Programming and the IBM 360 and 370 Computers*

[1]*belatedly:* late or too late. [2]*derive:* gain. [3]*justify:* show to be just, right, or in accord with reason.

Although the main body of the preceding example is devoted to a single, fully developed example, the writer also uses a few short examples in his introduction for a specific purpose. Wanting to flesh out his generalizations by explaining the kinds of information that can be processed on computers, he cites "mathematical formulas and data from experiments, a list of student names and grades, an airline schedule, and police records. . . ." Unfamiliar or difficult concepts in scientific or technical writing require careful presentation if they are to be made clear to the layman. Writing in specific terms can help in a major way.

Finally, observe how E. M. Forster, in discussing his beliefs, uses examples to clarify abstract terms. Forster's subject is a philosophical one. Unlike the writers of the previous example, he does not fill his paragraphs with examples. Yet he knows that, at key points in his passage, he must focus on specifics in order to deepen the reader's understanding. In which sentences does Forster use examples or concrete detail to make his points more specific?

I do not believe in Belief. But this is an age of faith, and there are so many militant[1] creeds that, in self-defence, one has to formulate a creed of one's own. Tolerance, good temper, and sympathy are no longer enough in a world which is rent[2] by religious and racial persecution,[3] in a world where ignorance rules, and science, who ought to have ruled, plays the subservient[4] pimp.[5] Tolerance, good temper, and sympathy— they are what matter, really, and if the human race is not to collapse they must come to the front before long. But for the moment they are not enough; their action is no stronger than a flower, battered beneath a military jack-boot. They want[6] stiffening, even if the process coarsens them. Faith, to my mind, is a stiffening process, a sort of mental starch, which ought to be applied as sparingly as possible. I dislike the stuff. I do not believe in it, for its own sake, at all. Herein[7] I probably differ from most people, who believe in Belief, and are only sorry they cannot swallow even more than they do. My law-givers are Erasmus and Montaigne, not Moses and St. Paul. My temple stands not upon Mount Moriah but in that Elysian Field where even the immortal are admitted. My motto is: "Lord, I disbelieve—help thou my unbelief."

I have, however, to live in an Age of Faith—the sort of epoch[8] I used to hear praised when I was a boy. It is extremely unpleasant really. It is bloody in every sense of the word. And I have to keep my end up in it. Where do I start?

With personal relationships. Here is something comparatively solid in a world full of violence and cruelty. Not absolutely solid, for Psychology has split and shattered the idea of a "Person" and has shown that there is something incalculable[9] in each of us, which may at any moment rise to the surface and destroy our normal balance. We don't know what we are like. We can't know what other people are like. How, then, can we put any trust in personal relationships, or cling to them in the gathering political storm? In theory we cannot. But in practice we can and do. Though A is not unchangeably A or B unchangeably B, there can still be love and loyalty between the two. For the purpose of living one has to assume that the personality is solid, and the "self" is an entity,[10] and to ignore all contrary evidence. And since to ignore evidence is one of the characteristics of faith, I certainly can proclaim that I believe in personal relationships.

[1]*militant:* aggressive, warlike. [2]*rent:* sharply divided. [3]*persecution:* continual annoyance or harassment. [4]*subservient:* helpful in furthering a cause. [5]*pimp:* one who serves the passions or base desires of others. [6]*want:* need. [7]*herein:* in this matter. [8]*epoch:* period of time notable for extraordinary events. [9]*incalculable:* unpredictable. [10]*entity:* something that has a real existence. [11]*chaos:*

Starting from them, I get a little order into the contemporary chaos.[11] One must be fond of people and trust them if one is not to make a mess of life, and it is therefore essential that they should not let one down. They often do. The moral of which is that I must, myself, be as reliable as possible, and this I try to be. But reliability is not a matter of contract —that is the main difference between the world of personal relationships and the world of business relationships. It is a matter for the heart, which signs no documents. In other words, reliability is impossible unless there is a natural warmth. Most men possess this warmth, though they often have bad luck and get chilled. Most of them, even when they are politicians, *want* to keep faith. And one can, at all events, show one's own little light here, one's own poor little trembling flame, with the knowledge that it is not the only light that is shining in the darkness, and not the only one which the darkness does not comprehend. Personal relations are despised[12] today. They are regarded as bourgeois[13] luxuries, as products of a time of fair weather which is now past, and we are urged to get rid of them, and to dedicate ourselves to some movement or cause instead. I hate the idea of causes, and if I had to choose between betraying my country and betraying my friend, I hope I should have the guts[14] to betray my country. Such a choice may scandalise[15] the modern reader, and he may stretch out his patriotic hand to the telephone at once and ring up the police. It would not have shocked Dante, though. Dante places Brutus and Cassius in the lowest circle of Hell because they had chosen to betray their friend Julius Caesar rather than their country Rome. Probably one will not be asked to make such an agonising[16] choice. Still, there lies at the back of every creed[17] something terrible and hard for which the worshipper may one day be required to suffer, and there is even a terror and a hardness in this creed of personal relationships, urbane[18] and mild though it sounds. Love and loyalty to an individual can run counter[19] to the claims of the State. When they do —down with the State, say I, which means that the State would down me.

"What I Believe," E. M. Forster, *Two Cheers for Democracy*

complete disorder and confusion. [12]*despised:* scorned, regarded as worthless. [13]*bourgeois:* middle class. [14]*guts* (colloquial): courage. [15]*scandalise:* shock the moral feelings of. [16]*agonising:* extremely painful. [17]*creed:* organized system of principles or beliefs. [18]*urbane:* polite, refined. [19]*counter:* in an opposite direction.

Forster's passage provides an illustration of examples being used with restraint. He refers to very few examples, but he mentions them when they are most needed. At the end of his first paragraph, having stated his philosophy in more or less general terms, he clarifies his viewpoint by mentioning the names of four men. Forster does this to show that he sympathizes, not with the Christian religious teachings of Moses and St. Paul, but instead with the humanistic doctrines of Erasmus and Montaigne, who valued human interests more highly than religious ones. The climax of Forster's selection comes when he says that, if he had to choose between betraying a friend and betraying his country, he would betray his country.

Forster realizes that this is a shocking statement. He knows that he must quickly supply some proof that other rational men have shared his point of view. So he immediately adds the example from the Italian Renaissance poet Dante, in whose *The Divine Comedy* the Romans Brutus and Cassius are given the most severe punishment because they betrayed their friend Julius Caesar rather than their country. Here an example is artfully used to convince the reader.

Because Forster is a British writer, his essay illustrates some of the differences between British and American English. One example is his use of the verb "want" in the sentence. "They **want** stiffening, even if the process coarsens them." In American English the verb "need" would be used in place of "want" in this context. Differences also occur in spelling. The letter "c" in many British words often becomes "s" in the American equivalents: **self-defence** (British), **self-defense** (American). The letter "s" in many British words often becomes "z" in the American equivalents: **scandalise** (British), **scandalize** (American); **agonising** (British), **agonizing** (American). The letters "ou" in many British words (**honour, colour)** are shortened to "o" in American usage: **honor, color.** In word choice and spelling, as in punctuation, you will want to follow British usage for British readers and American usage for American readers.

In this chapter's sample selections, writers have used examples to emphasize the controlling ideas of the passages. Choose examples for your own writing that do the same thing. In addition, pick examples that will have force and meaning for your reader. Your goal should be to supply fresh, unusual examples that suggest new connections and insights. Consider arranging your examples in order of increasing importance, saving your strongest examples for last.

EXERCISE 34
Outlining

First review the section on "The Composition Outline" in this chapter. Then reconstruct the outline the writer probably worked from in composing the model composition, "New Lifestyles from Old Philosophies."

Punctuation Points

THE SEMICOLON

The model paragraph contains an example of a sentence in which a semicolon joins two independent clauses: "His Islamic contributions express a profound humanism; Mohammed emphasized the dignity of man and viewed the whole of humanity as a single nation." If a comma had been used without a conjunction following it to join these independent clauses, it would have resulted in an error called the **comma splice** (see page 37).

Learning the following rules will help you to use the semicolon correctly:

1. Use a semicolon between independent clauses when they are not joined by the coordinating conjunctions **and, but, for, or,** and **nor.**

   Smoking is dangerous in the woods; it may result in a forest fire.

   Ask for directions at the gate; a guide is stationed there to help you.

   Delegates assembled for the convention; they expected to remain in Washington until late summer.

   (Often a writer may have to decide whether to join two main clauses with a semicolon, as has been done above, or to divide them into two sentences with a period and a capital letter. Generally speaking, the division into two sentences is preferable, even when a semicolon is possible. However, the semicolon is helpful in two situations: first, when the ideas in the two clauses are so closely related that a period would be too strong an interruption between them; second, when you want to give special emphasis to the ideas in two or more independent clauses.)

2. Use a semicolon between independent clauses joined by such connectives as **furthermore, moreover, for example, for instance, nevertheless, otherwise, that is, besides, therefore, accordingly, however, also, consequently, hence, still, instead, thus.**

   Nobody expected the injured football players to return to the game; however, the coach sent them in during the final quarter.

   Electronics is changing the habits of many people; for example, television viewing is becoming popular throughout the world.

   I waited for him; moreover, I saved him a seat.

3. Use a semicolon between independent clauses if there are commas within the clauses.

   The travel agency, the first one to open in our city, offered special tours to Europe, Latin America, and the Far East; and within three weeks over 200 people, including students and adults, had bought tickets.

4. Use a semicolon between items in a series if the items contain internal commas.

   Three men were elected to the board of directors: Arthur Crane, an insurance executive; George Blakeley, the owner of a lumber mill; and Fred Blankenship, the manager of a department store chain.

THE COLON

Remembering how to use the colon correctly is not difficult because it has only one general purpose: it signals the reader that something is to follow. For an example of this colon use, look at this sentence from the model paragraph: "Buddhism, Christianity, and many other beliefs recognize the value of the Golden Rule: 'Do unto others as you would have others do unto you.'" A colon often can be considered a substitute for the phrase "which is" or "such as" or for the word "including." Sometimes the colon appears between clauses and single words or phrases, as in the above example from the model paragraph. But it also appears after the salutation in a formal letter (*Dear Sir*:), between chapter and verse of Biblical reference (Luke 4:20), between hours and minutes in reports of time (8:05 P.M.), and in footnotes and bibliographies (Volume XI:20–25).

Study over these additional points governing the use of the colon:

1. Use a colon before an appositive at the end of a sentence, a list of appositives, or a list of any kind that is introduced by such words as "the following" or "as follows." (An appositive is a word placed beside another so that the second word adds to or explains the first. Both words have the same grammatical function.)

List of appositives	They unlocked the cabin and carried in our furniture: a couch, four chairs, a table, and two beds.
Using "the following"	We made appointments with the following people: the admissions officer, the dean of men, and the dormitory supervisor.

(When listed items directly follow the verb, no colon is required.)

Many children collect stamps, coins, or model airplanes.
Your dinner includes soup, dessert, and coffee.

Note that a colon is **not** used following *such as, including, like,* or any form of the *be* verb:

Colon not needed	The three soups we tried were: bird's nest, sweet and sour, and shark's fin.
Colon correct	We tried three soups: bird's nest, sweet and sour, and shark's fin.

2. Use a colon before a long, formal statement.

Professor Van Buren opened his commencement address with this statement: "Seldom in the history of education has a graduating class had a greater chance to shape world events than you have today."

3. Use a colon or a semicolon between independent clauses when the second clause explains or restates the idea in the first.

Exposure to the sun will not cause these drapes to fade: they are made of a color-fast synthetic material.

EXERCISE 35
The Semicolon and Colon

Write out the following sentences, placing commas, semicolons, and colons where they belong.

1. They rang the doorbell nobody answered.
2. The package contained three gifts a watch a hunting knife and a compass.
3. Only one word could describe the prisoner uncooperative.
4. Together they pulled on the oars the boat leaped ahead.
5. My English instructor had me revise my composition twice first to correct the spelling second to improve the sentence structure.
6. Tension rose during the meeting nevertheless most of the council members remained calm.
7. Take with you all the necessary items leave all others behind.
8. The boat was large enough for everything fishing rods bait cushions lunch boxes and five people.
9. At 2:30 P.M. the fire alarm sounded we rushed out of the building.
10. Our plans are to make a walking trip through Europe and to spend several weeks in Greece let's hope that we will be able to make the trip.
11. We had two choices the first was to plant a vegetable garden the second to plant a fruit orchard.
12. In footracing running records are all still far below human physiological limits the restraints on performance are psychological.
13. Solar energy is one of the nation's options nuclear energy is another one.
14. Museum directors often have special environmental problems to consider they must be sure that the temperature and humidity in galleries are controlled.
15. Agriculture is changing because of the new system for centerpoint irrigation water is applied from a central well by a novel rotating machine.

Grammar Skills

PARALLELISM

Up to this point in your study of composition, you have practiced using several different kinds of transitions to gain coherence in your writing. Parallelism, by clarifying the relationship between a writer's ideas, or between parts of a single idea, has a similar effect. The general principle of parallelism is this: similar ideas are expressed by similar grammatical forms. When a writer acquires the habit of frequently expressing himself in terms of parallel forms, he has taken a major step toward producing coherent essays.

Almost any kind of sentence element may be placed in a parallel construction:

Single words	Galileo **studied, thought,** and **experimented.** (Past tense verbs)
	The young actor was **tall, dark,** and **handsome.** (Adjectives)
	Late for the dance, Ruth dressed **hastily** and **carelessly.** (Adverbs)
	They waited four hours at the airport, **reading** and **sleeping.** (Participles)
Phrases	She has traveled **by land, by sea,** and **by air.** (Prepositional phrases)
	To support his family and **to put himself through college,** he worked seven hours a day. (Infinitive phrases)
	Fritz passes his time **doing crossword puzzles** and **building model airplanes.** (Participial phrases)
	Buying a car and **beginning her job** were the next steps in her life. (Gerund phrases)
Clauses	A father **who spends time with his son** and **who thoughtfully answers his son's questions** will be respected and loved. (Adjective clauses)
	If you write or **if you telephone,** wait for two weeks until I return from Singapore (Adverbial clauses)

Faulty parallelism occurs when elements that are similar in idea are not made similar in structure. Here are some typical examples of faulty parallelism, with revisions to make the structures parallel:

Faulty	*Knowing how to study* and *to learn to budget time* are important for college students.
Revised	**Knowing how to study** and **learning how to budget time** are important for college students.
Faulty	The doctor recommended plenty of *food, sleep,* and *exercising.*
Revised	The doctor recommended plenty of **food, sleep,** and **exercise.**
Faulty	Come to the meeting prepared *to take notes* and *with some questions to ask.*
Revised	Come to the meeting prepared **to take notes** and **to ask questions.**
Faulty	I forgot *that my research paper was due on Tuesday* and *my teacher had said he would not accept late papers.*

Revised   I forgot **that my research paper was due on Tuesday and that my teacher had said he would not accept late papers.**

Faulty parallelism can frequently be corrected in more than one way:

Faulty   *To chew carefully* and *eating slowly* are necessary for good digestion.

Revised   **To chew carefully** and **to eat slowly** are necessary for good digestion. *(Infinitive phrase paired with infinitive phrase)*

Revised   **Chewing carefully** and **eating slowly** are necessary for good digestion. *(Participial phrase paired with participial phrase)*

By improving the coherence of a sentence or paragraph, parallelism leads to clarity in writing. It also creates a pleasant rhythm in a prose passage. In addition, parallel structures often cut down on the number of words needed to express an idea. Suppose that you are writing about a student who is entering college as a freshman. You want to present three facts about him: first, he has been assigned a dormitory room; second, he has been given a part-time job; and third, he has been awarded a scholarship. Rather than stringing these ideas out in three separate sentences, you can group them compactly in a single sentence, following the principle of parallelism:

The entering college freshman was informed **that he had been assigned a dormitory room, that he had been given a part-time job,** and **that he had been awarded a scholarship.**

Sometimes it is possible to avoid repeating an article, a preposition, a pronoun, or a phrase in a parallel construction:

"For its" not repeated   The team was praised **for its courage and endurance.**

A general rule to follow is to repeat the introductory word or phrase in a parallel construction whenever it is necessary to make the meaning clear. In a series of *that* clauses, for example, the meaning is usually clearer if the introductory word is repeated in each clause.

Meaning not clear   The weather was a greater handicap *to the invading army* than *their enemy.*

Meaning clarified   The weather was a greater handicap **to the invading army** than **to their enemy.**

Meaning not clear   The boy denied *that he had entered the house* and *he had taken the money.*

Meaning clarified   The boy denied **that he had entered the house** and **that he had taken the money.**

EXERCISE 36
Parallelism

Write out these sentences, correcting the faulty parallelism by placing all similar elements in parallel structure.

1. Earlier in his life Antonio had been a waiter, a tour guide, an auto mechanic, and taught school.
2. We planned to buy a suitcase, an umbrella, to purchase our tickets, ask for a map of Rangoon, and leave a message for Jack at the Indian consulate.
3. The insurance clerk knew that we had paid our bill and we had our receipt.
4. The ambassador from Laos spoke with warmth and in a humorous way.
5. Several passengers were cut by flying glass but not being seriously injured.
6. Thomas Hardy gained success both as a church architect and writing poetry.
7. We met a Greek who had traveled throughout Southeast Asia but he knew very little about his own country.
8. To swim in a lake is more pleasant than swimming at the seashore.
9. The instructor recommended several books for outside reading and that we should attend a play dealing with our subject.
10. Dentists advise brushing the teeth after each meal and to avoid too much sugar in the diet.
11. The bookstore owner told us that the novel was timely, informative, and could hold our interest.
12. Galileo found it difficult to believe that the sun rotated around the earth and the earth to be the center of the universe.
13. My employer informed me that I would be sent to Hong Kong and I should make arrangements to leave in about two weeks.
14. Nuclear physics has led to research in improving communications and in how to make people healthier.
15. The American University of Beirut is noted for its students from many lands and for having a beautiful campus overlooking the Mediterranean.

CORRECT PRONOUN REFERENCE

As a writer of English, you can often use pronouns to good advantage. Such pronouns as "he," "she," and "one" provide you with greater flexibility of expression. Contrast the following sentences without such pronouns with the sentences containing them:

A student can learn if a student really tries.
A student can learn if **she** really tries.

A person should be careful when that person is crossing a street.
One should be careful when crossing a street.

But in using pronouns, you need to be aware of the possibilities of confusing pronoun usage. The word to which a pronoun is referring should be clearly identifiable within the sentence or within an earlier sentence. A pronoun should not be placed so that it can refer to either of two persons or objects. For example, in the sentence "Dr. Frye told Dr. Anderson that he should operate immediately," the reader is not really certain which doctor the pronoun "he" is referring to. Should Dr. Anderson operate, or should Dr. Frye? The meaning could be clarified by eliminating the ambiguous pronoun: Dr. Frye told Dr. Anderson to operate immediately.

Study over the three main kinds of pronoun reference errors:

1. **Divided reference.** This occurs when it is not clear to which of two nouns the pronoun is referring. The most direct solution is to substitute a noun for the ambiguous pronoun.

Divided reference	Before Ruth gave the dog its dinner, she washed *it*.
Clear reference	Before Ruth gave the dog its dinner, she washed **her pet.**

2. **Broad reference.** A pronoun should not refer to a verb or to an adjective or adverb clause.

Broad reference	If the Russians rejected communism, *it* would upset the balance of world power.
Clear reference	If the Russians rejected communism, **such an action** would upset the balance of world power.

3. **Weak reference.** A pronoun cannot refer to an implied, or understood, antecedent.

Weak reference	Daily practice is necessary in ballet training; in fact, *they* are often as highly trained as athletes.
Clear reference	Daily practice is necessary in ballet training; in fact, **ballet performers** are often as highly trained as athletes.

EXERCISE 37
Pronoun Reference

Rewrite these sentences, correcting them for faulty pronoun reference.

1. Mr. Smith told Mr. Brown that his chickens were in his garden.
2. Rice is an important crop in China, and many of them have little else to eat.
3. When we climbed up to the robin's nest, it flew away.
4. European dairy cattle can adjust themselves to a wide range of temperature, particularly if this changes gradually.

5. Before you give the baby its bottle, shake it well.
6. You had your choice of tooth powder or tooth paste, and you bought it without remembering that I don't like to use it.
7. A few pod diseases damage the beans if they are left to develop.
8. If a dog should bite any man in that gang of ruffians, he would die.
9. Only at ninety-nine degrees did the vegetation begin to wilt, and this was not surprising.
10. When I saw the advertisement for an electric train in that magazine, I bought it immediately.
11. If an upperclassman is displeased with something a freshman does, he is punished for it.
12. The farmer told his neighbor that his son had stolen his apples and that he ought to be spanked.
13. I had planned to become a lawyer, but I have lost my enthusiasm for it.
14. In Mongolia they don't have many railroad lines.
15. My roommate taught me how to water ski and scuba dive, and I have become very skilled at it.

REVIEW OF DEFINITE AND INDEFINITE ARTICLES

You first studied definite and indefinite articles in Chapter 2, and by this time you may have discovered it helpful to refer to Appendix 5 (Definite and Indefinite Articles). For some concentrated review in using articles, complete these exercises:

EXERCISE 38
Article Review

A. *Write out these sentences, placing the definite article* **the** *before nouns whenever necessary.*

1. Before driving up mountain we stopped at ranger station.
2. We were told to put chains on tires and to expect chance of heavy snowstorms.
3. Library of Congress, national library of United States, is situated near Capitol in Washington, D.C.
4. City has many stores in which people can buy all of goods they need to furnish their houses.
5. We learn in geography courses that valley surrounding Nile River is one of most fertile in world.
6. Perhaps sight English most enjoy is crowning of king.
7. In old days, rich land of Lebanon attracted many travelers.
8. End of movie brought tears to eyes of audience.
9. Pulling off road, truckdriver opened hood of truck to see what matter was.
10. Health, laughter, and love are important in everyone's life.

B. *Write out these sentences, placing the indefinite articles* **a** *or* **an** *before nouns whenever necessary.*

1. After long meeting, the union members decided to ask for new contract.
2. Newspapers sometimes expose scandals in government and business affairs.
3. The town council refused to allow foreigner to open small business.
4. In many countries assassin has ended the life of important political figure.
5. When son is born, the continuation of family's name is made more certain.
6. Nurse will sometimes need to tranquilize disturbed patient.
7. Olympic athlete trains to develop healthy, strongly muscled body.
8. After stepping on piece of coral, Scott discovered that he had superficial cut on his left foot.
9. The overcrowded dormitory was problem that required unique solution.
10. Sheila discovered easy way to wash her car: have elephant spray it with water.

Questions for Discussion and Review

1. One compound predicate is **boldfaced** in the model composition; can you find another?
2. Point out instances of subordination by adverb clauses and participial phrases in the model composition.
3. In the model composition, locate one essential clause that has not been set off by commas and one nonessential clause that has been set off by commas.
4. In the passage on using a computer, identify those transitions that link paragraphs together and those that appear within paragraphs.
5. Trace Barnett's use of transitions in the paragraph on the Newtonian Relativity Principle.
6. Where in his paragraph has Barnett placed pronouns for coherence?
7. Revise the following sentence so that the adjective clause is changed to an adjective phrase: "These words, which contain the essence of Greek thought, are simply expressed and profoundly thoughtful."
8. Has Forster's passage, "What I Believe," been developed by induction or deduction?
9. Find thesis statements in the three sample selections by Barnett, Rudd, and Forster.
10. Discuss life situations you have observed in which the Greek standards of "Know thyself" or "Nothing in excess" have been violated.

Vocabulary Growth

PARAGRAPH PUZZLE

Complete the paragraph by choosing the right word to fill in each blank. When choice is difficult, refer to neighboring words or sentences for help.

Words can be more powerful, and............treacherous, than we
(minor, major, less, more)

sometimes suspect; communication more............than we may think.
(difficult, easy, spiritual, unknown)

We............all serving life sentences of solitary confinement within
(were, are, is, have)

............own bodies; like prisoners, we............ ... to tap
(his, her, their, our)   (must, will, have, has)

in awkward code............our fellow men in their neighboring cells.
(to, at, of, for)

Further,............A and B converse [two characters don't take part
(why, when, how, what)

in their dialogue . . .],............they suppose, but six. For there
(as, if, of, by)

............A's real self—call it A;............is also A's picture of
(are, is, were, was)   (there, this, that, the)

............—A-1; there is also B's picture............A—A-2. And
(themselves, ourself, yourself, himself)   (for, of, at, on)

there are three corresponding............of B. With six characters in-
(charges, items, personalities, parcels)

volved even..........a simple tête-à-tête,[1] no wonder we fall..........
(on, in, up, over)   (into, onto, around, under)
muddles of misunderstanding.
"On the Fascination of Styles," F. L. Lucas, *Holiday* (March 1960)

[1]*tête-à-tête:* conversation between two people.

WORD CLUES

A. *Vocabulary words in the following exercise are boldfaced, but "Context Clues" have not been italicized; these you will have to identify. Take four steps in this exercise: (1) Write out the vocabulary word in the blank; (2) Find the word or word group in the selection that most clearly suggests the meaning of the vocabulary word and write these words in the "Context Clue" blank; (3) Enter your best guess as to the meaning of the vocabulary*

word in the "Probable Meaning" blank; (4) Look up the dictionary defini-
tion of the word and write it out concisely in the proper blank.

1. As dawn approached, the **sonorous** bells awakened the villagers and brought them **scurrying** to the square. So quickly did the natives gather that the marketplace filled with people even before the booming sound waves of the bell had completely died away.

Vocabulary Word. . . . .

Context Clue. . . . .

Probable Meaning. . . . .

Dictionary Definition. . . . .

Vocabulary Word. . . . .

Context Clue. . . . .

Probable Meaning. . . . .

Dictionary Definition. . . . .

2. As a governor Tom McCall was an innovator, and Oregon—once thought the most conservative of Pacific Coast states—is an **innovative** state. It was the first to adopt clean air and clean water laws, and the first to step up estuarine sanctuaries to protect its harbors from pollution. It was the first to decriminalize marijuana, so that an offender pays a fine like a traffic violator, incurring no criminal record. It was among the first to preserve its beaches for the public while legislating against honky-tonk development, among the first to adopt statewide land-use planning, one of the first states to adopt scenic river regulation.

   "The Pacific Northwest," Thomas Griffith, *The Atlantic Monthly* (April 1976)

Vocabulary Word. . . . .

Context Clue. . . . .

Probable Meaning. . . . .

Dictionary Definition. . . . .

3. As everyone suspects, violence is on the increase in the United States. Just how far we have come on the road to **mayhem** was the subject of some carefully calibrated research by Dr. J. Lawrence Angel, a physical anthropologist at the Smithsonian's National Museum of Natural History. His analysis of the remains of 82 Colonial and early 19th-century skeletons and of 188 modern-day skeletons showed that today's white males are twice as prone to bone fractures as their **forebears**. Worse, modern white males suffer four times as many head fractures as their Colonial **counterparts**.

   "Violence in America," *Smithsonian* (October 1976)

Vocabulary Word...

Context Clue..

Probable Meaning..

Dictionary Definition..

Vocabulary Word...

Context Clue..

Probable Meaning..

Dictionary Definition..

Vocabulary Word...

Context Clue..

Probable Meaning..

Dictionary Definition..

4. [Their] immense diversity [enables] human beings to express many trends in their individual lives and in their societies. Human beings can be selfish or **altruistic,** careless or **fastidious,** homeloving or eager to take to the open road.

"Recycling Social Man," René Dubos, *Saturday Review/World* (24 August 1974)

Vocabulary Word...

Context Clue..

Probable Meaning..

Dictionary Definition..

Vocabulary Word...

Context Clue..

Probable Meaning..

Dictionary Definition..

5. Most remarkable of all is that each bird finds its own way to its destination. The warblers do not follow a leader or make the journey as a group; they **navigate** individually. And young birds making their first migration reach their goal as surely as the experienced travelers. Somehow, purely by instinct, the warblers know exactly how to set their course.

"Celestial Navigation by Birds," E. G. F. Sauer, Warriner, et al., *Advanced Composition*

Vocabulary Word...

Context Clue..

Probable Meaning. . . . .

Dictionary Definition. . . . .

B. *In Chapters 5–10, you will find six English verbs in this section of Vocabulary Growth. You will be asked to guide your own vocabulary development by looking in a dictionary for meanings of these verbs and finding all the related forms of each verb you can. Make a list for verbs, nouns, adjectives, and adverbs.*

1. to absorb
2. to abandon
3. to decline
4. to activate
5. to resolve
6. to predict

Composition: Show What You Have Learned

Choose a composition topic from either Group I or Group II

GROUP I: TOPICS FOR WRITING A COMPOSITION DEVELOPED BY EXAMPLES

When a student is ready to enter college, he faces the bewildering and sometimes thorny problem of gaining admittance to the college he wants to attend. How can he prove to the Dean of Admissions that he is an eager, bright student with a diversity of interests?

On the opposite side of the fence, many American deans have pondered the same question, and some have come up with ingenious solutions. One of the most common is to have the student applicant respond in essay form to an unusual question. Although presumably you have already leaped the hurdle of gaining admission to college, you might enjoy trying your hand at writing a short expository essay on a subject that has intrigued many American students.

Write a short composition of from three to five paragraphs on one of the following topics, making sure your essay contains a thesis statement and transitions within and between paragraphs. Develop your composition by examples.

1. What do you think you will be like when you are 35?
2. Which science stimulates you the most?
3. Are you afraid that, if you started changing, the process might get out of control?
4. What person would you like to have been in history?
5. Stand aside and look at yourself objectively. Describe the person you see, as a separate person and as someone who relates to other persons and to a society or a culture.

6. Write about a recent significant action of yours and its apparent consequences.

GROUP II: TOPICS TO CHALLENGE YOUR IMAGINATION

Lewis Carroll wrote *Alice's Adventures in Wonderland* for the children of nineteenth-century Victorian England. But among twentieth-century readers, this fanciful tale is probably less popular with children than with adults, many of whom are fascinated with its whimsically violent visions. More than one critic has drawn a parallel between disturbing comic scenes in Carroll's book and certain serious sequences in Franz Kafka's novels *The Trial* and *The Castle*.

On her journey through Wonderland, Alice meets many memorable characters—the White Rabbit, the Queen of Hearts, the Cheshire Cat, the Mad Hatter, Tweedledum and Tweedledee. One of her most vivid encounters is the following one with the storybook character Humpty Dumpty. Their dialogue, which is at the same time nonsensical and quite meaningful, illustrates the unique tone in this work (see the discussion of "tone" in Chapter 10):

Illustration by John Tenniel.

Humpty Dumpty took the book and looked at it carefully. "That seems to be done right—" he began.

"You're holding it upside down!" Alice interrupted.

"To be sure I was!" Humpty Dumpty said gaily, as she turned it round for him. "I thought it looked a little queer. As I was saying, that *seems* to be done right—though I haven't time to look it over thoroughly just now—and that shows that there are three hundred and sixty-four days when you might get un-birthday presents—"

"Certainly," said Alice.

"And only *one* for birthday presents, you know. There's glory for you!"

"I don't know what you mean by 'glory,' " Alice said.

Humpty Dumpty smiled contemptuously. "Of course you don't—till I tell you. I meant 'there's a nice knock-down argument for you!' "

"But 'glory' doesn't mean 'a nice knock-down argument,' " Alice objected.

"When *I* use a word," Humpty Dumpty said, in rather a scornful tone, "it means just what I choose it to mean—neither more nor less."

"The question is," said Alice, "whether you *can* make words mean so many different things."

"The question is," said Humpty Dumpty, "which is to be master—that's all."

Lewis Carroll, Alice's Adventures in Wonderland

© 1976 United Features Syndicate, Inc.

Even though Wonderland's Humpty Dumpty lived in the nineteenth century and *Peanuts'* Lucy (in Charles Schulz's cartoon above) plays baseball in the twentieth century, the differences in time, place, and character between these two fictional creations are not as great as the similarity in the way they approach life. Both Humpty and Lucy bolster their egos by taking advantage of an important characteristic of English words: the ease with which they shift from one meaning to another.

The following composition topics are based on the passage from *Alice's Adventures in Wonderland* and the *Peanuts* cartoon strip. Choose one as the subject of a short composition of from three to five paragraphs. Include a thesis statement and transitions within and between paragraphs. Develop your essay by examples.

1. Sometimes, as in the exchange between Alice and Humpty Dumpty, verbal communication between people simply breaks down because of the shifting meanings of words. Describe an instance when this has happened to you, either in your own country or in the United States.

2. Lucy, the baseball-playing *Peanuts* character, uses the flexibility of the English language to excuse her missed catch. Can you recount another example when you, a friend, or a relative changed the meaning of words to excuse a mistake?

3. Have you ever had an amusing or embarrassing experience because of the fact that many American English words and phrases express more than one meaning? Explain.

4. Do words in your language change their meaning or add new meanings over a period of time? Discuss some examples.

5. Different age and ethnic groups in the American culture often use different words to say the same thing. For example, an American youth might say, "O.K., Dad, lay it on me. Tell me where your head's at, and maybe we can get it together. I want you to stay cool and not freak out. Like, can we generate some good vibes?" On the other hand, his father might say the same thing this way: "All right, son, be frank with me. Let me hear what you're thinking, and perhaps we can come to an understanding. I want you to remain calm and not become emotional. Now, can we have a friendly talk?" Do groups in your culture have different vocabularies, as in the above example? If so, give examples and explain them.

6. As your English vocabulary has grown, what American English words have been most useful to you? Least useful?

7. You can increase your ability to recognize the meanings of English words by using word stems (see Appendix 7). For example, if you know that the stem "spec" means "look," then it helps you to understand the meanings of many words, including "inspect," "respect," "prospector," and "spectacle." Choose five word stems to memorize that you think may be useful to you in increasing your English vocabulary; explain why you have selected these particular stems.

8. Refer to this week's Paragraph Puzzle. Then write a dialogue showing what a conversation would be like between the six people (A, A-1, A-2; B, B-1, B-2) *really* involved in any talk between two persons.

Chapter **6**

The Expository Composition

(Developed by Comparison and Contrast)

Japan and the U.S.A.: Different but Alike

Compound predicate

At first glance, Japan **astonishes** and **fascinates** the American because it seems so different. All that char-

Pair of dashes for emphasis

acterizes the United States—racial and ethnic hetero-geneity,[1] newness, vast territory, and individualistic ethic[2]—is absent in Japan. **Instead** one encounters an

Transition

ancient and homogeneous[3] population, traditions that emphasize the importance of groups and communal needs, with a rich panoply[4] of highly elaborate rites and ceremonies that cover every aspect of daily living, from drinking tea to saying hello.

Parallel development in paragraph's first three sentences

Where Americans pride themselves on a studied in-formality and openness, their Japanese counterparts employ formality and complexity. **If Americans value time,** the Japanese treasure space. **While Americans have always enjoyed** a sense of continental scale, employing metaphors of size to describe both the natural environment and industrial production, Japan has exerted its genius on the diminutive and the minia-ture. It seems appropriate for America to produce the world's airplanes, while Japan creates cameras and transistors.

[1]*heterogeneity:* dissimilarity. [2]*ethic:* system of morals. [3]*homogeneous:* similar or identical in nature or form. [4]*panoply:* covering that magnificently decorates.

159

Transition between
paragraphs

Commas for series

Short sentence
for variety

Semicolon
separating two
independent clauses

Yet these two cultures, so apparently opposite in almost every way, have always possessed a strange affinity[5] for each other. Like their descendants, 19th century American visitors found the world of Japanese art, philosophy, ceremonies, and social life to be compellingly attractive. **One reason is its very comprehensiveness.** Japan is a filled-in culture, with few imprecisions or empty spaces. Little has been left to chance; nothing has been too small to escape attention.

Restrictive clause

Transition

Opposites supposedly attract, but there is more to it than that. Japan and America share, to differing degrees, some large experiences and broad skills **which have bred a certain kind of sympathy.**

Colon for listing

Transition

Transition

Both, for example, have transplanted cultures. Each nation has a "mother" society—China and Great Britain—that has influenced the daughter in countless ways: in language, religion, social organization, art, literature, and national ideals. Japan, **of course,** has had more time than the United States to work out its unique interpretation of this older culture. **But** even today the debt to China is perceivable[6] and gracefully acknowledged. It has produced in some artists and philosophers the same kind of ambivalence[7] and self-consciousness dominating American cultural nationalists.

Transitions

Both societies, **moreover,** have developed the brokerage art, the business of buying and selling, of advertising and mass producing, to unprecedented levels. Few sights are more representative than the tens of thousands of bustling stores to be seen in Japan, above all the disciplined and enticing[8] department stores. To American eyes they seem comforting and reassuring as an expression of the commercial spirit.

Repeating a word
for coherence

Both peoples love to shop, to travel, and to record. And **both** peoples have always emphasized the importance of work and are paying penalties for their commitment to development and modernization.

"We're Different but Alike," Neil Harris, *San Francisco Examiner,* 4 July 1976

[5]*affinity:* natural attraction or inclination toward. [6]*perceivable:* able to be seen. [7]*ambivalence:* opposite thoughts or emotions experienced at the same time. [8]*enticing:* leading on or attracting by arousing hope of pleasure.

Writing Analysis

TRANSITIONS FOR COMPARISON AND CONTRAST

Transitions are important in every kind of expository development. But in writing a comparison or contrast, they are especially necessary. A reader needs clear signals in order to follow the many shifts of a writer's thought as he describes the similarities or differences of a subject.

Transitions work in more than one way in the model composition. Not only do such words as "instead," "for example," "but," "of course," "moreover," and "and" signal shifts in thought but also the key transition "yet" that begins the third paragraph informs the reader that the writer is moving from *contrasting* Japan and the U.S.A. in the first two paragraphs to *comparing* them in the final five paragraphs.

The following transitions are often used in writing comparisons:

first, second, third, etc.	furthermore	for one thing
another	too	moreover
equally important	then	at the same time
besides	in addition to	accordingly
in fact		like

Other transitions that are often helpful when dealing with contrasts are these:

on the contrary	yet	different from	but
on the other hand	unlike	in spite of	whereas
despite	in contrast	although	nevertheless
	however		instead

EXERCISE 39
Transitions for Comparison and Contrast

Write out the following passage, adding appropriate transitions in the places indicated.

There are both similarities and differences between the tourist-attracting countries Italy and Greece. ......, both the Italians and Greeks are friendly, gregarious people. ......, the antiquities of both countries are fascinating; Rome's Colosseum and Athens' Parthenon are two of the world's great sights. ......, both countries offer comfortable tourist accommodations. ......, the luxury hotels in Rome and Athens are excellent. ......there are important contrasts between Italy and Greece. ......, dining in Italy can be a memorable experience, ...food in Greece tends to be wholesome but plain. And the look of each country is different. The Italian countryside is green and lush. ......, the Greek terrain is dry and desertlike. ......the elegant Italian *signor* or *signorina*, the Greek citizen dresses and lives more simply. . . . . . .these differences, though, a tourist can expect a delightful holiday in either country.

Expository Development (by comparison and contrast)

One reason that you often find development by comparison or contrast is that this type of organization works well in many subject areas. History professors teach their students about the French Revolution by showing how it resembled and differed from the Russian Revolution. Some literary critics like to analyze one work in terms of another—pointing out, for example, ideas that are found in both Confucius' *Analects* and Lao Tzu's *Tao Te Ching*. Occasionally comparison or contrast seems to be the *only* way to explain something. A mother, trying to inform her young child what an Eskimo igloo is, might finally rely on a comparison: "Take a lot of ice cubes from the refrigerator. Build a big hollow snowball with them. Then cut it in half. . . ." By beginning with things that are familiar to the child, the mother makes the unfamiliar concept of the igloo understandable to the child. This is the heart of the method of comparison or contrast: explaining something that is unfamiliar to the reader in terms of something that is familiar.

For purposes of writing, comparison and contrast are essentially opposite approaches. When a writer is comparing, he is pointing out the **similarities** that exist between objects, terms, or ideas. For example, the fan belt of an automobile engine might be compared to the conveyor belt in a factory. When a writer is contrasting, though, he is focusing on the **differences** between objects, terms, or ideas. A large city like Istanbul could be contrasted with a small city like Izmir; a jet engine might be described by showing how it differs from a piston engine. Logically, however, you will find that comparison and contrast are, to some degree, always combined. In any set of items being compared, there is usually an element of contrast. Conversely, there is normally some point of comparison in any contrast. This is so both because completely identical things cannot be compared and because objects that have nothing in common do not provide a meaningful contrast. They are too different from each other in form, like a radio and a tree.

In writing either a comparison or a contrast, two basic methods of development, or a combination of them, are possible. Which one you choose will be determined by the nature of your subject matter. If you are dealing with two rather broad topics, not too complex or detailed, you may first fully discuss one, and then go on to discuss the second in a subsequent paragraph. But if your topics are complex or involve many small similarities or differences, it may be preferable to examine them in pairs, turning first to one and then to the other alternately as you write. Such a paired development of a comparison or contrast is especially suited to a topic containing statistics or many small details. In practice, development of parts of a comparison in two separate paragraphs may raise problems for the reader. By the time he reaches the second paragraph, he may not clearly remember the points that have been made in the first paragraph. Development by pairs tends to be more forceful and direct. Many times, though, you will want to combine these two approaches, placing comparative pairs within a broader framework.

Like the model composition, the next passage is developed through both comparison and contrast. The comparison here, though, is of a special type known as **analogy**. A dictionary defines analogy as "agreement or resemblance . . . between otherwise dissimilar things; similarity without identity." The paragraph below was written by a social scientist, whose discipline covers such fields as sociology, anthropology, or psychology. He is trying to persuade the reader that the work of social scientists is, in many ways, more difficult than the work of such physical scientists as chemists, physicists, or biologists. The writer uses analogy by comparing social scientists with swimmers and physical scientists with runners. Having established his thesis with this analogy, he then proceeds to a direct contrast of social and physical scientists:

> In discussing the relative difficulties of analysis which the exact and inexact sciences face, let me begin with an analogy. Would you agree that swimmers are less skillful athletes than runners because swimmers do not move as fast as runners? You probably would not. You would quickly point out that water offers greater resistance to swimmers than the air and ground do to runners. Agreed, that is just the point. In seeking to solve their problems, the social scientists encounter greater resistance than the physical scientists. By that I do not mean to belittle[1] the great accomplishments of physical scientists who have been able, for example, to determine the structure of the atom without seeing it. That is a tremendous achievement; yet in many ways it is not so difficult as what the social scientists are expected to do. The conditions under which the social scientists must work would drive a physical scientist frantic.[2] Here are five of those conditions. He can make few experiments; he cannot measure the results accurately; he cannot control the conditions surrounding the experiments; he is often expected to get quick results with slow-acting economic forces; and he must work with people, not with inanimate[3] objects. . . .
>
> Donald L. Kenmerer, "Are Social Scientists Backward?"

[1]*belittle:* minimize, make to appear less important. [2]*frantic:* madly excited, wild. [3]*inanimate:* lacking the qualities of a living being.

After labeling physical science an "exact" science and social science an "inexact" science, Kenmerer goes on to point out five ways in which the work of social scientists is more difficult than that of physical scientists. Can you think of an answer to the writer's argument that a physical scientist might be expected to give?

A second example of a comparative paragraph is this one by Rachel Carson. Like the writer of the model composition, Miss Carson has used comparative pairs in her development. Wanting to explain the nature of the continental shelf, she sets up in her topic sentence a comparison between the continental shelf and the land:

The continental shelf[1] is of the sea, yet of all regions of the ocean it is most like the land. Sunlight penetrates to all but its deepest parts. Plants drift in the waters above it; seaweeds cling to its rocks and sway to the passage of the waves. Familiar fishes—unlike the weird[2] monsters of the abyss[3]—move over its plains like herds of cattle. Much of its substance is derived from the land—the sand and the rock fragments and the rich topsoil carried by running water to the sea and gently deposited on the shelf. Its submerged valleys and hills, in appropriate parts of the world, have been carved by glaciers into a topography[4] much like the northern landscapes we know, and the terrain is strewn[5] with rocks and gravel deposited by the moving ice sheets. Indeed many parts (or perhaps all) of the shelf have been dry land in the geologic past, for a comparatively slight fall of sea level has sufficed,[6] time and again, to expose it to wind and sun and rain. The Grand Banks of Newfoundland rose above the ancient seas and were submerged again. The Dogger Bank of the North Sea shelf was once a forested land inhabited by prehistoric beasts; now its "forests" are seaweeds and its "beasts" are fishes.

"The Continental Shelf," Rachel Carson, *The Sea Around Us*

[1]*continental shelf:* submerged border of a continent, separating the land mass from the ocean depths. [2]*weird:* strange, bizarre. [3]*abyss:* lowest depths of the sea. [4]*topography:* physical features of a region. [5]*strewn:* covered with something scattered or sprinkled. [6]*sufficed:* been cause enough.

Here the author has taken advantage of the comparative method to describe undersea life, explaining the unfamiliar by relating it to the familiar. Developing her paragraph, she expands on the comparison between the continental shelf and the land by adding comparative pairs. Deep-ocean schools of fish are likened to herds of cattle wandering on the land. Underwater seascapes are pictured as similar to the landscapes of northern England. In the last sentence, comparisons are drawn between the forests and beasts found on land and the seaweeds and fishes found under water.

A passage containing an extended paired comparison follows. Its purpose is to compare a fictional shipwreck with a shipwreck that actually occurred:

In 1898 a struggling author named Morgan Robertson concocted[1] a novel about a fabulous Atlantic liner, far larger than any that had ever been built. Robertson loaded his ship with rich and complacent[2] people and then wrecked it one cold April night on an iceberg. This somehow showed the futility[3] of everything, and, in fact, the book was called

[1]*concocted:* made up, devised. [2]*complacent:* self-satisfied. [3]*futility:* lack of point, uselessness.

Futility when it appeared that year, published by the firm of M. F. Mansfield.

Fourteen years later a British shipping company named the White Star Line built a steamer remarkably like the one in Robertson's novel. The new liner was 66,000 tons displacement; Robertson's was 70,000 tons. The real ship was 882.5 feet long; the fictional one was 800 feet. Both vessels were triple screw and could make 24–25 knots. Both could carry about 3,000 people, and both had enough lifeboats for only a fraction of this number. But then, this didn't seem to matter because both were labeled "unsinkable."

On April 10, 1912, the real ship left Southhampton on her maiden voyage to New York. Her cargo included a priceless copy of the *Rubaiyat* of Omar Khayyam and a list of passengers collectively worth $250 million. On her way she too hit an iceberg and went down on a cold April night.

Robertson called his ship the Titan; the White Star Line called its ship the Titanic. This is the story of her last night.

"The Titanic," Walter Lord, *A Night to Remember*

This selection demonstrates how helpful the semicolon can be when a writer is comparing or contrasting things or events. In his second and fourth paragraphs, Lord has used semicolons to balance fiction against fact more sharply. The effect of the semicolon in such a sentence as "The real ship was 882.5 feet long; the fictional one was 800 feet" is to express the comparison clearly, forcefully, and in a very few words.

In scientific and technical writing, comparison is an extremely useful mode of development because it is one of the simplest and most graphic ways to make a difficult concept or object understandable. The following passage on designing a photographic lens begins with an analogy between a lens designer and a chess player:

Designing a lens can be compared to playing chess. In chess a player tries to trap his opponent's king in a series of moves. In creating a lens a lens designer attempts to "trap" light by forcing all the rays arising from a single point in the subject to converge on a single point in the image, as a consequence of their passing through a series of transparent elements with precisely curved surfaces. Since in both cases the ultimate goal and the means by which it can be attained are known, one is tempted to think there will be a single best decision at any point along the way. The number of possible consequences flowing from any one decision is so large, however, as to be virtually, if not actually, infinite. Therefore in lens design, as in chess, perfect solutions to a problem are beyond reach. Although this article will be concerned only with the design of photographic lenses, the same principles apply to all lenses.

The lens designer has one enormous advantage over the chess player: the designer is free to call on any available source of help to guide him through the staggering number of possibilities. Most of that help once came from mathematics and physics, but recently computer technology, information theory, chemistry, industrial engineering and psychophysics have all contributed to making the lens designer's job immeasurably more productive. Some of the lenses on the market today were inconceivable a decade ago. Others whose design is as much as a century old can now be mass-produced at low cost. With the development of automatic production methods, lenses are made by the millions, both out of glass and out of plastics. Today's lenses are better than the best lenses used by the great photographers of the past. Moreover, their price may lower, in spite of the fact that 19th-century craftsmen worked for only a few dollars a week and today's lenses are more complex. The lens designer cannot fail to be grateful for the science and technology that have made his work easier and his creations more widely available, but he is also humbled: it is no longer practical for a fine photographic lens to be designed from beginning to end by a single human mind.

"The Photographic Lens," William H. Price, *Scientific American* (August 1976)

Notice how the writer makes his intention clear in his first sentence by concisely stating his analogy. He then goes on to use parallelism to present his comparative pair in a lucid way: "in chess . . . ; in creating a lens. . . ." Continuing, he relies on a series of transitions (in both cases, however, therefore.)

By the end of the first paragraph, the writer has pretty well exhausted the analogy that introduced his subject. He makes one last use of the analogy, though, to state his "enormous advantage" point in the beginning of the second paragraph. Then he continues on to devote his full attention to explaining the lens design. Having done its job well, analogy can be retired until the next essay is written.

Let's shift now to another approach to comparison: development in separate sections. The next two-section passage draws a surprising comparison between two of the U.S.A.'s most influential media figures: Walt Disney and Hugh Hefner. Although at first glance Disneyland and *Playboy* Magazine seem to offer richer material for contrast than for comparison, writer Peter Schrag clearly feels differently:

The two great Puritan entrepreneurs[1] of culture in the twentieth century, Walt Disney of Disneyland and Hugh M. Hefner of *Playboy*, illustrate the transformation [of the U.S.A.'s middle class from accepting "square" values, which are rooted in a firm moral base, to accepting "plastic" values, which represent wanting to be fashionable and successful without paying the price]. Although they were born a generation apart, Disney in 1901, Hefner in 1926, and although they seem, at first, to be polar opposites, they came from similar Midwest WASP[2] backgrounds and might, but for the accidents of time, have followed similar careers. Disney, the son of an unsuccessful Missouri farmer, took the

[1]*entrepeneurs:* managers of business undertakings. [2]*WASP:* white, Anglo-Saxon Protestant. [3]*square:* traditional. [4]*plastic:* things that are sterile in nature,

square[3] values of rural America—or what sentiment later imagined them to have been—cleaned them up and turned them into plastic.[4] The barnyard was sterilized into clean mice, happy ducks, and bourgeois pigs; the small town was idealized into a blessed valley, and the frustrating universe converted into the sanitary Magic Kingdom of Disneyland. . . .

The issue here is not vulgarity (although Disney had his vulgar—and his violent—streak); it is, rather, the subtle process in which the puritanical compulsion to order the world, to control, to clean up, is coupled to technology and thereby lifted to a synthetic realm in which new deities[5] are created and old ones destroyed.

If Disney's attempts to employ technology to create a Middle American utopia[6] resulted in a plastic universe of dancing dolls, animated mermaids, shriveled heroes, and, finally, an enervated[7] and dehumanized world where technology was the only god, Hefner's parallel efforts to produce an antipuritanical freedom spewed forth[8] a cornucopia[9] of kitsch[10] which was considerably less horrible only because it so often parodied[11] itself. If you pass through the secret door in Disneyland, you will in short order be among the Playboy bunnies. But it is still, somehow, the same place. What Disney did with sentimentality, Hefner accomplished by inversion.[12] As the son of a Nebraska preacher, he grew up in the same landscape, learned the same lessons, and accepted the same descriptions of the good life. Then he reversed them, which is to say that he took the things that the Puritan had always imagined joy to be, and which he repressed, embraced them as healthy and valuable, and advertised them as freedom and self-expression. Like Disney he is enamored[13] of technology; like Disney he is a compulsive sanitizer;[14] and like Disney he converted his puritanical hangups into a vast enterprise which flourishes on the cultural refugees of the land which formed him. . . . Scratch a Puritan[15] and you find a hedonist.[16] Where it was once possible only to feel guilty about having sex, Hefner has now made it possible to feel guilty about not having it.

"Disney and Hefner, Birds of a Feather," Peter Schrag, *The Decline of the WASP*

without real substance or lasting qualities. [5]*deities:* gods. [6]*utopia:* ideally perfect society. [7]*enervated:* weakened physically, mentally, or morally. [8]*spewed forth:* created in a gushing torrent. [9]*cornucopia:* overflowing fullness, abundance. [10]*kitsch:* pretentious but shallow and tasteless art, writing, or bric-a-brac intended to have a popular appeal. [11]*parodied:* ridiculed or made nonsensical fun of something that was intended to be serious. [12]*inversion:* reversal. [13]*enamored of:* in love with. [14]*sanitizer:* person obsessed with cleanliness and hygiene. [15]*Puritan:* a person excessively strict in morals and religion. [16]*hedonist:* one who believes in the self-indulgent pursuit of pleasure as a way of life.

Sometimes, when you have an unusual thesis to present, it is wise to disarm the potentially doubtful reader by first acknowledging the exceptions to what you are going to say. Schrag does this in his opening two sentences by including an obvious contrastive pair (". . . they were born a generation apart . . .") and by admitting that the two men *seem* to be polar opposites. But he quickly counters these concessions by pointing out the similarity of the men's backgrounds. Then he immediately focuses in on Disney throughout the first paragraph.

Schrag's second paragraph shifts from examining Disney's achievements to concentrating on Hefner's. The paragraph's opening sentence accomplishes the transition by comparing Disney's "Middle American utopia" with Hefner's "cornucopia of kitsch." In the central section of the paragraph, Schrag continues to explain Hefner by referring back to Disney: "What Disney did with sentimentality, Hefner accomplished by inversion." And in his concluding sentences, the writer unleashes a string of short comparisons—three parallel clauses beginning with the words "Like Disney. . . ." By summing up his thesis in a short sentence ("Scratch a Puritan and you find a hedonist.") Schrag uses variety in sentence length to create a dramatic climax.

Moving now from comparison to contrast, you will find four examples to conclude your study. Three passages illustrate development by a contrastive pair, and one demonstrates development by separate contrastive sections. First, look at a tightly packed contrastive paragraph on the subject of small and large businesses:

> There are basic differences between the large and small enterprise.[1] In the small enterprise you operate primarily through personal contacts. In the large enterprise you have established "policies," "channels" of organization, and fairly rigid procedure. In the small enterprise you have, moreover, immediate effectiveness in a very small area. You can see the effect of your work and of your decisions right away, once you are a little bit above the ground floor.[2] In the large enterprise, even the man at the top is only a cog[3] in a big machine. To be sure, his actions affect a much greater area than the actions and the decisions of the man in the small organization, but his effectiveness is remote, indirect, and elusive. In a small and even in a middle-size business, you are normally exposed to all kinds of experiences and expected to do a great many things without too much help or guidance. In the large organization you are normally taught one thing thoroughly. In the small one the danger is of becoming a jack-of-all-trades[4] and master of none. In the large it is of becoming the man who knows more and more about less and less.
>
> "How to Be an Employee," Peter F. Drucker, *Fortune*, May 1952

[1]*enterprise:* business. [2]*a little bit above ground floor:* in a minor executive position. [3]*cog:* metal tooth projecting from the surface of a gear, to impart or receive motion. [4]*jack-of-all-trades:* one who can do almost any kind of work.

Drucker could, of course, have chosen to develop his contrast in separate sections, describing first, all of the aspects of a small business and second, all of the corresponding facts of a large business. But because his material consisted of three closely connected points of contrast, he wisely decided to pair them off within his paragraph.

In this chapter's model composition, Neil Harris has placed two cultures

—those of Japan and the U.S.A.—side by side and has proceeded to both compare and contrast them. In the following selection, Carlos Fuentes provides a second cultural study, this one wholly contrastive, by pointing out some major differences between Mexico and its neighbor the U.S.A.:

(1)   The American looks at the Mexican, the Mexican looks at the American, and what does each one see? A figure compounded[1] of clichés.[2] The American cliché of the Mexican—flickered in movies and inked in cartoons—boils down to a lazy, mustachioed, swarthy[3] man with a big sombrero;[4] a gentle, irresponsible child of nature sleeping the perennial[5] siesta under the sun; a Don Juan serenading dark-eyed girls under their balconies; a villainous, gun-toting bandit staging pocket-size revolutions every weekend.

(2)   To the Mexican the gringo is either a naïve,[6] freckled, dollar-lined tourist or a vulgar, time-is-money business shark. And the American woman is a love-starved blonde sleeping with her Latin Casanova while her gringo husband shoots photos or sells automobiles.

(3)   So much for the clichés. In spite of their cardboard dimensions, they indicate a contrast between the Latino and the gringo, not static or fixed to be sure, but rather a highly mobile one, created by differing values in their historic and personal lives.

(4)   Take, **for example,** the word success. The United States is perhaps the biggest success story the world has known. **Nowhere,** in so short a time, has a people risen to such heights of power, influence, and prosperity. **Nowhere,** in consequence, has a people been so bred by optimism and self-confidence; and also, perhaps, by a certainty that its values and remedies are the best that can, and *should,* be offered to other, and less fortunate, peoples.

(5)   **But** below the border, the key word, up to the 1910 Revolution, had been failure. In Mexico, history has been tinged with bloodshed, poverty, anarchy,[7] and national humiliation. **And** these, **in turn,** bred pessimism, rancor,[8] and fatalism,[9] a sense of guilt, of compassion and solidarity, and a collective shouldering[10] and cleansing of guilt.

(6)   Success and failure condition two opposing attitudes in time. **When a nation rides the crest of success and power,** its sights are set on the future; **when its history is shadowed with defeat,** it broods on the past. Mexico has been trapped in its history. In the United States John Smith, Sir Walter Raleigh, and Cotton Mather seem almost prehistorical; legend and reality fuse[11] as the past rushes back and is forgotten. **But** in Mexico the past is always present: the Indian civilizations, the Spanish Conquest, the Wars of

[1]*compounded:* made up of two or more separate elements. [2]*clichés:* trite expressions or ideas. [3]*swarthy:* having a dark complexion. [4]*sombrero:* broad-brimmed, tall-crowned hat. [5]*perennial:* lasting for a long time. [6]*naïve:* simple; unsophisticated. [7]*anarchy:* complete absence of government; lawlessness. [8]*rancor:* continued bitter hate or ill will. [9]*fatalism:* belief that all events are determined by fate and hence inevitable. [10]*shouldering:* bearing the burden of.

Independence, the Yankee Invasion, the French Intervention, and the social Revolution of 1910 are relived and refought every day.

(7)   **Or** what could be more contrasting than the American and Mexican attitudes toward sport? The American is concerned, chiefly, with the practical value of the individual competition, of the result of the competition—victory or defeat. Take the bullring, **for example.** The gringo tourist asks, on taking his seat in the **barrera,**[12] "Who do you think is going to win?" **But** for the Mexican, the bullring is a social, religious, and historical symbol, not simply a spectacle of sixty thousand people sitting under the sun and in the shadow, watching a gold-and-purple marionette slay a dumb beast in a blend of pageantry and sadism.[13] **For** the dark young men in shirtsleeves, the fat old men with straw hats, the dressed-up women in braids and satin are witnessing, perhaps unwittingly, the sacrifice of the bull to the sun.

(8)   The core of the Aztec faith—that the sun must be fed with a sacrifice every day lest it disappear, forever, one night—is being enacted once again in the center of the arena, but now fused with the Western belief that man through his own powers can dominate brute nature. The performance in the bullring is more than an act of courage, more than a display of pageantry. It is the reproduction of the conquest of Mexico, of its violation, surrender, and rebirth.

(9)   Then the trumpets blare, the drums roll, and the matador confronts the bull, the fury of blind nature; plays with it, step by step dominates it, slays it. Cortés, once again, has conquered.

(10)   The well-to-do smile; their alter ego, the man in the suit of lights, has shown his power. The others, the people, accept: the conqueror has conquered. But he has done it, this time, as an actor in the ancient ritual, in the sun sacrifice dictated by the Indian faith. For when the bull is dragged out—or, eventually, when the torn and bloodied bullfighter is carried away—both bull and bullfighter are seen for what they really are: actors of the sun sacrifice, minions[14] of the hot star now disappearing behind the dusky ring, sure to shine the next day.

"Latinos vs. Gringos," Carlos Fuentes, *Holiday* (October 1962)

[11]*fuse:* join together. [12]*barrera:* bullring. [13]*sadism:* taking pleasure from inflicting physical or psychological pain on another. [14]*minions:* subordinate officials or deputies.

Fuentes's introduction is a particularly lively and effective one. Notice that he relies heavily on examples in the first two paragraphs to lead up to his thesis statement in paragraph 3 that there exists "a contrast between the Latino and the gringo . . . created by differing values in their historic and personal lives." Then the writer selects two categories to use in building his contrast: success and sports. He develops each category by contrastive pairs, first discussing the importance of success in the United States and then the effect of failure in Mexico; first discussing a gringo's attitude toward a bullfight and then the meaning of a *barrera* to a Mexican. Throughout the passage, Fuentes infuses his writing with considerable force by including much specific detail.

By means of frequent transitions and parallelism, the writer has given his essay a firm coherence. Paragraph 4 begins with the transition "for example" and benefits from the parallel forms "nowhere . . . nowhere." Paragraph 5 contains three transitions: "but," "and," "in turn." Paragraph 6 opens with two sharply parallel statements ("when a nation rides . . . when its history is shadowed . . .") and its last sentence begins with the transition "but." Paragraph 7 begins with a transition "or" and contains several others: "for example," "but," "for."

The next writing selection, also a contrast developed by pairs, makes a perceptive point about a fundamental dichotomy ("division into two sharply opposed parts") in the U.S.A. The writer cites a major difference in the view of life expressed in American media—newspapers, magazines, television, and motion pictures—and in the view expressed in literature by serious American writers:

> The difference between the America of films, magazines and packaged goods and the America of Faulkner, Hawthorne, Saul Bellow, Carson McCullers, James Baldwin, Melville—I stab the names with a pin, hitting on past as well as present, because the *then* in every country is contained in its *now*—is extraordinary. (It is interesting that that marvelous American invention, sick humor, is based on this very difference: life as you've been told to want it, and life as it is.) One can't explain away the gap in terms of the difference between art and commercialism. For though shamelessly used by commerce, the American image is also held up by Americans in high and serious places, political ones, for example. The image exalts youth, success, unquestioning patriotism, the love of a good man/woman, the confidence of freedom and of being right. The best of American writers are concerned with the difficulty of fulfillment;[1] the corruption[2] of integrity;[3] the struggle for moral standards in public as well as private life; the truth of love, whatever its form, hetero- or homosexual; the battle of the individual against the might of society; and the doubt that one is right.
>
> "A Foreigner Looks at American Writers," Nadine Gordimer, *Holiday* (July 1963)

[1]*fulfillment*: realizing completely one's ambitions, potentialities, and desires. [2]*corruption*: decay. [3]*integrity*: the state of being upright, honest, sincere, and moral.

To find a paragraph more tightly packed with provocative ideas than the Gordimer one would be difficult. Fortunately, she has relieved the density of this passage by adding two informal stylistic touches: the pair of dashes and the parentheses. Notice, too, that she makes use of the colon in two places to stress the ideas that follow. Introducing ideas with a colon in this

way enhances the importance of what follows by shifting it to the conclusion of the sentence.

At one point in her paragraph, Gordimer might have added force to her
writing by including a needed transition. A phrase such as "in contrast" or
"on the other hand" placed at the beginning of the last sentence ("The best
of American writers are concerned with . . .") would highlight the final
contrasting point that the paragraph has been building to. Try inserting a
transition before the final sentence and then rereading the last three sentences to discover the force a single, well-placed transition can have.

Finally, read a well-written example of a contrast developed in separate
sections by Bruce Catton, an American historian. Catton's subject matter
concerns two American Civil War generals—Grant, who led the Northern
forces, and Lee, who was the commander of the Southern armies:

> When Ulysses S. Grant and Robert E. Lee met in the parlor of a
> modest house at Appomattox Court House, Virginia, on April 9, 1865, to
> work out the terms for the surrender of Lee's Army of Northern Vir-
> ginia, a great chapter in American life came to a close, and a great new
> chapter began.
>
> These men were bringing the Civil War to its virtual[1] finish. To be
> sure, other armies had yet to surrender, and for a few days the fugitive
> Confederate government would struggle desperately and vainly,[2] trying
> to find some way to go on living now that its chief support was gone. But
> in effect it was all over when Grant and Lee signed the papers. And the
> little room where they wrote out the terms was the scene of one of the
> poignant,[3] dramatic contrasts in American history.
>
> They were two strong men, these oddly different generals, and they
> represented the strengths of two conflicting currents that, through them,
> had come into final collision.
>
> Back of Robert E. Lee was the notion[4] that the old aristocratic concept
> might somehow survive and be dominant[5] in American life.
>
> Lee was tidewater[6] Virginia, and in his background were family, cul-
> ture, and tradition . . . the age of chivalry[7] transplanted[8] to a New
> World which was making its own legends and its own myths. He em-
> bodied[9] a way of life that had come down through the age of knighthood
> and the English country squire.[10] America was a land that was beginning
> all over again, dedicated to nothing much more complicated than the
> rather hazy belief that all men had equal rights and should have an equal
> chance in the world. In such a land Lee stood for the feeling that it was
> somehow of advantage to human society to have a pronounced[11] in-

[1]*virtual:* actual, real. [2]*vainly:* without success. [3]*poignant:* sharply painful to
the feelings. [4]*notion:* idea, belief. [5]*dominant:* controlling force. [6]*tidewater:* the
coastal region of Virginia; also applied to an aristocratic settler thereof.
[7]*chivalry:* qualifications of a knight, such as courage, nobility, fairness, loyalty,
courtesy, respect for women, and protection of the poor. [8]*transplanted:* removed from one place and planted in another. [9]*embodied:* gave bodily form to.
[10]*country squire:* large rural landowner. [11]*pronounced:* clearly marked. [12]*in-*

equality[12] in the social structure. There should be a leisure class, backed by ownership of land; in turn, society itself should be keyed to[13] the land as the chief source of wealth and influence. It would bring forth (according to this ideal) a class of men with a strong sense of obligation to the community, men who lived not to gain advantage for themselves but to meet the solemn obligations which had been laid on them[14] by the very fact that they were privileged. From them the country would get its leadership; to them it could look for the higher values—of thought, of conduct, of personal deportment[15]—to give it strength and virtue.

Lee embodied the noblest elements of this aristocratic ideal. Through him, the landed[16] nobility justified itself. For four years, the Southern states had fought a desperate war to uphold the ideals for which Lee stood. In the end, it almost seemed as if the Confederacy fought for Lee; as if he himself was the Confederacy . . . the best thing that the way of life for which the Confederacy stood could ever have to offer. He had passed into legend[17] before Appomattox. Thousands of tired, underfed, poorly clothed Confederate soldiers, long since past the simple enthusiasm of the early days of the struggle, somehow considered Lee the symbol[18] of everything for which they had been willing to die. But they could not quite put this feeling into words. If the Lost Cause, sanctified[19] by so much heroism and so many deaths, had a living justification,[20] its justification was General Lee.

Grant, the son of a tanner[21] on the Western frontier, was everything Lee was not. He had come up the hard way and embodied nothing in particular except the eternal toughness and sinewy[22] fiber of the men who grew up beyond the mountains. He was one of a body of men who owed reverence and obeisance[23] to no one, who were self-reliant to a fault, who cared hardly anything for the past but who had a sharp eye for the future.

These frontier men were the precise opposites of the tidewater aristocrats. Back of them, in the great surge[24] that had taken people over the Alleghenies and into the opening Western country, there was a deep, implicit[25] dissatisfaction with a past that had settled into grooves.[26] They stood for democracy, not from any reasoned conclusion about the proper ordering of human society, but simply because they had grown up in the middle of democracy and knew how it worked. Their society might have privileges, but they would be privileges each man had won for himself. Forms and patterns meant nothing. No man was born to anything, except perhaps to a chance to show how far he could rise. Life was competition.

Yet along with this feeling had come a deep sense of belonging to a national community. The Westerner who developed a farm, opened a

---

equality: lack of equality. [13]keyed to: dependent upon. [14]laid on them: necessary for them to fulfill. [15]deportment: behavior. [16]landed: landowning. [17]legend: story of some wonderful event, handed down for generations. [18]symbol: something that stands for or represents another thing. [19]sanctified: made holy. [20]justification: evidence of righteousness. [21]tanner: person whose work is making leather from animal hides. [22]sinewy: strong. [23]obeisance: submission. [24]surge: movement. [25]implicit: indirectly expressed. [26]grooves: fixed habits, settled

shop, or set up a business as a trader could hope to prosper only as his community prospered—and his community ran from the Atlantic to the Pacific and from Canada down to Mexico. If the land was settled, with towns and highways and accessible markets, he could better himself. He saw his fate in terms of the nation's own destiny. As its horizons expanded, so did his. He had, in other words, an acute[27] dollars-and-cents stake in the continued growth and development of his country.

And that, perhaps, is where the contrast between Grant and Lee becomes most striking.[28] The Virginia aristocrat inevitably[29] saw himself in relation to his own region. He lived in a static[30] society which could endure almost anything except change. Instinctively, his first loyalty would go to the locality in which that society existed. He would fight to the limit of endurance to defend it, because in defending it he was defending everything that gave his own life its deepest meaning.

The Westerner, on the other hand, would fight with an equal tenacity[31] for the broader concept of society. He fought so because everything he lived by was tied to growth, expansion, and a constantly widening horizon. He could not possibly stand by unmoved[32] in the face of an attempt to destroy the Union. He would combat[33] it with everything he had because he could only see it as an effort to cut the ground out from under his feet.

So Grant and Lee were in complete contrast, representing two diametrically[34] opposed elements in American life. Grant was the modern man emerging; beyond him, ready to come on the stage, was the great age of steel and machinery, of crowded cities and a restless, burgeoning[35] vitality. Lee might have ridden down from the old age of chivalry, lance[36] in hand, silken banner fluttering over his head. Each man was the perfect champion of his cause, drawing both his strengths and weaknesses from the people he led.

"Grant and Lee: A Study in Contrasts," Bruce Catton, *The American Story*

routines. [27]*acute:* critical, urgent. [28]*striking:* easily seen, conspicuous. [29]*inevitably:* unavoidably. [30]*static:* unchanging, not progressing. [31]*tenacity:* persistence. [32]*unmoved:* without resisting. [33]*combat:* oppose, fight.[34]*diametrically:* directly, exactly. [35]*burgeoning:* sprouting, growing. [36]*lance:* thrusting weapon consisting of wooden shaft with a sharp metal spearhead.

Observe that this contrastive essay is divided into two roughly equal parts. The first several paragraphs are devoted to Lee, the second several to Grant. The writer uses, not a word or phrase, but an entire sentence to give the reader the necessary information that Catton is about to shift from talking about Lee to talking about Grant: "Grant, the son of a tanner on the Western frontier, was everything Lee was not." Did this transitional device help to make your reading of the passage go more smoothly than it would have if the sentence had been left out?

Although Catton spreads his contrast over a number of paragraphs, he does not confuse his reader or permit him to forget the contrast that is taking shape. Catton avoids these dangers because he is dealing primarily with two ideas only: the aristocratic ideal contrasted with the democratic ideal and the idea of regionalism as opposed to the concept of national unity. Because he is not presenting a great number of points or considerable detail, Catton has selected the particularly appropriate method of developing his contrast in separate sections.

EXERCISE 40
Outlining

First review the section in Chapter 5 on "The Composition Outline." Then reconstruct the outline the writer probably worked from in composing the model composition, "Japan and the U.S.A.: Different but Alike."

USING FIGURATIVE LANGUAGE

Figurative language is a special type of comparison not touched upon earlier in this chapter. It is a highly flexible technique, used frequently by poets and occasionally by expository and scientific writers.

Because our thoughts have a habit of drifting upward to increasingly general and abstract levels, one of the most pressing problems any writer faces is that of bringing his ideas down to earth, of making them concrete and vivid. Figurative language, when carefully controlled, can help him to do this. It is the writer's way of making a picture say what it might otherwise take 1,000 words to state. Such figures of speech as the **simile,** the **metaphor,** and **personification** make direct or implied comparisons between two things. Often, figures of speech are used to help clarify the meaning of an unfamiliar thing by comparing it to something that is better known. For example, if you wanted to explain the game of ping pong to someone who had never heard of it, you could describe the size and markings of the table, the shape of the paddles, and the weight of the ball. But probably you could help the person to understand in a shorter time what ping pong is by saying "Ping pong is like a tennis game scaled down to a tabletop court."

The chief difference between a simile and a metaphor, both of which are figures of speech making comparisons, is that the former makes a direct comparison and the latter makes an indirect comparison. A simile includes such words as "like," "as," and "as if" to say that two things are *similar.* A metaphor, in contrast, declares that two things are *the same.* Compare these examples:

Similes

The snow was **like a white blanket** drawn over the field.
She was as noisy **as a mynah bird.**
His mouth tasted **as if it were lined with ashes.**

Metaphors

The sun was **a red wafer** in the sky.
His friend has become **a thorn** in his side.
For some music lovers, Bach's concertos are **a tonic.**

A third figure of speech—personification—attributes human qualities and abilties to inanimate objects, animals, abstractions, and events. The writer of this chapter's model composition uses a personification when he refers to China and Great Britain as "mother countries." Here are other examples:

The **racing car strained** impatiently at the starting line.
King of the jungle, the lion strode across the plain.
The **jet plane whined** its frustration at having to descend to the runway.

Since figurative language has a certain poetic quality, some people tend to associate it exclusively with creative writing. That this is far too limited an idea is shown by the figures of speech frequently appearing in all types of writing, expository as well as creative. With only a slight revision, the technical article on lens design earlier in this chapter could have opened with a simile: "Designing a lens is **like** playing chess." Similes, metaphors, and personification are prevalent both in writing and in speech because they provide one of the most useful ways of making our abstractions more concrete. Let's look at some examples of figurative language contributing to several different types of prose:

A biography

Everything that he was and did bore out this rigid face and played laughs against it. When he moved his eyes, it was **like seeing them move in a statue.**

"Buster Keaton," James Agee

A description

My town used to be **as bare as a picked bone,** with no tree anywhere around it larger than a ten-foot willow or alder.

Wallace Stegner, *Wolf Willow*

A scientfic explanation (of the tarantula spider)

The trichobothria, very fine hairs growing from **disklike** membranes on the legs, are sensitive only to air movement.

"The Spider and the Wasp," Alexander Petrunkevitch

A personal essay

Why should we be in such desperate haste to succeed and in such desperate enterprises? If a man does not keep pace with his companions, perhaps it is because he hears **a different drummer.**

Henry David Thoreau, *Walden*

Sometimes a writer will find it advantageous to create an extended figure of speech. He will make an initial comparison and then develop it, expanding his idea as he does. Examining the writings of Ernest Hemingway in "Nightmare and Ritual in Hemingway," Malcolm Cowley provides an example of such an extended simile:

> Going back to Hemingway's work after several years is like going to a brook where you had often fished and finding the woods as deep and cool as they used to be. The trees are bigger, perhaps, but they are the same trees; the water comes down over the black stones as clear as always, with the same dull, steady roar where it plunges into the pool; and when the first trout takes hold of your line you can feel your heart beating against your fishing jacket. But something has changed, for this time there are shadows in the pool that you hadn't noticed before, and you have a sense that the woods are haunted.
>
> "Nightmare and Ritual in Hemingway," Malcolm Cowley, *The Portable Hemingway*

In this passage the words "brook" and "woods" are metaphors for the stories and novels of Hemingway. "Water" is a metaphor for his prose style. What do you think "the first trout" stands for? The "shadows" in the pool? The "haunted" woods?

As you gain more experience writing in English, you will begin to develop a writer's sense that warns you if you are becoming too abstract in developing an idea. When this happens, a simile, metaphor, or personification can often help to make your thought more vivid. Figures of speech should be treated with caution, for they can easily be overused. But this does not at all detract from their power at the right time and in the right place.

Punctuation Points

PUNCTUATING PARENTHETICAL ELEMENTS

A parenthetical element is a word or group of words that is not closely related to the central thought of the sentence or is out of its normal order in the sentence. Parenthetical expressions or interrupters include nonrestrictive modifiers and appositives, connectives, transitional phrases, and words in direct address. Such elements are set off by commas.

The most common parenthetical elements are as follows:

Absolutes Absolutes are words or phrases, rarely clauses, that do not grammatically affect the sentences in which they appear. They are set off by commas. Note the punctuation of these absolutes:

1. Transitions.

The time has come, **however,** for a review of the policy.
In conclusion, we found three main causes of the French Revolution.

2. Words in direct address.

   Ladies and gentlemen, it is a pleasure to be here.
   For the next two hours, **George,** you must amuse yourself.

3. Speaker identifications in direct quotations.

   "I expect," **he said,** "that times will get better."

4. Absolute phrases. (Some absolute phrases are prepositional phrases with the preposition dropped.)

   She ran up the stairs, **a box of candy in her hands.** (Preposition **with** dropped)

   An *ablative absolute* is a noun plus a participle:

   The car washed, he went on to trim the shrubs. (Noun *car*; participle *washed*)

5. Adverbs of affirmation or negation.

   Yes, I rather like curry.
   No, we had expected to go, but the weather turned cold.

6. Interjections. (An interjection is a word expressing emotion or simple exclamation.)

   Well, perhaps she will change her mind.
   Oh, how could you say that!
   Why, I never expected to see you again.

Nonrestrictive modifiers and appositives   Adjective clauses, adverb clauses, and appositives may be either restrictive or nonrestrictive. When they are nonrestrictive, they are set off by commas:

1. Nonrestrictive adjective modifiers.

   Mr. Chang, **who left for Borneo yesterday,** forgot his attache case.

2. Nonrestrictive adverb modifiers.

   They will travel to Hong Kong, **unless the ship is delayed.**

3. Nonrestrictive appositives.

   Dostoevsky, **the Russian novelist,** wrote during the nineteenth century.

Elements out of order   Elements out of normal order in the sentence are set off by commas:

   The sea, **tranquil and smooth,** was sparkling in the sun.
   At the dock, a large yacht was anchored.
   Gratefully, he accepted the clothing for the war orphans.

Exceptions In four cases commas need not be used to set off parenthetical elements:

1. Elements that are only slightly parenthetical are usually not set off.

They went **instead** to the post office.
It was **indeed** a surprise to hear from you.

2. Parenthetical elements that are to be minimized are enclosed in parentheses, not commas.

The fact is **(if we can believe him)** that the order has been sent.
Confucius **(551?–478? B.C.)** was a Chinese philosopher and teacher.

3. Elements that are to be strongly emphasized are often set off by dashes, not commas.

The chief rule—**the one that must be followed**—has been given to all of you.

4. Parenthetical elements that would normally be set off by commas are often set off by dashes if they contain internal commas.

The three best students—**Gail, Nelson, and Edward**—were excused from taking the examination.

EXERCISE 41
Parenthetical Elements

Write out these sentences, punctuating all parenthetical elements.

1. Here as I see it is a universal problem.
2. Well ask your father the president of the group if we can go on the tour.
3. I believe Serge that you have guessed correctly.
4. His homework finished Frank began to read the newspaper.
5. My friend Bob who entered the track meet placed second in the pole vaulting competition.
6. Yes Mr. Allen I will give your message to the captain.
7. We found as we opened the door a deer in the living room.
8. The television set a gift from my cousin needs to be repaired.
9. "Men who are shy" said the speaker "do not make good detectives."
10. The purpose of the article as we have seen is to teach people how to train their dogs.
11. I was indeed sorry to hear of your illness.
12. The Eiffel Tower a Paris landmark is on many people's lists of attractions to visit.
13. The man who saved the drowning girl was given an award for his heroic act.

14. The race began the crowd's roar announced it before we had reached our seats.
15. Three students stood on the doorstep their hats in their hands.

Grammar Skills

THE ELLIPTICAL CLAUSE

An important aid to economy in writing English is the elliptical clause. In many cases, it is possible to leave out a relative pronoun that normally would join a dependent clause to an independent clause:

The movie **I wanted to see** was not playing. (*which* or *that* unexpressed)
We couldn't understand the point **he was making.** (*which* or *that* unexpressed)

Sometimes a dependent clause contains neither subject nor verb:

When in Barcelona, try to find a quiet hotel room. (For *When you are in Barcelona*)
While working in the store, I met many interesting people. (For *While I was working in the store*)

Whenever such words are left out of a dependent clause, it is known as an elliptical clause.

Another kind of elliptical construction occurs most commonly after the words "than" and "as." To avoid repetition in both speaking and writing, we usually drop the final verb in sentences such as these:

The chairman spoke longer than he. (*spoke* is not repeated)
Are you as old as she? (*is* is omitted)
We danced longer than they. (*danced* is not repeated)

After *than* and *as* introducing an incomplete construction, use the form of the pronoun you would use if the construction were completed. The pronoun chosen in such a construction depends upon the intent of the writer:

I like George better than **he.** (better than he likes George)
I like George better than **him.** (better than I like him)

Although the nominative case pronouns (*I, he, she, they, we*) are preferred usage in *than* and *as* constructions for formal writing and speaking, the objective case (*me, him, her, them, us*) is generally accepted colloquial usage:

Formal	They worked harder than **we.**
	Are you as hungry as **I?**
	Ann is older than **she.**
Colloquial	They worked harder than **us.**
	Are you as hungry as **me?**
	Ann is older than **her.**

EXERCISE 42
Elliptical Constructions

A. *Reduce the number of words in these sentences by making the introductory dependent clauses elliptical. Write out the revised sentences.*

Example: While **she was cooking dinner,** *she spilled the sugar.*
     While **cooking dinner,** *she spilled the sugar.*

1. Although he was expecting a telephone call, the doctor had to leave his office.
2. While she was driving into town, my mother ran out of gas.
3. If you are curious about your final grade, ask your professor.
4. When you are applying for a scholarship, you should write neatly.
5. After you finish cutting the grass, please water it.
6. Even though she is working every day, my sister still has time for a lot of reading.
7. When he is hammering a nail, he almost always hits his thumb.
8. After I had been looking for my key for half an hour, I found it under a chair.
9. When they are looking for an apartment to rent, newcomers to a city often read the newspaper advertisements every day.
10. While they were watching the football game on TV, the students often cheered.

B. *Choose the correct pronoun to complete each sentence. Write out the completed sentence. Then write in parentheses after each sentence the part of the sentence beginning with* than *or* as, *followed by the pronoun and the understood verb. Choose colloquial forms when indicated.*

Example: Janet is sleepier than (I, me).
     Janet is sleepier than **I.** *(than I am)*

1. You worked harder than (they, them).
2. Is he older than (I, me)?
3. Did you stay as long as (he, him)?
4. You don't seem as hungry as (I, me). (Choose colloquial form.)
5. Michael is more popular than (he, him).
6. Carl is stronger than (I, me). (Choose colloquial form.)
7. They don't dance as well as (we, us).
8. Is he older than (she, her)? (Choose colloquial form.)
9. Do you like to drive as fast as (they, them)?
10. I can do the job better than (she, her).

CORRELATIVE CONJUNCTIONS

Correlative conjunctions are pairs of words that have the same connecting function as single conjunctions. The chief correlative conjunctions are

both . . . and, either . . . or, neither . . . nor, whether . . . or, and **not only**
. . . but also. Here are examples of how they are used in sentences:

I like **both** his ambition **and** his energy.
Samuel will **either** get a raise **or** resign from his job.
Neither the students **nor** the professor attended the meeting.
The trains are **not only** old and dirty **but also** uncomfortable.
We had to decide **whether** to limit our club to seniors **or** to include lower
classmen.

Correlative conjunctions add to the clarity of writing in two ways. First,
they cut down on the number of words needed to express ideas:

The students did not attend the meeting, and neither did the professor.
(12 words)
Neither the students **nor** the professor attended the meeting. *(9 words)*

Second, correlative conjunctions add clarity by signaling the reader that
two related ideas are to be considered together. If the same ideas are put
in a compound sentence, the relationship between them is often not as
immediately clear:

Walking in the woods is enjoyable, and it is also healthful.
Walking in the woods is **not only** enjoyable **but also** healthful.

Note that the correlative construction causes the reader to anticipate the
second, related idea soon after he gets into the sentence. In the compound
sentence, though, he does not know that a comparison is to be added until
he reaches the last part of the sentence. When correlative conjunctions are
used, the comparison becomes sharper and more compact.

Strict English usage requires that elements following correlative conjunctions be expressed in parallel constructions. These elements should be equal
in grammatical form: verbs (*either* **sing** *or* **dance**), infinitives (*whether* **to**
rest *or* **to sleep**), adjectives (both **intelligent** *and* **beautiful**), *participles*
(neither **expecting** *nor* **hoping**), prepositional phrases (*not only* **in the**
garden *but also* **in the house**), and so on. Observe the following nonparallel
elements following correlative conjunctions that have been revised into
parallel forms:

Not Parallel	He had neither the *courage* nor *was his imagination* *active enough* for the job. *(noun; clause)*
Parallel	He had neither **the courage** nor **the imagination** for the job. *(noun; noun)*
Not Parallel	Mr. Carew hopes either *to be available* on Wednesday at 3 P.M. or *on Thursday* at 11 A.M. *(infinitive phrase, prepositional phrase)*
Parallel	Mr. Carew hopes to be available either **on Wednesday** at 3 P.M. or **on Thursday** at 11 A.M. *(prepositional phrase; prepositional phrase)*

Not Parallel   The professor likes both *teaching* and *to write*. *(participle; infinitive)*

Parallel   The professor likes both **teaching** and **writing**. *(participle; participle)*

EXERCISE 43
Using Correlative Conjunctions

Combine each pair of sentences into a single sentence by adding the correlative conjunctions in parentheses.

1. Felipe hopes to be a champion surfer. He also plans on graduating from college. (both . . . and)
2. I have no time to go roller skating tonight. I don't have the energy to go. (neither . . . nor)
3. You can listen to music on records. The radio also plays music for you to listen to. (either . . . or)
4. The diamond necklace is expensive. It is also a thing of beauty. (not only . . . but also)
5. He didn't know whether or not to telephone. He thought of writing a note. (whether . . . or)
6. The sale begins tomorrow. It also ends tomorrow. (both . . . and)
7. Her father will not allow her to go to the dance. He will not let her act in the play. (neither . . . nor)
8. Classes will begin on the last Monday of August. But they might begin on the first Monday of September. (either . . . or)
9. We spent the day catching fish. We also tried to look for crabs. (not only . . . but also)
10. They wondered whether to visit California first. They thought about going directly down to Mexico. (whether . . . or)
11. We can manipulate others by the words we use. The words we use can manipulate us. (either . . . or)
12. The trunk and branches of a tree grow. They become longer and thicker. (not only . . . but also)
13. We were amazed. He ordered frogs' legs and escargots. (both . . . and)
14. They were invited to a wedding and a concert on the same afternoon. They couldn't decide which event to attend. (whether . . . or)
15. He couldn't guess the meaning of the word. He couldn't find it in the dictionary. (neither . . . nor)

REVIEW OF PREPOSITIONS

You studied prepositions in Chapter 2, and each Paragraph Puzzle gives you some practice in using prepositions correctly. But you may benefit from the intensive review the following sentences provide:

EXERCISE 44
Preposition Review

Write out each sentence, placing the correct preposition in each blank. Refer to Appendix 6 if you need help in choosing prepositions.

1. The package consisted......three rolls......film, a camera......a viewfinder, and a carrying case made......leather.
2. They made arrangements to meet......the railroad station......a quarter......four.
3. ......the marketplace we found a rug which we bought......twelve dollars.
4. Can I depend......you to leave the room......good order when you leave......your vacation?
5. The telephone allows him to call......his family while he is...... special assignments......distant cities.
6. Stephen's letter.......acceptance.......Swarthmore College came ......airmail.
7. Several students signed up......their professor to travel......Europe ......the summer.
8. Mrs. Allen apologized......her neighbor......accidentally sprinkling her guests......the garden hose.
9. When the politician announced his decision......the afternoon, the roomful......newspaper reporters broke......confusion.
10. The poet lived......England......three years......moving...... Greece.
11. When you apply......admission......the university, you must first write a letter......inquiry......the Office......Admissions.
12. After the Admissions Office has received your letter, they will collect all......the necessary forms and information and mail them...... you.
13. The application form that you receive will ask you to write......all ......the high schools and colleges you have attended......the past, asking them to send transcripts......your academic record ......the university.
14. You will also be asked to request letters......recommendation...... counselors, teachers, and principals who know......your character and your school record.
15. Once you have filled out all......the forms and dropped them...... the mailbox, you may have to wait......two months to learn whether you have been admitted......the university.

Questions for Discussions and Review

1. Analyze the different types of composition beginnings used in this chapter's model composition and example passages. (Refer to "Writing an Introduction," Chapter 7.)
2. Identify any strong active verbs you find in the model composition.
3. Find an example of parallelism in the Schrag selection on Walt Disney and Hugh Hefner.
4. Locate the two introductory gerund phrases in Kenmerer's selection.
5. Explain why parenthetical statements appear in the Gordimer and Schrag articles.
6. How does Lord vary his sentence structure in writing comparative pairs in the second paragraph of *A Night to Remember?*
7. Construct an outline, from which a composition could be written, based on a comparative cultural study of two countries you are familiar with.
8. In his analogy Kenmerer compares social scientists to swimmers and physical scientists to runners. Try to create an analogy of your own— this one between college freshmen and graduate students.
9. Gordimer's view that there is a sharp difference between the idealized view of life in American media and the realistic view of life found in serious American literature offers an exceptionally acute insight into the U.S.A. If you have lived in the U.S.A. for some time, can you agree or disagree with Gordimer's idea? If you think she is right, how do you account for this contrast?
10. This chapter contains two comparative cultural studies, one by Harris on Japan and the U.S.A. and another by Fuentes on Mexico and the U.S.A. On the basis of content, style, and force of writing, which selection do you think is more successful in presenting its thesis?

Vocabulary Growth

PARAGRAPH PUZZLE

Beginning with this chapter's Paragraph Puzzle and through Chapter 8, some of the missing words in the paragraph will **not** *have word choices given beneath them. For these blanks, supply an appropriate word by studying the context.*

An unidentified wit once said, "Laugh. . . . . .the world laughs
(but, or, for, and)

with you. Snore, and . . . . .sleep alone." Yet snoring is far
(he, she, you, they)

. . . . .a laughing matter, as those unfortunates. . . . . .good
(from, toward, in, over)   (of, for, at, with)

hearing, who are subjected. . . . . .the sounds of the snoring disorder,
    (at, in, for, to)

. . . . .testify.
(will, wasn't weren't, which)

It has been estimated that one. . . . . .of eight Americans snores:
    (in, out, with, over)

this means. . . . . .there are approximately 21 million people—
    (this, for, then, that)

. . . . .as well as men—who render. . . . ., nocturnal can-
    (sonorous, slick, simple, orchestrated)

tatas when they are asleep. . . . ., assuming that each snorer dis-
    (But, For, And, Nor)

turbs the. . . . . .of at least one other person,. . . . . .necessar-
    (it, one, that, there)

ily follows that there are 21. . . . . .unhappy listeners.
    (hundred, dozen, trillion, million)

While a sleeping person. . . . ., either in or out, several struc-
    (perspires, rolls over, breathes, dreams)

tures. . . . . .his nose and throat generate snoring. . . . .
    (on, in, by, over)

sounds, coming from the soft palate and. . . . . .soft structures of the
    (rather, other, over, under)

throat, are caused. . . . . .vibratory responses to inflowing and out-

flowing. . . . . When the soft tissues of the. . . . . .and
(smoke, light, air, music)   (ear, eye, nose, mouth)

throat come close to the lining. . . . . .the throat, the vibrations that
    (on, of, at, by)

. . . . .are caused by the position of. . . . . .tongue. In short,
(occur, exert, display, decline)   (this, that, a, the)

the noise made. . . . . .snoring can be compared to the. . . . .
    (rumor, drift, lift, noise)

made when breezes flutter a flag. . . . . .a pole.
    (in, of, over, on)

WORD CLUES

A. *Vocabulary words in the following exercise are boldfaced.*

1. Today there [is 1] woman in the Cabinet, *no* women in the Senate,
   [1] woman governor, and only [17] women representatives (fewer

than in several previous Congresses). Our 4 women ambassadors serving abroad are in . . . [the United Kingdom,] Zambia, Togo, and Luxembourg.

There is no way by which even the most optimistic feminist can translate these **minuscule** figures into a record of feminine progress toward quality in politics.

"The 21st-Century Woman—Free at Last?" Clare Boothe Luce,
Saturday Review/World (August 24, 1974)

Vocabulary Word. . . . .

Context Clue. . . . .

Probable Meaning. . . . .

Dictionary Definition. . . . .

2. You can tell a lot about social change from the posters people buy. At $2.50 each, reproductions by Rembrandt, Renoir, and Van Gogh are moving well at the Re-Print Mint in Berkeley, as are the **languorous** scenes of turn-of-the-century illustrator Maxfield Parrish and his pretty women bending over waterfalls.

"The sense is away from social involvement of the '60s to **idealized** conceptions," says Berkeley poster shop owner Alice Shankar, whose Re-Print Mint sits on the edge of the college campus that carried the first banners of the '60s student protest movements. "Today, people just want to sit and look at something pretty."

San Francisco Examiner, 4 July 1976

Vocabulary Word. . . . .

Context Clue. . . . .

Probable Meaning. . . . .

Dictionary Definition. . . . .

Vocabulary Word. . . . .

Context Clue. . . . .

Probable Meaning. . . . .

Dictionary Definition. . . . .

3. For example, scientific criteria will increasingly be used in the definition of environmental quality; I shall mention one technical aspect of this problem that relates to economic policies. In the future, industrial and domestic **effluents** will be considered, not as wastes, but as resources; we shall develop new technologies to make use of them. In view of the expected world-wide shortage of many resources, recycling of wastes will become a socioeconomic necessity, and this

will prove to be the most important and effective method of pollution control.

"Recycling Social Man," René Dubos, *Saturday Review/World* (August 24, 1974)

Vocabulary Word...

Context Clue...

Probable Meaning......................................

Dictionary Definition.................................

4. In Soledad state prison, I fell in with a group of young blacks who, like myself, were in **vociferous** rebellion against what we perceived as a continuation of slavery on a higher plane. We cursed everything American—including baseball and hot dogs. All respect we may have had for politicians, preachers, lawyers, governors, Presidents, senators, congressmen was utterly destroyed as we watched them **temporizing** and compromising over right and wrong, over legality and illegality, over constitutionality and unconstitutionality. We knew that in the end what they were clashing over was us, what to do with blacks, and whether or not to start treating us as human beings. I despised all of them.

Eldridge Cleaver, *Soul on Ice*

Vocabulary Word...

Context Clue...

Probable Meaning......................................

Dictionary Definition.................................

Vocabulary Word...

Context Clue...

Probable Meaning......................................

Dictionary Definition.................................

5. Guatemala's **turbulent** [earthquake] . . . history finds explanation in the widely accepted geologic theory known as plate tectonics. The nation rides the boundary of the American and Caribbean plates. . . . These and some ten other great crustal slabs pave the planet with an ever-moving mosaic. The plates constantly interact at their boundaries—bumping, grinding, pulling apart, plunging one beneath the other. These jostlings breed most of the world's earthquakes.

Yet violent **convulsions** can and do occur thousands of miles from plate edges. One of the strongest series of earthquakes ever felt in North America **bludgeoned** New Madrid, Missouri, in 1811 and 1812. The area was sparsely settled, so few lives were lost.

"Can We Predict Quakes?," Thomas Y. Canby, *National Geographic* (June 1976)

Vocabulary Word.....................................

Context Clue.....................................

Probable Meaning.....................................

Dictionary Definition.....................................

Vocabulary Word.....................................

Context Clue.....................................

Probable Meaning.....................................

Dictionary Definition.....................................

Vocabulary Word.....................................

Context Clue.....................................

Probable Meaning.....................................

Dictionary Definition.....................................

B. *Look in a dictionary for meanings of each of the following verbs and for all the related forms of the verb you can find. Make a four-column list headed "verbs, nouns, adjectives, and adverbs."*

1. to avail
2. to condense
3. to conduct
4. to administer
5. to determine
6. to refer

Composition: Show What You Have Learned

Choose a composition topic from either Group I or Group II.

GROUP I: TOPICS FOR WRITING A COMPARISON OR CONTRAST

Since comparison has been the chief emphasis in this chapter, let's begin the writing assignment with a comparison: like some space missiles, this week's composition assignment consists of two stages. The first stage, A., gives you some suggested materials for writing a contrastive composition on the subject of "misinformation" in the U.S.A. You may want to go beyond what is given below, though, to write about misinformation that is common in another country.

The second writing stage, B., asks you to develop a longer comparative or contrastive composition based on a central theme. Depending on the topic you choose, you may develop your paper either in pairs or in separate sections. Having recently seen how helpful examples can be, you will want to use them liberally, choosing them always with your purpose and audience in mind.

A. *Develop a contrastive composition based on what a term is generally thought to mean and what is actually true about it.*

Most cultures contain a number of common sayings and beliefs that are not really based on fact but, when examined, prove to be misinformation. The United States is no exception. Many familiar U.S.A. sayings have no basis in fact. These are some of the common misconceptions:

abacus: Though an abacus is thought to be exclusively Oriental, it actually was used extensively in ancient Greece and Rome. Today, it is common in restaurants and money-changing border offices in the U.S.S.R.

French fries: This misnamed delicacy originated in Belgium, not France.

Galileo: Many people erroneously believe that Galileo invented the telescope (it was actually invented in 1608 in Holland) and that he did physics experiments at the Leaning Tower of Pisa (he didn't).

Lightning never strikes twice: This familiar saying has no factual basis. Actually, just the opposite is true. Because it follows the path of least resistance, lightning is *likely* to strike twice in the same place.

Moth-eaten: Many people think that moths chew holes in woolen clothing, but in fact moths don't; their larvae do.

Owls: Though owls have the reputation for being able to see only at night, they can see perfectly well in the daytime. They prefer to hunt at night because they rely more on stealth than on speed and because their favorite prey, mice and rats, are more active at night.

Porcupines shoot their quills: They cannot. Porcupines may slap at a tormentor with their tails, dislodging some quills in the process. But they cannot propel their quills through the air.

Still water runs deep: Here's another favorite U.S.A. expression that holds no water; still water doesn't run at all.

B. *Choose one of the following as your central theme for a composition primarily developed by comparison or contrast. Use examples liberally.*

1. The temperaments of two friends of yours.
2. Two ways to lose weight.
3. Two holiday resorts.

4. Two jobs you have held.
5. Family structure in two countries.
6. Two sports' personalities.
7. The same subject taught in high school and in college.
8. Life on the farm and life in the city.
9. Two public figures who serve humanity in different ways.
10. Two modes of travel.
11. Two cultures.
12. The teaching approach of two instructors or former teachers.
13. One college that is coeducational and one that is not.
14. Two ways to quit smoking.
15. Two family members with different value systems.

GROUP II: TO CHALLENGE YOUR IMAGINATION

Garry B. Trudeau, the artist who creates *Doonesbury* cartoons (one of which is on page 192), is not only a cartoonist. He is a social critic who artfully reflects the U.S.A. political and cultural scene. In *Time* Magazine, 9 February 1976, a writer said, "*Doonesbury* is more than mindless mirth. It is a climate of opinion, a mocking view of American life." As such, it has been read with considerable interest in top-level offices at Washington's White House. In 1976 President Ford said, "There are only three major vehicles to keep us informed as to what is going on in Washington—the electronic media, the print media, and *Doonesbury*, and not necessarily in that order."

Trudeau first produced cartoons for the Yale University campus news paper in 1968. (The title *Doonesbury* is a combination of two words: "doone," an old preparatory school term for someone who is out to lunch, and "Pillsbury," the name of Trudeau's Yale roommate, Charles Pillsbury, a flour-fortune heir.) Now his creation appears in over 450 newspapers and is read by 60 million people in the United States and Canada. Books of *Doonesbury* cartoons have sold over a million copies. In 1975 Trudeau was the first comic-strip artist to receive the Pulitzer Prize for editorial cartooning.

The following composition topics are based on the Trudeau cartoon strip. When possible, develop your composition through comparison or contrast, adding examples frequently:

1. Does the "generation gap" exist in your culture? Explain.
2. How is this *Doonesbury* cartoon a good example of irony?
3. What is an "analogy"? Is this statement of Mark's father a good analogy: "You know, you kids do the same thing to your bluejeans that you've done to the whole fabric of our national life!"?
4. Which values of the younger generation in the United States have most surprised you? Shocked you? Disappointed you? Pleased you?

Copyright, 1973, G. B. Trudeau / Distributed by Universal Press Syndicate.

5. In the United States, in what ways do you think the younger generation most misunderstands the older generation? In what ways does the older generation most misunderstand the younger generation?
6. Discuss the questions in number 5 in relation to your own country.

Chapter **7**

The
Expositry
Composition

*(Developed by
Cause and Effect)*

A Scientific Experiment

Recently an American manufacturer developed a scientific demonstrator named "The Swinging Wonder."

**Subordination by
participial phrase** **Intended for use in schools as an aid in understanding certain principles of physics or in the home as an educational toy,** this small demonstrator quickly became an object of fascination for both science teacher and layman. The purpose of this device is to demonstrate Sir Isaac Newton's third law of motion, in which he states that action and reaction are always equal and opposite.

Simile In its appearance the Swinging Wonder is a **boxlike** open wooden framework approximately ten inches square. Five lengths of strong string are attached to both the front and back top rails of the framework. Each piece of string hangs downward in a "V" shape, with a small steel ball attached at the base of the "V."

**Subordination by
prepositional phrase** **At rest** the five steel balls hang in an even row in which each ball touches the one beside it. The steel balls are suspended about two inches above the base of the framework.

Much of the effectiveness of the demonstrator comes from its simplicity.

**Subordination by
infinitive phrase** **To operate it** an experimenter may begin by **lifting the steel ball** at the extreme left of the

193

Parallelism

Subordination by
adverb clause

Transition

Compound predicate

Subordination by
participial phrase

Transition

Series of transitions

Subordinaton by
appositive

Subordination by
adjective clause

Transition
Parallelism

row of balls, **raising it** out beyond the side of the framework, and then **releasing it** so that it returns to strike the remaining four steel balls still hanging motionless in a row. **When this happens,** the released steel ball will stop in its original place at the left end of the row, and the corresponding[1] ball on the extreme right end of the row will automatically swing out and up for a distance equal to that to which the first ball had risen. **Next,** the experimenter **may grasp** the two steel balls at the left end of the row, **lift** them out to the side as he had done the first time, and **release** them together. Now they will return to place, **striking the row of balls and causing the two corresponding steel balls on the right hand side to swing out because of the transfer of momentum.** If three or four balls are raised on either side and let go, the same thing will happen. Three or four balls will detach themselves from the line of steel balls after it has been struck by the equal number of balls that have been raised and released. **Again,** the reacting balls will travel the same distance on the one side as you have lifted the balls on the other side.

An explanation for this phenomenon[2] can be expressed in five parts. **First,** when a steel ball is lifted, it is given energy. **Second,** when a ball is released, its energy is transformed into a type of motion called kinetic energy. **Third,** this energy of motion, **or kinetic energy,** is never truly conserved, being dissipated[3] by inefficiency in the system. **Fourth,** in addition to kinetic energy, a moving body also has momentum, **which is defined as the product of the mass[4] and its velocity.[5] Fifth,** unlike kinetic energy, momentum must be truly conserved and is not lost.

When the kinetic energy of the inelastic[6] balls is imparted[7] by impulse to other inelastic balls, the momentum of the first ball is transferred to the second. In order for the same momentum and nearly the same kinetic energy to be conserved, **however, the speed and mass of the balls traveling after the impact** must be nearly equal to **the speed and mass of those balls moving before the impact.**

[1]*corresponding:* similar in character or function. [2]*phenomenon:* unusual occurrence, something visible or directly observable. [3]*dissipated:* dispersed, dispelled, wasted. [4]*mass:* volume or magnitude of a solid body, size. [5]*velocity:* speed. [6]*inelastic:* inflexible. [7]*imparted:* bestowed upon, transmitted.

Writing Analysis

SYNONYMS AS TRANSITIONS

You have seen in Word Clues of each chapter that synonyms can be useful in pinning down the meaning of an unfamiliar word. Synonyms also serve another function in a paragraph; they act as transitions, moving the idea along from one sentence to another. Following are two sentences taken from a selection (Stephen Shafer's *Introduction to Criminology*) that appears in longer form later in this chapter (see page 200). In the following sentences a synonym is used as a transition:

> A **myth** suggests that both the poor and the wealthy are criminals, or at least potential lawbreakers, because the poor are pressed to crime by their poverty, and because the latter could hardly have gained their possessions with honesty and constructive work. This **fiction,** however, seems to be fading out gradually.

The word "fiction," a synonym for "myth," combines with the pronoun "this" to move the reader easily from the first long, rather complicated sentence to the second sentence.

As your English vocabulary grows, you will be in a better position to use synonyms as transitions. The following exercise will help you develop a feeling for this important expository technique.

EXERCISE 45
Synonyms as Transitions

Following is a list of words with their synonyms. Choose ten pairs of words. Write two sentences for each pair, the first sentence using the word, the second using its synonym as a transition.

	WORD	SYNONYM
1.	teacher	instructor
2.	plan	scheme
3.	remedy	cure
4.	economy	thriftiness
5.	weakness	frailty
6.	permanent	durable
7.	disagreement	dissension
8.	speed	velocity
9.	trip	journey
10.	darkness	obscurity
11.	slowness	sluggishness
12.	prediction	forecast
13.	disease	infirmity

WORD	SYNONYM
14. justice	fairness
15. duty	obligation
16. fear	terror
17. wealth	opulence
18. predicament	plight
19. danger	hazard
20. description	account

EXPOSITORY DEVELOPMENT (by cause and effect)

Unlike your process paragraph for Chapter 2, which told **how** something is done, analysis by cause and effect tries to explain **why.** Causal analysis is particularly well suited for writing about scientific subjects, as this chapter's model paragraph illustrates. But its usefulness as a mode of development extends far beyond the science classroom into every area of expository composition. A history student may be asked to write about the causes of World War I; a student of psychology may have to respond to an essay test question about the effects on a prisoner of war of prolonged internment; literature students may have to write term papers on the causes and effects of the rise of romanticism in English literature. Nor is causal analysis important only in schools, colleges, and universities. Professional and business men often adapt cause and effect to their affairs. It is essential, for instance, to a doctor diagnosing an illness, to a lawyer defending a client in the courtroom, to a businessman organizing a sales campaign. But our present concern with cause and effect centers upon its usefulness to the student writer.

Cause can be defined most concisely as that by which an effect is produced. Some causes are **immediate.** They can be discovered without much effort because they occur close in time to the effect produced. An example of an immediate cause is a broken gas line that causes an explosion and a subsequent apartment house fire. Other causes may be more **remote** and thus more difficult to uncover; these are the basic, underlying factors that help to explain the more obvious ones. The reason for the gas line breaking, for example, might have been that, several years earlier, a manufacturer supplied defective pipe to the apartment builder. Thus the remote cause for the apartment house fire would be the action of the careless or dishonest manufacturer.

How extensively you trace both immediate and remote causes and effects will depend on two factors: (1) The nature of your subject; (2) The audience you are writing to. Sometimes writers of causal analysis will tend to stress cause; at other times, they may place the chief emphasis upon effect. Later, in this chapter's examples of causal development, the selections from Jeans and Cousins discuss cause in considerable depth, and the model paragraph gives equal attention to both cause and effect. No matter what the balance, however, cause and effect must be considered as a single method. One is incomplete without the other.

In dealing with cause and effect, writers can commit certain fallacies of reasoning that should be guarded against:

1. Avoid assuming that something happening in connection with or after another incident is necessarily evidence of a causal relationship. For example, hearing a loud explosion after having seen a jet plane streak by may or may not mean that the noise is sonic boom. Nor does a rough-riding automobile necessarily mean that the car has a flat tire; the road might be uneven.
2. Consider all possibly relevant factors before settling on a cause. Perhaps a marriage failed because of the husband's short temper. But his being "difficult to live with" may itself be the result of his wife's extravagant ways. Sorting out possible causes is one of the writer's touchiest jobs.
3. Never omit any links in the chain of causes unless you are sure the audience you are writing to will automatically make the right connection— something you can rarely count on happening. It is much safer to detail carefully the network of causes that lead to an effect.
4. Try to be clear-minded, honest, and objective in your reasoning. Leave old prejudices behind when dealing with causal analysis. Equally important, open your mind to the probability of **multiple** causes and effects. Unless you take the complexity of causal analysis into consideration, your analysis could become embarrassingly shallow.

Normally, a writer approaching casual analysis works logically from the immediate cause (or effect) down to the most remote. Or he may start with the basic cause and work up to the immediate. Once you have sifted the subject through your mind, the most appropriate method of development will probably suggest itself.

When writing your causal analysis, make a conscious effort to support your assertions with **evidence.** Such evidence may include quotations from authoritative texts, statistics, or testimony of reliable experts in a field of study. Examples are as important in causal analysis as they are in other modes of development.

Look now at a scientific explanation whose development is similar in some ways to that of the model paragraph. This passage was written by a British scientist, Sir James Jeans, who presents the reason for the sky's color being blue:

Imagine that we stand on any ordinary seaside pier, and watch the waves rolling in and striking against the iron columns of the pier. Large waves pay very little attention to the columns—they divide right and left and reunite after passing each column, much as a regiment of soldiers would if a tree stood in their road; it is almost as though the columns had not been there. But the short waves and ripples find the columns of the pier a much more formidable obstacle. When the short waves impinge on[1] the columns . . . they are "scattered." The obstacle provided by the iron columns hardly affects the long waves at all but scatters the short ripples.

We have been watching a sort of working model of the way in which sunlight struggles through the earth's atmosphere. Between us on earth and outer space, the atmosphere interposes[2] innumerable obstacles in the form of air, tiny droplets of water, and small particles of dust. These are represented by the columns of the pier.

The waves of the sea represent the sunlight. We know that sunlight is a blend of lights of many colors—as we can prove for ourselves by passing it through a prism,[3] or even through a jug of water, or as Nature demonstrates to us when she passes it through the raindrops of a summer shower and produces a rainbow. We also know that light consists of waves, and that the different colors of light are produced by waves of different lengths, red light by long waves and blue light by short waves. The mixture of waves which constitutes[4] sunlight has to struggle through the obstacles it meets in the atmosphere, just as the mixture of waves of the seaside has to struggle past the columns of the pier. And these obstacles treat the light waves much as the columns of the pier treat the sea waves. The short waves which constitute blue light are scattered in all directions.

Thus, the different constituents[5] of sunlight are treated in different ways as they struggle through the earth's atmosphere. A wave of blue light may be scattered by a dust particle and turn out of its course. After a time a second dust particle again turns it out of its course, and so on, until it finally enters our eyes by a path as zigzag[6] as that of a flash of lightning. Consequently that is why the sky looks blue.

"Why the Sky Looks Blue," Sir James Jeans

[1]*impinge on:* strike, encroach upon. [2]*interposes:* causes to come between. [3]*prism:* instrument used to produce a spectrum or to refract light beams. [4]*constitutes:* makes up, composes. [5]*constituents:* necessary parts or elements. [6]*zigzag:* series of short, sharp turns or angles from one side to the other.

Cause and effect development here is supported by other methods of development. In Chapter 6 you studied the comparative technique of analogy, through which a person, object, or idea is explained more clearly by relating it to something it resembles. Notice in the above example that analogy is vital to the development of Jeans' causal analysis of the color of the sky. Relating the light waves of the sun to the waves of the sea, he simplifies and clarifies a rather complicated subject, avoiding the need for much technical vocabulary. The heart of his analogy is expressed in this sentence: "The mixture of waves which constitutes sunlight has to struggle through the obstacles it meets in the atmosphere, just as the mixture of waves of the seaside has to struggle past the columns of the pier." Another helpful point in this explanation is the author's use of example—the rainbow.

Following World War II, the British writer Dame Rebecca West wrote a brilliant book, *The Meaning of Treason,* in which she examined the causes of two prominent Britons having become traitors. The result of their treason was their trial and conviction by the state. Dame Rebecca is one of the great contemporary English prose stylists. As you read this short selection, notice that she uses words almost musically. If you closely analyze her writing, you will see that she relies on many of the techniques you are studying in this book: subtle changes in sentence structure and length, parallelism, subordination, transitions, figurative language, and word economy. Perhaps most interesting of all is that, though she is among the most sophisticated of writers, Dame Rebecca expresses herself *simply:*

The relationship between a man and a fatherland is always disturbed by conflict if either man or fatherland is highly developed. A man's demands for liberty at some point challenge the limitations the state imposes on the individual for the sake of the mass. If he is to carry on the national tradition, he must wrestle with those who, speaking in its name, desire to crystallize[1] it at the point reached by the previous generation. In any case national life itself must frequently exasperate[2] him because it is the medium in which he is expressing himself, and every craftsman or artist is repelled by the resistance of his medium to his will. All men should have a drop or two of treason in their veins, if the nations are not to go soft like so many sleepy pears. Yet to be a traitor is most miserable. All the men described in this book were sad as they stood their trials, not only because they were going to be punished. They would have been sad even if they had never been brought to justice. They had forsaken the familiar medium; they had trusted themselves to the mercies of those who had no reason to care for them; knowing their custodians'[3] indifference, they had lived for long in fear; and they were aware that they had thrown away their claim on those who might naturally have felt affection for them. Strangers, as King Solomon put it, were filled with their wealth, and their labors were in the house of a stranger, and they mourned at the last when their flesh and body were consumed. As a divorce sharply recalls what a happy marriage should be, so the treachery of these men recall what a nation should be; a shelter where all talents are generously recognized, all forgivable oddities forgiven, all viciousness quietly frustrated, and those who lack talent honored for equivalent[4] contributions of graciousness. Each of these men was as dependent of the good opinion of others as one is oneself; they needed a nation which was also a hearth.[5] It was sad to see them, chilled to the bone of their souls, because the intellectual leaders of their time had professed a philosophy which was scarcely more than a lapse of memory, and had forgotten, among much else, that a hearth gives out warmth.

"Man and the State," Dame Rebecca West, *The Meaning of Treason*

[1]*crystallize:* take on a definite form. [2]*exasperate:* irritate or very much annoy. [3]*custodian:* person who has the care of something. [4]*equivalent:* equal. [5]*hearth:* stone or brick floor of a fireplace, often extending out into a room.

In her first few sentences, Rebecca West points out some facts that may *cause* men to betray their country. Toward the middle of the passage, she shifts into talking of the *results* of treason; the key transitional sentence is, "Yet to be a traitor is most miserable." In her concluding sentences, she returns to causes, summarizing those conditions that, had they existed, might have eliminated any cause for a man to become a traitor.

A writer dealing with the subject of criminology often needs to present his material in terms of cause and effect. The purpose of the next short passage is to convince the reader that neither being poor nor gaining extreme wealth causes people to become criminals:

> A myth[1] suggests that both the poor and the wealthy are criminals, or at least potential lawbreakers, because the poor are pressed to crime by their poverty, and because the latter could hardly have gained their possessions with honesty and constructive work. This fiction, however, seems to be fading out gradually. It is becoming more strongly recognized that poverty *per se*[2] is not a cause of crime. A series of concentration camp, prison, and slum experiences indicate that there are millions of people with the necessary courage, fortitude,[3] honesty, and moral stamina[4] who would "rather starve than steal." At the same time, there is evidence that a great many wealthy persons accumulated their abundant riches without having been racketeers or white-collar criminals and generously share a part of their assets with socially worthy causes. Although the statistical truth shows that the poor dominate the volume of crime, not all the poor appear in these statistics. Although it is an almost common belief among the nonwealthy that the rich man has piled up his possessions through fraudulent[5] or other immoral crime-avoiding ways and that only his criminal skill or economic power enabled him to avoid accusation or conviction, most often only suspicion is available to fortify[6] these thoughts.
>
> "Myths about Crime," Stephen Shafer, *Introduction to Criminology*

> [1]*myth:* untrue account. [2]*per se:* by (or in) itself. [3]*fortitude:* strength to bear misfortune calmly and patiently. [4]*stamina:* endurance. [5]*fraudulent:* deceitful. [6]*fortify:* make strong.

Two transitional methods are used in this paragraph to help the reader follow the cause/effect thought line. The first is the pronoun "this" opening the second sentence; the second is the phrase "at the same time," signaling about halfway through the piece that the writer has finished discussing the poor and is moving on to talk about the rich. Finally, Shafer uses a parallel pair of adverb clauses opening with the same adverb, "although," to state his double conclusion—first for the poor, then for the rich.

Looking at the nature of these conclusions, do you find the writer's two arguments convincing? That is, do you think that "not all the poor appear in these statistics" proves that the poor are not necessarily criminals? Do you agree that "most often only suspicion is available" to support the idea that many wealthy people have gained their wealth through criminal means?

Analogy appears again with causal analysis in the final essay on the subject of man's survival in the nuclear age. Written by the American editor Norman Cousins, the article is essentially an argument developed by cause and effect:

It is a curious phenomenon of nature that only two species practice the art of war—men and ants, both of which, significantly, maintain complex social organizations. This does not mean that only men and ants engage in the murder of their own kind. Many animals of the same species kill each other, but only men and ants have practiced the science of organized destruction, employing their massed numbers in violent combat and relying on strategy and tactics to meet developing situations or to capitalize on[1] the weaknesses in the strategy and tactics of the other side. The longest continuous war ever fought between men lasted thirty years. The longest ant war ever recorded lasted six-and-a-half weeks, or whatever the corresponding units would be in ant reckoning.[2]

While all entomologists[3] are agreed that war is instinctive with ants, it is encouraging to note that not all anthropologists and biologists are agreed that war is instinctive with men. Those who lean on[4] experience, of course, find everything in man's history to indicate that war is locked up within his nature. But a broader and more generous, certainly more philosophical, view is held by those scientists who claim that the evidence of a war instinct in men is incomplete and misleading, and that man *does* have within him the power of abolishing war. Julian Huxley, the English biologist, draws a sharp distinction between human nature and the *expression* of human nature. Thus war is not a reflection but an expression of man's nature. Moreover, the expression may change, as the factors which lead to war may change. "In man, as in ants, war in any serious sense is bound up with the existence of accumulations of property to fight about. . . . As for human nature, it contains no specific war instinct, as does the nature of harvester ants. There is in man's makeup a general aggressive tendency, but this, like all other human urges, is not a specific and unvarying instinct; it can be molded into the most varied forms."

But even if this gives us a reassuring answer to the question—is war inevitable[5] because of man's nature?—it still leaves unanswered the question concerning the causes leading up to war. The expression of man's nature will continue to be warlike if the same conditions are continued that have provoked warlike expressions in him in the past. And since man's survival on earth is now absolutely dependent on his ability to avoid a new war, he is faced with the so-far insoluble[6] problem of eliminating those causes.

In the most primitive sense, war in man is an expression of his extreme

[1]*capitalize on:* take advantage of. [2]*reckoning:* act of counting. [3]*entomologists:* zooligists specializing in the study of insects. [4]*lean on:* reason from. [5]*inevitable:* certain, unable to be avoided. [6]*insoluble:* incapable of being solved. [7]*gave*

competitive impulses. Like everything else in nature, he has had to fight for existence; but the battle against other animals, once won, gave way[7] in his evolution to battle against his own kind. Darwin called it natural selection; Spencer called it the survival of the fittest; and its most over-stretched interpretation is to be found in *Mein Kampf*, with its naked glorification of brute force and the complete worship of might makes right. In the political and national sense, it has been the attempt of the "have-nots" to take from the "haves," or the attempt of the "haves" to add further to their lot at the expense of the "have-nots." Not always was property at stake; comparative advantages were measured in terms of power, and in terms of tribal or national superiority. The good luck of one nation became the hard luck of another. The good fortune of the Western powers in obtaining "concessions" in China at the turn of the century was the ill fortune of the Chinese. The power that Germany stripped from Austria, Czechoslovakia, Poland, and France at the beginning of World War II she added to her own.

What does it matter, then, if war is not the nature of man so long as man continues through the expression of his nature to be a viciously competitive animal? The effect is the same, and therefore the result must be as conclusive—war being the effect, and complete obliteration[8] of the human species being the ultimate result.

If this reasoning is correct, then modern man is obsolete,[9] a self-made anachronism[10] becoming more incongruous[11] by the minute. He has exalted[12] change in everything but himself. He has leaped centuries ahead in inventing a new world to live in, but he knows little or nothing about his own part in that world. He has surrounded and confounded[13] himself with gaps—gaps between revolutionary technology and evolutionary man, between cosmic gadgets and human wisdom, between intellect and conscience. The struggle between science and morals that Henry Thomas Buckle foresaw a century ago has been all but won by Science.

Given ample time, man might be expected eventually to span those gaps normally; but by his own hand he is destroying even time. Decision and execution[14] in the modern world are becoming virtually synchronous.[15] Thus whatever gaps man has to span he will have to span immediately.

This involves both biology and will. If he lacks the actual and potential biological equipment to build those bridges, then the birth certificate of the atomic age is in reality a *memento mori*.[16] But even if he possesses the necessary biological equipment, he must still make the decision which says that he is to apply himself to the challenge. Capability without decision is inaction and inconsequence.

Man is left, then, with a crisis in decision. The main test before him involves his *will* to change rather than his *ability* to change. That he is

way: changed. [8]*obliteration:* total destruction. [9]*obsolete:* out-of-date, out-moded. [10]*anachronism:* something out of its proper time. [11]*incongruous:* not suited to the circumstances, out of place. [12]*exalted:* intensified, heightened. [13]*confounded:* confused. [14]*execution:* accomplishment, fulfillment. [15]*synchro-*

capable of change is certain. For there is no more mutable[17] or adaptable animal in the world. We have seen him migrate from one extreme clime to another. We have seen him step out of backward societies and join advanced groups within the space of a single generation. This is not to imply that the changes were necessarily always for the better; only that change was and is possible. But change requires stimulus; and mankind today need look no further for stimulus than its own desire to stay alive. The critical power of change, says Spengler, is directly linked to the the survival drive. Once the instinct for survival is stimulated, the basic condition for change can be met.

That is why the power of total destruction as potentially represented by modern science must be dramatized and kept in the forefront of public opinion. The full dimensions of the peril must be seen and recognized. Only then will man realize that the first order of business is the question of continued existence. Only then will he be prepared to make the decisions necessary to assure that survival.

"Survival Is Yet Possible," Norman Cousins

nous: occurring at the same time. [16]*memento mori:* reminder of death. [17]*mutable:* capable of or subject to change.

Cousins carefully develops the analogy between men and ants throughout his first two paragraphs to establish the background for his discussion of the causes of war. By contrasting the war instinct of the ant with the lack of such an instinct in man, Cousins first eliminates one of the possible causes for human wars. Thus he is able to focus on the central problem: whether man can develop the will to suppress his "viciously competitive" behavior. Cause and effect development is notably used in the fifth paragraph to help the writer express his main point. Here Cousins says that, although man's war instinct is not the cause of war, his unbridled competitive impulse *is* the cause; and the ultimate result may be the extinction of the human species.

EXERCISE 46
Outlining

First review the section in Chapter 5 on "The Composition Outline." Then reconstruct the outline the writer probably worked from in composing the model composition, "A Scientific Experiment."

WRITING AN INTRODUCTION

An opening paragraph has at least two important purposes. First, it normally announces the writer's central topic and identifies his controlling idea. Second, it often contains some eye-catching information or an unexpected approach that will stimulate the reader to continue reading. The type of introduction that you select will be determined by several things. One of these is the tone (see page 303) of your paper—that is, whether it is serious, satirical, and so forth. Your choice of introduction will also depend on the nature of your material and the type of audience you are writing for; a writer reveals his taste and judgment in selecting an appropriate beginning. Of course, the length of an introduction should be in proportion to the overall length of the composition it appears in. Most important, the content of an introduction should be closely related to the writer's thesis statement.

When you are choosing a way to begin a composition, you have something in common with a fisherman. For just as a fisherman puts appetizing bait on his hook in order to attract fish to bite, so you will try in the beginning of your paper to interest your reader in following your written thoughts through to their conclusion. You do have an advantage over the fisherman, though. You have a wider variety of "bait" to select from. Here are some of the most frequently used possibilities for beginning compositions:

1. Thesis statement
2. Brief narration or description
3. Anecdote
4. Explanation of a writer's experience with a subject
5. Startling fact
6. Definition of terms
7. Statistics
8. Vivid contrast
9. Background information
10. Rhetorical question
11. Introduction of a person
12. Quotation
13. Historical detail
14. Humor
15. Figurative language

1. Thesis statement

Because expository writing can never be too clear, one of the surest ways to begin a composition is to place your thesis statement in the first paragraph. In the first example, the writer leaves little doubt that he is taking a firm stand against the threatening supremacy of machines over man. In the second example, the thesis is equally direct and, as in the earlier example, expressed in the final sentence: "new foods . . . are often costly, in terms of both dollars and, ultimately, health."

(In an article about computers):

The uneasy, half-embarrassed rivalry between man and machine has reached a peak with the thinking machine. We have become used to machines that are more powerful, more durable, more accurate, and faster than we are, but machines that challenge our intelligence are hard to take. At this point the competition becomes uncomfortable.

"The Thinking of Men and Machines," John H. Troll, *The Atlantic Monthly*

(In an article about nutrition):

If the bromide,[1] "You are what you eat," is true, we could all end up being very different people from our ancestors. Modern science and agriculture have freed the United States and many other nations from traditional diets based largely on natural farm products. New varieties of crops, transcontinental shipping, a wide spectrum of food additives, and new food-processing techniques have led, for better or worse, to diets different from any previously consumed by human populations. But these dietary changes reflect the decisions of business executives and investors, rather than nutritionists and public health officials. . . . Many of the new foods do save us time and trouble, but they are often costly, in terms of both dollars and, ultimately, health.

"Our Diets Have Changed, but Not for the Best," Michael Jacobson, *Smithsonian* (April 1975)

[1]*bromide:* trite statement.

2. Brief narration or description

Using a brief narrative or descriptive passage as an introduction eases the reader into the main body of the composition, establishing some background and setting the mood for what is to come. Here is a particularly dramatic narrative opening.

(In a book telling of the discovery of gold in California in 1849):

A January morning, crisp and clear. The sawmill foreman was up early. He was a loner—moody, and hard to get along with. But he was a good builder, anxious to complete the new structure. While his men dallied over breakfast, he was already busy down at the river. Each day the men cut the mill race ditch deeper, and each night the foreman let the river rush through it to sweep away the debris. Soon the current would be strong enough to power saws. James Marshall closed the sluice gate and waded down the drained, muddy ditch, checking its depth. Then something caught his eye. Stooping, he reached into the shallow water. What he found changed the course of American history.

Ghost Towns of the West, Sunset Books

3. Anecdote

Few readers ever outgrow their childhood pleasure of being told stories. A brief humorous experience or joke recounted in an opening paragraph can capitalize on this and whet a reader's interest in what is to come. Notice that both of the anecdotal openings below end with a statement of the essay's central idea. In the first example, the statement is direct: the paper will deal with a philosophical problem. In the second example, the statement is indirect. "You can get out of my light" is Jarrell's way of saying, "Give American intellectuals more breathing room."

(In a paper about philosophy):

When Gertrude Stein lay dying in Paris, her friend Alice B. Toklas leaned over her bed and whispered this question into her ear: "Gertrude, what is the answer?" Smiling weakly, Miss Stein turned to her and replied, "Alice, what is the question?" Seldom has the problem facing philosophers been more concisely stated.

(In an essay about the value of the intellectual in America):

The philosopher Diogenes lived in a tub in the market place. He owned the clothes on his back and a wooden cup; one morning, when he saw a man drinking out of his hands, he threw away the cup. Alexander the Great came to Athens and went down to the market place to see Diogenes; as he was about to leave, he asked, "Is there anything I can do for you?" "Yes," said Diogenes, "you can get out of my light."

"The Intellectual in America," Randall Jarrell, *Mademoiselle* (January 1955)

4. Explanation of a writer's experience with the subject

Sometimes a writer feels the need to establish his authority on a subject, particularly if the subject is a difficult or abstruse one. One of the best ways to do this is to open an essay by explaining his experiences with it.

(In an essay about writing):

During my years as an editor, I have seen probably hundreds of job applicants who were either just out of college or in their senior year. All wanted "to write." Many brought letters from their teachers. But I do not recall one letter announcing that its bearer could write what he wished to say with clarity, directness, and economy.

"How to Write Like a Social Scientist," Samuel T. Williamson, *The Saturday Review*

5. Startling fact

Perhaps you have seen a motion picture or a television show that immediately caught your interest because it opened with a startling scene. A composition beginning with a startling fact can do the same thing. The first example introduces a discussion of marriage and divorce with a surprising revelation. In the second example, the writer has chosen to open his article on Morocco with a short, realistic street episode that may capture the reader's attention through its shock effect.

(In a paper about American marriage):

Of every four couples who marry in the United States, one couple will seek a divorce. Consider what effect this high divorce rate seems to be having on society.

(In an essay on Morocco):

As the corpse went past, the flies left the restaurant table in a cloud and rushed after it, but they came back a few minutes later.

"Marrakech," George Orwell, *Such, Such Were the Joys*

6. Definition of terms

Often a writer may need to define essential terms before launching into the main development of his composition. In the example that follows, it was necessary to tell the reader what a fraction is before telling him how to work with fractions.

(In a college mathematics textbook):

Fractions are also numerals. In the same way that the Hindu–Arabic numeral 50 names the number of states in the United States, the numerals, $\frac{1}{2}$, $\frac{2}{4}$, $\frac{3}{6}$, $\frac{10}{20}$, are four equivalent names for the number that is exactly midway in value between 0 and 1. Although our language is often loose on this point, a fraction is actually a three-part symbol consisting of two numerals and a bar or mark between them. The numeral above the bar is called the *numerator,* and the numeral below the bar is called the *denominator.* Thus $\frac{1}{2}$, $\frac{3}{4}$, $\frac{5}{2}$ are fractions, as are $\pi/3$, x/y, and $2/\sqrt{5}$. In arithmetic we are concerned primarily with numbers whose fraction names can be expressed by whole-number numerators and whole-number denominators. Such numbers belong to a set of numbers called the *rationals.*

Francis J. Mueller, *Essential Mathematics for College Students,* 3d ed.

7. Statistics

Beginning a composition with statistics is a good way to gain the reader's confidence; specific figures tend to establish the writer as an authority on the subject, or at least as someone who knows what research is all about. Though useful in general writing, as in the first example, statistics are the lifeblood of scientific and technical writing, as the second example illustrates.

(In a paper about education in England):

The fact that less than 5 percent of the British population graduate from universities may seem surprising, especially when viewed beside the American percentage of over 30 percent. To understand this contrast, one needs to consider social differences between the two countries, as well as differences in their theories of education.

(In an article on uranium prospecting):

Nuclear power plants, which currently provide about 9 percent of the electricity generated in the U.S., last year consumed some 12,700 short tons of processed natural uranium ore (in the form of the oxide known as yellowcake, or U_3O_8). It is estimated that by 1985, when nuclear power is scheduled to account for perhaps a fourth of the total U.S. installed electric-generating capacity, the rate of consumption of fresh nuclear fuel will have reached at least 55,000 short tons of yellowcake per year (assuming that some of the spent fuel is by then being recycled in the form of reprocessed uranium and plutonium) or at most 62,000 short tons of yellowcake per year (assuming no recycling). And by the year 2000, when the nuclear share of the U.S. energy budget is expected to meet approximately half of the nation's electricity needs, the nuclear-fuel requirement is projected to reach anywhere from 127,000 to 164,000 short tons annually (again depending on the extent of recycling).

"Science and the Citizen," Scientific American (June 1976)

8. Vivid contrast

One way to give punch to an introduction is to put in it a strong contrast of facts or ideas. Although the first example does this more dramatically than the second, both use contrast to attract the reader.

(In an essay about existentialism):

Dostoevsky faced a firing squad but lived; Camus crashed his automobile into a tree by accident and died. Does man's experience with death prove the existentialist point that life has no pattern and no purpose?

(In an essay about the states of Washington and Oregon):

The Pacific Northwest coast is a land of contrasts. At times it is wild and wave-battered, at other times quiet and restful. All along its length there is variety: sandy beaches, steep headlands, lush pastures, rock coves, patches of deep forest. Industry is mostly lumbering and commercial fishing, but dairy farms and cheese factories spread out around Tillamook, cranberry bogs and oyster beds on the North Beach Peninsula, bulb fields near Brookings.

Travel Guide to Washington, Sunset Books

9. Background information

A no-nonsense way to begin a composition is to fill your first paragraph with necessary background material. The following example shows how this is done in a scientific article.

(In an article about photosynthesis):

Life on the earth is based on photosynthesis, through which the energy radiated by the sun is converted to drive the metabolic processes of living organisms. Only plants, some bacteria, and the blue-green algae are capable of photosynthesis because only they contain the critical chemical that captures the energy of light: chlorophyll. The absorption of light by chlorophyll initiates the transfer of electrons along a chain of other membrane-bound pigment molecules; the energy released in the course of electron transport is converted into the high-energy bonds of adenosine triphosphate (ATP), the primary energy carrier of living cells, and is made available for the synthesis of the earth's basic reserve of chemical energy in the form of starch, cellulose and free oxygen molecules.

"The Purple Membrane of Salt-Loving Bacteria," Walter Stoeckenius, *Scientific American* (June 1976)

10. Rhetorical question

What can a rhetorical question accomplish as an opener? One sure thing that it does is to make your reader think; he reads on to find the answer to the question you have raised. Test your own reaction by reading the two examples below.

(In a composition about art):

Do most people really know how to look at a painting? Many art critics, professors, historians, and even artists themselves would say no. The critic Bernard Berenson went as far as to say that people need a whole new set of responses to look at an art work with understanding. They have to be taught to look.

(In an article discussing the nature of time):

Why does time never go backward? The answer apparently lies not in the laws of nature, which hardly distinguish between past and future, but in the conditions prevailing in the early universe.

"The Arrow of Time," David Layzer, *Scientific American* (December 1975)

11. Introduction of a person

An often logical way to begin an article or book about a person is to introduce him. Observe how crisply and wittily the critic Brendan Gill introduces the subject of a biography, the American business magnate Henry Ford.

(In a book review):

One of the great subjects for biography is that spunky,[1] crotchety,[2] illiterate,[3] and wonderfully gifted maker of things, Henry Ford. Not to bring him to life, not to have the pages of a book about him crackle and spit with his ingenuities and perversities, is a writing feat of no mean proportions. This feat has just been accomplished by Alan Nevins, with the collaboration of Frank Ernest Hill. They have given their mound of baggage the baggagy[4] title of "Ford: The Times, the Man, the Company" (Scribner).

"Originals," Brendan Gill, *The New Yorker*

[1]*spunky:* courageous. [2]*crotchety:* full of eccentric or stubborn notions. [3]*illiterate:* unable to read and write. [4]*baggagy:* overloaded; ponderous.

12. Quotation

Like a rhetorical question, a quotation used to begin a composition catches the reader's attention. He becomes curious to know what is being said and who said it. An opening quotation should normally be related to the composition's thesis statement.

(In a composition about psychology):

"The proper study of mankind is Man," said Alexander Pope. Most psychologists have carried this idea further than Pope would have imagined.

(In an essay discussing man's responsibility to future generations):

"Will mankind survive?" Who knows? The question I want to put is more searching: Who cares? It is clear that most of us today do not care —or at least do not care enough. How many of us would be willing to give up some minor convenience—say, the use of aerosols—in the hope that this might extend the life of man on earth by a hundred years? Suppose we also knew with a high degree of certainty that humankind could not survive a thousand years unless we gave up our wasteful diet of meat, abandoned all pleasure driving, cut back on every use of energy that was not essential to the maintenance of a bare minimum. Would we care enough for posterity to pay the price of its survival?

> "What Has Posterity Ever Done for Me?," Robert L. Heilbroner,
> *New York Times Magazine* (19 January 1975)

13. Historical detail

When a writer wants to try a different approach to beginning a paper, he may decide to draw upon history. In the example that follows, the writer looks back to the 1960s:

(In an article about women's liberation):

Women's liberation formally began with the founding in 1966 of the National Organization for Women, which remains the largest and most influential movement group, the original umbrella under which other groups pressed their individual programs. Its membership has doubled to 18,000 in the past year; around 255 chapters now exist in [50] states. N.O.W. has led assaults in Congress and the courts on issues ranging from child care to abortion reform. Growing even faster is the National Women's Political Caucus, aimed at putting more levers of government power into female hands. . . . There is also the Women's Equity Action League, dedicated to pushing for equality via existing laws and executive orders.

> "Women's Liberation Revisited," *Time* (20 March 1972)

14. Humor

If your opening paragraph makes your reader smile, chuckle, or laugh, chances are he will still be reading by the time your conclusion rolls around. Notice the pleasing effect of the author's geniality in this example.

(In a book about California wines):

Vines, like humans, marry for better or for worse. California, afflicted with both phylloxera and nematodes, needs resistant rootstocks to carry its classic grapes. Some combinations work. Some do not. Some work in some conditions but not in others. Researchers are very busy at the mating game.

California Wine Country, Sunset Books

15. Figurative language

By using figurative language, a writer can often make an introduction more vivid than it otherwise might be. Here you see a metaphor at work. Providing a comparison between the actions of a sea otter and a carpenter is a fairly certain way to capture the reader's imagination.

(In an article about carpentry):

The sea otter uses an unusual dining tool. Swimming to the sea floor, he collects a clam and a small, hard stone. Then he uses the stone as a tool to crack the clam's shell on his chest while bobbing along the surface. Because a tiny one won't crack the shell, the otter is usually quite particular about the stone he chooses. Like the sea otter, the good carpenter knows that careful tool selection is the key to good carpentry.

Basic Carpentry Illustrated, Sunset Books

REVIEW OF WORDINESS

A first cousin to wordiness, first studied in Chapter 5, is **redundancy**—using more words than necessary to express an idea. Redundant words, phrases, or sentences merely repeat an already-stated idea in different words. Here are examples of some common redundancies: "~~still~~ continues," "continue ~~on~~," "~~still~~ retains," "~~still~~ remains," "climb ~~up~~ higher," "resumes ~~again~~."

Sometimes a redundancy is fairly obvious, as in the following sentence:

Archeologists have made meticulous, ~~painstaking~~ studies of the ruins.

But sometimes a redundant word is more subtle:

Stir ingredients in a ~~large,~~ 2 to 3-quart saucepan.

Now look at these 10 ways to eliminate redundancy and move toward word economy:

1. Avoid needless repetition.

Perhaps one of the most intriguing guides is an Italian professor who teaches ~~intriguing courses~~ at the University of Pisa in Italy.

2. Cut excess adjectives.

An ~~lively, colorful,~~ explosive fiesta . . .

3. Strike out redundant adverbs.

~~Slowly and~~ sluggishly, the river flows through the delta.

4. Compress adverb clauses into participial phrases.

~~Because they are~~ fond of travelers, the Balinese are magnificent hosts.

5. Delete prepositional phrases or shorten them to a possessive noun.

the world's richest nation ~~in the world~~
some ~~of the~~ celebrations feature . . .

6. Change relative clauses to participles.

          comprising
the countries ~~that comprise~~ . . .

7. Avoid weak sentence beginnings.

   About
~~Beginning some~~ twenty years ago . . .

8. Drop passive verbs.

We were invited . . .
~~The invitation was given to us~~ . . .

9. Delete unnecessary phrases.

~~of some kind; kind of; type of; a lot of; plenty of~~

10. Don't pontificate.

~~Specific dates are difficult to give because~~
The same festival may fall on different dates in different countries.
~~It would be wise to~~ check with the appropriate tourist office.

Finally, be alert to whole sentences that, because they are redundant, can be struck out:

> Ask yourself some questions. Coming up with a workable cabin design means careful consideration of one's expectations, lifestyle, and finances. Take as much time for planning as you can. ~~There is no such thing as "time wasted" when designing a shelter.~~

EXERCISE 47
Wordiness Review

Shorten the following sentences by removing any redundant elements.

1. The trip down the Nile still continues to be one of the Middle East's great travel experiences.
2. The Post Office noticed a large, substantial increase in mail at Christmas time.

3. Although the actress is middle-aged, she still retains the aura of youth.
4. Police made many fresh, renewed attempts to trace the stolen painting.
5. We ordered a kind of green vegetable to go with our main course of fish.
6. As they approached the summit of Mt. Rainier, the climbers felt that they had lost the energy to climb up any higher.
7. School resumes again on September 15.
8. Taiwan's National Museum of History in Taipei still remains one of the world's outstanding repositories of Chinese cultural treasures.
9. They wasted a lot of time trying to read the small print on the timetable.
10. After we had rested for a few days in Kyoto, we decided to continue on to Seoul.
11. The Australian clerk offered to show us a type of Aboriginal bark painting.
12. Since they are skilled in culinary art, Italians entertain at home with an unmistakable flair.
13. You can make exciting, fascinating discoveries on the islands that spread across the Mediterranean Sea.
14. The earthquakes in Peking are considered one of the most devastating, far-reaching natural disasters that has been known to the world's history.
15. Indications are that you will be well advised to avoid drinking the water in the villages of Guatemala.

Punctuation Points

USING THE APOSTROPHE

Three rules will help guide you to the correct use of the apostrophe:

1. **Use an apostrophe to show possession.** Unless a word ends in *s*, form the possessive of both singular and plural by adding *'s*.

SINGULAR	PLURAL
John's coat	children's games
the dog's collar	men's store
anybody's guess	people's choice

If a singular noun ends in *s*, add either *'s* or the apostrophe only, depending on the pronunciation:

the boss's son	Cummings' poems (or Cummings's)
Zeus's edict	Charles' throne (or Charles's)
Williams's plan	Dickens' novels (or Dickens's)

If a plural noun ends in *s*, add the apostrophe only:

citizens' rights	the Jones' car
witches' sabbath	the boys' bicycles

2. **Use an apostrophe to indicate the omission in contractions:**

He's gone. (He has gone.)
Who's there? (Who is there?)
It's time for dinner. (It is time for dinner.)
We *aren't* ready. (We are not ready.)

Some of the more common English contractions include *don't* (do not), *doesn't* (does not), *didn't* (did not), *I'm* (I am), *he's* (he is), *they're* (they are), *isn't* (is not), *aren't* (are not), *it's* (it is), and *let's* (let us). A frequently used irregular contraction is *won't* (will not).

In formal English writing contractions are rarely used; in informal writing, on the other hand, contractions are used almost as freely as in conversation. Ask your instructor if contractions are permissible in your writing.

3. **Use an apostrophe to form the plural of letters, figures, and words specified as words.** First italicize (underline) the element and then add a nonitalicized *'s.*

I will accept no *if's and's,* or *but's*; my decision is final.
Some people are superstitious about *13's*, but I worry whenever I see *9's* written out.
The only weakness in his handwriting is the way in which he forms his *f's*.

Dates are not italicized, and they are correctly made plural without an apostrophe.

Try to avoid two common errors in using the apostrophe:

1. Do not use the apostrophe to form the possessive of personal pronouns (*his, hers, its, ours, yours, theirs*) or of the relative or interrogative pronoun *whose*. Keep in mind the distinction between contractions and possessives:

CONTRACTIONS	POSSESSIVES
There's another key.	The trophy was theirs.
It's a clear day.	The horse lost its saddle.
Who's calling?	Whose camera is this?

2. Do not use the apostrophe in ordinary, nonpossessive plurals:

Wrong	The sailor's who want to go ashore for two day's must sign the roster in the cabin.
Correct	The sailors who want to go ashore for two days must sign the roster in the cabin.

EXERCISE 48
The Apostrophe

Write out the sentences, adding apostrophes whenever necessary.

1. The cows life was cut short because of Lewis poor driving.
2. Marsha wears dresses that were commonly worn in her grandmothers days—the 1930s.
3. My wife and daughters all take swimming lessons at the womens pool.
4. The horse showed its fear by running into the farmers barn.
5. Try another proprietors bookshop to see if he has the childrens story you are looking for.
6. The moons surface has many craters probably caused by falling meteorites.
7. The peoples faith in their leader was shaken when he declared, "Half a days pay for a full days work!"
8. His teacher said that Toms greatest problem in writing compositions was in using too many *ands*.
9. After you leave your friends house, remember to pick up your brothers books at school before five oclock.
10. Its time to decide whos going to cook dinner.

Grammar Skills

DANGLING ELEMENTS

A dangling element is a word or group of words that do not refer clearly and logically to some word in a sentence. Though a dangler can appear in any part of a sentence, it frequently occurs at a sentence's beginning.

There are four major kinds of danglers: (1) The participle (*Looking up at the sky*, the sun went under a cloud.); (2) The gerund (*By installing a birdbath*, the birds were given a source of water.); (3) The infinitive (*To ski properly*, a course of instruction is necessary.); (4) The elliptical clause (*While climbing the hill*, the rain began to fall.).

Introductory phrases like the ones in the preceding paragraph always refer to a sentence's subject. If, as in these sentences, the subject is *not* the one who is "looking," "installing," "skiing," or "climbing," then the phrase dangles. To eliminate this error, substitute the correct subject: (1) Looking up at the sky, **he** saw the sun go under a cloud.; (2) By installing a birdbath, **we** gave the birds a source of water.; (3) To ski properly **a beginner** should take a course of instruction.; (4) While climbing the hill, **she** felt the rain beginning to fall.

Dangling participle. Whether it stands alone or is part of a phrase, a participle dangles if the subject of a sentence is not the proper word for it to modify:

Dangling participle	*Reading,* the doorbell rang. **(Is the doorbell reading?)**
Corrected	Reading, **I** heard the doorbell ring
Dangling participle phrase	*Captured during the robbery,* the police questioned the suspect for hours. **(Were the police captured?)**
Corrected	*Captured during the robbery,* the **suspect** was questioned for hours by the police.

Dangling gerund. A gerund dangles when it is used in a phrase modifying the main verb and (1) when the agent doing the action is not named as the subject of the sentence, or (2) When the agent is not indicated by a possessive pronoun modifying the gerund:

Dangling gerund phrase	*From attending class,* the principles of chemistry were made clear.
Corrected by sentence subject	From attending class, **we** came to understand the principles of chemistry.
Corrected by possessive modifier	From **our** attending class, the principles of chemistry were made clear.

Dangling infinitive. When an infinitive begins a sentence as its subject— *To win* is our goal.—there is no dangling problem. But when an infinitive phrase opens a sentence, it will dangle if it refers to an inappropriate subject:

Dangling infinitive	*To apply,* an application form must be filled out.
Corrected	To apply, **you** must fill out an application form.
Dangling infinitive phrase	*To learn French cooking,* a lot of practice is necessary.
Corrected	To learn French cooking, **a student** needs a lot of practice.

Dangling elliptical clause. An elliptical clause will dangle if a writer does not make sure that the word it refers to is the subject of the main clause:

Dangling elliptical clause	*While running down the stairs,* the clock struck twelve.
Corrected	While running down the stairs, **I** heard the clock strike twelve.
Dangling elliptical clause	*Though tired from running,* our gym period ended with calisthenics.
Corrected	Though tired from running, **we** ended our gym period with calisthenics.

EXERCISE 49
Dangling Elements

A. Write out these sentences, eliminating dangling participles.

1. Making funny faces, the circus opened with the clowns.
2. Walking home from the movies, the street lights turned on.
3. Strung up on the Christmas tree, we were enchanted with the many-colored lights.
4. Impressed with his qualifications, Paul was hired by the printing firm.
5. Answering the telephone, no one was on the line.

B. Write out these sentences, eliminating dangling gerunds.

1. By leaning out the window, the full moon appeared in the sky.
2. From reading the timetable, no more trains were scheduled to depart today.
3. By comparing the plays of Marlowe and Shakespeare, Elizabethan literature can be better appreciated.
4. By studying throughout the night, the examination was passed.
5. From speaking with Giancarlo, the correct pronunciation of Italian was understood by the students.

C. Write out these sentences, eliminating dangling infinitives.

1. To plan your vacation, some books on Morocco should be read.
2. To start the car, the accelerator must be depressed twice.
3. To design the building, many consultants were hired by the architect.
4. To cross the bridge, the railing should be held on to.
5. To train for the Olympics, dieting was necessary for the athlete.

D. Write out these sentences, eliminating dangling elliptical clauses.

1. While studying chemistry, the barking dog disturbed me.
2. When crossing the Atlantic, a ship or plane may be taken.
3. Although unexpected, we found their visit to our home to be enjoyable.
4. When learning to spell English words, spelling rules should be memorized.
5. After working long hours, my bed was a welcome sight.

REVIEW OF SUBORDINATION

In Chapter 1 you studied various ways of subordinating one idea to another in sentences. You will remember that subordination clarifies the relationship between two ideas, thus adding to the coherence of your writing. Moreover, subordination often leads to greater economy in composition, permitting you to express yourself in the fewest possible words. Of course, the need for subordination depends both on the subject matter you are dealing with and on the context of a sentence within a paragraph. You would not often want to write a paragraph in which every sentence contained subordination. This would result in a monotonous style. Used wisely, however, subordination will help you to communicate better with your reader.

This chapter's model composition is virtually a case study of subordination serving a writer who has a complicated process to explain. In this case, no fewer than five adverb clauses, one adjective clause, two participial phrases, one infinitive phrase, one appositive, and five prepositional phrases have been used to subordinate ideas in sentences. Examples of each type of subordination are noted in the margin of the composition. Can you find the remaining examples of the same types of subordination in the model?

The following exercise will help you to review the various forms used in subordinating an idea:

EXERCISE 50
Subordination Review

Subordinate an idea in each of the sentences below in the ways indicated.

Subordinate by introductory adverb clauses (See explanation on page 21.)
1. They hoped to visit Indonesia, for they had heard that Bali was a paradise for travelers.
2. You reach the crossroads two miles from here, and you turn right to reach the ferry dock.
3. I want to graduate from college, but I hope to take a year off between my junior and senior years.
4. I took a course in gardening last fall, and my garden is bursting with blooms this summer.
5. The Lenten season arrives each spring, and there is a colorful festival in Viareggio.

Subordinate by adjective clauses (See explanation on page 23.)
6. George III was King of England during the American Revolution, and he was not in his right mind during the last ten years of his reign.
7. Isadora Duncan was a famous dancer in the 1920s, and she spent part of her career teaching in Russia.
8. American political conventions are lively affairs, and they take place every four years.
9. Television networks often change programs, and they are very competitive.
10. Julia Child has written a French cookbook, and she teaches French cooking on television.

Subordinate by prepositional phrases (See explanation on page 23.)
11. We took a trip over the holiday weekend; we went to Brighton.
12. The apartment building has several vacancies, and it is located on Wainaku Avenue.

13. The summer rainstorm quickly came and went; it happened on August 16.
14. We spent Sunday watching the new animals from Australia; they were in the zoo.
15. They left to pick up their new car, and it was at the automobile showroom on Van Ness Avenue.

Subordinate by participial phrases (See explanation on page 23.)
16. She opened the refrigerator, and she put the milk inside.
17. The actors were called onto the set, and they began to perform the scene.
18. Horticulturists have developed a new species of cucumber, and it is shaped like a lemon.
19. The Fredericks rented a condominium apartment on Maui for a week, and they sent a $50 deposit to confirm their reservation.
20. The patchwork quilt was made up of individual squares stitched by twenty different craftspeople, and it showed a broad range of creative talent.

Subordinate by appositives (See explanation on page 23.)
21. The wedding was a festive occasion, and it was held in August.
22. Nepal is an interesting country to visit, and it attracts many tourists each year.
23. Grant Avenue is in San Francisco, and it is an unusual shopping street.
24. Queen Victoria Arch is a massive stone structure, and it is on Bombay's waterfront.
25. The island of Hawaii's telephone book contains emergency information in case of tidal waves and volcano eruptions, and it is a unique publication.

Questions for Discussion and Review

1. Analyze the model compositions in Chapters 5, 6, and 7 to explain how the writers have linked together their paragraphs.
2. Identify the transitions used in describing the working of the machine in this chapter's model composition.
3. Can you find an introductory infinitive phrase in the model composition?
4. One compound predicate has been identified in this chapter's model composition. Can you locate two more?
5. What analogy does Jeans use to help clarify his explanation of why the sky is blue? What analogy does Cousins use in *his* passage?
6. Find a sample writing selection in any chapter from 1 through 7 that you think could be improved by removing words. Tighten this selection by eliminating its wordiness.

7. In paragraph 6 of the Cousins selection, what causes are given for modern man's obsolescence? In paragraph 7, what are the causes for the lack of time? In paragraph 9, what cause can produce change in man through the exercise of his will?

8. Does Cousins believe it would be better to eliminate the causes of war or treat the effects of war?

9. Identify examples of parallelism at the beginning and end of Shafer's "Myths about Crime."

10. Collect examples of the following expository techniques from Rebecca West's "Man and the State": transitions, subordination, parallelism, variety in sentence structure and length, figurative language.

Vocabulary Growth

PARAGRAPH PUZZLE

*In this Paragraph Puzzle some of the missing words in the paragraphs will **not** have word choices given beneath them. For these blanks, supply an appropriate word by studying the context.*

Along with the increasing employment . . . . American women
　　　　　　　　　　　　　　　　　　(by, of, with, at)

from middle- and upper-income families . . . . come a tremendous

improvement in . . . . educational qualifications of women workers.
　　　　　　　　(that, a, an, the)

As women . . . . received more and more education, those . . . .
　　　　　(has, have, is, was)　　　　　　　　　　　　(why, when, who, one)

have received the most have gone . . . . work in largest number.

Today more . . . . half of all women college graduates . . . .
　　　　　(that, this, their, than)　　　　　　　　　　　　(was, were, are, is)

employed, compared to four out of ten . . . . school graduates,
　　　　　　　　　　　　　　　　　　　　(high, low, up, down)

three out . . . . ten elementary school graduates, and only two
　　　　　(if, at, or, of)

. . . . of ten among those with less than five grades . . . .
(in, out, up, down)

school. Most of the working girls of 1890 . . . . ignorant and un-
　　　　　　　　　　　　　　　　　　　　(were, was, is, are)

skilled, but today's . . . . women have considerably more educa-
　　　(playing, working, driving, traveling)

tion than women...........do not work. Among those who...........
(has, have, was, were)

only recently completed school and.............to work, nearly three
(go, give, gave, gone)

fourths are high school............., and less than 10 percent have not
(principals, deans, teachers, graduates)

............to high school at all.
(be, been, went, go)

Most well-educated middle-class............women hold white-collar
(reading, writing, acting, working)

or professional jobs, ...now employ more than half of..........
(which, who, what, when)   (some, one, all, none)

working women. Although many other kinds............work have be-
(at, or, of, on)

come widely............to women, clerical work and teaching continue

............provide most of the jobs for women high school...........
(not, for, of, to)   (but, for, nor, and)

college graduates. About three fifths of............girls going to work

after graduating..........high school take clerical jobs, and...........
(at, to, of, from)   (around, under, about, less)

the same proportion of the young women............to work after college become teachers.

"Education of U.S.A. Women," Robert W. Smuts, *Women and Work in America*

WORD CLUES

A. *Vocabulary words in the following exercise are boldfaced.*

1. Seattle's civic **dynamism** was most severely tested by the Boeing cut-
   backs, which in 1971 led the city into a deep recession before the rest
   of the country. Volunteers rallied around to supply food to out-of-work
   neighbors in need. Recognizing the mistake it had made in letting itself
   become a one-industry aerospace town, Seattle has put new emphasis
   on reviving its **moribund** and shabby waterfront.

   "The Pacific Northwest," Thomas Griffith, *The Atlantic Monthly* (April 1976)

   Vocabulary Word.......................................

   Context Clue.............................:...............

   Probable Meaning.......................................

   Dictionary Definition...................................

Vocabulary Word..

Context Clue..

Probable Meaning......................................

Dictionary Definition.................................

2. Robert Frost's is a curious situation. Dead a dozen years, he remains something of an **enigma** to his readers and even to the biographer he himself selected to explain himself to his posterity. Not that Frost's achievement is in doubt. There is no question whatever of his achievement. He was a poet not only of his time but of his tongue: one of the very few who deserve that designation. . . .

But who the speaker in those poems *is* remains a question not only to intellectuals and academics, who live by putting questions to the past, but to children in schools who are given poems of Frost's to read at an early age.

"Robert Frost and New England," Archibald MacLeish,
National Geographic (April 1976)

Vocabulary Word..

Context Clue..

Probable Meaning......................................

Dictionary Definition.................................

3. One telling piece of evidence that has emerged from the study area has been the amount of stress a tigress experiences in feeding cubs. Recently, an animal with three well-grown cubs was **tranquilized** with a narcotic in order to be collared, only to have her die literally in the arms of the research group. On examination, the explanation of the **emaciated** tigress became apparent when it was found that one rear leg was gangrenous from an old wound and that a forelimb had broken bones. Either the stress of hunting for three big cubs had provoked her to fight with a large potential prey animal or she had been wounded fighting off a male tiger. In either case, the mother tiger's task had been greater than she could **cope** with.

"Ecologist Returns to South Asia for Another Look,"
S. Dillon Ripley, *Smithsonian* (October 1976)

Vocabulary Word..

Context Clue..

Probable Meaning......................................

Dictionary Definition.................................

Vocabulary Word..

Context Clue..

Probable Meaning. . . . .

Dictionary Definition. . . . .

Vocabulary Word. . . . .

Context Clue. . . . .

Probable Meaning. . . . .

Dictionary Definition. . . . .

4. Let me correct at the outset a common misunderstanding. Of course I recognize that language is a living and growing thing. I would not confine it in a straitjacket, fighting all innovation. On the contrary, I glory in the fact that English is a versatile and adaptable instrument, capable of meeting new needs and serving vigorous and inventive peoples. The question is not whether the English language shall grow. It is whether it shall grow in strength, beauty, and variety, or **degenerate** and decay and **proliferate** in feeble **gibberish**.

"You Americans Are Murdering the Language,"
Lord Conesford, Warriner, et al., *Advanced Composition*

Vocabulary Word. . . . .

Context Clue. . . . .

Probable Meaning. . . . .

Dictionary Definition. . . . .

Vocabulary Word. . . . .

Context Clue. . . . .

Probable Meaning. . . . .

Dictionary Definition. . . . .

Vocabulary Word. . . . .

Context Clue. . . . .

Probable Meaning. . . . .

Dictionary Definition. . . . .

5. The motion pictures and writings of Woody Allen are notable for their **facetious** tone. A comic genius, filling his works with outrageously funny perceptions of what life is like (or could be like), Allen also has a serious side. His farces, like those of Molière, have social and intellectual roots.

Vocabulary Word. . . . .

Context Clue. . . . .

Probable Meaning. . . . .

Dictionary Definition. . . . .

B. Look in a dictionary for meanings of each of the following verbs and for all the related forms of the verb you can find. Make a four-column list headed "verbs, nouns, adjectives, and adverbs."

1. to accelerate
2. to accompany
3. to illustrate
4. to assume
5. to detect
6. to combine

Composition: Show What You Have Learned

Choose a composition topic from either Group I or Group II.

GROUP I: TOPICS FOR WRITING A CAUSAL ANALYSIS

You can select a subject for writing a causal analysis this week in either of two ways:

1. Review the fifteen Word Clue passages in Chapters 5, 6, and 7 to find a composition topic. (Then follow the writing directions in 2.) The subjects touched upon in these Word Clues may stimulate you to choose one to develop further, or a Word Clue may suggest a related or different idea that interests you. These are some of the Word Clue topics you will find:
   a. Innovative state legislation (Chapter 5)
   b. Violence (Chapter 5)
   c. Women's equality (Chapter 6)
   d. Natural disaster (Chapter 6)
   e. Poster art (Chapter 6)
   f. Black liberation (Chapter 6)
   g. The future of the English language (Chapter 7)
   h. Civic resourcefulness (Chapter 7)
2. Analyze the immediate and remote causes and/or effects of one of the following subjects, or of another subject suggested by them. In developing your paper, avoid allowing your analysis to become a mere listing of superficial "reasons."
   a. The popularity of some hair style or clothing fad.
   b. Your need to succeed.
   c. The present-day emphasis on ecology.
   d. Student cheating.
   e. Airplane hijacking.

f. Some unreasonable fear or anxiety that afflicts you or someone you know well.
g. The popularity of some contemporary singer or entertainer particularly admired by young people.
h. The decision by someone to become a citizen of a country in which he was not born.
i. The attraction of motorcycles for young people.
j. Your need to conform.
k. Your urge toward individualism.
l. People's fascination with dieting.

GROUP II: TOPICS TO CHALLENGE YOUR IMAGINATION

ALFRED FRUEH

Drawing by Frueh: © *1959* The New Yorker *Magazine, Inc.*

Sometimes a cartoon has more impact if it tells its story in pictures alone, not relying on a written caption to explain its point. Such a cartoon is the one you have just looked at. Relying on symbolism (the church building as a symbol for religion, the space missile as a symbol for science), the artist makes the statement that science has become the religion of the twentieth century.

Following are composition topics related to the idea of this cartoon. To reply to most of these topics, you will need to write an argumentation. For this, you will want to supply *reasons* based on convincing *evidence* to support the stand you take. In many cases, you will partially or fully develop your paper by causal analysis.

1. Explain how you believe science has succeeded in becoming the twentieth-century religion.
2. Explain why you feel science has *not* become the twentieth-century religion.
3. Defend or refute this statement: "Governments are justified in spending huge amounts of money to develop space exploration programs."
4. Argue that the development of science has helped to improve human life.
5. Argue that the development of science has served to hinder human growth.
6. In what areas do you believe science will have the greatest impact over the next 100 years?

Chapter **8**

The Expository Composition
(Developed by Definition)

What Is a Rodeo?

A rodeo is perhaps the most genuinely American of all sports. The word "rodeo" is a Spanish one meaning "gathering place or marketplace for cattle." A rodeo itself is a competitive contest based loosely on traditional cowboy skills of riding and roping. It consists of six major events: (1) **Riding** an unbroken range horse (bucking bronco) in a saddle; (2) **Riding** a bucking bronco without a saddle (bareback); (3) **Riding** a bull; (4) **Roping** a calf; (5) **Wrestling** a steer to the ground (bulldogging); (6) **Racing** horses around barrels (with women riders).

Pronoun for coherence

Parallelism

The first rodeo took place following a cattle roundup in the **1880s.** From this informal cowboy pastime, a colorful spectacle has evolved that contains many familiar American elements—**the exciting action of bucking horses and bulls, the explosive masculine environment, the hot dog stands, beer barrels, boots, jeans, and cowboy hats.**

No apostrophe in plural number

Specific detail

Today most rodeos are staged in a large, flat arena that is fenced off to protect the viewing public. Grandstands are erected on two sides of the arena; on the other sides are pens to hold the horses, steers, calves, and bulls. **Nearby** are narrow chutes from which ani-

Transition between paragraphs

Semicolon joining independent clauses

Transition

227

mals are released into the arena. On a platform a loud-speaker system is set up for the announcer, who intro-duces the riders and comments on the events as they happen. Near the arena are refreshment stands where people gather to buy food and drink. Portable rest rooms are set up near the grandstand, and an ambulance is parked nearby in case of an accident.

An opening parade of proud riders on proud horses usually begins a rodeo; the performers carry flapping national and state flags. **Then the two-act performance begins.** Calf roping and steer wrestling are timed events. **In the fastest possible time, a man must rope and throw to the ground a calf and tie three of its feet together.** In steer wrestling, the object is to tumble the steer onto his back with its head and all its feet in line. Calf roping **has been done** under 15 seconds, and a steer **has been wrestled** in less than 10 seconds.

When riding an animal, a contestant mounts before the chute gates are opened. The rider must stay on the bucking animal for eight seconds; points are given for the performance of both the animal and the contestant. In all riding events the contestant is disqualified[1] if he touches the animal or its rigging with his free hand.

Probably the most difficult rodeo feat is Brahman bull riding. **During this event,** a rodeo comes to resem-ble a circus because gaily costumed clowns come into the arena to distract the bull's attention from fallen riders. **To stay** on a pitching bull for as long as eight seconds is one of the most challenging tasks in a rodeo. Spectators eagerly wait for this event.

The present circuit[2] extends far beyond the region in which the contests first developed. Now rodeos are popular throughout the western half of the U.S.A. and in major eastern and southern cities. Australia also stages these events. One of the biggest rodeos of all is held during the annual Calgary Stampede in Calgary, British Columbia, Canada.

Comma in compound sentence

Short sentence for variety

Periodic sentence

Passive voice verbs

Elliptical clause

Beginning sentence with prepositional phrase

Beginning sentence with infinitive

[1]*disqualified:* denied the right to participate. [2]*circuit:* group of rodeo areas where performers appear in turn.

Writing Analysis

COORDINATING CONJUNCTIONS AS TRANSITIONS

Earlier you have learned that the coordinating conjunctions *and*, *but*, *for*, *or*, and *nor* can serve as effective transitions between sentences or between paragraphs. Here is a chance to practice this form of transition

EXERCISE 51
Conjunctions as Transitions

A. *Write out each sentence pair, adding an appropriate coordinating conjunction to begin the second sentence.*

1. In the U.S.A. nuclear power reactors are fueled with enriched uranium and cooled by ordinary water. ......In Canada, the "Candu" system uses unenriched uranium and heavy water.
2. Dinosaurs were not obsolescent reptiles. ......They were a novel group of "warm blooded" animals. ......The birds are their descendants.
3. Although the eye has no shutter, the moving world does not appear as a blur. ......The visual system works not like a camera but more like a computer, with a program of specific mathematical rules.
4. Certain species of ants raid the nests of other species. ......They are looking for slave ants.
5. Natural diamonds and most manmade ones form at high pressure. ......It is possible to synthesize diamonds by growing them from existing diamonds in a low-pressure gas rich in carbons.
6. The tax revision bill was passed by a large majority in the House of Representatives. ......It was expected to win an even larger majority in the Senate.

B. *Write out four pairs of sentences. In two pairs, begin the second sentences with the coordinating conjunction* **or**. *Start the second sentence of the other two pairs with the coordinating conjunction* **nor**.

EXPOSITORY DEVELOPMENT (by definition)

To most people, the word "definition" brings to mind a dictionary, for it is to a dictionary that we turn to find the meanings of unfamiliar words. The English word "definition" comes originally from the Latin *de* and *finire*, meaning to set a limit or boundary. And that is what a dictionary sets out to do: to establish boundaries, fencing in those meanings which, by usage and logic, belong to a word and fencing out those which do not conventionally belong. Usually dictionary definitions are brief, logical, and formal.

The logical definition, by its nature, has two parts, as can be seen in the dictionary definition of the word "piano": "a stringed percussion instrument having steel wire springs that sound when struck by felt-covered hammers operated from a keyboard." The first part of a logical definition is its **genus** (class or category), consisting of items which can be grouped together because of their likenesses or common traits. In the above definition, the genus is "a stringed percussion instrument." The second part of a logical definition is its **species**, or those characteristics which differentiate it from other members of the same genus. Thus, in the definition of a "piano," the fact that it has "steel wire springs that sound when struck by felt-covered hammers operated from a keyboard" distinguishes it from any other stringed instrument, such as a zither or a harp.

Short definitions can be logical without being formal in the manner of most dictionary definitions. An example of an informal definition which has a proper genus and species is the poet Robert Frost's definition of "home" as "the place where, when you have to go there, they have to take you in." The individualistic Englishman Dr. Samuel Johnson, who devoted many years to compiling a dictionary, let his own attitudes creep into his work from time to time, most notably in his definition of a "fishing rod" as "a stick with a fish at one end and a fool at the other."

Three errors should be avoided in the writing of logical definitions. First of all, a definition should not be circular. In other words, the species should not include the word being defined, as in the faulty definition, "A stoic is an advocate of stoicism." Moreover, the genus in a definition should not be too small to include the thing being defined. If the definition of a "poem" read "two or more rhymed lines written to express an idea, mood, or emotion," the genus is too limited because it does not include blank verse and other nonrhyming poetry. But neither should the genus be so large that it becomes not really useful. If an "automobile" is defined as "a means of transportation," its genus is too large to be meaningful.

For purposes of expository writing, though, the brief logical definition that we have been examining plays a relatively small part. Of more interest to us is another form, called **extended definition.**

Extended definitions are sometimes developed by special expository techniques. Suppose we are dealing with the term "civil rights." One way to develop a definition is to give the **background of the term,** perhaps discussing the source of the civil rights movement and the various directions in which it has developed. Another method of definition is to **list the various elements** of what is being defined, possibly selecting one for further development. Using this method, we could break civil rights into political, social, and sexual categories. Still another way to define this term is by **negation,** clarifying civil rights by showing what it is *not*.

Yet probably the most common ways to construct definitions are the basic expository patterns found in other chapters of this book—examples, comparison and contrast, process, cause and effect, and logical division **or** classification. By using these modes of development, we could give **examples** of milestones in civil rights legislation for black Americans. We could **compare or contrast** civil rights advances of American blacks with those of American senior citizens. We could outline the **process** by which an important civil rights bill was passed. We could present the **causes and effects** of the sexual "consenting adults" legislation passed by several states. Or we could use **logical division** to examine the status of civil rights in a number of countries, among them the United States and South Africa.

Notice that, in the model composition "What Is a Rodeo?," several techniques have been combined for purposes of definition. In the first paragraph, background material for the term "rodeo" includes the derivation of the word and the origin of the event. Then the writer chooses the technique of logical division to outline the six main parts of a rodeo. Finally, the body of the composition depends on development by examples —the animals, the description of the arena, the rules for the contests, and the areas of North America and other countries where rodeos are popular.

Look now at some different approaches taken in writing extended definitions on a variety of subjects. First, read over a short definition of a teaspoon, considering as you read what form of development is used and how complete its genus and species are:

> A teaspoon is a utensil for scooping up and carrying small amounts of something. It has two joined parts: a flat, narrow, tapered handle, by which it is held, and a shallow, oval bowl to dip and carry liquid, food or other materials. The handle is about four inches long. It arches slightly upward at the wide end. It curves sharply downward at the narrow end. The shape of the handle allows it to fit easily in the hand when it is correctly held resting across the third finger and grasped between the thumb and first joint of the fore-finger of the right hand. When the bowl is level, the handle points upward at a shallow angle. A spoon is usually made of metal or some other hard-wearing, unbreakable material.
>
> "A Teaspoon," Roger H. Garrison, *A Guide to Creative Writing*

The preceding selection develops its definition of the teaspoon by describing its parts and its uses, first in general terms (genus, species) and then in more exact detail. Although it presents many identifying characteristics of a teaspoon, the definition could be more precise. It could, for instance, describe the bowl of the spoon as holding $1\frac{1}{3}$ fluid grams. Nor has the definition of the teaspoon eliminated from consideration the tablespoon or any other kinds of teaspoons that are similar in purpose and physical qualities. Moreover, the species is probably too small. It could be expanded to add to "scooping and carrying" a third function of a teaspoon—that of stirring a liquid. Still, the definition as it stands does a reasonably good job of defining a teaspoon, including information on how it is held and the materials it is made of.

Moving on from definition of objects, let us examine a definition of a type of person. Probably everyone has, at one time or another, been bored by another human being. But who has thought of defining a bore? Harold Nicholson gives his definition here:

It is not merely that a bore[1] is long-winded;[2] he is also touchy.[3] He knows that he is a bore; yet he persists. Unfortunately, he detests[4] the company of other bores, can recognize them immediately, and will avoid them as the plague. He enjoys reminiscences,[5] coincidences[6] and stories about imaginary circumstances and encounters. Wisecracks[7] are a specialty of bores, and I have met men in American club-cars[8] who will tell stories as long as the freight-trains that trundle[9] across the prairies through the night. The bore is irrelevant in that he will forget the point or concentration of his narrative to wander down by-paths and into hidden coppices.[10] He indulges also in unnecessary precision, wishing to fix names and dates that have little bearing on[11] his discourse. "It must," he will inform one at dictation speed, "have been in October '53—no it can't have been then because we were in Copenhagen—it may have been early in November—anyhow it doesn't matter, and to cut a long story short. . . ." He also much enjoys repeating Stock Exchange jokes of the "have you heard this one?" variety. "Clergymen," Vyvyan Holland has remarked acutely, "are seldom boring, unless they belong to the gaitered classes.[12] This is accounted for by the fact that, as they do not tell improper stories, they are forced to adopt more subtle forms of wit." Finally, the bore is invariably a nice man. Were he not kind, and virtuous, and honorable, we should not experience, as we do, both irritation at his insistence and remorse[13] at our own unkindness. He leaves us, when he does leave us, feeling, not angry only, but ashamed.

"A Bore," Harold Nicholson, *Good Behavior*

[1]*bore:* tiresome person. [2]*long-winded:* given to talking at length. [3]*touchy:* sensitive. [4]*detests:* hates. [5]*reminiscences:* remembered events. [6]*coincidences:* surprising accidental happenings. [7]*wisecracks:* humorous remarks, often disrespectful. [8]*club-cars:* railroad passenger cars furnished with lounge chairs and tables. [9]*trundle:* roll along. [10]*coppices:* thick growth of bushes or small trees. [11]*having little bearing on:* do not really pertain to. [12]*gaitered classes:* upper classes. [13]*remorse:* mental suffering caused by a sense of guilt.

Note that Nicholson relies upon quotation, example, and illustration in developing his definition of a bore. If he had not done this but had instead continued to remain on the same level of generalization as that found in his first four sentences, then the definition would be a far less effective one. In organizing the paragraph, Nicholson has chosen a certain order in which to arrange his examples. Can you detect what order he has followed? In thinking about this, ask yourself whether the last characteristic—that of the bore being a nice man—could have been presented first.

Defining by negation is demonstrated in the following selection. Concerned with communicating a specialized meaning for the word "resources," the writer first eliminates other possible meanings before he presents his particular definition:

> Resource is a word with many shades of meaning. Dictionary defini-tions range from "something in reserve" to "additional stores, ready if needed." But the definitions do not specify the "somethings" and the "stores." They could be resources of courage to face a personal crisis, of wood to fuel a stove through a winter, or of finances to meet a medi-cal expense. The resources discussed in this book are all linked by a common factor. They are all natural resources, which means that they are supplies we draw from a bountiful earth, such as food, building and clothing materials, minerals, water, and energy. . . .
>
> Natural resources fall into two distinct categories. Resources derived from living matter, such as food, clothing, and wood, are *renewable resources* because they are replenished each growing season. Even if one season's crop is consumed, the next season brings a renewed larder.[1] But *mineral resources* such as coal, oil, atomic energy, copper, iron, and fertilizers are not renewed each season. They are nonrenewable, one crop resources, and the earth's supplies are fixed. The kinds of mineral resources, their distribution, their quantities, the amounts we use, and our ever growing dependence on them are topics covered in this book.
>
> "Nonrenewable Resources," Brian J. Skinner, *Earth Resources*

[1]*larder:* supply of food.

Having first defined "natural resources," the writer goes on to break his term into two parts: renewable resources and mineral resources. By dis-carding renewable resources because they are irrelevant to his purposes, he effectively focuses on the actual subject of his book: mineral resources.

The next example also depends on definition by negation—telling what a term does *not* mean before you tell what it *does* mean. Scientific and tech-nical definitions need to be formulated with a great deal of precision. Sometimes, as in the following mathematical definition, the writer must resolve an ambiguity of terms before he gets down to the business of defining:

> In common usage, a *relation* means two or more things having some-thing in common. We say that a person's lifestyle is related to his income or that a person's career potential should be related only to his intelligence, his initiative, and his integrity.
>
> In mathematics we define a *relation* as a set of ordered pairs of the form (x, y). Sometimes a description or rule is also included that states the relationship between x and y. In an ordered pair the first element may be represented by any letter, but x is normally used. This first ele-ment is called the independent variable. The letter y is normally used as the second element of an ordered pair and is called the dependent variable.

All those numbers that are used as a first element of an ordered pair of a given relation form a set of numbers called the *domain*. The domain is often referred to as the set of all x's.

The *range* of a relation is the set of those numbers that are used as a second element of an ordered pair. The range may be referred to as *the set of all y's* [ys].

"A Mathematics Relation," Dale Ewen and Michael A. Topper,
Mathematics for Technical Education

This passage provides a timely illustration of two aspects of writing that you are very much concerned with: using examples for development and effective paragraphing. Notice that, in the first paragraph, the nonmathematical meaning of the term "relation" is concretely illustrated by two examples: one's lifestyle is *related* to one's income; one's career potential is *related* to one's personal qualities. Citing examples here allowed the writer to dismiss these general meanings of the word so that he could move on to his real concern, the mathematical definition of "relation."

Through disciplined paragraphing, the writer focuses sharply on the mathematical meaning of "relation." In his second paragraph, he discusses *together* both elements of an ordered pair, establishing the new terms "independent variable" and "dependent variable." Then he breaks the next step of his definition into two short paragraphs to discuss each element *separately*, introducing the new terms "domain" and "range."

Clearly the writer of this selection is concerned with communicating his meaning in the clearest possible way. Careful paragraphing has helped him to do this.

As in other modes of development, comparison is often an illuminating way to define a term. In the following selection, radar is more easily explained by comparing and contrasting radar and the human eye:

Radar is an electronic device that is used for the detection and location of objects. It operates by transmitting a particular type of waveform, a pulse-modulated sine wave for example, and detects the nature of the echo signal. Radar is used to extend the capability of man's senses for observing his environment, especially the sense of vision. The value of radar lies not in being a substitute for the eye, but in doing what the eye cannot do. Radar cannot resolve detail as well as the eye, nor is it yet capable of recognizing the "color" of objects to the degree of sophistication of which the eye is capable. However, radar can be designed to see through those conditions impervious to normal human vision, such as darkness, haze, fog, rain, and snow. In addition, radar has the advantage of being able to measure the distance or range to the object. This is probably its most important attribute.

The examples and specific terms that the writer includes in his closing sentences ("darkness, haze, fog, rain, snow"; the fact that radar can "measure the distance or range") communicate well two significant characteristics of radar. By controlling the lengths of his sentences throughout this passage, the writer adds force to his definition.

Finally, here is an extended and extremely perceptive definition of something that everyone is concerned with—friendship:

> . . . the desire for friendship is always with us but we do not always have friends. In fact, the first thing that our own experiences, as well as many of the great philosophers, tell us about true friendship is that it is very rare. A lot of our associations seem like friendships at first, only to languish and disappear in time. These lack what might be called the "prerequisites."[1] In trying to set down what they are, we must begin by clearly distinguishing between relationships that are accidental and transitory[2] and those that are essential and enduring.
>
> Aristotle offers us substantial[3] help here by pointing out that there are three kinds of friendship: the friendships based (1) on utility,[4] (2) on pleasure, and (3) on virtue.
>
> The friendships of utility and pleasure go together and are no doubt the most common. Everyone has experienced them. People are "friendly" to their business associates, neighbors, the members of their car pool,[5] and even casual acquaintances on trains, boats, and airplanes. This kind of civility is, to some degree, a form of friendship, the friendship of utility, of mutual convenience. Similarly, people are "friendly" to their golfing partners, to others at a cocktail party, and to acquaintances who entertain them. This is also a form of friendship, the friendship of pleasure, of mutual enjoyment.
>
> These lower forms of friendship are not necessarily bad, but they are inadequate. One of their defects results from the fact that they depend on and vary with circumstances. This is why they can quickly arise and just as quickly disappear. By contrast, when the Book of Proverbs says, "A friend loveth at all times," it is referring to a higher form of friendship that does not depend on circumstance. In order to surmount the effect of time and happenstance,[6] it must be based on the inherent[7] qualities of the individuals involved. A friendship so anchored cannot be a passing frendship.
>
> True friendship, then, surpasses[8] (although it often includes) both utility and pleasure. For Aristotle, such a friendship must be based on a good moral character. Only in that way can it last. Further, it must develop slowly, since it presupposes familiarity, knowledge, and—eventually—mutual trust.

Aristotle goes on to observe:

> This kind of friendship, then, is perfect both in respect of duration and in all other respects, and in it each gets from each in all respects the

[1]*prerequisites:* conditions necessary to something that follows. [2]*transitory:* existing for a short time only. [3]*substantial:* considerable and real. [4]*utility:* usefulness. [5]*car pool:* several passengers sharing a single automobile. [6]*happenstance:* chance occurrence, accident. [7]*inherent:* belonging to the very nature of a person or thing. [8]*surpasses:* goes beyond in degree or amount; exceeds.

same as, or something like what, he gives; which is what ought to happen between friends.

Perfect friendship, then, also presupposes a certain equality of status. Montaigne, speaking of the kinds of human relationships, confirms this when he says:

That of children to parents is rather[9] respect: friendship is nourished by communication which cannot, by reason of the great disparity,[10] be betwixt[11] these.

Parents can no more be friends to their children than teachers can be to their students. For the essence of friendship is reciprocity: giving and getting something like what you give. Parents see to the proper development of their children, and teachers guide the shaping of their students' minds. Children and students cannot reciprocate in kind.

It should be clear now why real friendship requires more than merely having "*something* in common." It is *what* people have in common that determines the kind of friendship they will have. True friendship requires at least a sound moral character out of the richness of which individuals are able to give and get this precious affection. And the more individuals give, the more they realize a genuine kind of selflessness, the better friends they are. A good man will not only do for his friend what he would do for himself, but will, if necessary, do more.

These prerequisites being hard to fulfill, true friendship is bound to be rare. To acquire a real friend, therefore, is one of the most praiseworthy accomplishments in life. Montaigne tells a story of Cyrus, the ruler of Persia. He was asked whether he would exchange a valuable horse, on which he had just won a race, for a kingdom. Cyrus replied, "No, truly, sir, but I would give him with all my heart to get thereby a true friend, could I find out any man worthy of that alliance."

"Friendship," Dr. Mortimer J. Adler, *Great Ideas from the Great Books*

[9]*rather*: instead. [10]*disparity*: inequality. [11]*betwixt*: between.

EXERCISE 52
Evaluating Definitions

The following short definitions of a pencil were written by two Arab students of English. Which definition is the stronger one, and why?

1. A pencil is an instrument for writing on paper. It is cylindrical and can be held by the first two fingers of the hand. It is about 4 inches long and ½ inch wide. At the end there is an eraser held to the pencil by a surrounding metal. Lead is the material which is used in making the marks on the paper, and a sharpener is needed to keep the pencil in good working order. Pencils are made of wood, although the kinds might differ.

2. A pencil is an implement for writing, drawing, or marking. The usual

pencils have four parts: a wooden case, a solid rod of graphite or other marking material, a small eraser, and a piece of metal fixing the eraser to the wood. The wooden cases of most pencils are either round or hexagonal with rounded edges. Inside the wooden case, there is a solid rod of marking material which gives the pencil its special writing characteristics. At the end of the wooden part, there is a small colored eraser for erasing the unwanted writings. The eraser is fixed to the main part by a colored piece of metal. Although the length, the weight, and the color differ from one pencil to another, the usual length and weight are 25 cm and 50 g. The shape of the pencil allows it to fit easily in the hand when it is correctly held between the thumb and third and fourth finger, and in the pocket when it is carried.

EXERCISE 53
Outlining

First review the section in Chapter 5 on "The Composition Outline." Then reconstruct the outline the writer probably worked from in composing the model composition "What Is a Rodeo?"

FORCE IN WRITING

Differences between Oral and Written Communication A person taking part in a conversation knows that the way he expresses himself is important. He wants to capture and hold the attention of the person he is speaking to. If he notices that the other person's attention is beginning to wander, he will try to make his manner of speaking more forceful. He can do this in several ways: through humor or irony, through unusual word choice, through intonation, or even through talking more loudly. The writer is faced with the same problem of attracting and keeping the attention of his reader. But the means he has to do this are more limited than those of the speaker. It is often more difficult, for example, for a writer to show a rise or fall in emphasis than it is for a speaker. A change in voice or volume can only be suggested in writing, not expressed with unmistakable impact, as in speech. Nor can a writer always be sure that his attempts at humor or ironic statement will be accurately interpreted. Therefore the writer needs to know well his particular means for achieving force in writing. Knowing this, he can practice and master the art of expressing himself in the manner that will most likely interest his reader.

Levels of Usage and Appropriateness Forceful writing is specific, direct, and active. Such writing is often found in newspapers, magazines, and popular fiction because these publications survive only through their appeal to a mass audience. The writing in these publications must interest the readers and communicate clearly to them. This is not to say that a college student should write in the style of a newspaper reporter. Yet the principles of forceful writing can be applied in even the most formal essays. For instance, some people believe that the lengthy, indirect, over-Latinized writing that characterizes many legal briefs would be greatly improved if made more active, specific, and direct.

Four Qualities of Forceful Writing   Now let's examine two paragraphs, judging them on the basis of their force:

A. In the large Eastern city, he doggedly pursued his primary objective of securing a position as a television performer. Three visits were made to every major television studio, and this led to his finally being given a small role in a nationally televised variety show.

B. In New York he worked hard at his goal of finding a job as a television actor. After applying to every major television studio three times, he finally won a small part on a nationally televised show.

Paragraph B is more forceful than paragraph A for several reasons. Below are two lists of words and phrases taken from each paragraph:

PARAGRAPH A	PARAGRAPH B
the large Eastern city	New York
doggedly pursued	worked hard
primary objective	goal
securing a position	finding a job
three visits were made	After applying . . . three times
being given	won

These lists show that the words in the forceful paragraph B are more *specific* than those in A. Choosing specific rather than general words can help you to write more forcefully.

A second reason for the greater force of paragraph B is its sentence structure. The second sentence of B, subordinated by an introductory adverbial clause, is more concise and emphatic than the corresponding compound sentence in paragraph A.

A third reason is the fact that the verb in the second sentence in paragraph A is in the passive voice (three visit **were made**), whereas the verb in the corresponding sentence in B is in the active voice (he **won**).

Finally, the combination of subordination and the use of the active voice allows the writer of paragraph B to say in only thirty-seven words what the writer of paragraph A needed forty-five words to say.

These, then, are four important qualities of forceful writing:
1. Use a majority of specific, rather than general, verbs and nouns.
2. Emphasize sentence variety, particularly subordination and parallelism.

3. Use active, rather than passive, voice verbs.
4. Express what you have to say in the fewest possible words.

EXERCISE 54
Force in Writing

A. *Revise the following paragraph so that it is more forcefully expressed.*

An attempt was made by him, while serving as a cabin boy on the whaling schooner, to learn to tie each and every knot that the various sailor members of the crew had so deftly mastered. Every humble action of the crew was learned by him, for he felt strongly in his heart the great passion to be relieved of the hated chores of bed-making and food-serving in order to participate in the more clearly manly activities of lifting the sails up the masts, pulling the anchor out of the water, and cleaning the decks with a mop.

B. *Explain, with examples related to the four categories above, which of the selections in the following pairs is the most forcefully written.*

1. White's "The Miracle of New York" and McCormac's "Levels for Surveying" (both in Chapter 1).
2. Ewen and Topper's "A Mathematical Relation" (Chapter 8) and Carson's "Mother Sea: The Gray Beginnings" (Chapter 1).
3. Schrag's "The Beatles and their Beat" (Chapter 3) and West's "Man and the State" (Chapter 7).
4. Nicholson's "What Is a Bore?" (Chapter 8) and "The U.S.A.'s Bicentennial" (Chapter 4).
5. Barnett's "The Newtonian Relativity Principle" (Chapter 5) and Gordimer's "A Foreigner Looks at American Writers" (Chapter 6).
6. De France's "Relays" (Chapter 2) and Schafer's "Myths about Crime" (Chapter 7).

WRITING A CONCLUSION

You're almost there—almost at home base. The carefully thought-out development of your ideas is behind you. Up to now, you have maintained unity and coherence in all of your paragraphs. All that remains is to tie off the composition, concluding it in a way that will be both meaningful and graceful. Are you ready?

You may not be. For one thing, you may be so tired from writing that you've run dry of ideas. For another, you may not realize the many possibilities that exist for conclusions. It might seem easier to just stop and turn in the paper as it stands. But doing this may lead to a disappointment: your abrupt ending might make the difference between a successful and unsuccessful composition.

Just as the end of a sentence is its most emphatic section, so the close of a composition is a position of major emphasis. Because the conclusion is the last section to be read, ideas placed here may have more impact than those mentioned earlier in the composition, and the reader may retain the concluding ideas longer.

Here are some effective ways of concluding a composition:

1. Summary
2. Restating the thesis statement
3. Anecdote
4. Rhetorical question
5. Dramatic narrative
6. Key climactic point
7. Quotation
8. First explicit statement of the thesis
9. Appropriate lines of poetry
10. Figurative language

The conclusion of a paragraph can be a place for great effects. But any pilot will tell you that it's a mistake to try to solo before you learn to fly. A good way to begin writing a conclusion is to practice **summary.** In an expository paper, the conclusion often figures importantly as the place for summing up your earlier ideas or restating your thesis. At this point in your paper, you can do your reader a real service by reminding him of your main point. The summary as conclusion is a primary tool of communication; you should practice it and use it often.

1. Concluding with a Summary

Throughout the essay that precedes the following concluding paragraphs, the writer has been examining the distrust, hostility, and contempt that women sometimes feel toward men. She cites several examples to show that if there are male chauvinists, there are female chauvinists, as well. Her conclusion sums up the case for equality between sexes that the essay has been presenting.

> Woman, who once was abandoned and disgraced by an unwanted pregnancy, has recently arrived at a new pride of ownership or disposal. She has traveled in a straight line that still excludes her sexual partner from an equal share in the wanted or unwanted pregnancy. A better style of life may develop from an assumption that men are as human as we. Why not ask the child's father if he would like to bring up the child? Why not share decisions, when possible, with the male? If we cut them out, assuming an old-style indifference on their part, we perpetrate the ugly divisiveness that has characterized relations between the sexes so far.
>
> Hard as it is for many of us to believe, women are not really superior to men in intelligence or humanity—they are only equal.
>
> "Confessions of a Female Chauvinist Sow," Anne Roiphe,
> *New York* Magazine (30 October 1972)

2. Concluding by Restating the Thesis Statement

In his two closing paragraphs, Isaac Asimov restates the thesis that appeared in the opening sentence of his essay: "It is not really the business of science-fiction writers to predict the future."

> But I repeat that all these predictions, however accurate and amazing they may be, are not our business. They are merely the side effects of our efforts to tell interesting and plausible stories outside the background of the humdrum everyday world.
>
> And when our ideas will work only if we make use of the scientifically impossible, which so far as we know, can never come true—such as time travel and antigravity—why, believe me, we do that, too, and without the tiniest compunction or remorse, provided only that we make it *sound* plausible.
>
> "Prediction as a Side Effect," Isaac Asimov, *Boston Review of the Arts* (July 1972)

Of course, you won't always want to conclude a composition with a summary or restatement of the thesis. Once you feel comfortable using these helpful methods, you can move on to many other possibilities. Here are some of them:

3. Concluding with an Anecdote

The following closing paragraph ends an essay that emphasizes the importance of the intellectual in American society. The writer chooses a brief anecdote to drive home his point about the worth of the intellectual; then he concludes by briefly enlarging upon the anecdote.

> That most human and American of Presidents—of Americans—Abraham Lincoln, said as a young man: "The things I want to know are in books; my best friend is the man who'll get me a book I ain't read." It's a hard heart, a dull one, that doesn't go out to that sentence. The man who will make us see what we haven't seen, feel what we haven't felt, understand what we haven't understood—he *is* our best friend. And if he knows more than we do, that is an invitation to us, not an indictment[1] of us. And it is not an indictment of him, either; it takes all sorts of people to make a world—to make, even, a United States of America.
>
> "The Intellectual in America," Randall Jarrell, *Mademoiselle* (January 1955)

[1]*indictment:* formal written accusation of one or more persons of criminal activity.

4. Concluding with a Question

Few writers have loved a river as deeply as the young Mark Twain loved the Mississippi. But once life on a steamboat had familiarized him with every aspect of the river, the romance of it faded away. In his conclusion, Twain compares a steamboat pilot to a doctor; he questions whether or not the sacrifice involved in learning a trade or skill is really worthwhile.

No, the romance and beauty were all gone from the river. All the value any feature of it had for me now was the amount of usefulness it could furnish toward compassing the safe piloting of a steamboat. Since those days, I have pitied doctors from my heart. What does the lovely flush in a beauty's cheek mean to a doctor but a "break" that ripples above some deadly disease? Are not all her visible charms sown thick with what are to him the signs and symbols of hidden decay? Does he ever see her beauty at all, or doesn't he simply view her professionally and comment upon her unwholesome condition all to himself? And doesn't he sometimes wonder whether he has gained most or lost most by learning his trade?

"Familiarity Breeds Regret," Mark Twain, *Life on the Mississippi*

5. Concluding with a Dramatic Narrative

In this selection the writer decribes the effects of the atomic bomb dropped on the Japanese city of Hiroshima in 1945. Miss Sasaki is one of six survivors who were working in a tin factory when the bomb exploded. Notice that the writer concludes with a strongly ironic incident: books, which are meant to nourish human life, instead nearly destroy it.

Everything fell, and Miss Sasaki lost consciousness. The ceiling dropped suddenly and the wooden floor above collapsed in splinters and the people up there came down and the roof above them gave way; but principally and first of all, the bookcases right behind her swooped forward and the contents threw her down, with her left leg horribly twisted and breaking underneath her. There, in the tin factory, in the first moment of the atomic age, a human being was crushed by books.

"The Day the Bomb Fell," John Hersey, *Hiroshima*

6. Concluding with a Key Climactic Point

What follows is the final paragraph of an essay on emotional development in the machine age. Joey, the subject of the essay, had been completely withdrawn from human contact as a child, "frozen" in the image of the machine. The essay traces the steps in Joey's gradual change from mechanical boy to human child. The climactic step in this transformation has been saved for the conclusion.

One last detail and this fragment of Joey's story has been told. When Joey was 12, he made a float for our Memorial Day parade. It carried the slogan: "Feelings are more important than anything under the sun." Feelings, Joey had learned, are what make for humanity; their absence, for a mechanical existence. With this knowledge Joey entered the human condition.

"Joey: A 'Mechanical Boy,'" Bruno Bettelheim, *Scientific American* (March 1959)

7. Concluding with a Quotation

A quotation placed at the end of a composition can serve several purposes. It might contain a piece of quoted wisdom to give final insight on a subject. Or it may be an authoritative statement by a specialist in the field about which you are writing. In the following case, though, a quotation is used to emphasize the shocking point of the essay: 38 people watched from their apartments in Queens while a woman was being fatally stabbed on the street below, but no one attempted to help the attacked woman.

> It was 4:25 A.M. when the ambulance arrived to take the body of Miss Genovese. It drove off. "Then," a solemn police detective said, "the people came out."
>
> > "38 Who Saw Murder Didn't Call the Police," Martin Gansberg,
> > *New York Times*, 17 March 1964

8. Concluding with First Statement of the Thesis

The essay that leads up to this closing paragraph tells the story of an American black's experiences living in a small European village. In his conclusion, the writer does several things: he generalizes from his experiences in the village, summarizes, and in his last sentence, states his essay's thesis for the first time. (Note that this type of conclusion is more suitable for a personal essay than for an expository composition.)

> The time has come to realize that the interracial drama acted out on the American continent has not only created a new black man, it has created a new white man, too. No road whatever will lead Americans back to the simplicity of this European village where white men still have the luxury of looking on me as a stranger. I am not, really, a stranger any longer for any American alive. One of the things that distinguishes Americans from other people is that no other people has ever been so deeply involved in the lives of black men, and vice versa. This fact faced, with all its implications, it can be seen that the history of the American Negro problem is not merely shameful, it is also something of an achievement. For even when the worst has been said, it must also be added that the perpetual challenge posed by this problem was always, somehow, perpetually met. It is precisely this black-white experience which may prove of indispensable[1] value to us in the world we face today. This world is white no longer, and it will never be white again.
>
> > "No More a Stranger," James Baldwin, *Stranger in the Village*

[1]*indispensable*: essential.

9. Concluding with Appropriate Lines of Poetry

This brief final paragraph concludes an essay in which Elizabeth Hardwick disagrees with many of the points made about women in Simone de Beauvoir's *The Second Sex*. The writer uses a few poetic lines to recapitulate her main point that women's liberation movements fail to take into account natural differences between women and men.

Coquettes, mothers, prostitutes and "minor" writers—one sees these faces, defiant or resigned,[1] still standing at the Last Judgment. They are all a little sad, like the Chinese lyric:

Why do I heave deep sighs?
It is natural, a matter of course, (all)
creatures have their laws.

> "The Subjection of Women," Elizabeth Hardwick, *A View of My Own*

[1]*resigned*: submissive; yielding and uncomplaining.

10. Concluding with Figurative Language

Here is the concluding paragraph of an article on style—style in writing and in living. Since throughout his essay the author has been praising simplicity as the key element of style, his choice of a Greek temple as a simile for simplicity in English prose is particularly appropriate.

In many ways, no doubt, our world grows more and more complex, sputniks[1] cannot be simple; yet how many of our complexities remain futile, how many of our artificialities false. Simplicity too can be subtle —as the straight lines of a Greek temple, like the Parthenon at Athens, are delicately curved in order to look straighter still.

> "On the Fascination of Style," F. L. Lucas, *Holiday* (March 1960)

[1]*sputniks*: space vehicles.

REVIEW OF VARYING SENTENCE OPENINGS

In Chapter 2 you studied and practiced ways to vary sentence openings. In the readings since then, you have seen many examples of authors adding interest to their writing by careful attention to how they begin sentences.

The possibilities for different sentence openings are many. Frequently consult the 24 listed below to add force to your writing:

1. Noun-verb:

   Winter arrives early in Denmark.

2. Personal pronoun-verb:

   She gained eminence in the field of china painting.

3. Inverted subject-verb:

   Displayed in the glass case **was** a rare **emerald.**

4. Prepositional phrase:

   a. **In containers** of various sizes grew tulips and daffodils.
   b. **With measurement marked,** you are ready to cut a pattern.

5. Adjective:

   Cold nights can be expected in many California national parks.

6. Adverb:

Slowly the ferry chugs across Hong Kong harbor.

7. Adverb of question:

Where can you find a room to experiment in?

8. Adverb phrase:

Ahead of time, arrange to have lunch at the railroad terminal.

9. Adverb clause:

When the building has reached 40 stories, the workers will top it off with a traditional ceremony.

10. Coordinating conjunction:

Nor is a hand saw as convenient as an electric one.

11. Direct object:

Coins you can store in small jars on the closet shelf.

12. Indefinite pronoun:

Such is the case when a new political party is established.

13. Series:

Time, place, and type of transportation were first arranged.

14. Participle:

Spattered, the paint covers the surface in an irregular and arresting way.

15. Participial phrase:

Selecting your home site, you will want to consider climate control.

16. Gerund:

Hiking can become a way of life.

17. Gerund phrase:

Tossing a salad should be done before, not after, it is served.

18. Infinitive:

To begin, lay your boards down in parallel rows.

19. Infinitive phrase:

To travel to the Orient seems more feasible these days.

20. Noun clause:

That you may master the art of leather craft is not an impossible dream.

21. Imperative with understood subject:

    Peel tomatoes, cut in cubes, and let drain for several minutes.

22. Transition:

    However, this approach to candle making can present difficulties.

23. Appositive:

    An expert in forest fire control, the ranger gives nightly talks to campers.

24. Absolute phrase:

    The turkey placed in the oven, you can turn to preparing dessert.

EXERCISE 55
Review: Varying Sentence Openings

Write out original sentences that begin in the ways indicated.

1. With a prepositional phrase.
2. With an adverb.
3. With an adverb phrase.
4. With an adverb clause.
5. With a coordinating conjunction.
6. With an indefinite pronoun.
7. With a participle.
8. With a participial phrase.
9. With a gerund.
10. With a gerund phrase.
11. With an infinitive.
12. With an infinitive phrase.
13. With a noun clause.
14. With an imperative with understood subject.
15. With an appositive.

Punctuation Points

PUNCTUATING APPOSITIVES

Nonrestrictive appositives are set off by commas wherever they appear in a sentence—beginning, middle, or end. Appositives may be as short as a single word; frequently they have one or more modifiers:

We arrived in our favorite city, **Lisbon.**
Luxor, **a city on the banks of the Nile,** was our next stop.
A frequent visitor to classrooms, the college president was known to most of the students.

A restrictive appositive, usually a single word, is one that is necessary in identifying the preceding noun. Here are four examples:

The poet **Quasimodo**   The preposition **in**
Your friend **Kevin**   The biography <u>**Queen Victoria**</u>

A sentence in Chapter 4's model paragraph shows a nonrestrictive appositive being used in a typical way, making another noun more specific and set off by commas: "It is as dangerous for man to model himself upon his invention, **the machine,** as it would be for God to model Himself upon His invention."

EXERCISE 56
Punctuating Appositives

Write out these sentences, punctuating the appositives whenever necessary.

1. The birthday gift a wool shirt was on my bed.
2. Mr. Thornsen told us that he had hired my brother a trained accountant.
3. A temperamental conductor Toscanini produced many great recordings.
4. My cousin James is coming to visit us in the spring.
5. Manuel Silva the oldest fisherman in Vera Cruz was photographed for the newspapers.
6. They introduced us to the young woman a famous ballet star.
7. The book a collection of poems fell off the table.
8. The popularity of the magazine *Sports Illustrated* has been proven by a rise in circulation.
9. We live next door to the Andersons a family of ten.
10. The novel *Siddhartha* a parable of the life of Buddha was written by Hermann Hesse a Swiss German.
11. The poet Burns wrote many simple and homely lyrics.
12. Robert Burns a Scottish poet wrote about the human condition.
13. The teacher a courteous and enthusiastic leader was popular with his students.
14. I always have a problem using the modal *may* correctly.
15. A modest and unassuming girl she was awarded the President's scholarship.

Grammar Skills

CORRECT AGREEMENT OF RELATIVE PRONOUNS

The relative pronouns *who, whom, whose, which, that,* and *what* are often used to introduce adjective clauses, as in the following sentences:

The man **who** came to dinner stayed overnight.
The job **that** was advertised in the newspaper had already been filled.
The camera **which** I ordered from Japan arrived today.

(Note that *who* or *whom* refer only to a person, *that* to a person, place, or thing, and *which* only to a place or thing. In modern English prose, *that* is often preferred to *which*.)

A problem sometimes arises in correctly placing the relative pronouns "which" or "that" within a sentence. A pronoun normally appears directly after the word it is referring to. If an adjective clause beginning with "which" is moved to another part of the sentence, confusion may result.

Misplaced adjective clause	The maid put a letter on my desk **which came from Prague.**
Corrected	The maid put a letter **which came from Prague** on my desk.

In the first sentence, the adjective clause *which came from Prague* refers to the noun "desk" immediately preceding it. Thus the sentence conveys the false idea that the *desk* came from Prague. What the writer really means to say, however, is that the *letter* came from Prague. By moving the adjective clause next to the word "letter" in the second sentence, the writer presents his idea more accurately. Here are additional examples of misplaced adjective clauses and their corrections:

Misplaced adjective clause	They sent a chair to the repair department **that was damaged.**
Corrected	They sent a chair **that was damaged** to the repair department.

Misplaced adjective clause	Nobody witnessed the accident after the election **which injured three people.**
Corrected	Nobody witnessed the accident **which injured three people** after the election.

Once you have understood the correct placement of relative pronouns, try to avoid using them too often. Many times an adjective clause can be reduced to a prepositional phrase, a participial phrase, or a single adjective to good effect:

Adjective clause	The maid put a letter **that came from Prague** on my desk.
Prepositional phrase	The maid put a letter **from Prague** on my desk.
Adjective clause	Beside it are a small prayer wheel from Tibet and six small figures **which represent Siamese musicians.**
Participial phrase	Beside it are a small prayer wheel from Tibet and six small figures **representing Siamese musicians.**

Adjective clause	They sent a chair **that was damaged** to the repair department.
Single adjective	They sent a **damaged** chair to the repair department.

EXERCISE 57
Relative Pronouns

A. *Write out these sentences, correctly repositioning misplaced italicized adjective clauses.*

1. The monsoon season occurs in Bangkok every year *which causes heavy rains.*
2. A dozen horses were put into the corral *that were to be trained for riding.*
3. The basket on the bus *which I found* contained eggs.
4. Several shops were set up along the river *that sold handmade rugs and jewelry.*
5. He wore a straw hat on the back of his head *that was obviously too small.*
6. In this book there are many facts about reptiles *which the librarian recommended very highly.*
7. Mr. Simmons left a book in the taxi *that he had been reading.*
8. She was carrying a leather purse over her shoulder *which she had bought in Australia.*

B. *Revise sentences 1–4 by changing the italicized adjective clauses to prepositional phrases.*

1. He delivered the rug *that was from Iran* to a customer in Philadelphia.
2. I found my glasses *which were under a newspaper* on the table.
3. On the piano she placed a photograph *which was of her family.*
4. They looked for the shop *that was around the corner.*

Revise sentences 5–8 by changing the italicized adjective clauses to participial phrases.

5. My uncle *who lives in Karachi* is working for a textile company.
6. The bus *that carried the football team* broke down.
7. A windstorm came up *which blew the roof off the house.*
8. The entertainer *who was brought from New Delhi* delighted the audience.

Revise sentences 9–12 by changing the italicized adjective clauses to single adjectives or noun modifiers.

9. We ordered a blanket *which was expensive* for the bride.
10. He would like to add some tropical fish *that are colorful* to his aquarium.
11. They sent a letter *which was friendly* to apologize for not having written to us sooner.
12. Fred proudly handed us his pictures *that showed his graduation.*

REVIEW OF MODAL AUXILIARIES

Reviewing now the modals you studied in Chapter 3 will give you some helpful practice. Test your mastery of these challenging words in the exercises that follow:

EXERCISE 58
Modal Review

A. *Change the following sentences from direct quotation to indirect quotation. Pay close attention to sequence of tenses and to pronoun forms. Make your statements complete sentences.*

Example: Her roommate asked, "Why can't you learn to study?"
Her roommate asked her why she couldn't learn to study.

1. Anne said, "I can't close the door."
2. The professor said, "I will explain the passage to you."
3. The foreign student remarked, "I can't seem to get used to American food."
4. Her mother always asks her, "Why don't you learn to cook?"
5. Her friend added, "Sandy, you'd better be sure that you come to the party."
6. Frank said, "I'm not going to the library tonight."
7. Her sister often complains, "You should not play the music so loudly."
8. The man at the airline counter remarked, "I don't like to travel."

B. *Change the following sentences so that a modal auxiliary appears in each. Choose the modal that best expresses the meaning.*

Example: My brother has permission to visit the White House.
My brother **may** visit the White House.

1. It is advisable for you to go shopping tomorrow.
2. She promises to appear this afternoon.
3. Teachers are obligated to help their students.
4. Ted's father promised to consult Ted.
5. She has permission to bring her dog to school.
6. He is not able to go at 10:00.
7. I guess she will leave at 3:00.
8. They told George it was possible for him to have an appointment on Tuesday.

C. *Write out the sentence, choosing the appropriate verb phrase from among those in parentheses.*

1. I haven't written to my uncle yet, but I (can, should, have, may) **to.**
2. (Do, Would, Will) you like to go to the theater tonight?
3. If you walk down the sidewalk, you (can find, will meet, will see, can come to) the outdoor café.

4. Andre (must go, could have gone, should go) to the Museum of Modern Art this morning, but he changed his plans.
5. (Shall, Will) these shoes be on sale tomorrow?
6. Emily (used to, had to, may) travel by bus, but now she travels by plane.
7. Since I can't find my key, I (must lose, must have lost, might lose) it.
8. If I had brought my old clothes, we (could go, could have gone, will go) on a hike.

D. *Add words to the end of each sentence to form a question.*

Example: Jane can dance.
           Jane can dance, **can't she?**

1. You like to play tennis.
2. People can't help falling in love.
3. They shouldn't write letters during class.
4. Kathy hopes to enter the University of Michigan.
5. The injured soccer player had better see a doctor.
6. She will do it.
7. Mrs. Larrimore would like to receive an invitation.
8. Joe might attend a tennis clinic this summer.

E. *Write one sentence to express each of the following.*

Example: Something that you don't have the ability to do.
           I can't speak Russian.

1. Something that you do have the ability to do.
2. An act that you had the opportunity to perform but didn't.
3. A conjecture about some time in the future.
4. A question of advisability.
5. A situation that is known to be impossible.
6. A present obligation.
7. Present or future permission.
8. A necessary action.

REVIEW OF PREPOSITIONS

Unless you keep after them, prepositions have a habit of slipping away from you. Check your skills by doing the following review exercise:

EXERCISE 59
Preposition Review

Write out each sentence, placing the correct preposition in each blank. Refer to Appendix 6 if you need help in choosing prepositions.

1. After arriving......Turkey......December, the couple stayed...... a small hotel......Ankara......a month.

2. Expecting a letter, he left......the post office to look......his mail box.
3. Have people ever told you that you remind them......Humphrey Bogart?
4. Most workers stay......the job......eight hours, but a doctor is ......call......twenty-four hours a day.
5. He smiled......me when I told him that I wanted to save money ......cooking......myself.
6. Roaring......anger, the female lion chased the monkey......a tree.
7. They live......a houseboat......the Ohio River......the summer.
8. We bought three oranges......breakfast and a bagful......apples ......the pound to take along......our picnic.
9. Every time he borrows a dollar......me, he forgets to give it back ......me unless I remind him......it.
10. ......my family I can talk......any subject, knowing that they will gladly share their ideas......me.
11. When we return......our house......an evening...... the movies, we drive our car......the garage.
12. Usually we walk.......the garage.......the front door.......our house, but sometimes we find this door locked, and so we have to walk ......the house......the back door.
13. A key......the back door is always kept......a high ledge...... the door.
14. Once we get......the house, we always go......the kitchen...... something to eat.
15. We have to kneel down to get the soft drinks which are stored...... the sink; then we stand......a chair to reach the crackers which are kept......a cabinet......the refrigerator.

Questions for Discussion and Review

1. Sometimes writers develop the monotonous habit of beginning several consecutive paragraphs with the article "the." List the variety of words the writer of the model composition has used in beginning his seven paragraphs.
2. List five examples of variety in sentence structure within the model composition.
3. Point out five different kinds of sentence openings in Adler's article on friendship.
4. Which mode of development do the writers use in the first paragraph of the definition of a mathematical relation?
5. Which of the sample passages in this chapter seems to you to be the most forcefully written? Why? The least forcefully written? Why?
6. You have read Robert Frost's definition of "home." What is yours?

7. Locate the thesis statements in the model compositions of Chapters 5 through 8.
8. When discussing such abstract terms as "friendship," a writer can fall into the trap of composing long, meandering sentences that obscure what he is trying to say. In writing about friendship, how has Adler varied his sentence length?
9. Find five examples of figurative language in the writing selections in Chapter 6.
10. Compare the definition of a surveying level in Chapter 1 with the student-written definitions of a pencil in this chapter. Does the "level" definition contain any unnecessary information? Which definition is most logical, complete, well-written, and interesting?

Vocabulary Growth

PARAGRAPH PUZZLE

In this Paragraph Puzzle some of the missing words will **not** *have word choices given beneath them. For these blanks, supply an appropriate word by studying the context.*

In every known human society, the male's need for achievement can be

.... Men may cook or weave or.............dolls or hunt
(called, lasted, reversed, recognized)   (dress, break, take, send)

hummingbirds, but if...........activities are appropriate occupations
                          (one, such, an, other)

of men, ...the whole society, men and women............,
                              (alike, himself, herself, itself)

votes them as important. When the...........occupations are per-
                          (some, same, latter, former)

formed by women, they are regarded as less important. In a............
                              (great, less, only, one)

number of human societies, men's sureness............their sex role

is tied up...........their right or ability to practice...........activ-
(what, with, which, when)

ity that women are not allowed...........practice.
                          (to, on, at, by)

The recurrent problem of civilization............to define the male
                          (are, is, give, gives)

role satisfactorily...........—whether it be to build gardens...........
        (enough, already, until, along)   (on, or, by, as)

raise cattle, kill game or kill............., build bridges............
(bread, enemies, friends, deer)

handle bank shares—so............the male in the course of...........
(what, which, this, that)

life reaches a solid sense of irreversible achievement, of............his
(which, what, that, this)

childhood knowledge of.............satisfactions of childbearing has

given him a glimpse. In the case of women, ...is only neces-
(their, one, it, this)

sary that they............permitted by the given social arrangements
(was, should, may, be)

to fulfill.............biological role, to attain this sense.............
(for, at, of, on)

irreversible achievement. If women are to be restless............questing,
(and, yet, up, down)

even in the face of child-bearing, they must............made so through
(are, be, was, is)

education. If men are............to be at peace, ever certain that their
(never, only, ever, want)

lives............been lived as they were meant to............, they
(is, was, be, are)

must have, in addition to paternity, culturally elaborated............of
(tables, books, shutters, forms)

expression that are lasting and sure.

Margaret Mead, *Male and Female*

WORD CLUES

A. *Vocabulary words in the following exercise are boldfaced.*

1. **Zealously** bending my thoughts toward the future, I have been scurrying around the Institution to learn from various staff members what will happen, what presumably will happen, what is planned to happen, and what just might happen around the Mall and beyond in the next few years. I am pleased to confirm that the Smithsonian is an **upbeat** organization. My minisurvey inspired not one suddenly tightened lip or despairingly clapped brow.

"What Will Go on Around the Mall," Edwards Park, *Smithsonian* (July 1976)

Vocabulary Word...

Context Clue...

Probable Meaning...

Dictionary Definition...

Vocabulary Word. . . . .

Context Clue. . . . .

Probable Meaning. . . . .

Dictionary Definition. . . . .

2. Because of **exorbitant** animal production, each Westerner requires two to six times more grain per day than does his **counterpart** in the hungry world. Few developing countries could allow themselves to use so much of their tilled land to raise animal feed (82 percent in the United Kingdom, 62 percent in the United States). The well-fed world has three times as much tilled land to feed each individual as does the hungry world and benefits additionally from being located in far more favorable climates.

"The Numbers Force Us into a World like None in History,"
Georg Borg-Strom, *Smithsonian* (July 1976)

Vocabulary Word. . . . .

Context Clue. . . . .

Probable Meaning. . . . .

Dictionary Definition. . . . .

Vocabulary Word. . . . .

Context Clue. . . . .

Probable Meaning. . . . .

Dictionary Definition. . . . .

3. At present, large quantities of nuclear wastes containing plutonium are stored in double-lined stainless steel and concrete containers buried at Hanford, Washington. The system is not perfect: a 1972 AEC report noted that at least 660 pounds of plutonium had been allowed to **leach** into the ground. And burial at Hanford is plainly a temporary solution because plutonium 239 remains radioactive for a quarter of a million years. Spent fuel is piling up at existing nuclear power plants because at the moment there are no **operational** recycling centers. The plant at West Valley, New York, is closed until at least 1983 for modifications. A plant built in Illinois by General Electric for $64 million does not work and has been shut down. A third, being built in Barnwell, South Carolina, awaits NRC licensing.

"Plutonium: 'Free' Fuel or Invitation to a Catastrophe?"
Peter Gwynne, *Smithsonian* (July 1976)

Vocabulary Word. . . . .

Context Clue. . . . .

Probable Meaning. . . . .

Dictionary Definition. . . . .

Vocabulary Word...

Context Clue...

Probable Meaning.......................................

Dictionary Definition...................................

4. If Atlanta is among the first to institutionalize neighborhood power, its citizens share with residents of almost every large city in the United States membership in a **nascent** popular movement which some call neighborhood (or community) decentralism. Decentralism may very well be the growing edge in citizen politics these days. Says Milton Kotler, a political scientist based at the Institute for Policy Studies in Washington, "This is the next, great citizen movement." In fact, it may be even greater than its **predecessors**—civil rights, environment, consumerism—because it combines elements of all of them. Municipal governments in more cities than Atlanta have recognized this and have provided means for its expression, although not in such a freewheeling way as Atlanta. Pittsburgh, Portland, Fort Worth, New York City, and Washington all have programs for neighborhood "input" to governmental decision-making. So do scores of other cities.

"Atlanta Renewal Gives Power to the Communities,"
Charles E. Little, *Smithsonian* (July 1976)

Vocabulary Word...

Context Clue...

Probable Meaning.......................................

Dictionary Definition...................................

Vocabulary Word...

Context Clue...

Probable Meaning.......................................

Dictionary Definition...................................

5. The sun is actually a gigantic, lustrous fusion reactor, far bigger, hotter, and—at a distance of ninety-three million miles from the earth—most probably safer than any we are ever going to build on earth. It **deluges** the planet with an enormous energy field, far beyond our energy needs. While the energy companies talk of energy crises, the surface area of the U.S. alone receives about nine thousand trillion kilowatt hours per year in solar energy, an amount roughly six hundred times our current energy use.

John Berger, *Nuclear Power*

Vocabulary Word...

Context Clue...

Probable Meaning..

Dictionary Definition.......................................

B. *Look in a dictionary for meanings of each of the following verbs and for all the related forms of the verb you can find. Make a four-column list headed "verbs, nouns, adjectives, and adverbs."*

1. to benefit
2. to convert
3. to emit
4. to investigate
5. to relate
6. to distinguish

Composition: Show What You Have Learned

Choose a composition topic from either Group I or Group II.

GROUP. I: TOPICS FOR WRITING A DEFINITION

In earlier paragraphs you have learned various methods of developing a composition—chronological order, space order, examples, cause and effect, and comparison and contrast. In this chapter you have studied how a definition is written. For this week's composition, you will need to combine these learnings.

Develop a composition in which you define one of the following terms. Develop your paper by choosing whatever methods and expository patterns will help to explain your meaning clearly.

1. Courage
2. Bigotry
3. Sophistication
4. Nationalism
5. Conscience
6. Morality
7. Social poise
8. Country Western music
9. Love
10. Pornography
11. A slide rule
12. A bicycle pump
13. A medical thermometer
14. An electric fan
15. An abacus
16. A drawing compass
17. A simple carburetor
18. A bunsen burner
19. A small, desk-size electric calculator
20. Any simple mechanical device used in your field of interest

GROUP II: TOPICS TO CHALLENGE YOUR IMAGINATION

The four short humorous passages that follow provide a background for this chapter's Group II writing topics. Does the first selection remind you of feelings you have had while waiting to be called into a dentist's office?

Too often has the scene in the dentist's waiting-room been described for me to try to do it again here. They are all alike. The antiseptic smell, the ominous hum from the operating-rooms, the ancient *Digests*, and the silent, sullen group of waiting patients, each trying to look unconcerned and cordially disliking everyone else in the room—all these have been sung by poets of far greater lyric powers than mine. (Not that I really think that they *are* greater than mine, but that's the customary form of excuse for not writing something you haven't got time or space to do. As a matter of fact, I think I could do it much better than it has ever been done before.)

I can only say that, as you sit looking, with unseeing eyes, through a large book entitled, "The War in Pictures," you would gladly change places with the most lowly of God's creatures. It is inconceivable that there should be anyone worse off than you, unless perhaps it is some of the poor wretches who are waiting with you.

That one over in the arm-chair, nervously tearing to shreds a copy of "The Dental Review and Practical Inlay Worker." She may have something frightful the trouble with her. She couldn't possibly look more worried. Perhaps it is very, very painful. This thought cheers you up considerably. What cowards women are in times like these!

"The Tooth, the Whole Tooth, and Nothing but the Tooth,"
Robert Benchley, *Inside Benchley*

Here is another, even more antic, view of dentistry. The humorist Woody Allen makes an imaginative leap, wondering what it would be like if the nineteenth-century French impressionist artists had been dentists, not painters. By writing in letter form, Allen satirizes the approach taken in a biography of Vincent Van Gogh, *Letters to Theo*. Allen composes three letters that could never have been written by Van Gogh to his brother Theo.

Dear Theo,
Will life never treat me decently? I am wracked by despair! My head is pounding! Mrs. Sol Schwimmer is suing me because I made her bridge as I felt it and not to fit her ridiculous mouth! That's right! I can't work to order like a common tradesman! I decided her bridge should be enormous and billowing, with wild explosive teeth flaring up in every direction like fire! Now she is upset because it won't fit in her mouth! She is so bourgeois and stupid, I want to smash her! I tried forcing the false plate in but it sticks out like a star burst chandelier. Still, I find it beautiful. She claims she can't chew! What do I care whether she can chew or not! Theo, I can't go on like this much longer! I asked Cézanne if he would share an office with me, but he is old and infirm and unable to hold the instruments and they must be tied to his wrists but then he lacks accuracy and once inside a mouth, he knocks out more teeth than he saves. What to do?

Vincent

Dear Theo,

I took some dental X-rays this week that I thought were good. Degas saw them and was critical. He said the composition was bad. All the cavities were bunched in the lower left corner. I explained to him that's how Mrs. Slotkin's mouth looks, but he wouldn't listen! He said he hated the frames and mahogany was too heavy. When he left, I tore them to shreds! As if that was not enough, I attempted some root-canal work on Mrs. Zardis, but halfway through I became despondent. I realized suddenly that root-canal work is not what I want to do! I grew flushed and dizzy. I ran from the office into the air where I could breathe! I blacked out for several days and woke up at the seashore. When I returned, she was still in the chair. I completed her mouth out of obligation but I couldn't bring myself to sign it.

Vincent

Dear Theo,

I am in love. Claire Memling came in last week for an oral prophylaxis. (I had sent her a postcard telling her it had been six months since her last cleaning even though it had been only four days.) Theo, she drives me mad! Wild with desire! Her bite! I've never seen such a bite! Her

Next Thusday I will give her gas
and ask her to marry me.

Drawing by Owen Finstad.

teeth come together perfectly! Not like Mrs. Itkin's, whose lower teeth are forward of her uppers by an inch, giving her an underbite that resembles that of a werewolf! No! Claire's teeth close and meet! When this happens you know there is a God! And yet she's not too perfect. Not so flawless as to be uninteresting. She has a space between lower nine and eleven. Ten was lost during her adolescence. Suddenly and without warning it developed a cavity. It was removed rather easily (actually it fell out while she was talking) and was never replaced. "Nothing could replace lower ten," she told me. "It was more than a tooth, it had been my life to that point." The tooth was rarely discussed as she got older and I think she was only willing to speak of it to me because she trusts me. Oh, Theo, I love her. I was looking down into her mouth today and I was like a nervous young dental student again, dropping swabs and mirrors in there. Later I had my arms around her, showing her the proper way to brush. The sweet little fool was used to holding the brush still and moving her head from side to side. Next Thursday I will give her gas and ask her to marry me.

Vincent
"If the Impressionists Had Been Dentists," Woody Allen, *Without Feathers*

An important aspect of any culture is its humor—what makes people laugh. Since the basis of humor is often sharply different from one culture to another, it is often helpful to read examples of a country's humor in order better to understand that country's values.

Many American humorists share the basic characteristic of treating a serious subject lightly, even irreverently. The examples you have just read illustrate this. Both writers, Robert Benchley and Woody Allen, write about the essentially serious subject of dentistry. But their approach is far from serious. As you think about the selections, try to decide what made these writers single out dentistry as a basis for humor.

When you have finished reviewing the Benchley and Allen passages, you should prepare to write your own composition. Approach this in one of four ways:

1. Select a serious subject (driving a car, operating a voting machine, becoming lost in a big city, for instance) and write about it humorously.
2. Select a humorous subject (a cooking disaster, learning to ice skate, your first kiss, for instance) and write about it seriously.
3. Explain how people's sense of humor in your country differs from people's concept of what is humorous in the United States.
4. Explore the reasons for some books, movies, jokes, or life experiences having made you laugh very loudly.

Chapter 9

The
Expository
Composition
*(Developed by Logical
Division)*

University Lore: U.S.A.

Subordination by
adjective phrase

Statement of logical
division; parallelism

Repeating a word
for coherence

Transition

Correlative
conjunction

Stanford University, **famous as one of northern California's several institutions of higher learning,** is sometimes called "the Harvard of the West." Its reputation
is based on **its location, its intelligent students, its distinguished[1] faculty, its growth opportunities offered
to students, its overseas programs, its substantial[2] endowment, and its recent extensive growth.**

The closeness of Stanford to San Francisco, a city
thirty-two miles to the north, gives the university a
decidedly **cosmopolitan**[3] flavor. Equally **cosmopolitan**
is the student body. Students enroll principally[4] from
the western United States. But most of the fifty states
send students to Stanford, and many foreign students
study here, as well. **And** standards for admission remain high. Young men and women are selected to enter
the university from the upper fifteen percent of their
high school classes.

Not only because of the high caliber[5] of its students
but also because of the desirable location and climate,
Stanford has attracted to its faculty some of the world's
most respected scholars. The university staff has in-

[1]*distinguished:* high in rank, merit, or esteem. [2]*substantial:* large, considerable.
[3]*cosmopolitan:* wordly. [4]*principally:* primarily. [5]*caliber:* quality, ability.

Specific detail

cluded such Nobel Prize winners as **Dr. Felix Bloch, Dr. Robert Hofstadter, and Dr. William Shockley in physics, Dr. Author Kornberg and Dr. Joshua Lederberg in medicine, and Dr. Paul J. Flory and Dr. Linus Pauling in chemistry. The Russian novelist Aleksandr Solzhenitsyn has been in residence.** Stanford's undergraduate school of engineering and its graduate schools of business, law, and medicine are especially well-regarded.

Rhetorical question

Correlative conjunctions

Commas in series

What is student life like on "The Farm"? Culturally, the campus is a magnet for **both** students **and** citizens of nearby communities. Plays, concerts, and operas are performed in the university's several auditoriums and in outdoor Frost Amphitheater, where graduations are also held. Several film series are presented during the school year. Guest lecturers from public and academic life frequently appear on campus. In the evenings, many students gather to socialize in the Student

Semicolon joining independent clauses

Union's coffee house; here the beverages and the atmosphere both have a decidedly European flavor. For the sports-minded, the Stanford campus offers highly

Subordination by adverb clause

developed athletic facilities. **Because its campus resembles a sprawling, wooded park backed by foothills and protected from the rather dense suburban life that surrounds it,** the university has been able to provide large athletic fields. Team sports, swimming, and track and field activity are all very much part of the Stanford picture. So are bicycling and jogging.

Specific detail

To enrich its educational offerings, the university has established **overseas branch study centers in Great Britain, Austria, Germany, Italy, and France** for third-year students. In addition to financial support from alumni, Stanford receives grants from the government and from private philanthropic[6] foundations. In recent years, government grants have made possible advanced studies in the fields of history, psychology, education, and atomic energy. At present Stanford is carrying out

Participial phrase at end of sentence

an ambitious building program, **financed in part by the Ford Foundation's 25 million grant.** Recently added to the campus are a new physics building, new school of business, new graduate school of law, new student union, and undergraduate library.

[6]*philanthropic:* charitable, generous.

Participial phrase
at beginning of
sentence

Founded only in 1891, Stanford is now generally considered comparable in quality to such other longer-established, major American universities as Harvard, Yale, Princeton, and Columbia. In the past decade, it has given young Americans increasing reason to follow Horace Greeley's advice: "Go West, young man."

Colon introducing
appositive

Writing Analysis

REPEATING A WORD FOR COHERENCE

Using transitions to link sentence to sentence and paragraph to paragraph helps to tie a composition together, to give it coherence. Another means of achieving coherence is to repeat a key word from one sentence to the next or from the ending of one paragraph to the beginning of the next one.

You have seen how the word "cosmopolitan" has been purposefully repeated in the model composition as a connective between two sentences. Of course, word repetition can detract from a person's writing as well as improve it, particularly if the repetition is unintentional or if it is overdone. On the other hand, most successful writers have mastered the art of word repetition and use it forcefully. Useful in the twentieth century, word repetition was also popular with nineteenth-century writers; examine how forcefully the British author Anthony Trollope applies this technique in his 1862 book, *North America:* "The taste of America is becoming **French** in its conversation, **French** in its comforts and **French** in its discomforts, **French** in its eating, and **French** in its dress, **French** in its manners, and will become **French** in its art."

A writer repeats a word to knit his ideas together, much as a bricklayer spreads mortar to fit one brick onto the next. A second purpose of word repetition is to emphasize an idea. Still another aim may be to generate emotional force. The American Negro essayist James Baldwin demonstrates all three functions of word repetition in the following passage in which he remembers his dead father, a former minister:

He was, I think, very handsome. I gather this from photographs and from my own memories of him, dressed in his Sunday best and on his way to preach a sermon somewhere, when I was little. Handsome, proud, and ingrown, "like a toe-nail," somebody said. But he looked to me, as I grew older, like pictures I had seen of African tribal chieftains: he really should have been naked, with war-paint on and barbaric mementos, standing among spears. He could be chilling in the pulpit and indescribably cruel in his personal life and he was certainly the most bitter man I have ever met; yet it must be said that there was something else in him, buried in him, which lent him his tremendous power and, even, a rather crushing charm. It had something to do with his **blackness**, I think —he was very **black**—with his **blackness** and his beauty, and with the fact that he knew that he was **black** but did not know that he was beautiful. He claimed to be proud of his **blackness** but it had also been the cause of much humiliation and it had fixed bleak boundaries to his life. He was not a young man when we were growing up and he had already suffered many kinds of ruin; in his outrageously demanding and protective way he loved his children, who were **black** like him and menaced, like him; and all these things sometimes showed in his face when he tried, never to my knowledge with any success, to establish contact with any of us.

"My Father," James Baldwin, *Notes of a Native Son*

In effect, Baldwin turns up the volume on the idea of "black" and "blackness" by skillfully repeating these words six times throughout the second half of his paragraph. Like a symphony conductor, he brings in the brass and percussion sections at appropriate moments; but, being a writer, he reaches this greater sound not by adding musical instruments but by repeating words. Consummate stylistic magician that he is, Baldwin artfully fits in the word "bleak" to echo the "black" refrain that he is insistently drumming out.

The second example of word repetition, composed not by a black American man but by a white American woman, touches on the same general subject—slavery and oppression—that underlies the Baldwin passage. But in this case, the object of the oppression is the American woman. After reading Clare Boothe Luce's selection, you may come to feel that controlled word repetition not only can generate an emotional response in a reader but also may be a technique natural to a writer who is emotionally involved with a subject:

The institution of slavery (**oppression** by the use of overt[1] force) existed at the dawn of history and lasted, with social approval in almost all civilizations, right down to the middle of the nineteenth century. (As forced labor, it still exists in Soviet Russia.) Our own Founding Fathers, as enlightened, scholarly, liberty-loving, and God-fearing a group of males as ever lived, did not question either the religious or political morality of black slavery. In America the institution of slavery was brought to an end only a century ago. And it took the bloodiest war on our soil to do it. Nevertheless—*it ended.*

The **oppressed** (the enslaved, the politically imprisoned, the exploited, the discriminated against) are **oppressed** because **oppression** is to the **oppressor's** interests, and because the **oppressed** lack the physical, political, economic, and psychological means to resist and throw them off. The **oppressed** never free themselves—they do not have the necessary strengths. They become free only when their **oppressors** lose the strength or the will to **oppress** them. A white President emancipates the black man. A male Congress grants woman the vote. A male-dominated Congress passes the equal-rights amendment.

The dominating, or **oppressor,** class relinquishes[2] its position of superiority either when another dominant class collapses it (the anti-slavery white North defeats the white slave-holding South), or when **oppression** no longer serves the political, economic, and psychological needs of the **oppressors.**

"The 21st-Century Woman—Free at Last?," Clare Boothe Luce
Saturday Review/World (24 August 1974)

[1]*overt:* not hidden; open. [2]*relinquishes:* gives up.

Here the twelve repetitions of the word "oppression" and its related forms (*oppress, oppressor, oppressed*) in a short selection strongly underscore the writer's central thesis, setting the stage for Mrs. Luce's pessimistic conclusion that there is little improvement at present for the U.S.A.'s women and only a distant hope.

EXERCISE 60
Repeating a Word for Coherence

Improve the coherence of the following paragraph, revising it by controlled word repetition.

Take cheese, for example. Here and there, in big cities, small stores and delicatessens specialize in such dairy products. In these stores, one can buy at last some of the first-rate ones that we used to eat—such as those we had with apple pie and in macaroni. The latter were sharp but not too sharp. They were a little crumbly. We called them American cheeses, or even rat types; actually, they were Cheddars. Long ago, this product began to be supplanted by a material called "cheese foods." Although some dairy product foods and "processed" ones are fairly edible, not one comes within miles of the old kinds for flavor.

"Science Has Spoiled My Supper," Philip Wylie, John E. Warriner, et al.,
Advanced Composition

EXPOSITORY DEVELOPMENT (by logical division)

Now that you have arrived at Chapter 9, it is time to shift your attention to a new aspect of analytical paragraph development—that of elaboration by logical division, or classification. Because an understanding of logical divison is fundamental to the mastery of American rhetoric, you will be studying this technique of breaking a subject into parts in this and the following chapter.

Actually, logical division is not really new to you. Much of the English writing that you have read has been organized in this way. Logical division as a form of development has frequently appeared in model selections in earlier chapters. It is particularly evident in Chapter 7's model composition, "A Scientific Experiment." In that model's final paragraph, the explanation for the scientific phenomenon that has been described earlier is divided into five parts. Transitions (first, second, third, fourth, fifth) introduce each of the reasons given.

A further example of a subject being broken down into workable parts by logical division is this chapter's model paragraph. The title "University Lore, U.S.A." tells only that the writer will describe a college. It does not suggest how the description may be developed. In choosing his controlling idea, the writer takes the first step in the process of logical division. For the model paragraph, he has chosen the controlling idea that Stanford is a prominent university. Then, to prove his thesis, he has broken down the idea of "prominence" into seven parts: ". . . its location, its intelligent students, its distinguished faculty, its growth opportunities offered to students, its overseas programs, its substantial endowment, and its recent extensive growth." These, then, are the structural parts of the logical division. The writer probably thought of others but eliminated them for a number of reasons. Some may not have been important enough; some may have been irrelevant to the thesis; about some he may not have had enough concrete information.

Logical division is also illustrated in a very direct way in the opening paragraph of E. B. White's "The Three New Yorks":

> **There are roughly three New Yorks.** There is, **first,** the New York of the man or woman who was born there, who takes the city for granted and accepts its size and its turbulence[1] as natural and inevitable. **Second,** there is the New York of the commuter[2]—the city that is devoured by locust each day and spat out each night. **Third,** there is the New York of the person who was born somewhere else and came to New York in quest[3] of something. Of these three trembling cities the greatest is the last—the city of final destination, the city that is a goal. It is this third city that accounts for New York's high-strung[4] disposition, its poetical deportment, its dedication to the arts, and its incomparable[5] achievements. Commuters give the city its tidal restlessness; natives give it solidity and continuity,[6] but the settlers give it passion. And whether it is a farmer arriving from Italy to set up a small grocery store in a slum, or a young girl arriving from a small town in Mississippi to escape the indignity[7] of being observed by her neighbors, or a boy arriving from the Corn Belt with a manuscript and a pain in his heart, it makes no difference: each embraces New York with the intense excitement of first

[1]*turbulence:* disorder, commotion. [2]*commuter:* person who travels daily or regularly between an outlying district and his place of work in the city. [3]*quest:* search. [4]*high-strung:* highly sensitive, nervous, tense, excitable. [5]*incomparable:* unequaled, matchless. [6]*continuity:* state or quality of being continuous, unbroken. [7]*indignity:* something that humiliates, insults, or injures dignity or

love, each absorbs New York with the fresh eyes of an adventurer, each generates[8] heat and light to dwarf[9] the Consolidated Edison Company.

"The Three New Yorks," E. B. White, *Here Is New York*

self-respect. [8]*generates*: produces. [9]*to dwarf*: to make to seem small by comparison.

From the start there is no doubt as to how Mr. White is going to develop his essay. He directly reveals his method of organization in his opening sentence: "There are roughly three New Yorks." In this sense we have logical division in its simplest form. But let us take a few steps backward in time, to the moment when White first decided to write a description of New York. At that time he must have put a lot of complex thought into selecting a suitable framework. This, in fact, is when the process of logical division begins. It is a process identical with the one you studied in Chapter 5 of breaking down an outline's subject into smaller main divisions.

White may first have thought of and have discarded a number of structural possibilities for developing a description of the city. He finally decided upon a delightful approach: to describe New York in terms of its people. This decision brought him to the second step in logical division. Next, he had to consider the many different **kinds** of people who inhabit America's largest city. Again, many possibilities probably came to his mind. He could have described New Yorkers by occupation or by race, by social level or by national background, by attitude or by political preference. Choosing and rejecting categories until one arrives at a workable one is the very essence of the method of logical division, a method that E. B. White clearly understands well. In this case, he chose three related categories of New Yorkers: those who are born there, those who commute, and those who have adopted New York.

In effect, a writer using logical division begins on the top rung of the ladder of generalization to establish his categories. Then he moves down the ladder to fill in the details more concretely. Perhaps more than any other method of development, logical division requires the writer to have an alert, resourceful mind. For if the development of a paper is too predictable, the paper might become dull. If the writer is also imaginative, so much the better. His organization and his subsequent writing will be stronger because of it.

Whether they are experimenting in the laboratory or writing at their desks, scientists and technologists must live by the word "precision." Because of this, logical division is for them a particularly suitable mode of development. See how logical division has been used in the following discussion of the pollution everyone is familiar with—noise pollution:

Noise is unwanted sound. **There are three basic types of noise: wideband, narrow-band, and impulse.**

Wide-band noise is, as the name implies, noise that is distributed across a broad range of frequencies. Narrow-band noises have their energies confined to a narrow range of frequencies or concentrated about a single frequency. The noise created by circular saws, planers, and similar power tools is narrow-band noise. Impulse-type noise is comprised of transient pulses which can occur repetitively or nonrepetitively. The noise associated with a jack hammer is an example of repetitive noise; the firing of a gun is a nonrepetitive noise.

"Noise," Robert W. Allen, Michael D. Ells, Andrew W. Hart, *Industrial Hygiene*

Starting with a brief but pointed definition ("Noise is unwanted sound."), the writers introduce a three-part breakdown of types of noise. Doing this allows the authors to state their case with the greatest economy of words and in the clearest possible way. Can a writer ask more of an expository technique?

Writing about the world's largest mammal, the whale, Rachel Carson also turns to logical division to help clarify her explanation:

Eventually the whales, as though to divide the sea's food resources among them, became separated into three groups: the plankton[1]-eaters, the fish-eaters, and the squid-eaters. The plankton-eating whales can exist only where there are dense masses of small shrimp or copepods to supply their enormous food requirements. This limits them, except for scattered areas, to arctic and antarctic waters and the high temperate latitudes. Fish-eating whales may find food over a somewhat wider range of ocean, but they are restricted to places where there are enormous populations of schooling[2] fish. The blue water of the tropics and of the open ocean basins offers little to either of these groups. But that immense, square-headed, formidably[3] toothed whale known as the cachalot or sperm whale discovered long ago what men have known for only a short time—that hundreds of fathoms below the almost untenanted[4] surface waters of these regions there is an abundant animal life. The sperm whale has taken these deep waters for his hunting grounds; his quarry[5] is the deep-water population of squids, including the giant squid Architeuthis, which lives pelagically[6] at depths of 1500 feet or more. The head of the sperm whale is often marked with long stripes, which consist of a great number of circular scars made by the suckers of the squid. From this evidence we can imagine the battles that go on, in the darkness of the deep water, between these huge creatures—the sperm whale with its 70-ton bulk, and the squid with a body as long as 30 feet, and writhing,[7] grasping arms extending the total length of the animal to perhaps 50 feet.

"Whales," Rachel Carson, *The Sea Around Us*

[1]*plankton:* microscopic animal and plant life living in water and used as food by fish. [2]*schooling:* swimming together. [3]*formidably:* causing dread, fear, or awe; fearsomely. [4]*untenanted:* empty, unpopulated. [5]*quarry:* anything being hunted or pursued. [6]*pelagically:* in the open sea, as distinguished from coastal waters. [7]*writhing:* twisting.

Miss Carson has clearly arranged the three parts of her logical division
—the plankton-eaters, the fish-eaters, and the squid-eaters—in a meaningful way. Her main interest in the paragraph centers upon the deep water
battle between the sperm whale and the giant squid. To place the strongest
emphasis upon this encounter, she places it last in her logical development.
If the squid-eaters had been placed as the first or second point in her organization, the resulting paragraph would have been strongly anticlimactic.

Perhaps J. B. S. Haldane, writing on "Science and Ethics," takes a less
imaginative approach than White does toward organization. But Haldane's
finished product is certainly no less thoughtful. He has carefully weighed
the relation of modern science to ethics; he has decided upon five main
points to discuss; and he has introduced them methodically, one by one,
before reaching the climax of his paper. Students should particularly
note how meticulously Haldane has apparently prepared his points by
thinking **before** writing. Few writers who expect to be taken seriously ever
begin to put pen to paper before carrying out rather extensive and pene-
trating dialogues on their topics with others and, importantly, with themselves.

> **Science impinges upon ethics in at least five different ways. In the first
> place,** by its application it creates new ethical[1] situations. Two hundred
> years ago the news of a famine[2] in China created no duty for Englishmen.
> They could take no possible action against it. Today the telegraph and
> the steam-engine have made such action possible, and it becomes an
> ethical problem what action, if any, is right. Two hundred years ago a
> workman generally owned his own tools. Now his tool may be a crane
> or steamhammer, and we all have our own views as to whether these
> should belong to shareholders, the State, or guilds representing the
> workers.
>
> **Secondly,** it may create new duties by pointing out previously unex-
> pected consequences of our actions. We are all agreed that we should
> not run the risk of spreading typhoid by polluting the public water sup-
> ply. We are probably divided as to the duty of vaccinating our children,
> and we may not all be of one mind as to whether a person likely to trans-
> mit club-foot[3] or cataract[4] to half his or her children should be com-
> pelled[5] to abstain from[6] parenthood.
>
> **Thirdly,** science affects our whole ethical outlook by influencing our
> views as to the nature of the world—in fact, by supplanting[7] mythology.
> One man may see men and animals as a great brotherhood of common
> ancestry and thus feel an enlargement of his obligations. Another will
> regard even the noblest aspects of human nature as products of a ruth-
> less[8] struggle for existence and thus justify a refusal to assist the weak

[1]*ethical:* conforming to moral standards. [2]*famine:* starvation, great hunger.
[3]*clubfoot:* congenital deformity of the foot into a twisted, often clublike, appearance. [4]*cataract:* eye disease causing partial or total blindness. [5]*compelled:*
forced, required. [6]*abstain from:* give up, voluntarily do without. [7]*supplanting:*
taking the place of. [8]*ruthless:* cruel, without pity.

and suffering. A third, impressed with the vanity of human efforts amid the vast indifference of the universe, will take refuge in a modified epicureanism.[9] In all these attitudes and in many others there is at least some element of rightness.

Fourthly, in so far as anthropology[10] is becoming scientific, it is bound to have a profound[11] effect on ethics by showing that any given ethical code is only one of a number practised with equal conviction[12] and almost equal success; in fact, by creating comparative ethics. But, of course, any serious study of the habits of foreigners, whether scientific or not, has this effect, as comes out plainly enough in the history of ancient Greek ethics. Hence science is not wholly responsible for the ethical results of anthropology.

Finally, ethics may be profoundly affected by an adoption of the scientific point of view; that is to say the attitude that men of science, in their professional capacity, adopt towards the world. This attitude includes a high (perhaps an unduly[13] high) regard for truth, and a refusal to come to unjustifiable conclusions which expresses itself on the plane of religion as agnosticism.[14] And along with this is found a deliberate suppression[15] of emotion until the last possible moment, on the ground that emotion is a stumbling-block[16] on the road to truth. So a rose and a tapeworm must be studied by the same methods and viewed from the same angle, even if the work is ultimately to lead to the killing of the tapeworms and the propagation[17] of roses. Again, the scientific point of view involves the cultivation of a scientific esthetic[18] which rejoices[19] in the peculiar forms of beauty which characterize scientific theory. Those who find an intimate[20] relation between the good and the beautiful will realize the importance of the fact that a group of men so influential as scientific workers are pursuing a particular kind of beauty. Finally, since the scientist, as such, is contributing to an intellectual structure that belongs to humanity as whole, his influence will inevitably fall in favour of ethical principles and practices which transcend[21] the limits of nation, colour, and class.

"Science and Ethics," J. B. S. Haldane, *Science and Human Life*

[9]*epicureanism:* fondness of luxury and sensual pleasures. [10]*anthropology:* study of the races of mankind. [11]*profound:* thorough-going, far-reaching. [12]*conviction:* strong belief. [13]*unduly:* excessively, unjustly. [14]*agnosticism:* doctrine that it is impossible to know whether there is a God or a future life, or anything beyond material phenomena. [15]*suppression:* restraining, keeping back. [16]*stumbling-block:* obstacle, hindrance. [17]*propagation:* raising, reproduction. [18]*esthetic:* doctrine of beauty. [19]*rejoices:* delights, is made happy. [20]*intimate:* very close. [21]*transcend:* go beyond, exceed.

Because of Haldane's interest in science, his precision in organizing and developing his essay is not surprising. In his opening paragraph, he begins immediately with a clear topic sentence setting forth his logical division: "Science impinges upon ethics in at least five different ways." Then he introduces his first point with the connective "in the first place. . . ." Notice how surely he prepares his reader to follow his thought development by placing a connective (secondly, thirdly, fourthly, finally) at the beginning of each of his four subsequent paragraphs.

You will notice that most of the writers of this week's sample passages, after having selected the structural parts of their logical division, took the further important step of arranging these parts in some kind of planned order; they did not just let them fall at random.

A reliable rule to follow is to arrange one's categories or structural parts in order of importance, beginning with the least important and ending with the most important. E. B. White did this in writing of the three New Yorks: he placed the "greatest" New York last, ending his discussion with it. The value of arranging in order of importance is that it permits your paper to build to a natural climax. In doing so, it carries your reader along, maintaining his curiosity, to a satisfying conclusion. Other possibilities for arranging structural parts include placing them in order of time, in order of area or space, or even in order of your most forceful supporting examples. The main goal here is to have some logical reason for both your division into structural units and your arrangement of these units.

In the model paragraph the seven structural parts were selected because they seemed to be the most important factors in the growing prestige of Stanford. They were arranged by a combination of order of increasing importance (its location is certainly less important than the caliber of its faculty) and order of increasing scope, ending with the impressive $25 million expansion program.

EXERCISE 61
Outlining

*First review the section in Chapter 5 on "The Composition Outline."
Then reconstruct the outline the writer probably worked from in composing the model composition "University Lore, U.S.A."*

STYLE IN WRITING

Having practiced forming definitions in Chapter 8, you should be ready to pin down the meaning of the word "style" as it applies to English prose. The concept of style applies to many areas in addition to that of English composition. It can refer to the shape of an automobile, the design of a building, or the manner in which a person swims. If we consider how style relates to these diverse things, we can better understand its meaning. For instance, style of automobile design and style of writing refer to the distinctive qualities of a car and of a composition, qualities that set them apart from the ordinary or usual. This is also true of style in swimming and in architecture. The Maserati automobile, the decathalon form of Bruce Jenner, the Barcelona cathedral, *Sagrada Familia*, designed by Gaudi, and the writing of James Baldwin all have a characteristic and unique quality. Each has a personal style.

What are the chief elements of a writer's style? Probably most apparent at first glance are his diction (word choice) and his sentence structure. Whether a writer's vocabulary is simple or complex, whether he uses words conventionally or in unusual ways, these choices contribute to the particular style he produces. The varying lengths and grammatical structures of his sentences are also fundamental in forming his style. Essentially, a writer's style is an expression of his individuality. But his style need not be the same at all times. The appropriateness of style varies according to time, place, occasion, subject, the writer's audience, and the writer's purpose.

This chapter is an especially appropriate one in which to begin study of writing style, for it contains some clear examples of quite different styles. By examining them, you may better understand what the components of an individual writing style are.

First, consider Mrs. Luce's writing style in "The 21st-Century Woman—Free at Last?" Because she is intent on giving her points maximum impact, she relies chiefly on short sentences. The following three Luce sentences might be compared to three boxer's jabs at a punching bag: "A white President emancipates the black man. A male Congress grants woman the vote. A male-dominated Congress passes the equal rights amendment."

Both Carson, in "Whales," and Haldane, in "Science and Ethics," have rather complex material to present. Carson's is factual, Haldane's abstract, and the contrast in their approach is revealing. Carson accomplishes a most difficult feat: she adds a fluidity and grace to scientific writing primarily through her sentence structure, word choice, and use of transitions. Equally important, she "humanizes" her subject, relating undersea life to human terrestrial life at key points (But that immense . . . whale . . . discovered long ago what men have only known for a short time . . . ; . . . we can imagine the battles that go on . . .). Haldane, on the other hand, bases his style purely on logic; he carefully weaves his ideas together with numerous transitions (in the first place, secondly, thirdly, another, but, hence, so, this, and, again, finally).

A second pair of writers also reveals highly individual (and highly polished) styles: E.B. White and James Baldwin. In "The Three New Yorks," the clarity of the development is directly related to White's extensive use of parallelism. Here is one example from the middle (**the city** of final destination, **the city** that is a goal) and one from the conclusion (**each embraces** New York . . . , **each absorbs** New York . . . , **each generates** heat and light . . .). The style of Baldwin's "My Father" is unique. Although many of the sentences begin with parallel pronoun-verbs (He was, He could, He claimed), the chief stylistic effects come from Baldwin's elegant simplicity of diction, his almost Biblical sense of word repetition and use of the conjunction "and," and his ability to weave phrases and clauses together with absolute clarity. The great achievement of this passage is that, in writing an elegy to his father, who had been a preacher, Baldwin recreates the same flowing type of incantation that his father probably chanted each Sunday from the pulpit. If style can be said to be a matter of achieving appropriateness, then Baldwin has excelled.

To get a broader picture of the gradations of English prose style, examine the following six passages taken from magazines, novels, an essay, and a letter:

1. A scientific description of a species of anemic fish, the ice fish

Without attempting to guess what further studies will show, I believe that the answer to the question of how these anemic fishes have managed to evolve is to be found in their unique ecological setting. In the case of the ice fish, for example, its major physiological asset—an unusually large volume of blood circulation—by itself would probably not be enough to keep the animal alive in temperate waters. Only when this characteristic is combined with the Antarctic's low and stable water temperature and that environment's abundant supply of food and oxygen is the survival of these peculiar animals possible. In fact, it is hard to imagine any other marine or freshwater environment that would offer a similar chance of survival should another family of anemic fishes begin to evolve elsewhere in the world.

"The Ice Fish," Juhan T. Ruud, *Scientific American* (November 1965)

The style of this passage is quite formal, its vocabulary somewhat scientific. Sentences are rather long and moderately complex. The writer is objective, logical, and direct.

2. A passage from a novel, describing stoic suffering

Silently Siddhartha stood in the fierce sun's rays, filled with pain and thirst, and stood until he no longer felt pain and thirst. Silently he stood in the rain, water dripping from his hair on to his freezing shoulders, on to his freezing hips and legs. And the ascetic stood until his shoulders and legs no longer froze, till they were silent, till they were still. Silently he crouched among the thorns. Blood dripped from his smarting skin, ulcers formed, and Siddhartha remained stiff, motionless, till no more blood flowed, till there was no more pricking, no more smarting.

"The Ascetic," Hermann Hesse, *Siddhartha*

Here is an artful and esthetic, almost poetic passage. In its word repetition and parallel structures, the selection recalls Biblical prose. Unlike the previous example, it is highly emotional and subjective.

3. A moment of fantasy in a children's book, in which Alice is falling down a seemingly bottomless pit

Down, down, down. There was nothing else to do, so Alice soon began talking again. "Dinah'll miss me very much tonight, I should think!"

(Dinah was the cat.) "I hope they will remember her saucer of milk at teatime. Dinah, my dear! I wish you were down here with me! There are no mice in the air, I'm afraid, but you might catch a bat, and that's very like a mouse, you know. But do cats eat bats, I wonder?" And here Alice began to get rather sleepy, and went on saying to herself, in a dreamy sort of way, "Do cats eat bats? Do cats eat bats?" and sometimes "Do bats eat cats" for, you see, as she couldn't answer either question, it didn't much matter which way she put it. She felt that she was dozing off, and had just begun to dream that she was walking hand in hand with Dinah, and was saying to her very earnestly, "Now, Dinah, tell me the truth, did you ever eat a bat?" when suddenly, thump! thump! down she came upon a heap of sticks and dry leaves, and the fall was over.

"Alice Falling," Lewis Carroll, *Alice's Adventures in Wonderland*

This style is humorous and whimsical. The word choice in the selection is simple, and it is written in an informal, colloquial manner.

4. A personal letter from Dr. Samuel Johnson to Lord Chesterfield, who had denied Johnson's earlier request for financial help at the beginning of Johnson's writing career

Seven years, my Lord, have now passed since I waited in your outward rooms or was repulsed from your door; during which time I have been pushing on my work through difficulties, of which it is useless to complain, and have brought it at last to the verge of publication, without one act of assistance, one word of encouragement, or one smile of favor. Such treatment I did not expect, for I never had a patron before. . . .

Is not a patron, my Lord, one who looks with unconcern on a man struggling for life in the water, and when he has reached ground encumbers him with help? The notice which you have been pleased to take of my labors, had it been early had been kind. But it has been delayed till I am indifferent, and cannot enjoy it; till I am solitary, and cannot impart it; till I am known, and do not want it.

I hope it is not very cynical asperity not to confess obligations where no benefit has been received, or to be unwilling that the public should consider me as owing that to a patron which Providence has enabled me to do for myself. . . . For I have long been wakened from that dream of hope in which I once boasted myself with much exultation, my lord— Your lordship's most humble, most obedient servant, Sam. Johnson.

From a letter written by Dr. Samuel Johnson to Lord Chesterfield

Writing in the eighteenth century, Johnson has a style that is very formal. The passage is filled with balanced sentences and parallel forms. Although the letter is extremely polite on the surface, the underlying feeling is one of bitter irony.

5. A sociological study of American society

The all-American radio heroes, from the Lone Ranger to Jack Armstrong, were for many reasons more sexless than their movie counterparts. Emotion was out, and sex wasn't for kids anyhow. The Shadow, who learned how to cloud men's minds in the Orient (dig?), may have had a little thing going with Margo Lane (not to be confused with Lois Lane, friend of Clark Kent, alias Superman), just as Perry Mason would, in later years of television, become a little cozy with Della Street. But for the most part, love and its problems were relegated to the soap operas, where the Americanism was either institutional, honoring the family and the small town, or nonexistent, leaving the mythic American unencumbered, either by family or by feeling, to press the fight.

"Love and Radio in the U.S.A.," Peter Schrag, *The Decline of the WASP*

Notable in this passage is the sharp contrast in style between the opening looseness of diction and the elevated word choice at the end. Even though many writers avoid using colloquialisms because they quickly go out of fashion, Schrag felt free to include one (dig), perhaps to reproduce more accurately the texture of the time. Having done this, he swings dramatically from relying on informal language (anyhow, had a thing going, become a little cozy with) to using formal words that suggest the university classroom (relegated, mythic, unencumbered).

Which style do you think is most effective, one like Schrag's, that mixes levels of languages, or one like Krutch's in the following selection, "The Mystique of the Desert," that maintains a single language level?

6. An essay about desert life

To those who do listen, the desert speaks of things with an emphasis quite different from that of the shore, the mountains, the valleys, or the plains. Whereas they invite action and suggest limitless opportunity, exhaustless resources, the implications and the mood of the desert are something different. For one thing, the desert is conservative, not radical. It is more likely to provoke awe than to invite conquest. It does not, like the plains, say, "Only turn the sod and uncountable riches will spring up." The heroism which it encourages is the heroism of endurance, not that of conquest. . . . The desert is "the last frontier" in more senses than one. It is the last because it was the latest reached, but it is the last because it is, in many ways, a frontier which *cannot* be crossed. It brings man up against his limitations, turns him in upon himself, and suggests values which more indulgent regions minimize. Sometimes it inclines to contemplation men who have never contemplated before. And of all answers to the question "What is a desert good for?" "Contemplation" is perhaps the best.

"The Mystique of the Desert," Joseph Wood Krutch, *Ten Contemporary Thinkers*

In contrast to the mixture of "pop" and scholarly styles in the previous passage, the style of this selection is unified, rhythmical, and flowing. The writer unfolds his ideas slowly and deliberately, in short, graceful sentences. Like some of the other writers, he uses repetition and parallel structure.

This style is representative of the reflective writing found in many personal essays.

As you contrast the writing styles represented in this book, you can see how flexible English prose is, how well it offers the opportunity for a variety of expression. After having read Dr. Samuel Johnson's letter to Lord Chesterfield, you can also gain insights into how English has changed over a two-hundred-year period. Sentences have become shorter. Vocabulary is generally simpler today; fewer words derived from Latin are being used. Elaborately balanced sentences have gone out of fashion. In their place have come sentences subordinated by such popularly modern means as participial phrases and adjectives and adverb clauses. Both concise parallel structures and the compound predicate have helped to make written expression in English become more direct. Transitions have become increasingly important. Elliptical phrases, appositives, and single-word modifiers permit the contemporary writer to express his ideas in fewer words than a writer of English a century ago would normally have used. Probably the chief trend in contemporary English prose style, as in modern clothing styles, is away from formality toward a greater informality.

THE RHETORICAL QUESTION

A rhetorical question differs from an ordinary question in this way: when a writer adds a rhetorical question, he does not expect the reader to answer it. Instead, a rhetorical question is used for emphasis. When a reader comes upon a rhetorical question, he generally pauses and reflects intensely for a moment. The question will fix an idea more firmly in his mind than a declarative statement would. Thus you can give special force to an idea by expressing it in the form of a rhetorical question. Such a question may appear at the beginning, middle, or end of a composition. But wherever it is placed, these points should be kept in mind:

1. A rhetorical question focuses and intensifies the reader's interest.
2. A rhetorical question should be used only to give force to the writer's main ideas; it should not be wasted on minor points.
3. The rhetorical question—like any stylistic device—should be used sparingly for best effect.

Note that the fourth paragraph of this chapter's model composition begins with a rhetorical question: "What is student life like on 'The Farm'?" Here the question both announces what is to come in the paragraph and arouses the reader's interest in what the paragraph's content will be. You will find other instances of rhetorical questions used for expository purposes in example selections throughout this book. Since a rhetorical question creates a strong effect, though, it should be used with restraint. Reserved for special occasions, it exerts its greatest force.

EXERCISE 62
The Rhetorical Question

List ten examples of rhetorical questions used in writings in Chapters 1–9.

REVIEW OF TRANSITIONS WITHIN A PARAGRAPH

Here is a paragraph from an article on the medical science of the future—predictive medicine, based on genetic profiles. Read it as the basis for the assignment that follows.

> If one of your grandparents is a **diabetic,** your chances of developing the disease in middle age are about 20 percent—nearly three times greater than average, but still not too alarming. . . . With closer relatives being **diabetic**—a parent and a sibling—your odds are raised to 50 percent. **But** in a few years, if a recently discovered biochemical defect in blood cells proves predictive, reacting positively to Dr. Blecher's test will be a warning that you are nearly certain to get the disease—unless you take radical steps to avoid it. **This** means stringent controls over your diet: no sugar, few starches, and a grand total of calories low enough to keep you slim, since even a 15 percent increase over your recommended weight could trigger the illness.
>
> "Genetic Profiles Will Put Our Health in Our Own Hands,"
> Maya Pines, *Smithsonian* (July 1976)

Each sentence in this passage is connected to the adjoining one by a different transitional device. Word repetition of the key term "diabetic" links the first and second sentences. The third sentence begins with a transition, the coordinating conjunction "But." The fourth sentence opens with the pronoun "This" acting as a transition.

EXERCISE 63
Review: Transitions within a Paragraph

Write a four-sentence paragraph on one of the subjects listed below (or on a subject of your own choice) that follows the same transition pattern as the example paragraph: (1) Begin the second sentence by repeating a key word; (2) Begin the third sentence with a coordinating conjunction; (3) Begin the fourth sentence with a pronoun.

TOPICS

A medical fact   A social experience
A dental fact   A dining experience
A scientific fact   A holiday experience

Punctuation Points

MISCELLANEOUS USES OF THE COMMA

In earlier chapters you have studied several different uses of the comma. Commas are also used conventionally in the following ways:

1. To separate day and year in dates:

July 4, 1776, was America's first Independence Day.

Often both commas are omitted when no day is given:

July 1776 was the month of America's first Independence Day celebration.

2. To separate places in addresses:

San Francisco, California 94102
Copenhagen, Denmark

3. To separate names from titles or degrees, or to separate last names from first names when names are reversed:

John Jay Wilson, Jr.
Arthur Knight, Vice-President
Harvey L. Andrews, Ph.D.
Smith, George L.

4. To set off direct quotation, especially in dialogue:

He said, "You need a brighter light," and walked toward the light switch.

Essential appositive phrases are not set off by commas:

As George was writing his history paper, the phrase "of the people, by the people, for the people" kept running through his mind.

5. After salutations in friendly letters:

Dear William,   Dearest Martha,

And after the complimentary close in all letters:

Yours truly,

   Michael Ferrington

6. To precede the last of three digits in numbers of 1,000 or higher:

1,003   175,000
$30,000,000 (or $30 million)   12,000

EXERCISE 64
Miscellaneous Comma Uses

Write out these sentences, adding commas wherever necessary.

1. Her daughter was born on October 15 1965 in Panama City.
2. I received a letter from Edward Small President.
3. Man will know much more about conditions on other planets by January 1 2000 scientists predict.
4. The house located at 251 Kensington Drive Stratford England is a very beautiful one.
5. The letter was signed "Sincerely yours Albert Nava."
6. They told us to write to Frank Ferris M.A.
7. The clerk said "You can sample the cheese" when we walked into the shop.
8. Mrs. Carl Reeves 1008 West End Avenue is the owner of the apartment building.
9. The July 1789 French Revolution was a major historical event.
10. Marie said that she had "run frantically" when the alligator started climbing out of the river.
11. The United Parcel Service stopped this morning and left a package that was addressed to Fred Koester Jr. 283 Poplar Lane Los Angeles California 98101.
12. The famous saying "I came, I saw, I conquered" applies to this situation.
13. Mark Rathwell treasurer received a calling card from Hollis Spaudling Ph.D requesting an interview.
14. His secretary suggested that he try some alternatives to his usual salutation "Dear Friend" and his customary close "Sincerely" in future letters.
15. Our advertising agency advised us that we had received 4018 replies to our questionnaire; they said that we might expect a gross income next year approaching $5000000.

Grammar Skills

IRREGULAR COMPARATIVES AND SUPERLATIVES

Several of the common adjectives and adverbs have irregular comparative and superlative forms that you may need to review:

	COMPARATIVE	SUPERLATIVE
good, well	better	best
bad, badly	worse	worst
little	less	least
much, many	more	most
far	farther	farthest

Here are examples of the correct use of irregular comparative and superlative forms:

She had **little** energy.
He has **more** energy.
She has **less** energy than he has.
She has the **least** energy of anyone I know.

They had a **good** vacation.
We had a **bad** vacation.
They had a **better** vacation than we did.
They had the **best** vacation they have ever had.

Honolulu is **far** from New York.
Honolulu is **farther** from London than from New York.
Honolulu is the **farthest** large American city from London.

Idiomatic Comparatives

Many commonly used idiomatic expressions in English contain comparative forms. You may find these useful in expressing your ideas in fewer words:

Sooner or later	**Sooner or later** we will read Sunday's paper.
More or less	They were **more or less** ready to get into the car.
For better or worse	I rented the summer cabin **for better or worse.**
Most people	**Most people** enjoy sleeping late on weekends.
Most of them	The child lost three marbles, but he found **most of them.**
At least	She expected **at least** a "B" in the art course.
At most	We can work for two hours **at most.**
At best	**At best,** his carpentry looks too crude to satisfy the supervisor.
At worst	The windstorm can uproot some small trees **at worst.**
At the earliest	I can answer your letter by Monday **at the earliest.**
At the latest	You must be at the airport by noon **at the latest.**

EXERCISE 65
Irregular Comparatives and Superlatives

A. *Answer these questions with complete sentences.*

1. What is better, war or peace?
2. What is better, being single or being married?
3. Which is worse, a fire or a flood?
4. Who is worse, a murderer or a traitor?
5. Which costs less, a bicycle or an automobile?
6. Which makes less noise, a drum or a violin?
7. Who studies more, a student or a businessman?
8. Who generally plays more games, children or adults?

9. Which is farther from the earth, the moon or Venus?
10. Which is farther from Tokyo, Manila or San Francisco?

B. *Write out the sentences, filling in the blanks with correct comparative and superlative forms.*

Example: *Ann has one cat, Sue has two cats, and Mary has three cats.*
Sue has **more** cats **than** Ann, but Mary has the **most** cats.
(much)

In the physics course John received a grade of A, Bob received a B, and George received a C.

1. Bob is a . . . . student . . . . George, but John is the
   (good)

   . . . . student.

2. Bob is a . . . . student . . . . John, but George is the
   (bad)

   . . . . student.

A person can travel by airplane from London to Paris, Moscow, or Singapore.

3. Moscow is . . . . from London . . . . Paris, but Singapore
   (far)

   is the . . . .

4. A ticket to Moscow costs . . . . than a ticket to Paris, but a ticket
   (much)

   to Singapore costs the . . . .

Aly can run for one mile: Mahmoud can run for two miles; Jamil can run for three miles.

5. Mahmoud has . . . . energy . . . . Jamil, but Aly has the
   (little)

   . . . . energy.

REVIEW OF DEFINITE AND INDEFINITE ARTICLES

How is your mastery of article usage progressing? Here are some review sentences to help you spot-check yourself:

EXERCISE 66
Article Review

Write out these sentences, adding articles whenever necessary.

1. We went to theater to see new play performed by French playwright.
2. When it is time to go to bed, I usually drink glass of milk.

3. After trip to Ceylon, we decided to write book about journey.
4. On Sunday I go to church; on Monday I go to work; but in future I hope to go to university.
5. We attended birthday party for Lucia at Hotel Flora on Via Veneto in Rome.
6. My friend invited me to lunch and later to see movie.
7. Some of most delicious food in Europe is served in small restaurants in Amsterdam.
8. Why do you put oil in car, when what it really needs is gasoline?
9. I didn't find book I was looking for, but clerk promised to order it for me next day.
10. Music is more enjoyable to listen to when you can watch symphony orchestra performing.
11. Long-sought goal has been brought into reach by recent technological advances.
12. Almost all cancers appear to be caused by exposure to environmental factors.
13. Sun tans skin, sets biological rhythms, and stimulates formation of vitamin D.
14. Scientists have recently discovered way to remove weakly magnetic particles from mixtures by generating strong magnetic fields.
15. Management of Swedish plant has tried to find new ways of organizing work along assembly line in order to reduce workers' boredom, reflected in high labor turnover and absenteeism.

Questions for Discussion and Review

1. Over the past nine chapters, you have read examples of writing that illustrate a wide variety of styles. Review these readings to find five examples of expository prose that seem most effective or pleasing to you. Be prepared to point out the expository techniques that have contributed to the success of these passages.
2. Three of the selections in this chapter's section on Style in Writing contain rhetorical questions. Identify these questions, explaining why each writer uses a question.
3. Repeating a word adds to the coherence of Chapter 6's model composition. Point out this example of word repetition.
4. In writing about "Whales," Carson has given an admirable smoothness to her description by subtle variations in sentence structure. Analyze the various ways in which she changes sentence patterns.
5. Point out two examples of subordination by participial phrases in this chapter's model composition.
6. Insert two transitions in the second paragraph of the Allen, Ells, and Hart passage on "Noise" to make it read more coherently.

7. Explain how the comma, semicolon, and colon have been used in White's "The Three New Yorks."
8. Identify examples of parallelism in the letter written by Dr. Samuel Johnson to Lord Chesterfield.
9. How do periodic sentences contribute to the expository force of Krutch's "The Mystique of the Desert"?
10. In Chapter 1 you studied the distinction between *inductive* and *deductive* reasoning. Has Mrs. Luce developed "The 21st-Century Woman —Free at Last?" by induction or deduction?
11. Analyze the model paragraphs and compositions that open Chapters 2–9 for variety in beginnings.

Vocabulary Growth

PARAGRAPH PUZZLE

In this chapter's Paragraph Puzzle, **no** *choices are given for the missing words. Use the context of the paragraph as a basis for choosing appropriate words to make the paragraph read meaningfully.*

One of the primary objectives......any animal population study is of course to determine......many animals there are. ......randomly sampling as much of the atoll......was practicable and counting......number of animals within plots of......known size, it was possible...... calculate average tortoise densities and......these figures to estimate the total population size. ......turned out to be much higher......anyone expected, at around 150,000 animals. They......not evenly distributed over the atoll. Although they occur......three of the four major islands ......bound the lagoon, the vast majority......found on Grand Terre, the largest island, ...bulk of them at the eastern end. There...... exist in much higher concentrations than...... other animal of comparable size......the wild, with as many as 9,000 per square mile.

Reptiles, ...mammals, are unable to control......internal temperature by sweating to keep cool......shivering to keep warm; their temperature......largely dependent......that of their environment. Tortoises are no exception, but they......geared their daily pattern of activity so ......their body temperature does not become dangerously high. ...... about 10 A.M. they start moving away......the open grasslands in which they have......feeding to the shade of......nearby shrubs and trees. Here they congregate to rest......shelter from the heat of the midday sun. ......some places hundreds of tortoises may......found asleep under favorite shade trees. ......mid-afternoon, with the sun lower in the sky, ...seemingly lifeless forms beneath the shade trees begin......stir, then slowly emerge and lumber......to feed.

"Giant Tortoises Do Almost Too Well on Island Reserve,"
David Bourn, *Smithsonian* (May 1976)

WORD CLUES

A. *Vocabulary words in the following exercise are boldfaced.*

1. In the people the Northwest sends to Congress, the region tolerates, takes pride in, politicians who are **mavericks.** Wayne Morse got elected over the years as Republican, Independent, and Democrat, and was unpredictable in all three **guises.** A more celebrated maverick was Idaho's isolationist Senator William Borah. He was classified as one of the Senate's Western progressives, though Hiram Johnson grumpily described him as 'our spearless leader.'

> "The Pacific Northwest," Thomas Griffith, *The Atlantic Monthly* (April 1976)

Vocabulary Word. . . . .

Context Clue. . . . .

Probable Meaning. . . . .

Dictionary Definition. . . . .

Vocabulary Word. . . . .

Context Clue. . . . .

Probable Meaning. . . . .

Dictionary Definition. . . . .

2. The vast majority of stars in a typical galaxy such as our own are extremely **stable,** emitting a remarkably steady output of radiation for millions of years. Occasionally, however, a star in an advanced stage of evolution will spontaneously explode, and for a few months it will be several hundred million times intrinsically more luminous than the sun. Such a star is a supernova, and at the time of its greatest brilliance it may **emit** as much energy as all the other stars in its galaxy combined.

> "Historical Supernovas," F. Richard Stephenson and David H. Clark,
> *Scientific American* (June 1976)

Vocabulary Word. . . . .

Context Clue. . . . .

Probable Meaning. . . . .

Dictionary Definition. . . . .

Vocabulary Word. . . . .

Context Clue. . . . .

Probable Meaning. . . . .

Dictionary Definition. . . . .

3. Certain **hypothetical dilemmas** [of the Central Intelligence Agency] are easily solved: the United States almost surely would have liked

to be able to assassinate Hitler before or during World War II; that act might have saved millions of lives and earned the gratitude of people the world over. In drawing up standards for peacetime, however, it is easier to **delineate** what should be prohibited than what should be permitted. No assassinations or even peripheral involvement in plots that might lead to them; no interference in the electoral processes of other countries; no more secret wars; no misleading propaganda that distorts the truth about the world situation; no drug-dealing or other activity that affects the health, livelihood, and well-being of people at home or abroad.

"The Intelligence Tangle," Sanford J. Ungar, *The Atlantic Monthly* (April 1976)

Vocabulary Word...

Context Clue..

Probable Meaning..

Dictionary Definition.....................................

Vocabulary Word...

Context Clue..

Probable Meaning..

Dictionary Definition.....................................

Vocabulary Word...

Context Clue..

Probable Meaning..

Dictionary Definition.....................................

4. Repeatedly throughout this essay I have stated that future trends will re-emphasize the locality—the spirit of place. One of the reasons is that human beings are at heart **sedentary**. They experience wanderlust only on rare occasions; moreover, they are learning that the open road commonly leads to the parking lot or even to the garbage dump.

"Recycling Social Man," René Dubos, *Saturday Review/World* (24 August 1974)

Vocabulary Word...

Context Clue..

Probable Meaning..

Dictionary Definition.....................................

5. Environmental quality, however, includes much more than chemical and physical cleanliness. Privacy, space, and quietness may not be essential for survival, but they are needs deeply rooted in human nature, and the demand for them increases with prosperity. Rural

America came as close as any society has to providing these **amenities** when most people lived in freestanding, isolated houses. This kind of dwelling, however, is not likely to be common anywhere in the world of 2024.

"Recycling Social Man," René Dubos, *Saturday Review/World* (24 August 1974)

Vocabulary Word...

Context Clue..

Probable Meaning..

Dictionary Definition..

B. *Look in a dictionary for meanings of each of the following verbs and for all the related forms of the verb you can find. Make a four-column list headed "verbs, nouns, adjectives, and adverbs."*

1. to confer
2. to associate
3. to connect
4. to expose
5. to reflect
6. to reduce

Composition: Show What You Have Learned

Choose a topic for composition from either Group I or Group II.

GROUP I: TOPICS FOR WRITING A COMPOSITION DEVELOPED BY LOGICAL DIVISION

"University Lore, U.S.A.," this chapter's model composition, is basically a factual piece of writing. Its purpose is to report information about the nature of an American university—its programs, its students, its faculty, its facilities. There is no first-hand opinion in this essay; the few value judgments are reported: "Stanford University . . . is sometimes called 'The Harvard of the West.'" Because of its factual nature, this selection can be termed an **objective** piece of writing.

In contrast to **objective** writing is **subjective** writing, in which the emphasis is not on fact but instead on opinion. To examine how great the contrast can be between objective and subjective writing, let's look at another view of Stanford expressed in 1966 by a well-known former Stanford student, David Harris.

Born in Fresno, California, Harris grew up to be named Fresno High School Boy of the Year and went on to attend Stanford. Politically alert, he left school in 1964 to work in the civil rights movement in Mississippi. Returning to Stanford, he was elected Student Body President and gained recognition as a leader of the opposition to the Vietnam War. He married folk singer Joan Baez. In 1968 he resisted the draft, declaring, "The last resort a citizen has against an unjust law is to openly and publicly break it and accept the consequences." As a result, he spent nearly two years in Federal prisons. Most recently, he has been a writer and a political candidate for a seat in the United States Congress.

In an American magazine, Harris summarized his feelings about his Stanford educational experience, speaking about his campaign for Student Body President. Harris's thoughts—tape recorded during a conversation and later written out by the interviewer, Gina Berriault—reflect the difference between spoken and written English. Although this passage conveys deep conviction, it lacks expository force, particularly in its last five sentences. Here you find pronouns without antecedents, an unjustifiable sentence fragment, excessive colloquialisms, and awkward sentence structure. What make this selection valuable are its ideas, not particularly how they are expressed:

My [political] platform was a long list of change based on the attitude that Stanford is not educating and has no understanding of what education is. Students have no right of control over their own lives. It's a system calculated on the impotence of the students in that it makes everything the student does something outside himself. What that does is teach people to be powerless. We started from the initial statement that education is something that happens in your mind, the mind learning itself, learning how to use itself. It's a very inner process, and the function that teachers traditionally serve in most of the cultures of the world—where they haven't gotten to modern industrial teaching which is essentially a training mechanism—is one of spiritual guidance. Not only should a teacher know things but he should have an understanding, a wisdom about things, beyond simply knowing them. So that a teacher provides himself as a mirror to the other person's mind and gives that person a glimpse into his own mind so he can then start educating himself. That's what education is, and it isn't this whole social system at Stanford, the superficialities. They rigidify the students here into cogs for the great American wheel. Most people who teach at colleges are doing it for very simple security reasons, and they don't like people to rock the boat even though they make a big thing about intellectual inquiry and all that. A professor will allow you to put down the administration but will get offended if you say the faculty is irrelevant, which they are, by and large, except for maybe ten people, and they're relevant as people because they've devloped a style of living that really has relevance to other lives.

"The New Student President," Gina Berriault, *Esquire* (September 1967)

Now that you have read both an objective and subjective view of one American university, you have the necessary background to approach this week's writing assignment. Your subject this week will be one that you know a great deal about: your own educational experiences. Using logical division as your mode of development and stocking your paper well with specific examples, write a composition of several paragraphs on one of the following topics:

1. Write an **objective** composition telling about the programs, students, faculty, and facilities of an educational institution you have attended or know well.
2. Write a **subjective** composition in which you give your opinion about the quality of the education offered in some school or college you have attended. (Your opinion, of course, may be favorable, unfavorable, or mixed.)
3. Many writers have expressed their ideas about what an ideal society would be. What are your ideas about what an ideal *educational experience* would be? Explain how the approach to higher education could be changed so that a university would more fully meet the needs of its students.
4. The Greek philosopher Socrates said that the ideal classroom was a fallen log with a student sitting on one end of it and a teacher sitting on the other end. Comment on this idea.

GROUP II: TOPICS TO CHALLENGE YOUR IMAGINATION

THE LION WHO WANTED TO ZOOM

There was once a lion who coveted an eagle's wings. So he sent a message to the eagle asking him to call, and when the eagle came to the lion's den the lion said, "I will trade you my mane for your wings." "Keep talking, brother," said the eagle. "Without my wings I could no longer fly." "So what?" said the lion. "I can't fly now, but that doesn't keep me from being king of beasts. I became king of beasts on account of my magnificent mane." "All right," said the eagle, "but give me your mane first." "Just approach a little nearer," said the lion, "so that I can hand it to you." The eagle came closer and the lion clapped a huge paw on him, pinning him to the ground. "Come across with those wings!" he snarled.

So the lion took the eagle's wings but kept his own mane. The eagle was very despondent for a while and then he had an idea. "I bet you can't fly off the top of that great rock yonder," said the eagle. "Who, me?" said the lion, and he walked to the top of the rock and took off. His weight was too great for the eagle's wings to support, and besides he did not know how to fly, never having tried it before. So he crashed at the foot of the rock and burst into flames. The eagle hastily climbed down to him and regained his wings and took off the lion's mane, which he put about his own neck and shoulders. Flying back to the rocky nest where he lived with his mate, he decided to have some fun with her. So, covered with the lion's mane, he poked his head into the nest and in a deep, awful voice said *"Harrrrooo!"* His mate, who was very

nervous anyway, grabbed a pistol from a bureau drawer and shot him dead, thinking he was a lion.

Moral: Never allow a nervous female to have access to a pistol, no matter what you're wearing.

"The Lion Who Wanted to Zoom," James Thurber, *Fables for Our Time*

Much of the humor in "The Lion Who Wanted to Zoom" lies in the irony of the eagle's outwitting the lion only to be defeated by his own mate. (A motion picture director once asked Charles Chaplin what he thought the most humorous sequence would be in filming a fat woman walking down the street and slipping on a banana peel: to show first a closeup of the walking woman's smiling face, then the banana peel, then the fall; or to show first the banana peel, then the woman's face, then the fall. Chaplin replied, "Neither." He went on to explain that the best comic effect would be to show first the woman's smiling face, then the banana peel, then the woman seeing the banana peel and carefully stepping around it, then the woman's smiling face again, then the smiling woman stepping into an open manhole in the sidewalk and disappearing out of sight.)

Like Chaplin, Thurber has shown a firm grasp of the basis for comedy in this fable. But he suggests some serious points, as well: both the lion and the eagle come to grief because of their character flaws. Since "The Lion Who Wanted to Zoom" has both its humorous and serious sides, you may want to approach writing this week in either a comic or serious vein, depending on your mood.

Following are some of the qualities that the lion and the eagle revealed in the fable:

LION	EAGLE
Covetousness	Gullibility
Greed	Naivete
Pride	Failure to anticipate the conse-
Excessive ambition	quences of his actions
Deceit	Lack of knowledge of his mate
Specious reasoning	Shallowness
Aggressiveness	

1. Base a **serious** composition, developed by logical division, on one of these traits. Include examples to illustrate the thesis you have selected.
2. Base a **humorous** composition on one of these traits. Develop your essay by logical division, supplying examples when possible.

Chapter **10**

The Expository Composition
(Developed by Logical Division)

Let's Go to the Movies . . .

Beginning with an anecdote

Commenting on the motion picture version of *Macbeth*, a critic once wrote, **"In this film of Shakespeare's tragedy, Orson Welles played Macbeth. Macbeth lost."** Many producers of films also **lose,** in another sense.

Repeating a word for transition

Commas setting off parenthetical element

They **lose** in their efforts to create meaningful and artistic films. For the modern film industry, **generally speaking,** emphasizes business rather than art. Despite this fact, a few brilliant films are produced each year.

Statement of logical division

Most successful films have a number of qualities in common. **These include creative photography, a sense of style, and meaningful ideas.** Because the camera makes it possible for movies to be the most flexible[1] of the performing arts, imaginative camera work is a pleasure to watch. In the field of black and white photography, the British director David Lean poetically filmed the English countryside in *Great Expectations* and the

Transition

slums[2] of London in *Oliver Twist.* **Similarly,** in the American movie *Citizen Kane*, Orson Welles **applied**

Parallelism

the technique of perspective[3] **to the motion picture** in the same way that Breughel the Elder **had applied it to**

---

[1]*flexible:* adaptable to many uses or means of expression. [2]*slums:* overcrowded section of a city, marked by poverty and poor living conditions. [3]*perspective:*

291

Simple sentence for variety	Flemish painting 300 years earlier. **Color photography has given new opportunities for creativity.** Often a color film will reflect the art of the country in which it
Comparative pair	was made. **Like** Teinosuke Kinugasa's masterpiece *Gate of Hell*, which has the delicate coloring of a Japanese print, Franco Zeffirelli's *The Taming of the Shrew* is filmed in the same richly muted Italian colors that the Renaissance painter Raphael might have used.
Transition	A **second** important feature in the films I have most
Correlative conjunctions	enjoyed is style. A film gains its style **not only** from camera work **but also** from set design, costume design, sound track, film editing, and the performances of the
Commas in a series	actors. Jean Cocteau's *Beauty and the Beast*, Billy Wilder's *Sunset Boulevard*, Arthur Penn's *Bonnie and Clyde*, and Stanley Kubrick's *Barry Lyndon* are movies in which style is a vital element. Details from these
Colon for listing	films stick in the mind: the human arms changed into candelabra[4] in Cocteau's surrealistic[5] production; the
Semicolon separating elements having internal commas	zebra-skin upholstery of an aging actress's Rolls-Royce in *Sunset Boulevard*; Faye Dunaway running through a dead, sun-bleached cornfield as the sunlight briefly passes over it in *Bonnie and Clyde*; the stunning glow of candlelit, eighteenth-century rooms, photographed for *Barry Lyndon* with a special lens normally used in
Short sentence for variety	space exploration. **An actor who personifies[6] cinematic style is the comedian Charles Chaplin.** Who could forget Chaplin as a hungry tramp in Alaska, using a knife and fork to eat his shoe?
	What usually give a film its most enduring value, though, are the ideas it presents. For this reason, the work of the Swedish director Ingmar Bergman is espe-
Specific detail	cially powerful. One of his most ironic films, *Wild Strawberries*, concerns an aging professor who wins high academic honors but loses the love and respect of his family. The Frenchman Jean-Luc Godard and the
Commas setting off nonrestrictive element	Spaniard Luis Buñuel, also concerned with man's role in life, focus in their films on the alienation[7] of modern man. **Both** the Japanese director **Akira Kurosawa,** in
Comparative pair	*Seven Samurai*, **and** the Indian director **Satyajit Ray,** in *Pather Panchali*, examine the social structure of their re-

art of representing solid objects on a flat surface so that they appear in depth and at a distance. [4]*candelabra:* large, branched candlesticks. [5]*surrealistic:* incongruous presentation of subject matter, expressing the subconscious mind. [6]*personifies:* represents as a person, typifies. [7]*alienation:* removal or disassocia-

spective cultures, with an emphasis on the values of peasant life. And few male directors have shown the vigor, daring, and political awareness that explode in such films by Italian director Lina Wertmuller as *Love and Anarchy, The Seduction of Mimi, Swept Away . . .,* and *Seven Beauties.*

Significant changes are taking place in cinema in the second half of the twentieth century. New dramatic subjects, from childbirth to space travel, are being filmed. The camera is becoming more versatile than ever before. Slow motion scenes and speeded-up action

Commas in a series   are combined at a normal speed. Color, sepia, and black and white photography are combined in a single film. Motion picture editing is growing in new directions: cross cutting[8] makes some experimental movies resem-

Transition   ble abstract art.[9] **In recent years,** multiple screen viewing has been gaining popularity.

No matter what its future development may be, the

Comparative pair   motion picture industry will bear watching. **Just as** opera was the typical art form of the eighteenth century, **so** film seems likely to become the representative art form of the twentieth century.

tion from society. [8]*cross cutting:* producing a rapid succession of different film images or scenes. [9]*abstract art:* art that does not depict identifiable objects.

Writing Analysis

REPEATING A STRUCTURAL UNIT FOR COHERENCE

Having studied examples in Chapter 9 of writers repeating a word for coherence, you will be interested to see how other writers use structural units for the same purpose. Perhaps you have noticed this technique in earlier readings. One graceful example appeared in the last chapter in a selection by Krutch, "The Mystique of the Desert." Notice how the writer picks up the words "the last" from a short quotation and repeats this phrase twice to carry along his idea:

> The desert is '**the last** frontier' in more senses than one. It is **the last** because it was the latest reached, but it is **the last** because it is, in many ways, a frontier which *cannot* be crossed.

Following are three further examples of writings in which repeated word groups give a strongly cohesive quality to the writing. In the first passage, the writer, imagining what life will be like in 2024, repeats the opening clause "I imagine" halfway through the paragraph to remind the reader that the ideas being presented are suppositions:

I imagine that the achievements in physics and chemistry (perhaps employing computer modeling) will lead not only to the creation of synthetics superior to the natural materials in every significant way (the first steps have been taken in this field) but also to the artificial reproduction of many unique aspects of entire systems existing in nature. **I imagine** that automatons of the future will have efficient and easily directed "muscles" of contractive polymers and that there will be highly sensitive analyzers of organic and inorganic mixtures of the air and water operating on the principle of an artificial "nose." Artificial diamonds will be created from graphite through special underground atomic blasts. Diamonds, of course, play a major role in contemporary technology, and cheaper production methods will heighten their importance.

"Tomorrow: The View from Red Square," Andrei D. Sakharov,
Saturday Review/World (August 24, 1974)

Notice that, in addition to the repeated structural unit, the transition "of course" and the correlative pair "not only . . . but also" help to bind this paragraph together.

A second selection, this one dealing with forestry, is even more emphatic in repeating a structural unit. Here the verb "means," followed by several modifiers, appears four times in two consecutive sentences:

Modern forestry **means scattering seeds** by helicopter in remote areas, **means sprinkling young trees** from the air with growth-spreading nutrients in the form of pellets, **means aerial logging** by chopper[1] or by balloon where valued trees are hard to get at. But above all it **means new techniques** in silviculture,[2] making trees grow faster, straighter, and healthier than does nature in its profligate,[3] random way.

"The Pacific Northwest," Thomas Griffith, *The Atlantic Monthly* (April 1976)

[1]*chopper:* helicopter. [2]*silviculture:* art of producing and tending a forest and forest trees. [3]*profligate:* recklessly extravagant; in great profusion.

Finally, here is a third example of phrase repetition demonstrating that a skilled writer with an ear for the rhythms of English words and sentences can successfully break the rules of style. Although the expletive "it" can contribute to dull writing when used unnecessarily, in this case repeating the element "it is" seven times only adds to the emotional force of the paragraph. Note, too, how the writer has planned for variety in sentence length. The first seven relatively short sentences (one has only six words) pleasantly contrast with the longer eighth sentence. Because short sentences concisely convey the earlier ideas in the paragraph, the reader will have a reserve of patience left to propel him through the longer, more complex concluding sentence:

Central Park is many things. **It is** the calm eye in the center of a hurricane. **It is** the vision of men who knew men's needs. **It is** the measure of seasons in a city which tries to insulate itself from them. **It is** the refuge of wild things escaping stone. **It is** a zone of danger. **It is** the only sleeping land in a sleepless city. And **it is** the only place, aside from the Jersey and Brooklyn shores and the Lower Bay, from which the dream of Manhattan is wholly visible because the eye has room to embrace it and the heart and distance to love it.

"The New York I Know," Marya Mannes, *The New Yorker* (21 January 1960)

As you add to your vocabulary the many transitions that will help you to express your thoughts more clearly, remember that transition can be accomplished not only by the addition of words to a sentence or a paragraph but also by the internal arrangement of its parts.

EXERCISE 67
Repeating a Structural Unit for Coherence

Look through Chapters 1–10 to find five writing selections that could be strengthened by repeating a structural unit in one or more sentences as a transition. Write out the revised sentences, adding repeated structural units.

EXPOSITORY DEVELOPMENT (by logical division)

The model composition "Let's Go to the Movies . . ." illustrates how logical division can supply the framework to which a writer often adds other modes of development. At the opening of the second paragraph, the model's basic three-part logical division is announced: "These include creative **photography,** a sense of **style,** and meaningful **ideas.**" Then, in developing the essay, the writer makes frequent use of comparison. He first likens the photography in *Citizen Kane* to Flemish painting. Comparative pairs continue: the Japanese *Gates of Hell* and the Italian *Taming of the Shrew* are linked as films whose color photography reflects the art of their respective cultures; *Seven Samurai* and *Pather Panchali* provide a second comparison.

In addition to development by comparison, the model is well stocked with examples. Notice especially how well the five examples of style in the third paragraph serve to make an abstract idea concrete and meaningful to the reader. Moreover, if the several specific examples of changes in motion picture technology (slow and speeded-up motion, color versatility, cross cutting, multiple screen viewing) had not been mentioned in the next to last paragraph, the force of this paragraph would have been considerably diminished.

Now read four selections that show how other writers have used logical division for development. First, writing on the general topic of "words," Warren Weaver organizes his approach by naming several different categories that words can fit into. He adds color to his writing by following each general statement of category with at least one specific example:

For the past forty years I have been building a cage large enough to hold some of the more difficult and tricky words. I have tried to divide this cage into sections. One section, for example, is for those words that have two opposite meanings. *Fast* is one such word. It obviously means in rapid motion; but it can also mean motionless, as when a ship is tied fast to a dock. . . .

A second and closely associated category contains pairs of opposite words with the same meaning. A *blunt* remark is often equivalent to a sharp or pointed remark. . . .

Another compartment of my collection contains words whose proper dictionary meanings differ substantially from the sense in which they are properly used. . . . When one speaks of a person being *livid* with rage, he commonly thinks that livid means red or mottled purple, whereas it means pale or leaden. . . .

Still another part of my collection, and one of which I am particularly proud, since I invented the category myself, contains nouns which are very unfamiliar names of very familiar objects. . . . In at least an impersonal sense we are all familiar with the bottom of the sea, but do you know the name *benthos*? . . .

Closely connected with this question is specificity in words. . . . When an object is of overwhelming concern to a culture, then a whole array of special words is developed. Spectacular examples . . . are furnished by the Eskimo language, which has some dozen different words for snow in all of its special states and manifestations . . . and by Arabic, which has over 6,000 words for camels, for the parts of a camel, and for camel equipment.

                                   Warren Weaver, "The Case of the Wayward Words"

Notice that, in his treatment of his five-part logical division, Weaver has chosen *not* to list the five parts first before examining each one in detail. The reason for this is probably that each item in the division requires several words to explain it. Therefore the items can be dealt with more concisely in separate parts. Through the use of transitions, though, Weaver makes clear each shift to a new division. (He uses these transitions: a second and closely associated . . . ; another compartment . . . ; still another part . . . ; closely connected with. . . .)

In a graduation address delivered at Columbia University in New York, Nicholas Murray Butler spoke about the qualities that make up an educated man. In developing his paper, he chose five essential qualities to emphasize; in his second paragraph, he announced that his logical division will fall into five parts (controlling idea and transitions are boldfaced):

A question often asked is: "What are the marks of an educated man?" It is plain that one may gain no inconsiderable[1] body of learning in some special field of knowledge without at the same time acquiring those habits and traits which are the marks of an educated gentleman. A reasonable amount of learning must of course accompany an education, but, after all, that amount need not be so very great in any one field. An education will make its mark and find its evidences in certain traits, characteristics, and capacities which have to be acquired by patient endeavor,[2] by following good example, and by receiving wise discipline and sound instruction.

These traits or characteristics may be variously described and classified, but among them are five that should always stand out clearly enough to be seen of all men.

The first of these is correctness and precision in the use of the mother tongue. The quite shocking slovenliness and vulgarity of much of the spoken English, as well as not a little of the written English, which one hears and sees proves beyond peradventure[3] that years of attendance upon schools and colleges that are thought to be respectable have produced no impression. When one hears English well spoken, with pure diction, correct pronunciation, and an almost unconscious choice of the right word, he recognizes it at once. How much easier he finds it to imitate English of the other sort!

A second and indispensable[4] trait of the educated man is refined and gentle manners, which are themselves the expression of fixed habits of thought and action. "Manners makyth the man," wrote William of Wykeham over his gates at Winchester and at Oxford. He pointed to a great truth. When manners are superficial, artificial, and forced, no matter what their form, they are bad manners. When, however, they are the natural expression of fixed habits of thought and action, and when they reveal a refined and cultivated nature, they are good manners. There are certain things that gentlemen do not do, and they do not do them simply because they are bad manners. The gentleman instinctively knows the difference between those things which he may and should do and those things which he may not and should not do.

A third trait of the educated man is the power and habit of reflection. Human beings for the most part live wholly on the surface or far beyond the present moment and that part of the future which is quickly to follow it. They do not read those works of prose and poetry which have become classic because they reveal power and habit of reflection and induce[5] that power and habit in others. When one reflects long enough to ask the question *how?*, he is on the way to knowing something about science. When he reflects long enough to ask the question *why?*, he may, if he persists, even become a philosopher.

A fourth trait of the educated man is the power of growth. He continues to grow and develop from birth to his dying day. His interests expand, his contacts multiply, his knowledge increases, and his reflection becomes deeper and wider. It would appear to be true that not many human beings, even those who have had a school and college education, continue to grow after they are twenty-four or twenty-five years

---

[1]*inconsiderable:* small, trivial. [2]*endeavor:* effort. [3]*peradventure:* doubt, question. [4]*indispensable:* essential, necessary. [5]*induce:* produce, cause. [6]*zeal:* enthusiastic devotion.

of age. By that time it is usual to settle down to life on a level of more or less contented intellectual interest and activity. The whole present-day movement for adult education is a systematic and definite attempt to keep human beings growing long after they have left school and college, and, therefore, to help educate them.

A **fifth trait** of the educated man is his possession of efficiency, or the power to do. The mere visionary dreamer, however charming or however wise, lacks something which an education requires. The power to do may be exercised in any one of a thousand ways, but when it clearly shows itself, that is evidence that the period of discipline of study and of companionship with parents and teachers has not been in vain.

Given these five characteristics, one has the outline of an educated man. That outline may be filled in by scholarship, by literary power, by mechanical skills, by professional zeal[6] and capacity, by business competence, or by social and political leadership. So long as the framework or outline is there, the content may be pretty much what you will, assuming, of course, that the fundamental elements of the great tradition which is civilization, and its outstanding records and achievements in human pernality, in letters, in science, in the fine arts, and in human institutions, are all present.

Nicholas Murray Butler, "Five Evidences of an Education"

Notice that Butler follows many of the principles of effective composition that you have studied earlier in this book. He begins his composition with a rhetorical question, one that is likely to capture his audience's attention and make them wonder what his answer to this question will be. Throughout his paper he achieves coherence through transitions (however, therefore) and transitional phrases (after all, of course). He knits his paragraphs together by transitions (the first of these . . . , a second and indispensable trait . . . , a third trait . . . , a fourth trait . . . , a fifth trait . . . , given these five characteristics. . . .). In the fifth paragraph, he illustrates how coherence can also be increased by means of a repeated pronoun, in this case "they." The final two sentences in the fifth paragraph, as well as the second and third sentences in the final paragraph, illustrate Butler's frequent use of parallelism. The author also appreciates the need for variety in sentence length. The shortest sentence in his fourth paragraph contains six words; the longest sentence twenty-seven words.

Writing on the subject of the English language, C. L. Wrenn has also devised a five-part logical division of his topic. Unlike Butler, Wrenn does not announce early in his paper that he is dividing his subject into five parts. Instead, he relies upon transitional phrases at the beginning of each paragraph to make this clear:

The English language is spoken or read by the largest number of people in the world, for historical, political, and economic reasons; but it may also be true that it owes something of its wide appeal to qualities and characteristics inherent[1] in itself. **What are these characteristic features** which outstand in making the English language what it is, which give it its individuality and make it of this worldwide signficance?

First and most important is its extraordinary receptive and adaptable heterogeneousness[2]—the varied ease and readiness with which it has taken to itself material from almost everywhere in the world and has made the new elements of language its own. English, which when the Anglo-Saxons first conquered England in the fifth and sixth centuries was almost a "pure" or unmixed language—which could make new words for new ideas from its own compounded[3] elements and had hardly any foreign words—has become the most "mixed" of languages, having received throughout its history all kinds of foreign elements with ease and assimilated[4] them all to its own character. Though its copiousness[5] of vocabulary is outstanding, it is its amazing variety and heterogeneousness which is even more striking: and this general receptiveness of new elements has contributed to making it a suitable and attractive vehicle[6] in so many parts of the world.

A second outstanding characteristic of English is its simplicity of inflection[7]—the ease with which it indicates the relationship of words in a sentence with only the minimum of change in their shapes or variation of endings. There are languages, such as Chinese, that have surpassed English in the reduction of the language in the matter of inflections to what looks like just a series of fixed monosyllabic[8] roots: but among European languages, taken as a whole, English has gone as far as any in reducing the inflections it once had to a minimum. A natural consequence of this simplifying of inflection by reduction, however, is that since the relationship of words to each other is no longer made clear by their endings, this must be done in other ways.

A third quality of English, therefore, is its relatively fixed word order. An inflected language like Latin or Russian can afford to be fairly free in the arrangement of its words, since the inflections show clearly the proper relationship in the sentence, and ambiguity[9] is unlikely. But in a language which does not change the forms of its words according to their relationship in the sentence-significance, the order of the words is likely to be relatively fixed; and a fixed word order in relation to meaning in the sentence takes the place of the freedom made possible by the system of inflections.

Another consequence, fourthly, of the loss or reduction to the minimum of the inflections which English once had, is the growth of the use of periphrase or roundabout ways of saying things, and of the use of prepositions to take the place of the lost inflections. The English simplified verb uses periphrases and compound tenses made with auxiliary

---

[1]*inherent:* forming a permanent and essential element of something; inborn. [2]*heterogeneousness:* being composd of parts or elements that are dissimilar or unrelated. [3]*compounded:* combined. [4]*assimilated:* absorbed. [5]*copiousness:* abundance. [6]*vehicle:* language. [7]*inflection:* change in the form of words to express grammatical and syntactical relations, as of case, number, gender, person, and tense. [8]*monosyllabic:* having only one syllable. [9]*ambiguity:* expres-

verbs to replace the more elaborate system of tenses that once existed (though tenses had already become fairly simple before the Anglo-Saxons came to England). Similarly, English, which once had nearly as many case endings as Latin, has come to use prepositions instead of these, as can easily be seen if one translates any piece of Latin into English.

A fifth quality of English—though this, like the loss of inflections and its consequences, is shared with some other languages—is the development of new varieties of intonation[10] to express shades of meaning which were formerly indicated by varying the shapes of words. This is perhaps somewhat comparable (though only in a small way) to the vast use of intonation in Chinese in what would otherwise seem like a series of unvarying monosyllabic roots. Consider, for instance, the wonderful variety of shades of meaning we may put into the use of the word *do*, merely by varying the intonation—that is, the pitch and intensity, the tone of the voice.

Not all the above qualities are in themselves necessarily good, nor have they all contributed to the general success of English. But it seems probable that of them all it is the adaptable receptiveness and the simplicity of inflection that have done most in this regard. On the other hand, the very copiousness and heterogeneousness of English leads to vagueness or lack of clarity. Its resources are too vast for all but the well educated to use to full advantage; and such phenomena as "pidgin English," "journalese," jargon, woolliness[11] of expression, and slatternly[12] speech and writing are everywhere likely to be met with. It may fairly be said that English is among the easiest languages to speak badly, but the most difficult to use well.

"The Characteristics of English," C. L. Wrenn, *The English Language*

sion of thought that can be interpreted in more than one sense. [10]*intonation:* meaning and melody given to speech by higher and lower levels of pitch. [11]*woolliness:* lack of clarity. [12]*slatternly:* careless, untidy.

Wrenn's opening paragraph has some features in common with Butler's opening paragraph, but it also has a basic difference. In both essays, the topic sentence of the paper is expressed in a rhetorical question. But in Butler's composition, the topic sentence is the first sentence in the opening paragraph. In Wrenn's, it is the last sentence in the opening paragraph. You have learned in Chapter 1 that a topic sentence may appear in any position within a paragraph. Yet the opening paragraph of a composition is a special case. It is often desirable to begin the first paragraph, as Wrenn has done, with a generalization about the subject and then to narrow this generalization down to a quite specific statement of the controlling idea in the paragraph's final sentence. By doing this, the writer leads the reader into his subject with a general observation that will arouse interest, at the same time saving his most vital piece of information—the direct announcement of his controlling idea—for the most emphatic position in the paragraph, its ending. Try to pattern your organization of opening paragraphs after Wrenn's approach.

In supplying transitional phrases for his five central paragraphs, Wrenn has been conscious of the need for variety in phrasing. Note the changes he makes in the phrasing, at the same time keeping the orderly development of this controlling idea before the reader: "first and most important. . . ."; "a second outstanding characteristic. . . ."; "a third quality of English. . . ."; "another consequence, fourthly, ..."; "a fifth quality of English. . . ." Within the paragraphs, as well, he inserts transitions (but, however, therefore, similarly, though, for instance) at appropriate places to insure coherence.

Several short passages in earlier chapters have been constructed by more than one method, just as this week's model composition, "Let's Go to the Movies . . ." has been. The following short composition on the subject of personal crisis is a further example of development by a combination of methods.

To develop her thought, the writer of the next selection has chosen three approaches. Her first three paragraphs depend on definition; in the fourth and fifth paragraphs, she shifts to logical division; and she generously sprinkles examples throughout the last four paragraphs to give the composition specific force:

One dictionary broadly defines the word "crisis" as "a crucial turning point in the progress of an affair or of a series of events, as in politics, business, a story, or play. . . ." This paper will attempt to define a much narrower but extremely significant aspect of crisis: personal crisis.

Sometimes our more or less steady progress through life comes to a jolting halt. Something unexpected, shocking, frightening, threatening, and disastrous happens—a crisis. Such a development can disturb relationships, interfere with work efficiency, and cause confusion, disorganization, and serious emotional upheaval. Solutions that have worked for us in solving past problems no longer prove adequate. As anxiety increases, our powers to cope with it correspondingly decrease. The crisis quickly leads to frustration; we feel helpless either to escape from the problem or to resolve it successfully.

Many people think of crisis as being connected only with unhappy or unpleasant events. This is not the case. Crisis can occur as a result of any change, even one that is generally welcomed: marriage, birth of a child, graduation from school or college, or election to public office.

Crises are generally of two types. First, there are the expected, maturational[1] crises we experience at times of life development and change. Examples of this include a child's first enrollment in school or his transfer at a later age to a new school. These events may precipitate[2] a crisis—both for the youngster and his parents. Another time when crisis can be expected is during adolescence.

The second type of crisis is the unexpected, accidental kind. This can stem from many sources: becoming involved in a legal suit, having an automobile crash, being fired from a job, losing a large sum of money,

[1]*maturational:* related to growth and maturity. [2]*precipitate:* hasten the occur-

or falling suddenly ill. Severe illness will create a crisis not only for the individual concerned but also for his family. And an illness may itself be caused by an emotional crisis, such as the death of a spouse,[3] offspring,[4] or sibling.[5]

In a recent attitude survey, researchers gathered information to determine which crisis situations in life were most likely to precede[6] illness. The study showed that the three most stressful life events were death of a spouse, divorce, and marital separation. Other events that fell toward the top of the crisis scale were a jail term, death of a close family member, personal injury or illness, marriage, losing one's job, marital reconciliation, retirement, change in the health of a family member, pregnancy, sex difficulties, gain of a new family member, business readjustment, and change in financial state.

"The Nature of Crisis," adapted from Malinda Murray, *Fundamentals of Nursing*

rence of. [3]*spouse:* husband or wife. [4]*offspring:* son or daughter. [5]*sibling:* brother or sister. [6]*precede:* come before.

Clearly the preceding composition has many of the essential expository elements that you have already studied. First, note that a thesis statement appears at the close of the first paragraph. Next, the passage depends for coherence on a number of transitions (such this, first, second, these, another, and, other). A variety of punctuation has been correctly used: the comma in series and setting off nonessential and parenthetical elements, the semicolon, the colon, quotation marks, the dash for desired emphasis. (Note that the dash really *works* both times it appears: first, to stress the word "crisis"; second, to reinforce the idea that the parents will also experience crisis when a child does.)

In addition, the correlative conjunctions "either . . . or" and "not only . . . but" also function effectively here. Sentence length varies from very short (This is not the case.) to extremely long—the composition's last sentence. Finally, notice that subordination has an important purpose in the sentence "As anxiety increases, our powers to cope with it correspondingly decrease." By downplaying the clause "anxiety increases," the writer throws her emphasis where she wants it, on the idea that "our powers to cope . . . decrease."

In the passages from Weaver, Butler, Wrenn, and Murray, you have seen four experienced writers giving form to their compositions by means of logical division. You can best demonstrate your control of English composition by mastering this important expository technique.

EXERCISE 68
Outlining

First review the section in Chapter 5 on "The Composition Outline." Then reconstruct the outline the writer probably worked from in composing the model composition, "Let's Go to the Movies. . . ."

TONE IN WRITING

Although its exact definition is hard to arrive at, tone may be roughly said to be the attitude of an author toward his subject matter as it is reflected in his style. Tone is closely related to a writer's emotion and to his intent. If he is amused by his material, he may set it down in a light, humorous tone. If he is outraged by a social injustice, he may express himself in bitter, indignant words. If he wishes to criticize in a subtle way, he may choose to write in an ironic tone, making his words mean just the opposite of what they appear to mean.

To understand an author's tone, a reader will examine such stylistic points as the choice of words, the position and interrelation of words in a sentence, the length and rhythm of sentences, and the use of figurative language. A piece of writing may convey a tone that is gay or somber, sentimental or cynical, reverent or mocking, literal or ironic, or any shading of emotion that represents a human attitude.

Why is the understanding of tone important to a student writer? Learning to recognize tone in another person's writing helps a student to recognize and control the tone of his own compositions. Often, beginning writers make the mistake of opening their papers with an apology for their weaknesses in English composition or for their lack of knowledge of subject matter. Such a humble, apologetic opening, however, frequently has the opposite effect from what has been intended. The reader tends to lose trust in the writer's power; he expects the paper to be weak. On the other hand, a confident tone on the part of the writer serves to inspire confidence in the reader.

You may also need practice in recognizing tone in order to handle irony well. Irony can be a most effective tool, particularly for the writer of persuasive or argumentative papers. But if irony is exaggerated or overdone, it soon loses its effectiveness. By observing the restrained use of irony in professional writers, a student can learn to moderate and polish his own ironic powers.

Here are four examples to examine for tone:

1. In the first selection, a description of a midwestern American town by the English writer Charles Dickens, the hostile tone is unmistakable:

> Nor was the scenery, as we approached the junction of the Ohio and Mississippi rivers, at all inspiriting in its influence. The trees were stunted in their growth; the banks were low and flat; the settlements and log cabins fewer in number; their inhabitants more wan[1] and wretched than any we had encountered yet. No songs of birds were in the air, no pleasant scents, no moving lights and shadows from swift passing clouds. Hour after hour, the changeless glare of the hot, unwinking sky shone upon the same monotonous objects. Hour after hour, the river rolled along, as wearily and as slowly as time itself.

At length, upon the morning of the third day, we arrived at a spot so much more desolate than any we had yet beheld that the forlornest places we had passed were, in comparison with it, full of interest. At the junction of the two rivers, on ground so flat and low and marshy that at certain seasons of the year it is inundated to the housetops, lies a breeding-place of fever, ague,[2] and death; vaunted[3] in England as a mine of Golden Hope, and speculated in, on the faith of monstrous representations, to many people's ruin. A dismal swamp on which the half-built houses rot away: cleared here and there for a space of a few yards; and teeming, then, with rank unwholesome vegetation, in whose baleful[4] shade the wretched wanderers who are tempted hither droop, and die, and lay their bones; the hateful Mississippi circling and eddying before it, and turning off upon its southern course a slimy monster hideous to behold; a hotbed of disease, an ugly sepulchre,[5] a grave uncheered by any gleam of promise: a place without one single quality, in earth or air or water, to commend it: such is this dismal Cairo [Illinois].

"Cairo, Illinois," Charles Dickens, *American Notes*

[1]*wan:* pale. [2]*ague:* malarial fever, marked by chills and sweating. [3]*vaunted:* boasted of. [4]*baleful:* sorrowful; miserable. [5]*sepulchre:* burial place.

Through the use of the word "dismal" in his last sentence, Dickens makes clear his attitude toward the town of Cairo, Illinois, in this very literal passage. The strength of his aversion for the place, though, is expressed by the gradual accumulation throughout the passage of a number of words that suggest unpleasant images: *stunted, wan, wretched, monotonous, wearily, swamp, slimy monster, disease, sepulchre, grave, death.* In addition, the repeated sentence openings in the final two sentences of his first paragraph reinforce the feeling of monotony. In its word choice and its structure, then, this selection emphatically expresses a tone of loathing and revulsion.

2. The tone of the second passage, Mark Twain's recipe for a breakfast dish, is perhaps not so easy to recognize:

To make this excellent breakfast dish, proceed as follows: Take a sufficiency[1] of water and a sufficiency of flour, and construct a bullet-proof dough. Work this into the form of a disk, with the edges turned up some three-fourths of an inch. Toughen and kiln-dry it a couple of days in a mild but unvarying temperature. Construct a cover for this redoubt[2] in the same way and of the same material. Fill with stewed dried apples; aggravate with cloves, lemon peels, and slabs of citron; add two portions of New England sugar, then solder on the lid and set in a safe place till it petrifies.[3] Serve cold at breakfast and invite your enemy.

"Recipe for a Breakfast Dish," Mark Twain, *A Tramp Abroad*

[1]*sufficiency:* proper amount. [2]*redoubt:* fortress. [3]*petrifies:* becomes like a stone.

Here word choice again leads the reader to the tone of the selection. Although he might be misled by the statement "excellent breakfast dish" in the opening sentence, such words and phrases as "bullet-proof dough," "toughen," "redoubt," "aggravate," "solder," and "petrifies" soon show that Twain is being ironic when he says that this breakfast dish is excellent. In case the reader should miss the ironic tone in reading the recipe, however, Twain gives it extra emphasis in his short final sentence: "Serve cold and invite your enemy." Having eaten an unappetizing breakfast dish in a foreign country, Twain indirectly criticizes it by writing in an ironic, satirical tone. Without directly saying so, he conveys the message to the reader that this foreign food is decidedly unappetizing.

3. Here is a passage in which James Thurber writes in a humorous vein about the problems faced by the males of many species in courting females:

> The male fiddler crab has a somewhat easier time, but it can hardly be said that he is sitting pretty.[1] He has one enormously large and powerful claw, usually brilliantly colored, and you might suppose that all he had to do was reach out and grab some passing cutie.[2] The very earliest fiddler crabs may have tried this, but, if so, they got slapped for their pains. A female fiddler crab will not tolerate any caveman stuff;[3] she never has and she doesn't intend to start now. To attract a female, a fiddler crab has to stand on tiptoe and brandish[4] his claw in the air. If any female in the neighborhood is interested—and you'd be surprised how many are not—she comes over and engages him in light badinage,[5] for which he is not in the mood. As many as a hundred females may pass the time of day with him and go on about their business. By nightfall of an average courting day, a fiddler crab who has been standing on tiptoe for eight or ten hours waving a heavy claw in the air is in pretty sad shape.[6] As in the case of the males of all species, however, he gets out of bed next morning, dashes some water on his face, and tries again.
>
> "Courtship," James Thurber, *My World—and Welcome to It*

[1]*sitting pretty:* without problems, well off. [2]*cutie:* attractive girl. [3]*caveman stuff:* rough treatment, brutality. [4]*brandish:* wave triumphantly, menacingly, or defiantly. [5]*badinage:* playful conversation. [6]*pretty sad shape:* tired and discouraged.

Word choice also plays an important part in creating the comic tone of this passage. The incongruity of such phrases as "sitting pretty," "passing cutie," "caveman stuff," "pretty sad shape," and "gets out of bed" in referring to the fiddler crab quite clearly points up the humor here. By applying essentially human slang terms to animals, Thurber sets the comic tone for his essay on the courtship of females and males.

4. Last of all, a student of English composition can hardly fail to recognize the plight of a professional writer, Brendan Gill, who, after work-

ing for almost forty years on *The New Yorker* magazine staff, still feels insecure about his ability to write well:

> In some cases, the pressure of all those doubting eyes upon his copy is more than the writer can bear. When the galleys of a piece are placed in front of him, covered with scores, perhaps hundreds, of pencilled hen-tracks of inquiry, suggestion, and correction, he may sense not the glory of creation but the threat of being stung to death by an army of gnats. Upon which he may think of nothing better to do than lower his head onto his blotter and burst into tears. Thanks to the hen-tracks and their consequences, the piece will be much improved, but the author of it will be pitched into a state of graver self-doubt than ever. Poor devil, he will type out his name on a sheet of paper and stare at it long and long, with dumb uncertainty. It looks—oh, Christ!—his name looks as if it could stand some working on.
>
> "How Much Can a Writer Stand?," Brendan Gill, *Here at the New Yorker*

Irony ("being stung to death by an army of gnats"), melodrama ("lower his head . . . and burst into tears"), and incongruity ("his name looks as if it could stand some working on") combine in Gill's writing to create a witty and urbane tone.

When considering the tone of your own writing, remember these points:
1. Adopt a tone appropriate to your subject matter.
2. Avoid sudden shifts in tone within your paper.
3. Be personal in your writing but not familiar.
4. Avoid being either overly modest or excessively boastful.
5. Avoid exaggeration.
6. Handle humor with special restraint.
7. Do not become pompous or oversolemn.
8. Do not try to achieve a certain tone in your writing by overpunctuating.

TWO MATTERS OF WORD ARRANGEMENT

Sometimes the contrast between what a student learns in school and what he sees happening in the outside world is surprising. In the case of language, many U.S.A. students have been taught that they should not end a sentence with a preposition.

In reading books, magazines, newspapers, and even letters, though, one quickly finds that sentences *can* end with prepositions. Let's look briefly at this and one other word arrangement situation.

Should You End a Sentence with a Preposition?

Winston Churchill, an illustrious British statesman and prose stylist, once made this ironic comment about writing: "Ending a sentence with a preposition is something up with which I will not put." Here Churchill has intentionally garbled the English idiom "to put up with," meaning "to accept" or "to agree to." Clearly his sentence would have been much more graceful if it *had* ended with a preposition in this way: "Ending a sentence with a preposition is something I will not put up with."

Because prepositions appear frequently in English writing, sooner or later the problem of where in a sentence to fit one in will arise. In contemporary American English rhetoric, ending a sentence with a preposition is something no student should feel guilty about in informal writing.

Should a Subject and Predicate Be Separated?

A second point about word arrangement concerns the relationship between a sentence's subject and predicate. Sometimes a word or phrase falls naturally between a subject and predicate. This often happens with a transition (The most economical way, *though*, is to build a compost pile.) or with an appositive (Salisbury, *the capital of Rhodesia*, is in a state of unrest.). Generally speaking, however, you should try not to separate the subject and predicate of a sentence by intervening words and phrases. Particularly when the intervening element is a prepositional phrase, the force of the sentence can sometimes be weakened.

Here are two examples showing how subjects and predicates separated by prepositional phrases can be joined:

Separated	**Traffic** in London **moves** on the left.
Joined	In London **traffic moves** on the left.
Separated	**Totem poles** throughout the city **add** color to the scene.
Joined	Throughout the city, **totem poles add** color to the scene.

EXERCISE 69
Word Arrangement

A. *The following sentences would all read better if they ended with prepositions. Revise them so they do.*

1. That is the most amazing coincidence of which I have ever heard.
2. Todd didn't ask for a large salary; he only wanted enough on which to live.
3. For what are you looking?
4. The salesgirl pointed out the dressing room where Louise could take the three dresses on which to try.
5. Martha considered Patricia to be a valued friend on whom she could always count.

B. *Revise the following sentences so that their subjects and predicates are not separated.*

1. San Francisco in the summer has a cool, foggy climate that most people welcome.
2. The French during the colonial period controlled Indochina.
3. The actor between his two films slipped away to Brazil for a short vacation.

4. Traffic in large cities all over the world is congested.
5. A celebration on John's birthday was arranged at Disneyland.

Review of Transitions between Paragraphs

Since you have been writing compositions of more than one paragraph since Chapter 5, you will want to review how to bridge the break between the end of one paragraph and the beginning of the next. It is important to provide continuity between paragraphs so that your reader is sure of the direction that your thought is taking.

You will remember from the discussion in Chapter 5 the four useful ways to link paragraphs:

1. Use a pronoun (*this, that, these, those*) in the first sentence of a paragraph to refer back to the subject discussed in the last sentence of a preceding paragraph.
2. Repeat a key word from the end of one paragraph to the beginning of the next.
3. Repeat a key phrase from the end of one paragraph to the beginning of the next.
4. Use a transitional expression at the beginning of a new paragraph.

Look again at the examples of linking paragraphs together on page 135 before starting the following review exercise.

EXERCISE 70
Review: Transitions between Paragraphs

A. *Look back over the sample writing passages containing more than one paragraph in earlier chapters. Find five examples where word repetition could have been used (but was not) to link paragraphs together. Copy the last sentence of one paragraph and the first sentence of the next, adding the linking word or words.*

B. *Write a short composition of four paragraphs on any subject. Supply the following transitions between paragraphs: (1) Between the first and second paragraphs, use a pronoun; (2) Between the second and third paragraphs, repeat a key word or phrase; (3) Between the third and fourth paragraphs, use a transitional word or phrase.*

Punctuation Points

PUNCTUATION REVIEW

In earlier chapters you have studied various uses of the comma. Since it is one of the most frequently used marks of punctuation, a review of the comma at this stage will help you to be more certain of the rules.

The following exercise reviews the use of commas in series, in compound sentences, after introductory clauses and phrases, around nonrestrictive elements, and in dates and addresses.

EXERCISE 71
Review: Comma Usage

Write out the sentences, inserting commas wherever needed. Not all sentences need commas.

Commas in Series (See explanation on page 48.)

1. I'll have to beg borrow or steal a dress for Saturday's party.
2. I'll have to beg or borrow a dress for Saturday's party.
3. His kindness patience and courtesy won him many friends.
4. My parents never coaxed bribed or forced me to eat.
5. We made six hits three runs and two errors in the first inning.
6. The scouts hiked through the woods over a mountain and across a stream.
7. My father and I will pick up Betty and Ruth at the station.
8. Our beds and our clothes and our food were full of sand.

Commas in Compound Sentences (See explanation on page 44.)

9. The chairman rapped on the table and the audience quieted down.
10. The chairman rapped on the table and waited for order.
11. Earl painted the porch and his father paid him for the job.
12. Hot air rises but cold air falls.
13. You can lead a horse to water but you cannot make him drink.
14. Paul drove to the side of the road and let the other car pass.
15. Larry has worked after school and on Saturdays and he has saved nearly $500.
16. The product must be advertised or the public will never ask for it.
17. I had heard about the Brazilian soccer teams and wanted to see them play.

Commas after Introductory Phrases and Clauses *(Not all the phrases and clauses are introductory; not all sentences need commas.)* (See explanation on page 46.)

18. When some article disappears around the house Ralph is always blamed.
19. It began to rain at the very beginning of the game.
20. If I have to do it alone the job will take all day.
21. Lois has wanted to be a nurse ever since she was a little girl.
22. With icy shivers in my spine I reached for my flashlight.
23. Seeing nothing ahead of me on the road I increased my speed.

24. When we first met Harvey was a sophomore in high school.
25. Although he shouted the name could not be heard.

Commas for Setting off Nonrestrictive Elements (See explanation on page 104.)

26. It happened I suppose on an icy pavement.
27. English on the other hand is easier for me.
28. This model by the way is more expensive.
29. I was worried by the way he acted.
30. Yes we do own a dog.
31. Well this is all the news I have to tell.
32. Why did you change your mind?
33. Why this story is ridiculous.
34. Our target a small tin can was nailed to a post.
35. Our target was a small tin can.
36. The editor of our paper Harvey Brooks is graduating.
37. Harvey Brooks the editor of our paper is graduating.
38. A heavy snowstorm held up our train the Trans-Europe Express.
39. With the help of Bob Morley the boy across the street I built a model jet plane.
40. I have decided my friend to take your advice.
41. The next time you come Dave you must bring Earl along.
42. You must admit that Ross won the game for Steve.
43. I am reading *Doctor Zhivago* for my book report.
44. I am reading an interesting book *Doctor Zhivago* for my book report.
45. The church which we visited yesterday was built in 1901.
46. The Milan Cathedral which was constructed over several centuries is an impressive sight.

Commas in Dates and Addresses (See explanation on page 335.)

47. Mr. A. C. Roe of 461 Avery Road is the owner.
48. Mr. A. C. Roe 461 Avery Road is the owner.
49. We moved to 1700 Lakeshore Avenue Sydney Australia on September 5 1960.
50. The Dionne quintuplets were born on May 28 1934 in Callander Ontario.
51. We drove from Munich to Salzburg in one day.
52. Mr. John Porter of 2211 Pinecrest Road is in charge of ticket sales.
53. Nairobi Kenya is the newly chosen convention site.

Review of Commas

54. Can you come to my graduation Rafael on Friday June 21?
55. In the early days of the industry each automobile was virtually made by hand and the price was very high.

56. I wrote to the Sterling Stamp Co. 1600 Jefferson Ave. Buffalo N.Y. for a price list.
57. When we first met Carlos had dark brown hair and wore glasses.
58. Yes I have complete faith ladies and gentlemen in our incoming chairman.
59. Tim of course apologized to Miss Bromley and she accepted his apology graciously.
60. I was still holding the king of spades the queen of spades and two aces in my hand.
61. If you know what's good for you you won't cross Mr. Kronk's lawn when you deliver his paper.
62. You can read *Huckleberry Finn* in one or two evenings.

Grammar Skills

MISPLACED MODIFIERS

Deciding upon the proper word order or syntax in English is a problem that constantly confronts the speaker of another language. And, of course, mistakes in word arrangement are much more obvious in writing than they are in speaking. One of the most common mistakes is called the misplaced modifier. This happens when a writer fails to place a word or phrase in a sentence beside the word it modifies. Being out of order, the word or phrase changes the sense of the sentence and sometimes even makes it seem meaningless.

As a general rule, English sentence structure follows this pattern:

SUBJECT + VERB + OBJECT + ADVERB OF PLACE + ADVERB OF TIME

Exceptions in word order occur, of course, especially when a writer purposefully varies his sentence structure in the twenty-four ways illustrated in Chapter 8's Review of Varying Sentence Openings.

What beginning writers also need to remember about English word order is that the modifiers of each part of the basic sentence pattern should normally be placed as close as possible to the part modified. For example, you should not write, "The dog won first prize *with the red collar*." In this sentence, the prepositional phrase properly modifies (or gives further information about) the noun subject *dog*. Correctly written, the sentence reads: "The dog *with the red collar* won first prize." Review these additional examples of misplaced modifiers and their corrections:

Misplaced modifiers	A car drove down the street **decked with ribbons.** (Is the street decked with ribbons?)
Corrected	A car **decked with ribbons** drove down the street.

Misplaced modifier	She was wearing a colorful scarf around her shoulders, **which she had bought in Mexico.** (Did she buy her shoulders in Mexico?)
Corrected	Around her shoulders she was wearing a colorful scarf **which she had bought in Mexico.**

Misplaced modifiers	He worked hard in the fields, raising crops that would bring in money **without complaint.** (Is the money not complaining?)
Corrected	**Without complaint,** he worked hard in the fields, raising crops that would bring in money.

To see how the fifth sentence in the model paragraph in Chapter 9 was revised from its original form in order to correct a misplaced modifier, note this change:

Misplaced modifier	Young men and women are selected from the upper fifteen percent of their high school classes **for admission to Stanford.**
Corrected	Young men and women are selected **for admission to Stanford** from the upper fifteen percent of their high school classes.

As this example shows, whenever you have two or more modifiers to place after a verb, normally place *first* the modifier that answers the question "What?". Place *second* the modifier that answers the question "How?" or "Why?" or "Where?" or "To whom?". Place *third* the modifier that answers the question "When?". There is one major exception to this rule. In English, the indirect object of a verb nearly always precedes the direct object. (In the sentence "She gave him a gift," *him* is the indirect object; *gift* is the direct object.)

EXERCISE 72
Placing Modifying Elements

Rewrite these sentences to eliminate misplaced modifiers.

1. The car is in that garage which he smashed.
2. He looked at the angry boy with sad eyes.
3. They talked about going on a second honeymoon frequently, but they never did.
4. Fortunately, the fire was put out before any damage was done by the volunteer firemen.
5. There is a lecture tonight about juvenile delinquency in the student lounge.
6. I listened while he talked attentively.
7. Gary Cooper played the sheriff who refused to compromise with outlaws superbly.

8. He showed his drum to his father that he had won as a prize.
9. There was a noisy disturbance when the speaker began his address at the back of the hall.
10. Everyone stared at the girl who was dancing with the bearded dean in the low-cut dress.
11. The newsboy walked his bicycle to the house of his first customer who was burdened with newspapers.
12. She poured the wine into the chilled carafe which was a domestic brand.
13. It is fashionable in America for most college students to wear informal clothing who want to keep up with fashion trends.
14. Recent findings reveal that, prior to the Spanish-American War, the sinking of the battleship "Maine" was caused by an accidental explosion which was anchored for a time in Cuban waters.
15. Many faculty members at Hastings Law School in San Francisco who have previously retired from teaching are men over 65 years of age.

REVIEW OF PARALLELISM

Since studying the principles of parallelism in Chapter 5, you have read many examples of this technique. Here in review is a paragraph that shows clearly how well parallelism can contribute to a rich English prose style (parallel forms are boldfaced):

> Today's young couples seem to be freer to express themselves, in words and physically. **Perhaps** they will succeed in incorporating into their sexual lives a new philosophy of touch. **Perhaps** they do understand **that touching**—like seeing, hearing, tasting and smelling—nourishes the pleasure of being alive; **that touching** another human being satisfies the profound creature need not to feel alone; **that being touched** by another human being satisfies the need to be desired as a physical presence; and **that in touching and being touched,** one can experience not only the pleasure of being alive but also the joy of being a sexual creature—a joy that ultimately and inevitably, as a natural extension of life itself, expresses itself in the sexual embrace.
>
> "Touching—and Being Touched," William H. Masters and Virginia E. Johnson, *Reader's Digest* (December 1972)

Parallelism is introduced here with the second and third sentences both having the same structure and some of the same words ("perhaps they will succeed"; "perhaps they do understand"). Then follow three parallel noun clauses ("that touching . . . nourishes"; "that touching . . . satisfies"; "that being touched . . . satisfies") and a fourth parallel relative pronoun introducing an adjective phrase ("that in touching and being touched").

Of course, the writers could simply have numbered the four benefits of touch and listed them efficiently in a column. But by placing their points in parallel forms, Masters and Johnson present a tender subject in graceful rhetoric.

Although parallelism assures the coherence of this paragraph, the authors make certain that their important final point is not overlooked. They do this by adding two expository elements: a pair of correlative conjunctions "not only . . . but also" and the word "joy," repeated for coherence. By carefully shaping their paragraph for clear communication, Masters and Johnson demonstrate the control over words that professional writers must exercise.

EXERCISE 73
Parallelism Review

Find five examples of parallelism that have not been previously identified in the sample writing selections of Chapters 1–10.

REVIEW OF PREPOSITIONS

Try your hand at choosing prepositions this week to see how sharp your ear has become:

EXERCISE 74
Preposition Review

Write out each sentence, placing the correct preposition in each blank. Refer to Appendix 6 if you need help in choosing prepositions.

1. ......the time she walked......the staircase, I had waited impatiently......an hour and a half.
2. Men are supposed to be......the peak of their creative powers...... the age......forty-seven.
3. Stopped......a policeman......driving his car too fast, Mr. Brown explained that he was......a hurry to take his wife......the hospital.
4. If you are looking......information......magnets, you should go ......the library.
5. You must be......time......the movie, or you won't be able to sit ......us.
6. Paul has a comfortable life, living......a small apartment and driving ......work......a sports car.
7. When we come......the end......the semester, we will travel...... another class to visit the Louvre.
8. He flew......Rio de Janiero......a business trip.
9. After looking carefully......the room, he decided to leave the party ......8 o'clock if his friend wanted to leave......him.
10. ......Sunday I will have time to play bridge......the evening...... a few hours.
11. ......October 10 the Abbey Players will open......the Arena Theater......a revival......Oscar Wilde's comedy, *The Importance of Being Earnest.*

12. When the play opened......Edinburgh a week ago, the critics praised the Abbey Players, who have thrilled audiences......their perform-ances......many years.
13. The acting company was so enthusiastically acclaimed......Paris ......their production......*Waiting for Godot* that the play ran ......ten months.
14. Tickets are now......sale......the box office......the Arena The-ater......the four-week engagement.
15. There will be a performance every night except Sunday......8:30 P.M. and matinees......Wednesdays and Saturdays...... 2:30 P.M.

Questions for Discussion and Review

1. Find examples of especially forceful writing in this chapter's model composition.
2. Identify three writing passages in Chapters 1–10 whose tone is in-formal and three passages whose tone is formal.
3. Analyze the model compositions in Chapters 9 and 10 to determine what means writers have used to link their paragraphs together.
4. Compare the style and tone of White in "The Three New Yorks" (Chapter 9) with those of Mannes in this chapter's "The New York I Know."
5. Explain the use of parentheses in Wrenn's essay, "The English Lan-guage."
6. Reread the last five sentences of the Harris passage in the Group 1 composition section of Chapter 9. Then rewrite these sentences so that they express Harris's ideas with greater expository force.
7. Identify the repeated pronouns (not including "they") that add co-herence to Butler's essay, "The Marks of an Educated Man."
8. Find additional examples of parallelism in Butler's selection, not includ-ing the ones already identified.
9. List all the specific terms you can find in the selection from Murray's *Fundamentals of Nursing.*
10. Contrast Mark Twain's tone in this chapter's "Recipe for a Breakfast Dish" with his tone in Chapter 9's "Familiarity Breeds Regret."
11. Analyze the model paragraphs and compositions that open Chapters 2–10 for variety in conclusions.

Vocabulary Growth

PARAGRAPH PUZZLE

In this chapter's Paragraph Puzzle, **no** *choices are given for the missing words. Use the context of the paragraph as a basis for choosing appropri-ate words to make the paragraph read meaningfully.*

Unlike fossil or fissile energy, the energy......the sun is virtually inexhaustible and can......tapped without exhausting limited energy resources, save......those used in constructing and maintaining......solar plant. And because no fuels are burned......the course of plant operation, solar power plants will not foul the air......particulate or radioactive discharges. Thus divorced......fossil and fissile fuels, solar power......an inherent simplicity and elegance that no......technology can match. Another great asset......solar power is that it is available from......sun in large amounts......the late afternoon—when the greatest electrical demand occurs. Moreover,......large proportion of the solar energy needed ......distributed free by nature to......point of use. We do not need ......pay an energy conglomerate to bring sunshine to......, unless we let those corporations "pull a fast one" on us as......have done with nuclear fission.

Using solar energy effectively is especially challenging......the sun is a diffuse and......intermittent energy source that varies......intensity daily, seasonally, and by geographic region. ......characteristics add to the complexity......solar systems and hence to their costs. ......the problems are being successfully overcome. ......reason for this success is that, ...contrast to nuclear fission or fusion, ...technology, along...... other energy alternatives, can provide many citizens......total energy independence from power utilities......relative independence from big energy conglomerates.

John Berger, Nuclear Power

WORD CLUES

A. *Vocabulary words in the following exercise are boldfaced.*

1. In this sixty-year period (1890–1950), America changed from rural to **urban,** but few who knew the conditions of life in the large cities would contend that Americans had come to terms with their cities as their grandparents had come to terms with the countryside: American civilization was urban, but it was not yet an **urbane** civilization. Americans had conquered leisure for themselves on a scale never before thought possible; yet never before had men seemed so hurried, and when they thought of a leisurely society it was always in terms of a past innocent of labor-saving devices: no twentieth-century statesman accomplished so much as Jefferson, none enjoyed so much leisure.

Henry Steele Commager, The American Mind

Vocabulary Word..

Context Clue...

Probable Meaning...

Dictionary Definition......................................

Vocabulary Word. . . . .

Context Clue. . . . .

Probable Meaning. . . . .

Dictionary Definition. . . . .

2. Wilson's **eminence** as a literary critic and literary historian overshadowed his distinction as a journalist. For his part, he would perhaps have liked more attention to be paid to his short stories, poems, and plays. In a **laudatory** piece, the *London Times Literary Supplement* once described him as America's foremost man of letters, and by his standards a man of letters was one who could accomplish any literary task that happened to come his way.

Brendan Gill, Here at the New Yorker

Vocabulary Word. . . . .

Context Clue. . . . .

Probable Meaning. . . . .

Dictionary Definition. . . . .

Vocabulary Word. . . . .

Context Clue. . . . .

Probable Meaning. . . . .

Dictionary Definition. . . . .

3. Insect **fecundity** is frightening. Many species lay hundreds or thousands of eggs after each mating. Some insects pass through their entire life cycles, from egg to adult, in a matter of days or weeks, producing dozens of generations a season. This gives insects an enormous evolutionary advantage over man.

Vocabulary Word. . . . .

Context Clue. . . . .

Probable Meaning. . . . .

Dictionary Definition. . . . .

4. We have recently discovered another photosynthetic mechanism powered by a different pigment, one that is closely related to rhodopsin, which has hitherto been known only as a visual pigment in the eye of animals. This new system is found in the halobacteria: microorganisms that require high concentration of sodium chloride for growth and that therefore **proliferate** in natural salt lakes and in salterns, where seawater is evaporated to produce salt.

"The Purple Membrane of Salt-Loving Bacteria," Walter Stoeckenius,
Scientific American (June 1976)

Vocabulary Word. . . . .

Context Clue. . . . .

Probable Meaning. . . . .

Dictionary Definition. . . . .

5. It seemed at times the cruelest kind of **juxtaposition.** Crises were breaking nearly everywhere at home and abroad, demanding official attention
and perhaps action. Terrorism: a siege at the headquarters of the Organization of Petroleum Exporting Countries in Vienna; a bomb explosion
at a baggage claim area of La Guardia Airport in New York. International tension: a civil war in the new independent African nation of
Angola between **factions** loyal to the Communists and the "free world";
a situation that threatened to reach the same point in Angola's former
colonial parent, Portugal, a NATO ally.

"The Intelligence Tangle," Sanford J. Ungar, *The Atlantic Monthly* (April 1976)

Vocabulary Word. . . . .

Context Clue. . . . .

Probable Meaning. . . . .

Dictionary Definition. . . . .

Vocabulary Word. . . . .

Context Clue. . . . .

Probable Meaning. . . . .

Dictionary Definition. . . . .

B. *Look in a dictionary for meanings of each of the following verbs and
for all the related forms of the verb you can find. Make a four-column list
headed "verbs, nouns, adjectives, and adverbs."*

1. to conform
2. to denounce
3. to reject
4. to extend
5. to penetrate
6. to expand

Composition: Show What You Have Learned

Choose a composition topic from either Group I or Group II.

**GROUP I: TOPICS FOR WRITING A COMPOSITION DEVELOPED BY LOGICAL
DIVISION**

If one travels around the world, one soon realizes that a woman's role
in society differs—sometimes sharply—from one country to another.

Great Britain, for instance, has been called "a man's country"; some people, on the other hand, see the U.S.A. as "a woman's country."

In all parts of the world, of course, basic similarities occur in the way men think about women and in the way women think about themselves. But more significant than the similarities are the *differences* in how men think about women—and especially in how women think about themselves. Some observers feel that the U.S.A.'s reputation as a feminist stronghold began with such memorable women as Susan B. Anthony (woman's suffrage), Frances Willard (temperance), Ellen Swallow Richards (first woman graduate and first woman faculty member at Massachusetts Institute of Technology), and Margaret Sanger (birth control). Today, for every *macho* Burt Reynolds, there is a *magnifica* Gloria Steinem or Betty Friedan; for every issue of *Playboy* Magazine, there is a women's counterpart in *Playgirl*.

A prominent American historian, Henry Steele Commager, has expressed this view of woman's place in American society:

> Twentieth-century America, even more than nineteenth, seemed to be a woman's country. The supremacy of woman could be read in the statistics of property ownership, insurance, education, or literature, or in the advertisements of any popular magazine. Women ran the schools and the churches, they determined what would appear in the magazines and the movies and what would be heard over the radio. As many girls as boys attended college, and women made their way successfully into almost every profession. There were a hundred magazines designed especially for their entertainment or edification, and among them some with the largest circulation, while most metropolitan newspapers had a page for women and every radio station a series of programs directed exclusively to their supposed needs. As women spent most of the money, the overwhelming body of advertisements was addressed to them, and advertisers found it advisable to introduce the feminine motive even, or especially, where they hoped to attract men. Traditionally women had ruled the home, but only in America did they design it, build it, furnish it, direct its activities, and fix its standards. Most American children knew more of their mothers' than of their fathers' families, and it was the opinion of many observers of World War II that the silver cord[1] bound American youth more firmly than the youth of any other land. It was appropriate enough that an American, Lester Ward, should have propounded the theory of the natural superiority of the female sex, which he called gynecocracy, and American experience appeared to validate[2] the theory.
>
> "America: A Woman's Country," Henry Steele Commager, *The American Mind*

[1]*silver cord:* close tie between mother and son. [2]*validate:* support; verify.

Having read Commager's selection, and possibly having observed how women fit into two or more societies, choose one of the following composition topics to develop by logical division. Stock your paper liberally with examples:

1. Agree or disagree with Commager's view that the U.S.A. is a woman's country.
2. Explain how the role of women in your country compares with the role of women in the U.S.A.
3. Do you believe that equal opportunity for men and women in all areas of life is desirable? Explore this issue.
4. As women become more active in business and political life, do you think that men should become more domesticated, possibly staying home, keeping house, and caring for the children?
5. During the past decade, much publicity has been given to women's liberation. If you feel that a male liberation movement may be in order, discuss what you think might be its issues.
6. Clare Boothe Luce, in Chapter 9's "The 21st-Century Woman—Free at Last?," and Henry Steele Commager, in this chapter's selection from *The American Mind*, express conflicting views about American women's progress toward equality with men. Contrast the ideas of these two passages, concluding with evidence to support your opinion as to which viewpoint seems presently to be the more accurate one.

GROUP II: TOPICS TO CHALLENGE YOUR IMAGINATION

One of the quickest ways to begin to understand a country's value system is to look at the advertisements appearing in various places—in magazines and newspapers; on television; on such public transportation vehicles as subways, streetcars, and taxicabs; in movie theaters; in programs; in mailings. For in their desire to sell a product, advertisers strive to appeal to urges they believe are shared by the greatest number of people.

The American oil company advertisement on page 321 communicates a basic insight about the U.S.A. It is revealing that in 1976 (the nation's Bicentennial year), advertising executives should have looked ahead a hundred years to the U.S.A.'s Tricentennial in 2076. As the advertisement says, "We have always been a nation more interested in the promise of the future than in the events of the past."

Certainly tradition plays a far less important part in the United States than it does in most other countries of the world. In fact, many of the differences that visitors notice in the texture of American life stem from the essentially untraditional nature of the country.

The following composition topics are based on ideas suggested by the advertisement. Check a topic, developing it by logical division and writing in specific terms:

1. The Americans' general lack of concern with tradition has had both positive and negative effects. Evaluate from both sides the role of tradition in American life.
2. Discuss the place of tradition in your country.

Use this coupon to send us your Tricentennial idea.

Send your idea to:
Tricentennial
Atlantic Richfield Company
P.O. Box 2076
Los Angeles, CA 90053

From:_____

Address_____

City_____State_____Zip_____

My idea is:

We have always been a nation more interested in the promise of the future than in the events of the past.

Here at Atlantic Richfield we see the future as an exciting time. The best of times. And we know that all of us can achieve a splendid future by planning for it now.

We'd like your help. We need your vision. America will change a great deal by the year 2076. We want you to tell us what you think those changes should be.

What do you envision as the best way to solve our energy problems?

Should we have a universal language?

How do you think architecture of the future can improve on that of the present?

Or, if those topics don't appeal to you, pick one that does.

Please note that all ideas submitted shall become public property without compensation and free of any restriction on use and disclosure.

ARCO ◆
AtlanticRichfieldCompany

Celebrate America's Tricentennial 100 years early.

Reprinted by permission of the Atlantic Richfield Company Tricentennial Program.

3. What traditions do you think are essential for a country to preserve?
4. Predict what changes you think may occur over the next hundred years in the United States. (Touch on the ideas the advertisement suggests—energy, language, architecture—or select others.)
5. Explain the social and economic transformation that may occur in your country by 2076.

Chapter **11**

Advanced Composition Topics

The four units in this chapter offer topics for compositions to be developed by whatever expository methods or combination of methods you choose. In writing on these subjects, apply the learning gained from Chapters 1–10 to help you organize your ideas in the most forceful way.

Topic 1: Censorship—A Burning Issue

How much freedom of expression should writers and artists have? In the past, many heads of state have asked themselves this question, and the issue of censorship is as alive today as it has ever been.

Censorship—the suppression of writings, art works, and performances—is often imposed, either directly or indirectly, by authorities who feel it necessary to suppress published ideas or images that might subvert official policies or endanger accepted morality. A difficulty arises, though, in deciding what the limits of censorship will be, and excesses often occur.

The following list shows that, in the past, censorship has not been confined to any single period or to any single country. For students interested in cultural differences, censorship is an especially illuminating subject because the type of works suppressed and the reasons for keeping works from the public reveal much about a society's standards during a given time:

CENSORED OR SUPPRESSED WORKS

Homer, *The Odyssey*
  35 A.D.—Rome: Caligula tried to suppress the book because it expressed Greek ideals of freedom.

Confucius, *Analects*
  250 B.C.—China: The first ruler of the T'sin dynastry burned all books relating to the teachings of Confucius.

Dante, *The Divine Comedy*
  1497—Florence: Savanorola burned this book during the "Burning of the Vanities."

The Koran
  1542—Switzerland: This was confiscated by Basel authorities.

Molière, *Tartuffe*
  1664—France: Molière's play was banned because it was a satire on religious hypocrisy. The ban was lifted in 1669.

Whitman, Walt, *Leaves of Grass*
  1881—Boston: The book was withdrawn at the insistence of the Society for Suppression of Vice.

Clemens, Samuel, *Huckleberry Finn*
  1885—Concord, Massachusetts: Called "trash and suitable only for slums," this book was banned.

Shaw, Bernard, *Man and Superman*
  1905—New York: This play was withdrawn from the New York Public Library.

Joyce, James, *Dubliners*
  1912—Ireland: The entire first edition, less one copy, was burned.

The Bible
  1926—Russia: Because only antireligious books were authorized, this was banned in libraries.

London, Jack, *The Call of the Wild*
  1929—Yugoslavia: All London's works were banned in Yugoslavia.

Carroll, Lewis, *Alice's Adventures in Wonderland*
  1931—China: Officials banned this work on the grounds that animals should not use human language.

Shakespeare, William, *The Merchant of Venice*
  1931—Buffalo, New York: This play was eliminated from schools because it was declared to be anti-Semetic.

Connelly, Marc, *Green Pastures*
  1933—Norway: The play was forbidden to be shown in this country.

Disney, Walt, *Donald Duck*
  1954—East Germany: Disney's cartoon character was declared "decadent" by members of the Free German Youth, and publications containing the animal's image were burned.

Mozart, Wolfgang, *Don Giovanni* (Film of the opera)
  1961—Chicago: The right of the Chicago Police Commissioner to require prior viewing and approval of films before public release of the films was upheld by the United States Supreme Court in a 5–4 decision.

Williams, Tennessee, *Plays and other works*
  1965—Portugal: All Williams' writings were banned.

Baldwin, James, *Tell Me How Long the Train's Been Gone*
  1969—Washington: One of the United States Information Agency's overseas libraries banned this book on the grounds that it represents Americans in an unattractive way.

Hersey, John, *Hiroshima*
  1969—California: A decision in January by the Board of Education to ban this book was reversed in February, 1969.

Cleaver, Eldridge, *Soul on Ice*
  1970—California: The California State Superintendent of Public Instruction warned that teachers using this book in schools could lose their certificates.

Miller, Henry, *Tropic of Capricorn*
  1970—Greece: After this work was ruled obscene, all copies were ordered destroyed.

Salinger, J. D., *The Catcher in the Rye*
  1970—South Carolina: This was removed from the Kershaw County List of acceptable books.

Vidal, Gore, *Myra Breckinridge*
  1970—Australia: This book was banned on moral grounds.

Baez, Joan, *Daybreak*
  1971—California: The Orange County Board of Education banned the book from school libraries, declaring that the author was a "radical."

Vonnegut, Kurt, *Slaughterhouse-Five*

> 1971—Michigan: A County Circuit Judge in Pontiac ruled that the book should be banned from high school libraries because it was anti-Christian.

"Censored or Suppressed Works," Palo Alto (California) City Library

Use the information supplied by this list of censored works as a basis for choosing one of the following composition topics. Select the most useful method or (combination of methods) to develop your paper:

1. Have you ever read a book or seen a movie that has been censored? What was your reaction?
2. How is censorship handled in your country? Do you feel it is successfully dealt with?
3. Discuss similarities and differences in the approach to censorship between your country (or some other country) and the United States.
4. Support or refute this statement: "Censorship is an essential governmental function in any culture."
5. Select an important work of fiction or nonfiction that you admire. Write an essay defending it against possible objections. Present reasons why this work might be attacked. Base your defense on a consideration of such matters as its language, characters, artistic purpose, and value for readers.
6. Choose a book you have read or a movie you have seen that you feel *should be* censored. Explain your reasons.
7. Read one of the censored works mentioned above and explain why you think censorship *was* or *was not* justified.

Topic 2: Letting the Public Voice Be Heard

People can express themselves in many ways. If they are literate, they can write; if they are artistic, they can draw; if they are extroverted, they can perform. But how can the person who is not a writer, artist, or actor visibly transmit his message to the world? One popular way to do this in the U.S.A. is to march in a demonstration, carrying a placard bearing a brief statement.

The cartoon on the next page showing the animal parade reflects the popularity of public demonstration in the United States. Unlike most political or social protesters, though, these animals are not expressing a partisan stand or opposition to an issue. Their placards are of a more personalized nature than the "Ban the Bomb" or "Flower Power" signs carried to catch the television camera's roaming eye. Each animal's sign bears a familiar saying inspired by that animal's name.

Such sayings are commonly heard in the U.S.A. Although the ones on the placards are so well known that they might be considered trite (no

Drawing by Lorenz; © *1970*
The New Yorker *Magazine, Inc.*

doubt the cartoonist is commenting on the predictability of poster slogans), animal-based sayings can be both original and highly expressive. For instance, a person can be described as "happy as a clam" or as "nervous as a long-tailed cat in a room full of rocking chairs."

1. You can take your cue for this composition assignment from the ideas underlying the statements on these ten signs. Read the brief explanation of each; then select one statement as basis for a composition related to its central idea. For example, suppose you are intrigued by the meaning of "The Cat's Pajamas"—"something especially elegant." Then you would write a composition on the idea of elegance, perhaps explaining what elegance means to people of different ages, different classes, or different countries. Or perhaps "I'll Be a Monkey's Uncle," which is an expression of surprise, will give the idea of writing about the five greatest political surprises of the past year. Let your imagination break one of these subjects into a number of different possibilities; select the most promising one to write about. Develop your paper by a method of your choice or by a combination of methods.

a. **Lord Love a Duck:** This expresses surprise, amazement, or astonishment. It is equivalent to saying, "Would you believe that?"
b. **A Bear for Punishment:** Someone who voluntarily and frequently does things the hard way; an excessively eager worker.
c. **I'll Be a Monkey's Uncle:** This is an expression of extreme surprise.
d. **In a Pig's Eye:** A way to state doubt or disbelief.
e. **The Cat's Pajamas:** Something that is especially elegant.
f. **See You Later, Alligator:** A colloquialism for "Goodbye."
g. **It's a Dog's Life:** This is a negative statement; it implies frustration, servility, and futility.
h. **Drunk as a Skunk:** Someone who is extremely inebriated.
i. **You Can Lead a Horse to Water but You Can't Make Him Drink:** This suggests stubbornness.
j. **Snug as a Bug in a Rug:** A way to indicate extreme coziness.

2. Here are three alternative composition topics:
   a. Explain what means are available to citizens of your country for publicly stating their views.
   b. How far should citizens of any country be allowed to go in voicing their opinions on social and political matters? What avenues of expression should be open to them, and what avenues, if any, should be closed?
   c. Write a letter to the editor of a newspaper or magazine, expressing your agreement or disagreement with an article you have read in the publication.

Topic 3: A Delicate Balance: Women's Liberation and Family Life

Chapters 9 and 10 presented two opinions about the role of the American woman: one from an American man, Henry Steele Commager, who calls the United States a "woman's country," and one from an American woman, Clare Boothe Luce, whose opinion of women's status is somewhat less optimistic.

To help round out the picture of women in the world, the following composition topics are based on the ideas expressed by a European woman, the Italian writer Oriana Fallaci, who was the subject of an interview in the publication *Rolling Stone* (U.S.A.). Fallaci has gained prominence through her own in-depth interviews with the world's leading political figures. Jonathan Cott, interviewing the interviewer, wrote this about her work: "It is clear that, at their best, Oriana Fallaci's brilliantly theatrical interviews remind us of the aims of historians and playwrights such as Thucydides and Ben Jonson, in whose works history and human relations are seen as nothing less than moral drama."

In the following excerpt from Cott's talk with Fallaci, they speak of two women who have led nations as chiefs of state: India's Indira Ghandi and Israel's Golda Meir:

COTT: I was struck by a moving moment during your interview with Mrs. Ghandi when you talked about "the solitude that oppresses women intent on defending their own destinies." You mention that Mrs. Ghandi, like Golda Meir, had to sacrifice her marriage for her career. And I got the feeling that here you were somehow also talking about your sense of yourself.

FALLACI: The first difference between me and them is that I never give up. Marriage is an expression that to me suggests "giving up," an expression of sacrifice and regret. I never wanted to get married, so I didn't make that sacrifice—it was a victory for me. The solitude I was referring to wasn't a physical solitude. Nor was it, for instance, for Indira Gandhi, because everybody knows that at the time I interviewed her she wasn't alone at all. She likes men, thank God, and she makes use of that. It was an internal solitude that comes about from the fact of being a woman—and a woman with responsibilities in a world of men.

That kind of solitude is a victory for me, and I've been searching for it. Today, you are interviewing me in 1976. If you had interviewed me in '74 or '73 or '65, I would probably have answered a little differently—but not too much. Like a photograph, an interview has to crystallize the moment in which it takes place. Today, I need that kind of solitude so much—since it is what moves me, intellectually speaking—that sometimes I feel the need to be physically alone. When I'm with my companion, there are moments when we are two too many. I never get bored when I'm alone, and I get easily bored when I'm with others. And women who, like Indira and like Golda, have had the guts to accept that solitude are the women who have achieved something.

You must also consider that, in terms of the kind of solitude we've been talking about, women like Golda and Indira are more representative because they are old. A person of my generation and, even more so, a woman younger than myself, really *wants* that solitude. Golda and Indira were victimized by it, since they belonged to a generation in which people didn't think as we do today. They were probably hurt, and I don't know how much they pitied themselves. Golda cried at a certain moment during the interview. When she spoke of her husband, she was regretting something.

As for myself, in the past I felt less happy about this subject. It was still something to fight about inside myself, trying to understand it better. But today I'm completely free of it; the problem doesn't exist anymore. And I don't even gloat over the fact that what could have been considered a sacrifice yesterday is today an achievement. We must thank the feminists for this because they've helped not only me but everybody, all women. And young people, both men and women, understand this very much.

Golda spoke of having lost the family as a *great* sacrifice—she was crying then. But to me, the worst curse that could happen to a person is to *have* a family.

COTT: That's not a very Italian attitude, is it?

FALLACI: You'd be surprised. We know about Marriage Italian Style. But people in Italy today are getting married less and less. We have an unbelievable tax law that makes two persons who are married and who both work pay more taxes than they would if they were single. So they get separated or divorced. And there's nothing "romantic" or "Italian" about this. No, the family, at least morally and psychologically, is disappearing in Italy, as well as all over Europe.

COTT: What should exist in its place?

FALLACI: Free individuals.

COTT: But no community.

FALLACI: You ask me too much. If I could answer you, I would have resolved the problem. If you said to me: "All right, socialism as it's been applied until now hasn't worked. Capitalism doesn't work. What should we do?" I'd have to respond: "My dear, if I could answer these questions, I'd be the philosopher of my time."
"How to Unclothe an Emperor," Jonathan Cott, *The Rolling Stone* (17 June 1976)

The following composition topics are based on the viewpoints expressed by Oriana Fallaci in the interview you have just read. Choose one topic to develop by whatever method seems most appropriate, or by a combination of methods.

1. Agree or disagree with this statement: ". . . the worst curse that could happen to a person is to *have* a family."
2. Do you believe in the importance of the "internal solitude" that Fallaci speaks of? Elaborate.
3. Agree or disagree with this idea: Family in the United States is "morally and psychologically" disappearing.
4. Agree or disagree with this idea: Family in your country is "morally and psychologically" disappearing.
5. Can you imagine a society restructured without the family as its basis? Expand on this.
6. Agree or disagree with Fallaci's statement: "Marriage is an expression that . . . suggests 'giving up,' an expression of sacrifice and regret."

Copr. © 1940 James Thurber. Copr. © 1968 Helen Thurber.
From Fables for Our Time, *published by Harper & Row, New York,*
Originally printed in The New Yorker.

Topic 4: The Trials of Love

THE CROW AND THE ORIOLE

Once upon a time a crow fell in love with a Baltimore oriole. He had seen her flying past his nest every spring on her way North and every autumn on her way South, and he had decided that she was a tasty dish. He had observed that she came North every year with a different gentleman, but he paid no attention to the fact that all the gentlemen were Baltimore orioles. "Anybody can have that mouse," he said to himself. So he went to his wife and told her that he was in love with a Baltimore oriole who was as cute as a cuff link. He said he wanted a divorce, so his wife gave him one simply by opening the door and handing him his hat. "Don't come crying to me when she throws you down," she said. "That fly-by-season hasn't got a brain in her head. She can't cook or sew. Her upper register sounds like a streetcar taking a curve. You can find out in any dictionary that the crow is the smartest and most capable of birds—or was till you became one." "Tush!" said the male crow. "Pish! You are simply a jealous woman." He tossed her a few dollars. "Here," he said, "go buy yourself some finery. You look like the bottom of an old teakettle." And off he went to look for the oriole.

This was in the springtime and he met her coming North with an oriole he had never seen before. The crow stopped the female oriole and pleaded his cause—or should we say cawed his pleas? At any rate, he courted her in a harsh, grating voice, which made her laugh merrily. "You sound like an old window shutter," she said, and she snapped her fingers at him. "I am bigger and stronger than your gentleman friend," said the crow. "I have a vocabulary larger than his. All the orioles in the country couldn't even lift the corn I own. I am a fine sentinel and my voice can be heard for miles in case of danger." "I don't see how that could interest anybody but another crow," said the female oriole, and she laughed at him and flew on toward the North. The male oriole tossed the crow some coins. "Here," he said, "go buy yourself a blazer or something. You look like the bottom of an old coffeepot."

The crow flew back sadly to his nest, but his wife was not there. He found a note pinned to the front door. "I have gone away with Bert," it read. "You will find some arsenic in the medicine chest."

Moral: Even the llama should stick to mamma.

James Thurber, Fables for Our Time

You have read fables by James Thurber that presented a variety of animals in situations that illustrated certain human foibles. The fairly intelligent fly wasn't intelligent enough; the lion who wanted to zoom crash landed instead. The fable you have just read deals with the most basic of human dilemmas: love.

Thurber has relied on puns and figurative language in part to achieve his comic effect. Puns include "fly-by-season" (the customary expression is "fly-by-night," meaning "scatterbrained") and the verbal reverse when the crow "pleaded his cause—or . . . cawed his pleas."

Figurative language is used extensively. "A tasty dish," for example, is an attractive woman (or, in this case, bird), and a "mouse" is a colloquial term for a young girl. The crow thinks the lady oriole is "cute as a cuff link." The crow's wife compares the lady oriole's voice to a "streetcar taking a curve." And the crow's admonition to his wife, "You look like the bottom of an old teakettle," is paralleled by the male oriole's later disparaging remark to the crow: "You look like the bottom of an old coffeepot."

Although "The Crow and the Oriole" is lighthearted in tone, it suggests a number of serious issues dealing with human relationships. Select one of these and develop it in a way that suits the topic. If it is appropriate to do so, use a combination of methods.

1. Is a marriage a good risk between two people of greatly different ages or racial backgrounds? In answering this question, cite examples that have (or have not) worked.
2. Do you favor *"open* marriage" or *"closed* marriage"?
3. Compatibility between people is an important element in any relationship. How accurately can a person determine early in an acquaintanceship whether the two people involved will be compatible over a long period of time?
4. Hazards in marriage are known to be the "seven-year itch" and the maturing husband who, in his forties and fifties, sometimes breaks away from family life to seek a younger companion. (The crow has illustrated this kind of impulse.) Do you feel that these or other signs indicate that the traditional system of monogamy in the United States (or in your country) is in need of change? What changes do you think would represent an improvement?
5. If monogamy is not practiced in your country, explain what system of relationship is socially acceptable.
6. Write on an aspect of one of these subjects suggested by the fable:
   a. Fidelity
   b. Promiscuity
   c. Jealousy
   d. Sexual attraction
   e. Foolish pride
   f. Self deception
   g. Impulsiveness
   h. Divorce

Appendix

1. RULES FOR PUNCTUATION
2. RULES FOR CAPITALIZATION
3. RULES FOR SPELLING
4. PRINCIPAL PARTS OF IRREGULAR VERBS
5. DEFINITE AND INDEFINITE ARTICLES
6. PREPOSITION USES
7. WORD STEMS, PREFIXES, AND SUFFIXES
8. GLOSSARY OF STANDARD USAGE
9. GLOSSARY OF GRAMMATICAL TERMS
10. USING PRINCIPLES OF PHONICS TO RECOGNIZE AND PRONOUNCE ENGLISH WORDS

1. Rules for Punctuation

1. The Period (.)

A period is used at the end of a statement or command.

He is a student.
Take this medicine three times a day.

Periods are often used after abbreviations.

A.M.   Fig.   i.e.   R.F.D.   U.S.

Exceptions: Many abbreviations made up of the first letters of words that name an organization are written without periods (UN, NATO, TVA). Periods are also often omitted after many technical abbreviations.

2. The Question Mark (?)

A question mark is placed at the end of a question.

Is it time for the train to arrive?
Did you see the eclipse?

3. The Exclamation Point (!)

An exclamation point is used after a forceful or emotional statement and sometimes after a command.

Listen to me!   Watch out!   Shut that door!

4. The Comma (,)

Commas are used in the following situations:

a. A comma separates independent clauses that are connected by a correlative conjunction (and, but, for, or, nor).

> We left the house early to drive to the airport, but heavy traffic caused us to miss our plane.
> The sound of the pounding surf lulled her to sleep each night, and the crowing of roosters woke her up every morning.

Note: The comma is often omitted from a compound sentence if its clauses are very short.

> I called and she answered.

b. A comma follows an introductory clause or phrase.

> Although they had only two weeks to travel, they managed to see many villages in Mexico.
> After hiking for three hours, we stopped to rest.
> In the middle of the first semester, he began to understand the principles of economics.

Note: The comma is often omitted following a very short introductory prepositional phrase.

> At work he was friendly and industrious.

c. Commas set off nonrestrictive clauses or phrases within a sentence.

> The new church, which was built with donated funds, will open next week.

d. Commas set off nonrestrictive appositives.

> Carl Sandburg, the biographer of Lincoln, won the Pulitzer Prize.

e. Commas separate words, phrases, or clauses in a series.

> We gave them food, clothing, and shelter for the night.
> At the beach they learned to swim, to fish, and to water ski.
> I saw the celebrity when he arrived at the hotel, when he went shopping downtown, and when he entered the restaurant that evening.

f. A comma sets off a contrasted element.

> The boy's uncle, not his aunt, will meet you at the airport.

g. Commas set off geographical names.

> Leningrad, Russia, used to be named St. Petersburg.
> Osaka, Japan, was selected as the site of the 1970 Exposition.

h. Commas set off items in dates and addresses.

> The convention was to be held on March 18, 1970, in San Francisco, California.
> Address the letter to Mr. F. J. Barnes, Denver, Colorado.

i. Commas set off parenthetical expressions.

> As a matter of fact, I never expected him to complete his studies.
> The house is, for the most part, very satisfactory.
> "If you leave this afternoon," he said, "you will arrive in plenty of time."

j. Commas set off direct address.

> Come inside, Michael, and join us.
> You see, my friends, the problem is not a simple one.

k. Commas set off absolute elements.

> Rain or shine, he plays tennis every day.
> I wonder what will happen next, his ambition being what it is.

l. A comma is used to set off interjections.

> Well, I decided to try to turn the boat around.
> Oh, how beautiful the tropical sunset is!

m. A comma is used whenever it is necessary to prevent misreading.

> In the morning, light began to flood our room.
> The problem is, is there time to shower before lunch?

n. A comma is used after last names when the normal order of names is reversed.

> Kennedy, John F.

o. A comma is used to precede the last three digits in numbers of 1,000 and higher.

> 1,200   15,000   750,000
> 45,000,000 (or $45 million)

p. A comma is often used preceding a direct quotation.

> He said, "I have found the key."

5. The Semicolon (;)

A semicolon is used in these cases:

a. Between two main clauses not joined by a coordinating conjunction.

> The debate was drawing to a close; each team gathered together to prepare its final remarks.
> I closed the book; I had grown tired of reading.

b. To separate coordinate elements containing internal punctuation.

> The conference, short as it was, gave us the facts we needed; and at dinner that night, we shared opinions, questions, and conclusions about the labor dispute.

6. The Colon (:)

A colon is used to direct attention to what is to follow:

a. A colon may introduce an appositive.

> Poetry may be divided into three classes: narrative, lyric, and dramatic. All of his energy was directed toward his chief goal: graduation from college.

b. A colon may introduce a quotation.

> The advertisement for the Hawaiian trip read as follows: "Visit six islands, and learn for yourself what Paradise of the Pacific means."

c. A colon may separate two independent clauses when the second clause explains the first.

> Not all of the students agreed to participate in the public demonstration: several preferred to write letters to the newspaper editor.

d. A colon is used after the salutation of a business letter, between a title and subtitle, and between figures indicating the chapter and verse of a Biblical reference or the hour and minute of a time reference.

> Dear Sir:
> 10:50 A.M.
> *Science Problems: A Handbook for Students*
> according to Ecclesiastes 3:9

7. The Apostrophe (')

An apostrophe is used for these reasons:

a. It indicates the possessive case, except for personal pronouns.

　1) If the word (either singular or plural) does not end in an /s/ or /z/ sound, add the apostrophe and s.

the girl's dress
yesterday's problem
the car's upholstery

2) If the singular ends in an /s/ or /z/ sound, add the apostrophe and *s* unless the second *s* makes the pronunciation difficult; in such cases, add only the apostrophe.

Lois's coat
Charles's dog

But

Moses' story
Aristophanes' comedies
(The addition of a second *s* would change the pronunciation of Moses to *Moseses* and Aristophanes to *Aristophaneses*.)

3) If the plural ends in an /s/ or /z/ sound, add only the apostrophe.

ladies' dresses (dresses for ladies)
boys' shoes (shoes of the boys)
five dollars' worth

4) In compound words, make only the last word possessive.

brother-in-law's books (singular possessive)
mothers-in-law's books (plural possessive)
someone else's book

5) In nouns of joint possession, make only the last noun possessive; in nouns of individual possession, make both nouns possessive.

Jane and Alice's book (joint possession)
Jane's and Alice's books (individual possession)

b. An apostrophe indicates the omission of a letter or a number.

shouldn't
doesn't
can't
o'clock
the gold rush of '49

c. An apostrophe and *s* form the plural of letters, figures, symbols, and words. (Such forms are also italicized.)

Writers should cross their *t*'s and dot their *i*'s.
Count to 100 by *5*'s.
Try to cut down on the number of *and*'s you use in your writing.
We live in the *70*'s.

8. The Dash (—)

A dash is used in these cases:

a. A dash marks a sudden break in thought.

> She had her reasons—or did she?
> Could he—I mean, would he be willing to work with us?

b. A dash sets off an appositive or brief summary.

> One food grown in Southeast Asia—rice—is of the highest quality.
> The white sand, tall palm trees, and rolling surf—all these combine to make Hapuna Beach my favorite vacation spot.

c. A dash sets off a parenthetical element that is very abrupt or that has commas within it.

> Her eyes lighted up with love—or was it pity?—when she read the letter.
> He stood up—small, bent, and frightened—waiting for us to speak first.

9. The Hyphen (-)

Use the hyphen in the following cases:

a. Hyphenate compound numbers between twenty and one hundred:

> thirty-five
> sixty-three
> ninety-nine

b. Place a hyphen between the numerator and denominator of a fraction unless either part contains a hyphen:

> two-thirds
> five-eighths

> **But:** twenty-two sixteenths

In an expression like *one half of* and in a fraction intended as merely roughly approximate, the hyphen is generally omitted:

> About three fourths of the students attended the game.

c. Hyphenate a combination of two or more words used as a single adjective modifier immediately before a noun:

> a well-known actor
> a devil-may-care attitude

If the combination does not stand immediately before a noun, it is not hyphenated unless it is a permanent compound:

He is a well-liked man.
He is well liked.

She is old-fashioned. (Permanent compound)

It is an up-to-date book.
This book is up to date.

The hyphen is also omitted if the first word of a compound adjective is an adverb ending in *-ly* or if the combination is a proper noun with a fixed meaning:

a generally accepted rule
New England schools

d. Hyphenate a compound noun in which the second element is a preposition or adverb:

take-off
kick-off
runner-up
hanger-on

e. Use a hyphen to indicate that a word has been divided. (Words of one syllable should never be divided. Other words are divided between syllables, often between prefix and stem, or between stem and suffix.) If a word is divided between two lines, the hyphen should be placed at the end of the first line, never at the beginning of the second:

In the opinion of the press, the defendant was convicted on circumstantial evidence.

f. In compounds not covered by the above rules, a writer must depend chiefly upon memory of the individual words and upon help from a reliable, up-to-date dictionary. As with spelling in general, hyphen usage cannot be reduced to a logical system. The general tendency is to use the hyphen only if joined elements are not felt to be thoroughly fused or if the omission of the mark between separate elements might cause a misreading.

10. Parentheses ( )

Parentheses are used for two main purposes:

a. To enclose figures.

The treaty stipulated that the countries would (1) cease fighting, (2) respect each other's boundaries, and (3) resume trade.

b. To set off parenthetical, supplementary, or illustrative material.

He said (and we assumed that he was sincere) that he would attend the ceremony without fail.

As we drove down the mountain road (could this truly be called a road?), our brakes began to smoke.

11. Brackets ([ ])

Brackets are used to set off editorial corrections or additions to quoted matter.

On his desk he found a note: "Do not try to find me for i [sic] will be far away when you read this." (A bracketed *sic*—meaning *thus*—tells the reader that the error appears in the original and is not a misprint.)

The Cardinal sent a message to his trusted subordinate in Rome [Bishop Francetti] to ask for further information.

12. Italics (*slanting print*)

Italics are printed letters that slant toward the right. In a typed or hand-written manuscript, however, italics are indicated by underlining words. Italics are used for the following reasons:

a. Italicize the titles of books, newspapers, magazines, and all independently published works. (Separate parts of a published work, such as stories, poems, or articles appearing in a book, are placed in quotation marks, not italicized.)

the London *Times*
Webster's New Collegiate Dictionary
Stories of Mystery and Adventure
Paris-Match
Life
Modern British Poetry
Scientific American
Roget's Thesaurus

b. Italicize the names of ships, aircraft, works of art, movies, and plays.

the *Queen Elizabeth II*
Michelangelo's *Pietà*
the *Spirit of St. Louis*
Romeo and Juliet
Hair
Who's Afraid of Virginia Woolf?

c. Italicize letters, words, and numbers used as words.

Your *r*'s look very much like your *l*'s.
She wrote a *7* but I thought it was a *1*.
You should try to eliminate the *um*'s and *er*'s from your speech.

d. Italicize foreign words and phrases that have not yet been accepted into the English language. (Consult a dictionary to determine whether a foreign word should be italicized.)

> The senator's fiery speech gave the *coup de grâce* to the housing bill.

e. Use italics to give special stress to a word.

> She *never* expected such a welcome.
> "You've been *such* a perfect host," the departing guest said.

13. Quotation Marks (") (')

Follow these rules in punctuating quoted material:

a. Use double quotation marks to enclose a direct quotation from both spoken and written sources.

> He said, "Wait for me at the corner."
> The handbook says, "Students are responsible for keeping their rooms clean."

Notice that *indirect* quotations are not punctuated:

> He said that I should wait for him at the corner.

b. Use single quotation marks to enclose a quotation within a quotation.

> She replied, "Look for the letter that ends, 'Most sincerely yours.' "

c. If you are quoting several paragraphs, use quotation marks at the beginning of each paragraph and at the end of the final paragraph. Quotation marks are not needed at the ends of internal paragraphs.

> "At this time Bernini's personal religious convictions seem to have strengthened and deepened. He consorted with Jesuits and Oratorians, and devotions became an important feature of each day. For years he walked to the church of the Gesu every evening for vespers; we are told that he always had a keen awareness of death. Despite his association with the nobility of Europe, he lived a simple life. His diet was largely fruit, and we see him in his self-portraits and through descriptions as a small, thin, fiery man, 'terrible in wrath.'
>
> "Shortly before the death of Urban VIII, the famous Cardinal Mazarin, who was Italian and very friendly with Bernini, tried to lure him to France with the promise of an annual salary of 12,000 scudi. The Pope would not hear of it: 'Projects in France are begun in heat,' he advised, 'but end in nothing.' Besides, and this was surely the truth, Bernini 'was made for Rome, and Rome was for him.' After Urban's death in July of 1644, Mazarin tried again, to no avail. Twenty years later a new king and a new minister persuaded him to go.
>
> "Bernini was more than a great artist; he was virtual artistic dictator of Rome during the second half of Urban's pontificate. No

Italian artist since Giotto had been so completely triumphant, and Bernini's position naturally earned him the envy and enmity of all those who sought preferment in vain. A hostile biographer wrote of him: 'That dragon who ceaselessly guarded the Orchards of the Hesperides made sure that no one else should snatch the golden apples of Papal favour. He spat poison everywhere and was always planting ferocious spikes along the path that led to rich rewards.' As long as Urban was alive, Bernini was unassailable; after his death Bernini's fortunes took an almost fatal turn for the worse."

Howard Hibbard, *Bernini*

Long quotations are normally not enclosed in quotation marks, however. Instead, quotations of more than five lines are single-spaced and indented from the left-hand margins and sometimes from the right as well.

d. Use quotation marks to set off titles of poems, songs, and of articles, short stories, and other parts of a longer work.

The class liked the story "A Rose for Emily" in our text *Stories for Our Time.*
"Get Me to the Church on Time" is a song from the musical play *My Fair Lady.*
Look for the article in *Time* titled "A New Approach to the Monetary Problem."

e. Use quotation marks to set off words used in a special sense.

What he calls "stylish" I would consider to be very out of date.
The professor referred to the student as a "frisky colt."

f. Always place a comma or period inside quotation marks.

"If you try again," she said, "I think you will succeed."
Although he told us that he is "restless," I think a more appropriate word would be "lazy."
He said, "The note read 'No milk today.' "

g. Always place a colon or semicolon outside quotation marks.

I looked blankly at my music instructor when he said "Andante"; I did not understand the meaning of the term.
He gave us what he called his "recipe": think well, listen carefully, speak cautiously.

h. Place a question mark, dash, or exclamation point inside the quotation when it applies only to the quotation. Place it outside the quotation when it applies to the whole statement.

He asked, "Will you be ready to recite tomorrow?"
Did you hear her say, "I overslept yesterday"?

> He cried out, "I will never agree to that!"
> I can't describe the horror of that "unfortunate incident"!

i. Use a comma to separate an opening quotation from the part of the sentence that follows unless the quotation ends with a question mark, exclamation point, or dash.

> "This case is closed," he said firmly.
> "Is it time to eat?" she asked.
> "I can't believe it!" he exclaimed. "Our house can't have burned down!"
> "You've misunderstood—" he began. "I meant something quite different.

j. When a quotation is interrupted by explanatory words (*he said*, or similar ones), use a comma after the first part of the quotation. In choosing the punctuation mark to place *after* the explanatory words, follow the rules for punctuating clauses and phrases.

> "I have been told," he said, "of the dangers of skiing."
> "You follow directions well," the supervisor said. "Your first two weeks with us have been very satisfactory."
> "Michael was an imaginative tour leader," the girl said; "every day brought some new adventure."

k. In punctuating explanatory words preceding a quotation, be guided by the length and formality of the quotation.

No punctuation	She cried out "Wait!" and ran for the bus.
Punctuation with a comma	The clerk said politely, "If you need any help, please call on me."
Punctuation with a colon	The politician began his lengthy speech with these words: "Never in the history of our country has there been a greater need for unity among us. Never have the words 'United we stand, divided we fall' had greater meaning than they do today, my fellow citizens."

2. Rules for Capitalization

1. Beginnings of Sentences

The first word in a sentence is capitalized.

> Nobody knew where the sound was coming from.

2. The Pronoun *I*

The pronoun *I* is always capitalized:

After two weeks, I had finished reading the novel.

3. Proper Names

Proper names, and nouns used as proper names, are capitalized:

a. Names of people and races

Albert Schweitzer
Katherine
Oriental
Negro

b. A title preceding a proper noun

Dr. Tom Dooley
Prince Charles
President Marcos
Ambassador Humphreys

c. Specific geographical locations

Budapest
Via Veneto
Mount Rainier
the Amazon River
San Diego
Ecuador

d. Nationalities and names of languages

Russian
Turkish
Swahili
Australian

e. Points of the compass when they refer to a section of a country

the West (western United States)
the Northeast
the South

f. Names of religions, deities, and sacred terms

Moslem
Buddhist
Catholic
the Ten Commandments

g. Days of the week, months, and holidays

> Wednesday
> July
> Easter
> Christmas

h. Titles of books, articles, journals, newspapers, and magazines. (The first word and all other important words are capitalized. Articles, coordinate conjunctions, and prepositions are usually not capitalized.)

> *The Call of the Wild*
> *To Kill a Mockingbird*
> *Time*
> *Tulane Drama Review*

i. Names of steamships

> the *Statendam*
> the *Cristoforo Colombo*

j. Certain college courses (languages and official catalogue titles)

> Latin (We study Latin.)
> Geology I (We study geology.)
> Spanish
> Interdisciplinary Studies 190

k. Documents, organizations, and historical events

> the Louisiana Purchase
> World War II
> the Lions Club
> the Chamber of Commerce
> the Bill of Rights
> the Constitution

3. Rules for Spelling

Because English is so irregular, it presents problems to many writers of the language, both native and nonnative. Mastering English spelling may require several approaches, including memorizing lists of words, creating memory devices to learn the spelling of especially difficult words, and memorizing spelling rules.

Although there are exceptions to most of the rules of English spelling, a knowledge of these rules can help a writer to fix in his mind the correct spellings of many commonly used words. Listed below are the chief rules of English spelling:

1. Drop the final *e* in a word when adding a suffix beginning with a vowel.

tide	+	*-al*	=	tidal
combine	+	*-ation*	=	combination
come	+	*-ing*	=	coming
fame	+	*-ous*	=	famous
guide	+	*-ance*	=	guidance
locate	+	*-ion*	=	location
please	+	*-ure*	=	pleasure
ride	+	*-ing*	=	riding

Exceptions:

a. In some words the final *e* is retained to prevent confusion with other words.

singeing (to distinguish it from *singing*)
dyeing (to distinguish it from *dying*)

b. A final *e* is retained to keep *c* or *g* soft or before *a* or *o*.

notice	+	*-able*	=	noticeable
change	+	*-able*	=	changeable
practice	+	*-able*	=	practiceable

2. Retain the final *e* in a word when adding a suffix beginning with a consonant.

care	+	*-ful*	=	careful
sure	+	*-ly*	=	surely
arrange	+	*-ment*	=	arrangement
like	+	*-ness*	=	likeness
entire	+	*-ly*	=	entirely
hate	+	*-ful*	=	hateful

Exceptions:

a. Some words taking the suffix "-ful" or "-ly" drop the final *e:*

awe	+	*-ful*	=	awful
due	+	*-ly*	=	duly
true	+	*-ly*	=	truly

b. Some words taking the suffix "-ment" drop the final *e:*

judge	+	*-ment*	=	judgment
acknowledge	+	*-ment*	=	acknowledgment

3. Except before "-ing," a final *y* is usually changed to *i* when a suffix is added to a word.

defy	+	-ance	=	defiance
happy	+	-ness	=	happiness
forty	+	-eth	=	fortieth
mercy	+	-ful	=	merciful
modify	+	-er	=	modifier

BUT

cry	+	-ing	=	crying (Not changed before ing)

4. Double a final single consonant before a suffix beginning with a vowel when (a) a single vowel precedes the consonant, and (b) the consonant ends an accented syllable or a one-syllable word. Unless both of these conditions are met, the final consonant is not doubled.

stop, sto*pping* (In a word of one syllable preceded by a double vowel: *stoop, stooping.*)

admit, admi*tted* (In an accented syllable preceded by a single vowel. But in an unaccented syllable: *benefit, benefited.*)

5. Form the plural of nouns by adding *s* to the singular but by adding *es* if the plural makes an extra syllable.

girl, girls; hat, hats; radio, radios; train, trains
bush, bushes; match, matches; bus, buses (The plural makes an extra syllable.)

Exceptions:

a. If a noun ends in *y* preceded by a consonant, change the *y* to *i* and add *es*: *army, armies*; comedy, comedies. But after final *y* preceded by a vowel, *y* is retained and only *s* is added: *joy, joys.*

b. If a noun ends in *f* or *fe*, the *f* or *fe* is sometimes changed to *ve* and an *s* is added: *life, lives; knife, knives; hoof, hooves; thief, thieves.* (Exceptions: *roof, roofs; fife, fifes.*)

c. A few nouns ending in *o* take the *es* plural, even though the plural does not make an extra syllable: *Negro, Negroes; potato, potatoes; tomato, tomatoes.*

d. Plurals of such compound words as *mother-in-law* usually add the *s* to the chief word, not to the modifier: *mothers-in-law; sons-in-law; maids of honor.*

Consult a dictionary for the spellings of other plurals that are formed irregularly. (Dictionaries list irregular plurals only.)

6. To distinguish between *ei* and *ie* spellings:

a. Write *ie* when the sound is /*ee*/ (except after *c*, in which case write *ei*).

niece	relief	thief
believe	pierce	chief
wield	yield	field
grief		

(After *c*)

receive	ceiling	conceive
decieve	conceit	

b. Write *ei* when the sound is other than *ee*.

eight	neighbor	vein
foreign	sleigh	stein
height	heir	feign
deign	weigh	reign

Exceptions: leisure, financier, weird, seize, fiery, species.

Spelling Lists

Studying the following lists according to the directions that precede them will help to resolve many of your possible spelling dilemmas.

HOMONYMS

Homonyms are words that are identical in pronunciation but different in meaning and, usually, in spelling. Make sure that you can distinguish between homonyms in the following list. Learn the meanings along with the spellings. Comparing the derivations given in a dictionary will help you remember the distinctions.

aisle, isle	die, dye
altar, alter	dying, dyeing
arc, ark	faze, phase
bare, bear	fiance, fiancee
berth, birth	forth, fourth
brake, break	foul, fowl
buy, by, bye	hear, here
canvas, canvass	heard, herd
capital, capitol	hole, whole
cereal, serial	its, it's
cession, session	lead, led
chord, cord	lessen, lesson
cite, sight, site	mantel, mantle
coarse, course	marshal, martial

medal, meddle
passed, past
peace, piece
plain, plane
principal, principle
rain, reign, rein
right, rite, wright, write
ring, wring
role, roll
scene, seen
shone, shown
sole, soul
stake, steak
stationary, stationery

steal, steel
straight, strait
tail, tale
their, there, they're
threw, through
throne, thrown
to, too, two
troop, troupe
vain, vane, vein
waist, waste
weak, week
who's, whose
your, you're

WORDS SIMILAR IN SOUND OR FORM

The words in the following groups, despite their similarities in sound or form, have important differences in pronunciation, spelling, and meaning. Study these words carefully, using a dictionary whenever necessary, until you are certain that you will not confuse them.

accept, except
adapt, adept, adopt
advice, advise
affect, effect
alley, ally
allusion, illusion
angel, angle
author, Arthur
bases, basis
bath, bathe
born, borne
breath, breathe
Calvary, cavalry
casual, causal
censor, censure
choose, chose
close, clothes, cloths
cloth, clothe
collar, color
coma, comma
complement, compliment
costume, custom
council, counsel, consul
dairy, diary
decent, descent, dissent
desert, dessert

device, devise
dining, dinning
dual, duel
elicit, illicit
emigrant, immigrant
eminent, immanent, imminent
ever, every
farther, further
foreword, forward
formally, formerly
holly, holy, wholly
hoping, hopping
human, humane
later, latter
loath, loathe
loose, lose, loss
marital, martial
moral, morale
of, off
personal, personnel
poor, pore, pour
prophecy, prophesy
quiet, quite, quit
respectfully, respectively
sense, since
speak, speech

statue, stature, statute
suit, suite
than, then
though, thorough, through
trail, trial

vary, very
wander, wonder
weather, whether
woman, women

COMMON SUFFIXES

Certain endings (for example, *-able, -ible; -ance, -ence; -ant, -ent; -sion, -tion, -xion*) cause difficulty because they are often pronounced alike but spelled differently. Since no rules apply to the use of such endings, learn to spell the individual words and, when in doubt, consult a dictionary. Here are examples of words with the above endings.

-able	*-ible*
acceptable	audible
advisable	compatible
available	convertible
dependable	credible
desirable	discernible
imaginable	feasible
justifiable	gullible
movable	legible
sizable	tangible
suitable	terrible

-ance	*-ence*
abundance	coincidence
acceptance	competence
accordance	confidence
balance	excellence
endurance	insistence
extravagance	obedience
reluctance	persistence
repentance	preference
resemblance	residence
resistance	reverence

-ant	*-ent*
attendant	coherent
defendant	competent
defiant	confident
distant	existent
extant	expedient
intolerant	innocent
irritant	insistent
observant	intelligent
radiant	precedent
vigilant	recurrent

-sion	-tion	-xion
collision	attrition	complexion
collusion	condition	crucifixion
division	creation	prefixion
extension	fiction	
fission	location	
impression	mention	
incision	mutation	
lesion	radiation	
tension	retention	

Grammar

A knowledge of grammar is an invaluable aid to spelling. For example, you can avoid confusing these words if you know that *advise, devise, breathe, clothe,* and *prophesy* are verbs and that *advice, device, breath, cloth,* and *prophecy* are nouns. Knowing the principal parts of common verbs will also help you choose the correct forms; you'll find these in Appendix 4.

4. Principal Parts of Irregular Verbs

Many frequently used English verbs have irregular past tense and past participle forms. The following list of the principal parts of irregular verbs is based in part on an unpublished manuscript by Merle Fifield, "The English Verb" (Muncie, Indiana: Ball State University). Consulting this list will help you to choose correct verb forms for your writing.

PRESENT	PAST	PAST PARTICIPLE
Group 1. Identical forms		
beat	beat	beat, beaten
bet	bet	bet
bid (offer)	bid	bid
burst	burst	burst
cast	cast	cast
cost	cost	cost
cut	cut	cut
hit	hit	hit
hurt	hurt	hurt
let	let	let

PRESENT	PAST	PAST PARTICIPLE
put	put	put
quit	quit	quit
rid	rid	rid
set	set	set
shed	shed	shed
shut	shut	shut
split	split	split
spread	spread	spread
upset	upset	upset
wet	wet	wet

Group 2. Spelling change; /d/ ending on last two forms

lay	laid	laid
pay	paid	paid
say	said /ɛ/	said /ɛ/

Group 3. No change in vowel sound; last two forms identical with /t/ ending

bend	bent	bent
build	built	built
lend	lent	lent
send	sent	sent
spend	spent	spent

Group 4. Vowel change from /i/ to /ɛ/; last two forms identical with /t/ or /d/ ending

/i/	/ɛ/	/ɛ/
bleed	bled	bled
read	read	read
deal	dealt	dealt
feed	fed	fed
flee	fled	fled
mean	meant	meant
lead	led	led
keep	kept	kept
creep	crept	crept
sleep	slept	slept
sweep	swept	swept

Consonant change (v to ft)

leave	left	left
bereave	bereft	bereft

PRESENT	PAST	PAST PARTICIPLE

Group 5. Vowel change from /aɪ/ to /aʊ/; last two forms identical with /d/ ending

/aɪ/	/aʊ/	/aʊ/
bind	bound	bound
find	found	found
grind	ground	ground
wind	wound	wound

Group 6. Vowel change from /ɪ/ to /ə/; last two forms identical

/ɪ/	/ə/	/ə/
cling	clung	clung
dig	dug	dug
spin	spun	spun
stick	stuck	stuck
sting	stung	stung
swing	swung	swung
win	won	won

Group 7. Vowel change to /ɔ/ or /o/; last two forms identical with /t/ or /d/ ending

	/ɔ/	/ɔ/
lose	lost	lost

Consonant change to ght

bring	brought	brought
buy	bought	bought
catch	caught	caught
fight	fought	fought
teach	taught	taught
think	thought	thought

	/o/	/o/
sell	sold	sold
tell	told	told

Group 8. Irregular vowel changes; last two forms identical

bite /aɪ/	bit /ɪ/	bit, bitten /ɪ/
get /ɛ/	got /ɑ/	got, gotten /ɑ/
hang /æ/	hung /ə/	hung /ə/
hear /ɪ/	heard /ər/	heard /ər/
hide /aɪ/	hid /ɪ/	hid, hidden /ɪ/
hold /o/	held /ɛ/	held /ɛ/
stand /æ/	stood /ʊ/	stood /ʊ/
shoot /u/	shot /ɑ/	shot /ɑ/

PRESENT	PAST	PAST PARTICIPLE

Group 9.   Vowel series /ɪ/, /æ/, /ə/

begin	began	begun
drink	drank	drunk
ring	rang	rung
shrink	shrank	shrunk
sing	sang	sung
sink	sank	sunk
spring	sprang	sprung
swim	swam	swum

Group 10.   Vowel series /aɪ/, /o/, /ɪ/; past participle with -en or -ne

drive	drove	driven
ride	rode	ridden
rise	rose	risen
shine	shone	shone
	(transitive shined)	(transitive shined)
write	wrote	written

Group 11.   Vowel series irregular; past participle with -en, -in, -ne, or -n

arise	arose	arisen
bid (command)	bade	bidden
do	did	done
eat	ate	eaten
fly	flew	flown
give	gave	given
lie (recline)	lay	lain
see	saw	seen
take	took	taken

Group 12.   Vowel change to /ɔ/ or /o/ in last two forms; past participle with -en or -n

bear /ɛ/	bore	borne, born
break /e/	broke	broken
choose /u/	chose	chosen
freeze /i/	froze	frozen
speak /i/	spoke	spoken
steal /i/	stole	stolen
swear /ɛ/	swore	sworn
tear /ɛ/	tore	torn
wear /ɛ/	wore	worn

Group 13.   Vowel change in past tense only; past participle with /ən/

blow	blew	blown
draw	drew	drawn

PRESENT	PAST	PAST PARTICIPLE
fall	fell	fallen
grow	grew	grown
know	knew	known
shake	shook	shaken
take	took	taken
throw	threw	thrown
wake	woke	waken

Group 14.   Irregular forms

go	went	gone
have	had	had
make	made	made
come	came	come

5. Definite and Indefinite Articles

1. Articles with Singular Countable Nouns

Either a definite **(the)** or indefinite **(a, an)** article is used with a **singular countable noun** (a noun representing a person or thing that can be counted as a single item). You can write either **a pencil** or **the pencil, an eraser** or **the eraser, a student** or **the student, an instructor** or **the instructor.**

a. Sometimes the indefinite article **a** or **an** has approximately the same meaning as the number "one."

I'll be in the library for **an** hour or two.
(Or: I'll be there for **one** or two hours.)

More often **a** or **an** has the meaning of "one" in the sense of a single unit or item. In situations of this kind, "one" cannot be substituted for the indefinite article without changing the meaning. Compare:

The lifeguard saved **one** swimmer's life. (But the other swimmer drowned.)
I drank **a** cup of coffee this morning.
I drank only **one** cup of coffee this morning, but I usually drink two.

b. The definite article **the** is mainly used to single out a specific or particular person or thing. Before a singular countable noun, **the** has much the same meaning as the demonstrative "that," although "that" is more emphatic in pointing something out. Compare:

Did you buy **the** book?
Did you buy **that** book?

When using the definite article in this way, the speaker may further identify the book by adding a qualifying word, phrase, or clause.

Did you buy **the chemistry** book?
Did you buy **the** book **recommended by the instructor?**

c. Whether a definite or indefinite article is placed before a single countable noun is further illustrated in the following sentences:

She rented **a** bicycle. (A single item)
She rented **the** bicycle. (A specific bicycle, such as the Italian bicycle)

Sometimes a writer begins with an indefinite article and then shifts to a definite article once the identity of the person or thing has been established.

A package arrived from Alicia. We put **the package** on the dining room table.

2. Articles with Plural Countable Nouns

Since a plural countable noun refers to more than one person or thing, the definite article *can* be used with it but the indefinite article *cannot*. You would write either **pencils** or **the pencils, students** or **the students,** and so forth.

a. Even though indefinite articles are not used with plural nouns, such indefinite adjectives as **few, a few, fewer, some, any, several,** and **many** may be used to indicate an indefinite number.

He put **ice cubes** in the glass.
    (Or: He put **some** ice cubes in the glass.)
There aren't **any** magazines on the desk.
I don't see **many** people at the box office.
We brought **a few** apples on the picnic.

b. An article is not used before a plural noun that refers to persons or things as a group or in general.

Newspaper critics can often determine the fate of New York plays.
They like to collect **stamps.**

c. With plural countable nouns, as with single countable nouns, **the** singles out or identifies a specific or particular person or thing. Before a plural countable noun, **the** has much the same meaning as the demonstrative "those," although "those" is more emphatic. As with singular countable nouns, a qualifying word, phrase, or clause is often used to identify further the persons or objects.

> I shopped for **the cooking utensils.**
> He used **the ice cubes** we brought for the party.
> **The basketball players** will be given awards tomorrow.

3. Articles with Uncountable Nouns

The indefinite article *is not used* with an uncountable noun (a noun representing something that cannot be counted as a single unit or item). The definite article *can be used* to limit or restrict uncountable nouns. You would write **water** or **the water, strength** or **the strength, sound** or **the sound.**

> **Laughter** is a tonic. (Uncountable)
> **The laughter** of the audience pleased the actress. (Limited by a definite article.)

The following types of noun are generally considered uncountable:

a. *Mass nouns,* such as **sugar, coffee, tea, water, oil, air, ink, oxygen.**

> They will serve either **coffee** or **tea.**
> He checked the car's **oil, water,** and **gasoline** and filled the tires with **air.**

Indefinite adjectives may be used with mass nouns to indicate indefinite quality.

> She spilled **some** sand on the rug.
> There isn't **any** pepper in the shaker.
> It takes **much** energy to jog for five miles.

Countable units of measure may be used with mass nouns to indicate definite amounts. Compare:

> Buy **a bottle** of milk.
> The recipe calls for **a cup of** sugar.
> He drank **a glass of** orange juice.

b. *Abstract nouns,* such as **peace, truth, liberty, justice, beauty, honesty.**

> **Darkness** comes about 6 o'clock every night.
> **Wisdom** is the goal of many scholars.
> She has shown a lot of **patience** with her daughter.

c. *Names of general areas of subject matter*, such as **music, economics, history, English, art, science.**

> His courses included **English, biology, mathematics,** and **political science.**

d. *Names of sports or recreational activities*, such as **football, baseball, tennis, golf, dancing, chess, singing.**

> She is studying **ballet dancing.**
> He plays **hockey** well.

> The name of a sport or recreational activity that functions as a modifier may be preceded by an article:

> He is **a valuable hockey player.**

4. Summary of Articles with Countable and Uncountable Nouns

Some nouns normally considered uncountable may also function as countable nouns, depending on whether they are being used in an abstract or more specific sense.

> A favorite North African drink is mint **tea.** (A mass noun)
> The **teas** served in the Orient are varied. (A plural countable noun meaning "the types of tea")
> **Wisdom** is **strength.** (Abstract nouns)
> She doubted **the wisdom** of his decision. (A singular countable noun meaning "act of deciding")
> The **strengths** of your paper are clear. (A plural countable noun meaning "good points")
> **Science** is a subject that interests many people. (A general area of subject matter)
> Would you call astrology **a science?** (A countable noun meaning "a branch of science")

The following groups of nouns are used either as countable or uncountable nouns, depending on the meaning to be expressed:

a. **Breakfast, lunch, dinner, supper, town.** Compare:

> Mrs. Allen drove to **town** this afternoon.
> **The town** has many points of historical interest.

The chart that follows summarizes the use of articles with countable and uncountable nouns:

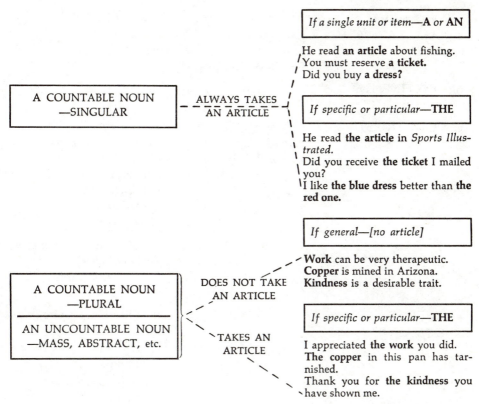

If a single unit or item—**A** or **AN**

He read **an article** about fishing.
You must reserve **a ticket.**
Did you buy **a dress?**

A COUNTABLE NOUN
—SINGULAR

ALWAYS TAKES
AN ARTICLE

If specific or particular—**THE**

He read **the article** in *Sports Illustrated.*
Did you receive **the ticket** I mailed you?
I like **the blue dress** better than **the red one.**

If general—[no article]

Work can be very therapeutic.
Copper is mined in Arizona.
Kindness is a desirable trait.

A COUNTABLE NOUN
—PLURAL

AN UNCOUNTABLE NOUN
—MASS, ABSTRACT, etc.

DOES NOT TAKE
AN ARTICLE

TAKES AN
ARTICLE

If specific or particular—**THE**

I appreciated **the work** you did.
The copper in this pan has tarnished.
Thank you for **the kindness** you have shown me.

5. Articles with Proper Names

By proper name we mean the name of a person or the name of a particular place or thing. As with common nouns, **the** before a proper name singles out or identifies that which is specific or particular. Generally speaking, no article is required before a proper name when the name is sufficient in itself to establish identification. **The** would be used only in a situation in which the identification was not clearly established. Compare:

I met **George Anderson** last week.
The George Anderson whom I knew in college telephoned yesterday.

The is necessary when a person is referred to by a title composed of what would ordinarily be considered a common noun plus an identifying phrase.

The Emperor of Japan rarely travels abroad.
The Secretary of State flew to Riyadh for the meeting.

Since the use of articles with proper names involves many exceptions, the following list may be helpful:

TYPES OF NAME	WITHOUT ARTICLE	WITH THE
a. GEOGRAPHIC AREAS	Eastern Europe, North Africa, Southern California	the North Pole the South Pole
b. CONTINENTS	Africa, North America	
c. COUNTRIES	Colombia, Thailand, Canada, Russia, England, Lebanon	the Republic of Colombia, the Kingdom of Thailand, the Dominion of Canada, the Soviet Union, the United States (of America)[1]
d. STATES, PROV-INCES, COUNTIES, CITIES	Oklahoma, Quebec, Cook County, Boston, Salt Lake City	the State of Oklahoma, the Province of Quebec, the City of Boston, The Hague
e. EMPIRES, DYNASTIES, etc.		the Ottoman Empire, the Ming Dynasty, the British Commonwealth of Nations
f. OCEANS, SEAS, RIVERS, CANALS, DESERTS, and FORESTS		the Atlantic Ocean,[2] the Red Sea, the Tigris River, the Suez Canal, the Sahara Desert, the Black Forest
g. ISLANDS, LAKES, and MOUNTAINS	-*Singular:* Wake Island, Lake Geneva, Mount Whitney	-Plural: the Canary Islands, the Great Lakes, the Andes Mountains
h. PARKS	Central Park, Hyde Park, Kruger Park	
i. STREETS	Maple Street, Fifth Avenue, Elderberry Road, Sunset Boulevard	

[1] We do not usually refer to countries, states, and so forth by their official titles; that is, we refer to France, rather than the Republic of France. However, *the United States*, *the United Kingdom*, and *the Soviet Union* are commonly used titles.

[2] The word "ocean" is often omitted, and the words "sea," "river," and "desert" are often omitted when the place is well known.

The Panama Canal connects **the Atlantic** and **the Pacific.**
The Nile flows into **the Mediterranean.**

TYPES OF NAME	WITHOUT ARTICLE	WITH THE
j. UNIVERSITIES, COLLEGES, SCHOOLS, INSTITUTES	Yale University, New York University, Wellesley College, San Francisco State College	the University of Maryland, the College of Holy Names, the State College of Washington
k. MUSEUMS, LIBRARIES		The Metropolitan Museum, the Louvre, the Library of Congress, the Huntington Library
l. BUILDINGS	Independence Hall, Carnegie Hall, Wheeler Auditorium	the Empire State Building, the Medical-Dental Building, the Civic Auditorium
m. BUSINESSES (stores, restaurants, firms, etc.)	Penney's, Joe's Cafe, Mary's Beauty Shop, Sears, Roebuck (and Company), Hotel Ambassador	the J. C. Penney Company, the All-Nite Grocery Store, the Feather Mattress Company, the Fox Theatre, the Statler Hotel
n. HOLIDAYS	Christmas, Thanksgiving, New Year's Day, Washington's Birthday	the Fourth (4th) of July
o. CHARTERS, CLUBS, COMMITTEES, DOCTRINES, etc.		the United Nations Charter, the Rotary Club, the Foreign Relations Committee (of the Senate), the Monroe Doctrine

Whether or not an article is used with the names of nationalities depends on the way the name is used.

a. When the name of a nationality functions as a noun, the principles governing the use of articles with countable nouns apply.

> There is **a Brazilian** in the store.
> He is **the Russian** I told you about.

b. In referring to an entire group of people, no article is required if the name has a plural form; **the** may be used to single out one group from another.

Norwegians are fond of winter sports.
Do **the Americans** eat as much ice cream as **the Italians?**

c. **The** is ordinarily used if the name does not have a plural form.

The British are known for their civilized ritual of high tea.
The French have made their mark in the fashion world.

d. When the name of a nationality functions as an adjective complement, no article is used.

The Mitsubishis are Japanese.
Hans is German.

6. Preposition Uses

Prepositions are frequently used in English to relate a noun or pronoun to some other word in the sentence. They express a number of relationships, including time, location, manner, means, quantity, purpose, and state or condition. You will find many examples of preposition usage in your reading. Study them in the context in which they appear.

Uses of Common Prepositions

A. TIME

about:	about noon (approximately)
after:	after the game
	after lunch
	after three
at:	at five o'clock
	at last (finally)
by:	by midnight (not later than)
for:	for an hour (duration)
from:	from Monday to Friday
in:	in the morning (evening)
	in the fall (spring)
	in April (month)
	in 1969 (year)
	in six months (at the end of)
	in time (early enough)
of:	quarter of three
on:	on Tuesday (day of the week)
	on May 8 (date)
	on time (punctual)
past:	quarter past three
to:	quarter to three

B. PLACE OR DIRECTION

around:	She walked around the car.
at:	They are at home.
	We were at the restaurant.
	He smiled at her.
down:	They lived down the hall.
from:	We left from Peru to go to Singapore.
	a mile from here
in:	He lives in a trailer.
	We waited in the bus.
	He is in Paris.
of:	inside of the house
	south of Montreal
on:	on the ocean pier
	on the train (bus, plane)
	on the table
through:	They drove through the tunnel
to:	He went to Prague.
	Give it to me.
up:	He walked up the stairs.
with:	He went with me.

C. MEANS OR AGENT

by:	He was hit by a ball.
	She came by train.
	He did it by hard work.
	It came by special delivery.
	He got there by swimming.
from:	His success results from careful planning.
in:	He takes pleasure in it.
on:	They live on fruit.
with:	He chased the mongoose with a stick.

D. MANNER

by:	By doing it yourself, you save time.
in:	He left in confusion.
	The room was in a turmoil.
	You can do it in a day. (in several days)
like:	He looks like a hero.
on:	I swear it on my word of honor.
with:	He ate it with a fork.

E. STATE OR CONDITION

at:	My friend is at work.
	She is at home.
by:	They are by themselves. (alone)
in:	He is in a state of confusion.
on:	He is on duty. (subject to duty)

F. QUANTITY OR MEASURE

for: We drove for twenty miles.
        We bought it for ten cents. (two dollars)
by: We bought them by the kilo.

G. PURPOSE

for: He bought it for them.
        She went to the city for sightseeing.
        He loved her for her thoughtfulness.
        I asked you for it.
        We looked for it.

Uses of Prepositions after Certain Verbs

account for
agree on (something)
agree with (someone)
apologize to
apply for
approve of
argue with (someone)
ask for
believe in
belong to
blame (someone) for (something)
blame (something) on (someone)
borrow from
call on (upon)
care for
compliment (someone) on
come from
consent to
consist of
convince (someone) of
   (something)
decide on, upon
depend on, upon
get rid of
hear about
hear from

hear of
insist on, upon
invite (someone) to
laugh at
listen for
listen to
look at
look for
look forward to
object to
plan on
provide for
provide with
recover from
remind (someone) of
search for
see about
substitute for
talk about
talk of
telephone to
think about
think of
wait for
wait on (meaning serve)

Uses of Prepositions with Certain Adjectives and in Idiomatic Expressions

according to
accustomed to
angry about (something)

angry at (someone), or
   angry with (someone)
based on

capable of
composed of
content with
dependent on (or *upon*)
different from (or *than*)
disappointed in
due to
followed by
fond of
have respect for
in accordance with

independent of
in regard to
interested in
limited to
married to
proud of
related to
resulting from
similar to
tired of

7. Word Stems, Prefixes, and Suffixes

Many English words are built of parts that have been borrowed from other languages, particularly from Greek and Latin. Borrowed elements may appear as *stems* (word roots to which are added various combinations to form words), *prefixes* (word elements added at the beginnings of words), and *suffixes* (word elements added at the ends of words). To a student attempting to increase his English vocabulary, the study of stems, prefixes, and suffixes is a major tool.

A. Stems

Stems form the base of many large word families. An example is the stem "path," meaning *feeling*. This stem is central to many common words, such as *sympathy*. A student who recognizes the meaning of the stem "path" can more easily understand related words such as *empathy*, *pathos*, and *antipathy*.

The following list gives you some of the more frequently used stems from which many English words are built. Examine this list, thinking of words other than the examples that are based on these stems. Then memorize five stems at a time. You will find this a profitable approach to vocabulary learning.

STEM OF THE ORIGINAL GREEK OR LATIN WORD	MEANING	PRESENT-DAY EXAMPLES
AMO	love	amiable, amorous
ANIM	breath, soul, mind	animated, inanimate
ANTHRO	man	anthropology, philanthropy, misanthrope

STEM OF THE ORIGINAL GREEK OR LATIN WORD	MEANING	PRESENT-DAY EXAMPLES
AQUA	water	aqueduct, aquarium
ANN (ENN)	year	annual, annuity, biennial
ARCH	highest, most important	matriarch, patriarch, architect, archbishop
AUD	hear	audible, audience
AUTO	self	autocrat, autobiography, automobile
AV	bird	aviary, aviation, aviator
BELL	war	antebellum, postbellum, belligerent, bellicose
BENE	well	benediction, benefactor, benevolence
BIBL	book	bibliography, bibliophile, Bible, bibliomania
BI	two	bimetallism, binocular, bigamy, biplane
BIO	life	biography, biology, biochemistry
CAD (CID, CAS)	fall	casualty, casual, coincide, occasional, deciduous, accident, decadent
CANT	sing	cantata, chant, cant, incantation
CAP (NOUN)	head	capital, capitol, decapitate
CAP, CIP (VERB)	take	recipient, anticipate, capture
CED (CESS)	go, yield	precede, intercession
CID (CIS)	cut, kill	matricide, parricide, insecticide
CINIS (CINERIS)	ashes	incinerator, cinder, Cinderella
CLAUS (CLOS, CLUD)	shut	include, closet, cloister, claustrophobia
COGN (COGNIT)	notice, understand	incognito, recognize
COR	heart	core, courage
CORPUS (CORPOR)	body	corporation, corpulent, corpuscle, incorporate, corps, corpse, corporal
COSMO	world	cosmopolitan, cosmopolite, cosmos
CRED (CREDIT)	believe	creed, credit, credible, credo

STEM OF THE ORIGINAL GREEK OR LATIN WORD	MEANING	PRESENT-DAY EXAMPLES
CULP	fault	culprit, exculpate, culpable
CURA	care	curator, manicure, cure, sinecure, curative, pedicure
CURR (CURS)	run	current, course, currency, cursory, incur, excursion, precursor, occurrence
DIC (DICT)	say, tell	diction, dictate
DOC (DOCT)	teach	document, doctor, docile, doctrine, indoctrinate
DOL	suffer, grieve	dolorous, indolent, doleful
DOM	home	domestic, domicile
DUC (DUCT)	lead	abduct, viaduct, aqueduct
EQUE (EQU)	horse	equestrian, equine
ERR	wander	errant, erroneous, error
FAC (FACT)	make, do	factor, malefactor, bene-factor, fact, factotum manufacture, factory
FALL	make a mistake	fallible, infallible, fallacious
FER	bear, carry	pestiferous, floriferous, coniferous, Lucifer
FID	faith, trust	fidelity, confide, infidel
FIN	boundary, end	finite, finish
FLUEN (FLUX)	flowing	fluent, confluence, affluence, fluid, influence, flue, influenza
FORM	form	deform, formative
FRATER	brother	fraternize, fraternal, fraternity
FUG (FUGIT)	flee	fugitive, centrifugal, fugue, refuge
GAM	marriage	monogamy, bigamy, polygamy, misogamy
GEN (VERB)	to beget, to be born	primogenitor, congenital, genesis, progenitor, generation
GEN (NOUN)	kind, species, race	homogeneous, genus, heterogeneous, genealogy, gender
GEO	earth	geometry, geology, geography
GRAND	great	grandeur, grandiose

STEM OF THE ORIGINAL GREEK OR LATIN WORD	MEANING	PRESENT-DAY EXAMPLES
GRAPH	write, draw	graphite, stenographer, photograph
GNOT (GNOS)	know	prognosticate, prognosis, agnostic
GREG (GRES)	gather	congregate, congress, gregarious
HELIO	sun	helium, heliotrope, heliocentric
HIPPO	horse	hippodrome, hippopotamus
HOMO	man	homicide
IMPED (IMPEDIT)	hinder	impediment, impede, impedimenta
IMPERI	supreme power	empire, emperor, imperial, imperious
ITER (ITINER)	journey, route	itinerant, itinerary, reiterate
JAC (JACT, JECT)	throw, cast	ejaculate, reject
JUNC	join	junction, conjunction, injunction, adjunct
JUR (JUD)	swear	jury, jurist, jurisdiction, judge, judicial
LABOR	work	laboratory, laborious, elabrate, collaborator, laborer
LEX (LEG)	law	legal, illegal, legalize, legislate, legality, legitimate, illegitimate
₌INGUA	tongue, language	linguist, language, lingual, lingo, bilingual, multilingual
LOQU	talk	monologue, loquacious, dialogue, soliloquy, colloquial
LOGY (LOG)	a study, science	zoology, meteorology, conchology, biology
LUCENT	showing light	lucent, lucid, translucent
MAL	bad	maladjustment, malnutrition, malefactor, malediction, maladroit
MARI	sea	marine, submarine, aquamarine, maritime
MAN (MANU)	hand	manual, manacles, manuscript, manufacture
MATER (MATRI)	mother	maternal, matrimony, matricide, maternity

STEM OF THE ORIGINAL GREEK OR LATIN WORD	MEANING	PRESENT-DAY EXAMPLES
MERC	sell, buy	merchant, mercantile, mercenary
MIGRO	go	migrate, migration, emigrate, immigration, immigrant, migratory
MENT	mind	demented, mental, mentality
MIN	less	minimize, minute
MIT (MIS)	send, throw	mission, missile, missive, missionary, omit, admit
MOB (MOV)	move	mobile, automobile, immobile, move, moveable
MONO	alone, single	monologue, monk, monogamy, monotheism, monocle, monosyllable
MORALE	custom	moral, morality, immoral, morale
MORT	death	mortal, immortal, mortify, morgue, mortuary, mortgage
NASC (NAT)	be born	nascent, native
NEO	new	neolithic, neology, neon, neophyte
NOC	harm	innocuous, innocent, obnoxious
NOMEN (NYM)	name	cognomen, antonym, anonymous
NOV	new	novelty, novel, novitiate, innovate
OMNI	all	omnipresent, omnibus, omnivorous, omniscient, omnipotent
OPTIM	beat	optimist, optimum
ORA	speak, pray	oratoric, oracle, oratory
ORIENT	rising	orient, oriental
OSE	full of (in chemistry), related to	bellicose, verbose, glucose, cellulose, grandiose
PART	part, portion	partition, particle
PATER (PATRI)	father	paternity, patricide, patriarch
PATH (PATI, PAS)	feeling	sympathy, pathetic, antipathy, patient, osteopathy, compatibility, passion, com-

STEM OF THE ORIGINAL GREEK OR LATIN WORD	MEANING	PRESENT-DAY EXAMPLES
		passion, pathos, empathy, psychopath
PECUNIA	money	pecuniary, impecunious
PED (POD)	foot	centipede, millepede, biped, quadruped, expedite, expedition
PEL (PULS)	drive	propel, propulsion
PHIL	love, liking	Philadelphia, philharmonic, philanthropist, philosophy, bibliophile
PHOB	dislike of, fear of	hydrophobia, claustrophobia, Francophobia
PLAC	please	placid, complacent, complaisant
PLIC	fold	complicate, duplicate, multiplication
POND	weight	ponderous, ponder
PORT	carry	porter, portage, deport, import, export, report
PSEUDO	false	pseudonym, pseudoscience
RAP (RAPT)	seize	rapture, rapt, rapacious
REGENT	ruling	regent, regal, regality
ROTA	wheel	rotate, rotary, rotation
RUPT	break	bankrupt, rupture, disrupt
RUS (RUR)	country	rural, rustic
SALUT	health	salutary, salute
SCOP	see	telescope, microscope, horoscope, periscope, scope, stethoscope
SCRIB (SCRIPT)	write	scripture, postscripts, scribble, scribe, prescription
SCRUT	scan, peer into	inscrutable, scrutiny, scrutinize
SED (SID)	sit, settle	president, resident, sediment, sedentary, sedulous
SENT (SENS)	feel, know	sense, sentient, assent, dissent, resent, presentiment, consent
SEQU	follow	sequel, sequence, consequence
SPIC (SPEC)	look	retrospect, prospect, inspect

STEM OF THE ORIGINAL GREEK OR LATIN WORD	MEANING	PRESENT-DAY EXAMPLES
SPIR	breathe	inspire, inspiration, perspire, conspiracy, expire, respiratory
STUD	being eager	student, studious, study
TAC (TACIT)	to be silent	reticent, tacit, taciturn
TANG (TAC)	touch	tangent, tangible, tactile, contact
TEMPOR	time	contemporary, temporal
TEN	hold	tenure, tenacious
TORT	twist	contortionist, distort
TRAC (TRACT)	draw	extract, attraction
VERS (VERT)	turn	invert, controvert
VID (VIS)	see	provide, vision
VIV (VICT)	live	revive, victual
VOC (VOK)	call	vocation, invoke
VOL	wish	volunteer, voluntary

B. Prefixes

A prefix is a syllable or group of syllables placed at the beginning of a word to form a new word. The word "prefix" itself is made up of a prefix "pre-" (meaning *before*) and a stem, "fix." Recognizing this prefix, you can see at a glance that the word "prefix" means something that you *fix or place before.* This same prefix, "pre-," is found in dozens of other English words such as *predict* (say in advance), *precede* (go before), *precaution* (care or caution taken in advance), and *preview* (see beforehand). Knowing the meanings of the many commonly used prefixes will help you better to analyze the words in which they appear.

Generally speaking, prefixes change the meaning of a word or stem in six different ways:

1.	TIME	*ante*date, *post*graduate
2.	PLACE	*para*llel, *sub*marine
3.	NUMBER	*bi*sect, *tri*mester
4.	DEGREE	*hyper*sensitive, *ultra*modern
5.	DIRECTION	*trans*oceanic, *de*plane
6.	NEGATION	*in*convenient, *mis*interpret

Among the most important prefixes are those that change a positive meaning to a negative one. These include the Greek *a-*, the Latin *de-, in-, dis-,* and *non-,* and the Old English *mis-* and *un-.* Related to these are the prefixes that indicate the reversal of an idea, such as the Latin *contra-* and *ob-*.

Now study the meanings of the most frequently used prefixes, noticing how they help in determining word meanings.

PREFIX	MEANING	EXAMPLES
A- (AN-)	not, without	anomalous, atypical
AB- (A-, ABS-)	from, away from	avert, abstain
AD- (AP-, AL-, AT-, AC-)	to, toward	advert, admit
AMBI-	both	ambidextrous, ambivert
ANTE-	before	antecedent, antedate
ANTI-	against	antibiotic, antipathy
BENE-	well, good	benefit, benevolent
BI-	two, twice	bimonthly, biennial
CENT- (CENTI-)	one hundred	centipede, centennial
CIRCUM-	around	circumscribe, circumference
COM- (CO-, CON-, COL-)	with, together with	combine, cooperate
CONTRA-, CONTRO- (COUNTER-)	against	contradict, counteract
DE-	down or down from, reversal, wholly, away from, off	descend, defrost, defunct, detract, detrain
DI- (Compare BI-)	two, twice	diacid, dibasic
DIA-	across, through	diagonal, diameter
DIS-	reverse, not	disappear, disown
E-	See EX-	
EN-	See IN-, IL-, IR-	
EU-	well, good	euphony, eulogize
EX (E-)	from, out from, former	excavate, ex-president
EXTRA-, EXTRO-	outside, beyond	extracurricular, extraordinary
FOR-	away, apart, off	forbid, forget
FORE-	ahead, first, before, future	forearm, foretell
HETER- (HETERO-)	other	heterogeneous, heterosexual
HOMO-	same, similar	homosexual, homonym, homogenized
HYPER-	above, beyond	hypersensitive, hypertension
HYPO-	below, under	hypoglossal, hypodermic
IN- (IL-, IR-, EN-)	in, on, into	inject, infiltrate

PREFIX	MEANING	EXAMPLES
IN- (I-, IL-, IM-, IR-)	not	inconsistent, ignoble
INTER-	between, among	intercollegiate, intervene
INTRA-, INTRO-	within	intrastate, intramural
MAL-	bad, badly	maladroit, maladjusted
MIS-	wrong, wrongly	mishap, misshapen
MONO-	one	monopoly, monoplane
MULTI-	much, many	multimillionaire, multiple
NON-	not	non-Christian, nonpayment
OB- (OC-, OF-, OP-)	against	opposition, obstinate
PAR- (PARA-)	beside, contrary	parallel, parasite
PER-	through	pervade, permeate
POST-	after	postgraduate, postscript
PRE-	before, in front	preeminent, prefix
PRO-	before, forward, favoring, acting or substituting for	prophet, proceed, protariff, pronoun, proconsul
RE-	again, back	recur, recede
RETRO-	back, backward	retroactive, retrospect
SEMI-	half	semicircle, semiconscious
SUB-	under, below	submarine, substandard
SUPER-	over, above	supersensitive, superimpose
SYN-	with, together	synthesis, synchronize
TEL- (TELE-)	far	telescope, television
TETRA-	four	tetrachord, tetrameter
TRANS-	across	transition, transoceanic
TRI-	three	triumvirate, triune
ULTRA-	beyond, excessively	ultramodern, ultraconservative
UN-	not, reverse	unimportant, unlock
UNI-	one only	uniform, unique

C. Suffixes

A suffix is a syllable or group of syllables placed at the end of a word or stem to form a new word. Whereas prefixes are primarily used to change the meanings of words, suffixes serve to change the grammatical function of words. That is, a word being used as one part of speech, such as a noun, may be changed to a different part of speech, such as an adjective, by the addition of a suffix. Examples include the suffix "-ful" being added to the noun "joy" to form the adjective "joy*ful*," the suffix "-er" being added to the verb "speak" to form the noun "speak*er*," the suffix "-ice" being added to the adjective "just" to form the noun "jus*tice*," and the suffix "-ly" being added to the adjective "slow" to form the adverb "slow*ly*."

The English language contains many more noun-forming and adjective-forming suffixes than verb-forming or adverb-forming ones. A number of noun-forming suffixes, including -*al*, -*ity*, and -*ness*, form such abstract nouns as *betrayal, purity,* and *newness.* Many others show an association of a person with what the stem of the word indicates. For instance, such suffixes as -*an*, -*er*, -*ian*, -*ist*, and -*or* make up the words *Presbyterian, receiver, politician, soloist,* and *captor.* Similarly, certain adjective-forming suffixes state "a resemblance to," others, "full of," and still others, "capable of." Typical of the first group are -*al* and -*ic*, occurring in such words as *regal* and *moronic;* of the second, -*ous* and -*ful*, in such words as *perilous* and *mournful;* of the third, -*ile*, in such a word as *mobile.*

On the other hand, verb-forming suffixes have only one general meaning, "to make," with an occasional meaning of "become" appearing in intransitive verbs (verbs that do not take an object). Adverb-forming suffixes have only two meanings: "way" and "manner."

The following lists of suffixes are divided into four parts: (1) those used to form nouns; (2) those used to form adjectives; (3) those used to form verbs; and (4) those used to form adverbs. You may find it easiest to memorize suffixes by grouping together those that have the same meaning and those that produce the same change in function.

Some Noun-Forming Suffixes

SUFFIX	MEANING	EXAMPLES
-AGE	act of, state of, related to	tillage, vassalage, mileage
-AL	act of, process of	dismissal, portrayal
-AN	one who is born or lives in, one who believes in or follows	American, San Franciscan, Parisian Republican
-ANCE (-ENCE)	act of	continuance, reference
-ANCY (-ENCY)	state of	buoyancy, regency
-ANT (-ENT)	one who	participant, combatant
-ARD (-ART)	one who does something excessively	braggart, laggard
-ATION	act of, state of	flirtation, desperation
-DOM	state of	freedom, serfdom
-EER	one who	auctioneer, profiteer
-ER (-AR, -IER)	one who	worker, liar, financier

SUFFIX	MEANING	EXAMPLES
-ERY	act of	robbery, snobbery
-ESS	female	lioness, governess
-HOOD	state of, the whole group of	womanhood, priesthood
-IAN	See -AN	Italian, Bostonian, Christian, Confucian
-ICE	quality of being	cowardice, prejudice
-ION (-SION, -TION)	act of, state of	extension, corruption
-ISM	act of, state of, characteristic of	baptism, invalidism, communism
-IST	one who does or performs, one who believes in or follows	soloist, typist, Buddhist, egoist
-MENT	act of, of state of, that which	postponement, bewilderment, inducement
-NESS	state of	blindness, rudeness
-OR	one who	debtor, administrator
-SHIP	state of, art or skill	apprenticeship, penmanship
-TY (-ITY)	state of	obscurity, loyalty
-TH	act of, state of	growth, width
-Y (-ACY)	state of	jealousy, accuracy

Some Adjective-Forming Suffixes

SUFFIX	MEANING	EXAMPLES
-ABLE (-IBLE)	inclining to, having the quality of	changeable, intelligible
-AC	resembling, tending to	demoniac, maniacal
-ANT (-ENT)	having the character of	repentant, independent
-ATE (-ENT)	having	proportionate, infinite
-FUL	full of	sorrowful, joyful
-IC (ICAL)	resembling	dramatic, problematical
-IL (ILE)	capable of	civil, mobile
-ISH	resembling	clownish, shrewish
-IVE	having, tending to	secretive, demonstrative
-LESS	without	worthless, hopeless
-LY	like	motherly, saintly

SUFFIX	MEANING	EXAMPLES
-ORY	relating to	sensory, illusory
-OUS (-OSE)	full of	gracious, wondrous
-LENT	full of	benevolent, fraudulent
-Y	resembling, full of	gloomy, slimy

Some Verb-Forming Suffixes

SUFFIX	MEANING	EXAMPLES
-ATE	make	perpetuate, activate
-EN	make	strengthen, fasten
-FY (-IFY)	make or make like	falsify, liquefy
-IZE (-ISE)	make	familiarize, antagonize

The Adverb-Forming Suffixes

SUFFIX	MEANING	EXAMPLES
-LY	way, manner	truculently, ponderously
-WISE	way, manner	lengthwise, clockwise

8. Glossary of Standard Usage

A, an. The article "an" is used only before an unpronounced *h*—for example, *an honor* or *an heir.* If the *h* is pronounced, the article "a" is the correct choice: *a hotel, a historical site.*

Accept, except. "Accept" means *to receive willingly.* (He *accepted* the reward.) "Except" means *with the exclusion or omission of.* (Everyone was invited except my youngest son.)

Affect, effect. These two words can be confusing because "affect" serves mostly as a verb and "effect" serves as both a verb and a noun. The meaning of the verb "affect" is to *influence* or *to make a show of.* (The hot weather *affected* his disposition. He *affected* a deep interest in the sermon.) "Effect" is most commonly used as a noun meaning *result.* (The *effect* of his speech on the audience was remarkable.) "Effect" is less frequently used as a verb meaning *to bring about.* (The ambassador *effected* a truce between the warring factions.)

Aggravate. This word is incorrect in the sense of *irritate* or *annoy.* (He *aggravated* me by interfering with my work.) It is correct in the sense of *intensify* or *make worse.* (His interference *aggravated* my difficulty.)

All ready, already. "All ready" is used to mean *completely prepared.* (She is *all ready* to eat.) *"Already"* is used as an adverb of time. (The boy has *already* eaten.)

All right, alright. Although some student writers fall into the habit of using "alright," it is not acceptable usage. The only correct form consists of the two words "all right." (It's all right to go out tonight.)

All together, altogether. Use "all together" when you mean *all in the same group or location.* (We saw them *all together* at the races.) Use "altogether" as a synonym for *totally.* (He has *altogether* a different idea.)

Also. It's weak to begin a sentence with "also." Fit it within the sentence instead. Or substitute "too," preceded by a comma, at the end of the sentence.

Among, between. "Among" is used to refer to more than two persons or objects (The cake was divided *among* the guests.). "Between" is used in reference to two only (The profits were divided *between* the two owners.).

Amount, number. "Amount" refers to quantity of bulk material (The *amount* of grain in storage was impressive.). In contrast, "number" refers to objects that can be counted. (The *number* of dogs in the kennel is decreasing.)

Because of, due to. Many writers incorrectly use the adjective phrase "due to" when the correct usage is the adverb phrase "because of." One test: *due to* is always wrong as a sentence opener—*"Because of* its thin walls, copper pipe must be soldered." Another test: *due to* is correct only when it follows a "to be" verb—"The delay was *due to* rain." BUT: "The baseball game was called off *because of* rain."

Beside, besides. "Beside" means *by the side of.* (I sat *beside* my sister.) "Besides" has two opposite meanings: *furthermore* or *except.* (I'm too tired to swim; *besides,* I have to study. Everyone, *besides* Jim, is passing the course.)

Between, among. As a preposition, "between" properly takes only two objects or a plural object which denotes just two things: *"between* you and me" or *"between* the two brothers." On the formal level, it is improper to use *between* when the objects are more than two: *"between* you and me and him" or *"between* all the members of the football team." In these latter examples the right word to use is "among."

Can, may, might. In formal English the modal auxiliary "can" means *to be able to;* the corresponding sense of "may" is *to have permission to.* The use of *can* has spread into this second sense, the one proper to *may*—"Can I go now?"; but this is questionable usage above the colloquial level. "May I go now?" is preferable. "Might" is the past tense of "may." The difference between them is that *may* implies a greater probability than *might*— "He *might* be on time, but don't depend on it."

Capitol, capital. Writers often run into difficulty distinguishing between these two words. "Capitol" is a building—the statehouse in which legislature convenes; "capital" is the seat of government—the *capital* city or town of a country or state. *Capital* is also the word when the topic is money, letters, or punishment.

Comprise. Avoid the temptation to write *comprised of*. The verb "comprise" means *consist of* or *include*; it's correctly used as follows—"The building *comprises* three wings."

Contact. As a verb meaning *to get in touch with* a person, "contact" has only colloquial status. "Why not *communicate* with the president?" is better usage than "Why not *contact* the president?"

Data. This word is plural; the singular is *datum*. "Data," therefore, when it is a subject, requires a plural verb; when it is modified by an adjective that shows number, it requires the plural form of the adjective: "*These* data *are* important."

Different from, different than. Some people favor "different from" (His car is *different from* mine.), but "different than" is often common American usage in speaking and even in writing. *Different from* is the preferred usage.

Etc., such as. "Etc." means *and other things*. Though it is often used in technical writing, in formal writing it is not recommended, for "etc." often suggests that a point has been hastily and incompletely developed or thought through. In its place a writer may use the expressions "and the rest," "and others," "and so forth," or "and so on" when he wants to conclude a sentence with a general summary more gracefully expressed than by using "etc."

"Etc." should not be confused with the expression "such as," which means *for example*. (Do you have your supplies, *such as* your pencils and notebooks?) or *of a particular kind or degree* (The result of the trial was *such as* might be expected.)

Farther, further. A distinction is made by careful writers between "farther," referring to actual distance, and "further," referring to quantity or degree. (We spoke *further* about his desire to move *farther* away.)

Fewer, less. "Fewer" refers to things that can be counted, "less" to things that cannot. (I am taking *fewer* classes this semester. He has *less* ambition than you do.) The word "lesser," an adjective in the comparative degree, is the antonym of "greater." (He has the *greater* need for approval; I have the *lesser*.)

Fine. "Fine" is often employed as an adjective approximately synonymous with "very good," or indicating general favor or approval. This usage is established and entirely proper in certain familiar contexts: to the casual greeting "How are you?" the customary response "Fine, thank you" is certainly acceptable. In other contexts, however, the word in this sense is too vague to be very expressive—"We took a fine trip," "We had a fine time," "We saw a great deal of fine scenery." Other words, at least somewhat more specific, are ordinarily preferable. In the examples above, "enjoyable," "exciting," or "beautiful," respectively, would represent some improvement.

Good, well. In both formal and informal writing, "well" is either an adverb (He played *well.*) or an adjective. (He was *well.*) "Good" is only an adjective. (He was a *good* boy. His playing was good.)

Its, it's. "Its" (without the apostrophe) is the possessive pronoun (*its* owner, *its* meaning.) However, "it's" (with the apostrophe) is the contraction of "it is" or "it has." (*It's* time to leave. *It's* been a lovely day.) There is *no* form its' (with an apostrophe after the "s").

Lie, lay. "Lie" is an intransitive verb meaning to *recline* or *repose.* (The books *lie* on the table.) "Lay" is a transitive verb meaning to *put* or *place.* (Please *lay* the books on the table.) One reason these two verbs are sometimes confused is that the past tense of "lie" is "lay." (The books *lay* on the table yesterday.) Anyone who has difficulty with these words should make a point of learning the principal parts of each.

PRESENT	PAST	PAST PARTICIPLE
lie	lay	lain
lay	laid	laid

Like, as. In formal writing, a strict distinction is still made between "like," a preposition, and "as," a conjunction. (He talks *like* me, but he doesn't think *as* I do.) In colloquial English, however, "like" is commonly used as a conjunction. (The guava tasted good *like* I thought it would.)

Lot(s). In formal English it is better to use "very much" or "a great deal" than "a lot" or "lots of" to mean the same thing. (I admire her *very much*" rather than "I admire her *a lot*"; "He has a *great deal* of money" rather than "He has *lots* of money.")

Many, much. "Many" refers to things that can be counted, "much" to things that cannot. (I ate *many* ice cream cones. I ate too *much* ice cream.)

Nice. "Nice," like "fine," is sometimes used as an adjective indicating general favor or approval. (It's a *nice* day.; They are *nice* people.; We had a *nice* time.) Though such expressions are acceptable in casual conversation, in careful usage the meaning can be better represented by words such as "pleasant," "charming," and "agreeable."

Predominate, predominant. Correct only as a verb, "predominate" is sometimes misused as an adjective. The adjective form is "predominant"— "Hoopskirts were a *predominant (not predominate)* fashion of the time." The adverb is predominantly—"The population is *predominantly (not predominately)* Chinese."

Prejudice toward. This expression is ambiguous. Since a prejudiced attitude may be either favorable or unfavorable, the writer should make clear which kind he means by using *prejudiced in favor of* or *prejudiced against.*

Principal, principle. As an adjective, "principal" means *chief*. (His *principal* virtue is kindness). As a noun, it means either *chief* or *head* (the school *principal*) or a sum of money (the interest will be paid in a *principal* of two thousand dollars). In contrast, "principle" is always a noun meaning a rule, law, or fundamental truth. (Conciseness is an important *principle* of English composition.)

Sit, set. "Sit" and "set" are analogous to "lie" and "lay" respectively. "Sit" is most commonly an intransitive verb; "set," a transitive verb meaning *put, place, lay.* (*Set* it down on the floor.) There are some proper intransitive senses of "set" (e.g., the sun *sets*), and a few, rather rare transitive meanings of "sit" (e.g., to *sit* a horse); but it is incorrect to say "She was *setting* in the chair" or "*Sit* it down on the floor."

So. Two precautions should be observed in the use of "so." First, it should not be overused as a loose kind of coordinating conjunction. (I was tired, *so* I decided to go home, *so* I got my hat and coat.) The second precaution is that "so" as an adverb of degree ordinarily requires a result clause to complete its meaning. (I was so tired that I could hardly walk.) The use of "so" as an intensive, with no result clause following—simply "I was *so* tired!"—is questionable, at least on the formal level.

Stationary, stationery. "Stationary" means *in a fixed position*. It's easy to remember that "stationery" is *writing paper* if you associate the *e* in the *ery* ending with the two *es* in the word "letter," for which stationery is used.

There, their, they're. "There" is often used as an adverb (Look for it *there*.), a noun (Are you from *there*, too?), or an expletive. (*There* are six cylinders in that car.) "Their" is a possessive pronoun. (The hikers lost *their* maps.) "They're" is the contraction of the two words "they are."

To, too, two. "To" is used as a preposition or adverb, indicating *in a direction toward* (He walked *to* the store); "to" is also the sign of an infinitive (She liked *to dance*). "Too" is an adverb, meaning either *also* (They wanted to go, *too*) or *to a greater degree than desirable or possible* (The pressure was *too* much for him). "Two" is a numeral (They rested in Taos for *two* days).

While. "While" is a time word. Don't use it as a conjunction when no sense of time is involved: "Some of the city's magnificent ruins have been restored, *while* the others are undergoing excavation," is incorrect. It is correct to say, "At the old Chiang Mai Cultural Center, diners are served a Northern Thai meal *while* hill tribe members perform dances in regional costumes."

Who's, whose. "Who's" is the contraction for *who is*; "whose," the possessive form of the pronoun *who*. (Who's knocking at *whose* door?)

You're, your. "You're" is the contraction for *you are*; "your," the possessive form of the pronoun *you*. (*You're* doing good work in *your* studies.)

9. Glossary of Grammatical Terms

Absolute. Group of words not grammatically connected to the sentence where it occurs; sometimes called a "nominative absolute."

The letter being mailed, we returned home.

Adjective. One of the parts of speech. Modifies (describes or limits) a noun or pronoun.

cool night, **yellow** flowers, **angry** man

Adjective clause. Clause used as an adjective to modify a noun or pronoun.

An ax **that is dull** is unsatisfactory. (The clause **that is dull** modifies the noun **ax.**)
Someone **who telephoned** left his number. (The clause **who telephoned** modifies the pronoun **someone.**)

Adverb. One of the parts of speech. Modifies verbs, adjectives, or other adverbs.

He swims **well.** (**Well** modifies the verb **swims.**)
The bread is **very** fresh. (**Very** modifies the adjective **fresh.**)
Your brick wall is **more** rigidly constructed than mine. (**More** modifies the adverb **rigidly.**)

Adverb clause. Clause used as an adverb to modify any part of speech that an adverb might modify, usually a verb. Such a clause often tells how, when, where, or why.

Society begins to degenerate **when people become too materialistic.** (The boldfaced clause modifies the verb **begins.**)
If you want to buy a used car, you had better shop carefully. (The boldfaced clause modifies the verb **had better shop.**)

Agreement. Necessary correspondence between a subject and verb in person and number; between a pronoun and its antecedent in person, number, and gender; and between a demonstrative adjective (**this, these**) and the noun that it modifies, in number.

Antecedent. Noun or pronoun to which a pronoun refers.

After boarding the **ship,** he began to inspect **it.** (**Ship** is the antecedent of **it.**)

Appositive. Noun or other substantive placed next to some other noun, used in the same way grammatically and referring to the same thing or person.

The old building, **a former church,** was restored as a restaurant.
The valedictorian, **an exchange student from Turkey,** gave an impressive speech.

Article. Any of three words—**a, an,** or **the. A** and **an** are indefinite articles, **the** a definite article. (See Appendix 5.)

Auxiliary. Word used as part of a verb to assist in indicating the tense, voice, mood, and so on of the main verb.

is calling, **have** worked, **might have** entered, **shall** or **will** write

Clause. Grammatical unit containing a subject and a finite verb. At least one independent clause is necessary in any complete sentence. A main or independent clause is one that makes an independent assertion. (Sometimes part of the clause may be implied rather than expressed; in this case it is called an elliptical clause.)

A subordinate or dependent clause is one that is not self-sufficient, does not of itself make an assertion, but is used as part of a main clause. It always functions as if it were a single word—noun, adjective, or adverb.

Independent clause: The air is clear.
Subordinate clause used as a noun: We saw **that the party was ending.**
Subordinate clause used as an adjective: The brochure described a tour **that sounded fascinating.**
Subordinate clause used as an adverb: Please return the book **after you have read it.**

Comparison. Change of form in an adjective or adverb, indicating change of degree, as in **good, better, best; long, longer longest; easily, more easily, most easily.**

Complement. Element that ordinarily follows a verb and completes the assertion made by the verb about the subject. Types of complements appear below:

Direct object: The jeweler repairs **watches.**
Indirect object: Her employer offered **her** a raise.
Predicate adjective as subjective complement: The car is **new.**
Predicate adjective as objective complement: Her son's birth made her **happy.**
Predicate noun as subjective complement: The dessert is **chocolate cake.**
Predicate noun as objective complement: The publisher named Fred White **executive editor.**

Complex sentence. See *Sentence.*

Compound sentence. See *Sentence.*

Compound-complex sentence. See *Sentence.*

Conjunction. One of the parts of speech. A word used to connect words, phrases, or clauses. Coordinating conjunctions connect elements that are equal in grammatical rank. Subordinating conjunctions are used to connect subordinate clauses to main clauses.

Coordinating conjunctions: **and, but, or, nor, for.** See also *Correlative conjunctions.*
Subordinating conjunctions: **after, so, as, because, since, when, where, yet,** etc. For example, in the sentence "He did not call *because he was away,*" *because* subordinates the clause it introduces.

Conjunctive adverb. An adverb that functions also as a conjunction (**also, however, moreover, consequently, furthermore,** and so on). Ability to discriminate between conjunctive adverbs and coordinating conjunctions is important as a means of avoiding the serious error known as the "comma splice" (see page 72).

Correlative conjunctions. Conjunctions used in pairs to join elements of equal rank.

either . . . or; neither . . . nor; not only . . . but also; both . . . and

Ellipsis. Omission of words that are necessary for the grammatical completeness of the sentence, the words omitted being implied by what is expressed.

While (she was) washing her hair, she ran out of shampoo.
The new television set performs better than the old (one did).
(You) Reply promptly to the letter.

Since the subject of an imperative sentence is normally **you** implied, an imperative sentence is almost always elliptical.

Expletive. A word that bears no real meaning but is used to fill out a sentence. An expletive at the beginning of a sentence is sometimes necessary but may cause postponement of the word that should be the subject.

It is a sandstorm.
It is nine o'clock.
There are signs that inflation will lessen.

Finite. Verb form that can assert action or existence, ask a question, or give a command (such as **take, did take, was taking, have taken, will take, has been taken, had taken, had been taken**).

Gender. Status of a noun or pronoun as masculine **(man, waiter, he)**, feminine **(woman, waitress, she)**, neuter **(tree, house, it)**, or common **(mouse, person, you)**.

Gerund. Verb form ending in **ing** used as a noun.

Gerund: **Diving** is a popular water sport.
Gerund Phrase: **Sighting a meteor** is an exciting experience. (Gerund used as subject of the sentence.)
Gerund Phrase: **By studying all night,** he passed the examination. (Gerund used as object of preposition "by.")

Idiom. When we refer to the *idiom of a language,* we refer to the particular manner of using words to convey ideas—a manner that cannot be entirely accounted for by rules or by the meaning of individual words. The use and meaning of prepositions, especially, depend upon the idiom of the language.

The more the merrier (meaning "Everybody is welcome") is a typical idiom. It conveys more meaning than can be accounted for by the words and is acceptable as a sentence even though it does not have the elements a sentence calls for.

Make off with is a phrasal verb meaning "take away." Since the meaning of phrasal verbs changes with each different preposition a verb is joined to, these verbs are a form of idiom.

Infinitive. Verb form that is used after *to,* though sometimes the *to* is implied rather than expressed. (He hoped **to be** chosen. He can **ski.**) When it is part of the verb phrase, as in the examples above, an infinitive is called a complementary infinitive because it completes the verb.
An infinitive can also be used as a noun, adjective, or adverb:

Infinitive as a noun: **To practice** is essential for a pianist. (**To practice** is subject of the verb **is.**)
Infinitive as an adjective: She has a diet **to follow. (To follow** modifies the noun **diet.**)
Infinitive as an adverb: They were unhappy **to see** the business go bankrupt. (**To see** modifies the adjective **unhappy.**)

Inflection. Variation in the form of words to indicate change of number, gender, person, tense, or mood. Inflection of nouns is referred to as declension; inflection of verbs as conjugation; inflection of adjectives and adverbs as comparison.

Interjection. One of the parts of speech. A type of word placed at the beginning of a sentence or inserted into a sentence but not connected with the grammatical structure. Words such as **Oh, alas,** and **well** (as an exclamation) are interjections.

Linking verb. Verb that expresses neither action nor condition but merely establishes a connection between its subject and a noun, pronoun, or adjective in the predicate. A noun or pronoun following a linking verb is in the nominative case. The commonest linking verb is the verb **to be.** Other characteristic linking verbs are **become, appear, seem, smell** (in the sense of "possess an odor"), **taste** (in the sense of "possess a flavor"), and **feel** (in the sense of "experience or provide a sensation").

The apple juice **is** tasty.
The water **feels** warm.
The sale **seems** attractive.

Modifier. Word, phrase, or clause used to limit or change the meaning of some other word, or of a phrase or clause.

Word as a modifier: His **slightly** shy manner was amusing. (**Slightly,** an adverb, modifies **shy,** an adjective, which in turn modifies the noun **manner.**)
Phrases and clauses as modifiers: Construction **of the dam** will be postponed **until the storm passes. (Of the dam,** an adjectival prepositional phrase, modifies **construction. Until . . . passes,** an adverb clause, modifies the verb **will be postponed.)**

Mood. Form, in a verb, that indicates how the action or condition expressed by the verb is conceived by the writer or speaker. In stating a fact or asking a question, the indicative mood is used. In giving a command, the imperative mood is used. In expressing doubt, wish, or condition contrary to fact, the subjunctive mood is used.

Indicative: The chair **is** heavy. **Can** you **lift** it?
Imperative: **Examine** the surface carefully.
Subjunctive: If I **were** you, I **should approve** the plan.
   I wish he **were** not so aggressive.

Nonrestrictive modifier. Modifier that merely gives information about the term modified rather than limiting or identifying it.

The barn, **which was very old,** was damaged by the wind.
His oldest son, **who was more experienced,** handled the case efficiently.

Noun. One of the parts of speech. A word used to name a person, place, thing, quality, etc.

Alan; Shakespeare; architect; San Diego; iron; truth

Many words can be used, of course, as more than one part of speech. Such words cannot be classified until they are actually used. For example, **green** is a noun in the sentence, "**Green** is its natural color." but an adjective in "The **green** grass is attractive."

Noun clause. Subordinate clause used as a noun.

I know **what you want.** (Noun clause used as object of the verb **know.**)
How he had survived was a puzzling question. (Noun clause used as subject of the verb **was.**)

Object. Word, phrase, or clause identifying the person or thing that receives the action indicated by a transitive verb, or the substantive referred to by a preposition.

Direct object of a verb. The company ordered a **helicopter.** (**Helicopter** is the direct objective of **ordered.**)
Indirect object of a verb: He offered **me** a ride. (**Me** is the indirect object of **offered,** for it indicates the person to whom the offer is made. **Ride,** like **helicopter** in the preceding example, is a direct object).
Object of preposition: He worked on a **ranch.** (**Ranch** is the object of **on.**)

Participle. The present form of a verb ending in **ing** (though this ending also characterizes a gerund); the past participle usually ends in **ed.** A participle may be used as the main element in a verb phrase or as an adjective.

Participles as verbs: I am **taking** the cure I have **taken** before.
Participles as adjectives: **Running** water makes a pleasant sound. The **unstamped** letter was returned. The runner was **tired.**

Parts of speech. Classification under which all words are grouped. The eight parts of speech in traditional grammar are nouns, pronouns, verbs, adjectives, adverbs, prepositions, conjunctions, and interjections. (Each of these terms is defined in this glossary.)

A word qualifies as one or another part of speech only on the basis of its use in a sentence or phrase; it is possible for the same word to be used as more than one part of speech. Good usage, though, limits the uses of many words. To determine whether it is correct to use a word as a certain part of speech, consult a dictionary.

Person. Some pronouns and most verbs vary in form to indicate whether they refer to the person speaking or writing (first person), the person addressed (second person), or the person spoken or written about (third person).

FIRST PERSON	SECOND PERSON	THIRD PERSON
I am	you are	he is
I can	you can	he can
I see	you see	he sees
I have	you have	he has
I shall try	you will try	he will try
We shall find	you will find	they will find

Phrasal verb. Verb whose meaning is changed by the addition of another word, often a preposition.

Example: From the verb "to take" comes the phrasal verb "to take in," meaning *to see* (We *took* in the movie last night).

Phrase. A group of related words that does not include a subject and predicate and that is usually used as a single part of speech—adjective, adverb, verb, or noun. Phrases may be prepositional, participial, gerund, infinitive, or verb forms.

Prepositional phrase: The lawyer discovered the file **of the case.** (Adjective phrase, modifying the noun "file.")
Participial phrases: **Entering the room,** I noticed that the woman **standing in the corner** was laughing. (Adjective phrases, modifying, respectively, *I* and *woman*)
Gerund phrase: **Climbing hills** is strenuous work. (Used as noun subject.)
Infinitive phrase: **To predict the winner** is impossible. (Used as noun subject.)
Verb phrase: The results **have been found** to be inconclusive.

Predicate. Portion of a clause or sentence consisting of a verb, its complements, and the modifiers of both. Except for interjections and absolute phrases, neither of which appear frequently, the predicate consists of everything in a clause or sentence except the subject.

Preposition. One of the parts of speech. A word used to introduce a noun or pronoun object and establish its relationship to the sentence.

He will arrive **in** the afternoon **on** the train **from** Amsterdam.

Principal parts. Three forms of a verb from which, by help of auxiliary verbs, the various tenses are derived. These forms are the present infinitive, the past tense, and the past participle. (The past participle is the form used after *have*.)

PRESENT INFINITIVE	PAST TENSE	PAST PARTICIPLE
work	worked	worked
sing	sang	sung
begin	began	begun
catch	caught	caught

Pronoun. One of the parts of speech. A word used in place of a noun.

Personal pronouns: **I, you, he, she, it, we, they**
Interrogative pronouns: **who, which, what**
Relative pronouns: **who, which, what, that**
Demonstrative pronouns: **this, that, these, those**
Indefinite pronouns: **each, either, neither, any, anyone, some, someone, one, no one, few, all, none**

Reciprocal pronouns: **each other, one another**
Reflexive pronouns: **myself, yourself, himself**
Intensive pronouns: **myself, yourself, himself**

Relative clause. A clause, always dependent, introduced by a relative pronoun. The clauses used as restrictive modifiers below are examples.

Restrictive modifier. Modifier that limits, and thus restricts, the meaning of whatever it modifies.

All pilots **who fly recklessly** should be grounded.
The bottles **that were damaged** have been returned.

Sentence. Group of words expressing a thought and containing, either actually or by implication, a subject and a finite verb (predicate). In grammatical form a sentence may be simple, compound, complex, or compound-complex.

1. **A simple sentence** consists of a single independent clause, though as indicated by the second example below, its subject, its verb, or both may be compound.

Simple sentence: The bus is old.
Simple sentence: Both husband and wife signed the first copy and initialed the second.

2. **A compound sentence** consists of two or more independent clauses.

Compound sentence: Attendance was decreasing, and income was shrinking.

3. **A complex sentence** contains a single independent clause and one or more dependent clauses.

Complex sentence: The sheriff recovered the car that had been stolen.

4. **A compound-complex sentence** contains at least two independent clauses, one being compound, and at least one complex dependent clause.

Compound-complex sentence: The tide was coming in, and the sky had darkened when we finally reached the path leading up the cliff.

Subject. The substantive (see below) that a verb or verbal makes an assertion about, asks a question about, or gives an order to.

Subject of a sentence: **Tourists** often head south in the winter.
Subject of an infinitive phrase (a verbal): I know **him** to be creative. (*Him* is the subject of *to be.*)

Substantive. Noun, or any word or group of words used as a noun. Any of the following, in addition to a noun, may be a substantive: pronoun, infinitive phrase, gerund, or noun clause. (See separate listing for each of these terms.)

Tense. Distinctive form in a verb that indicates time.

Present tense: It **fits** well.
Past tense: It **fitted (fit)** well.
Future tense: It **will fit** well.
Present perfect tense: It **has fit** well.
Past perfect tense: It **had fit** well.
Future perfect tense: It **will fit** well.

Tenses appear in the progressive and emphatic forms of verbs, as well as in the simple forms:

Present progressive: I **am sewing.**
Present emphatic: I **do sew.**

Verb. One of the parts of speech. A word or phrase that indicates action, being, or state of being. In a declarative sentence the verb is the word or phrase that actually makes the assertion.

A transitive verb takes an object:
He **sold** the **trailer.**

An intransitive verb cannot take an object:
The sun **sets** in the west.

Some verbs may be either transitive or intransitive:
Transitive: I **baked** a cake.
Intransitive: I **was baking.**

Verbal. Word or phrase derived from a verb but not making an assertion. Infinitives, gerunds, and participles (participles used either in participial phrases or as adjectives) are the three types of verbals. (Each is listed here as a separate entry.)

Voice. Form of a verb that shows whether the subject of a verb or verbal performs the action indicated (active voice) or has the action performed upon it (passive voice). Only transitive verbs can be used in the passive voice.

Active voice: The government **signed** the treaty.
Passive voice: The treaty **was signed** by the government.

10. Using Principles of Phonics to Recognize and Pronounce English Words

The majority of English words are formed according to phonetic principles. By learning the rules below, you will improve your recognition and pronunciation of English words.

I. Learn the vowels and the consonants:

1. The vowels are *a, e, i, o,* and *u.*

2. All the other letters are consonants. But two of them, *w* and *y,* are sometimes used as vowels.

   W is a vowel when used in combination with another vowel, as in *sew* or *town.*

   Y is a vowel when used in combination with another vowel, as in *day* and *they. Y* is also used alone as a vowel when it is the only vowel in the syllable or word, as in *gym,* and when it is at the end of a word or syllable, as in *by* or *pretty.* When *y* is used alone as a vowel, either long or short, it has the sound of *i,* either long or short.

II. Learn the single consonants with one sound:

b	as in *boy, rob*	*p*	as in *pet, mop*
f	as in *fun, if*	*r*	as in *run, fry*
h	as in *hat, he*	*v*	as in *vest, love*
j	as in *jam, Jane*	*w*	as in *win, warm*
k	as in *key, seek*	*y*	as in *yes, young*
l	as in *let, coal*	*z*	as in *zone* (exception z (zh) as in
m	as in *meat, am*		*azure)*
n	as in *new, in*		

III. Learn the consonant blends:

bl	as in *black*	*pl*	as in *place*
br	as in *bread*	*pr*	as in *pray*
cl	as in *clean*	(kw) *qu*	as in *queen*
cr	as in *cream*	(sk) *sc*	as in *scald*
dr	as in *draw*	(sk) *sch*	as in *school*
dw	as in *dwarf*	*scr*	as in *scream*
fr	as in *free*	*sl*	as in *slow*
gl	as in *glass*	*sm*	as in *small*
gr	as in *grass*	*sn*	as in *snow*
nk	as in *bank*	*sp*	as in *spot*

spl	as in	*splash*	*tch* as in *catch*	
sq	as in	*square*	*thr* as in *three*	
st	as in	*stick*	*tr* as in *tree*	
str	as in	*street*	*tw* as in *twist*	
sw	as in	*swing*	*wh* as in *wheel*	

IV. Learn the short sounds of the vowels (they are usually marked this way in a dictionary: ă):

    a as in *hat, man*   *y* as in *gym*
    e as in *let, hen*   *o* as in *hop, Tom*
    i as in *it, rip*   *u* as in *up, tub*

V. Learn the long vowel sounds (they are usually marked this way in a dictionary: ā):

    a as in *hate, lane*   *y* as in *type, my*
    e as in *Eve, me*   *o* as in *hope, dope*
    i as in *nice, like*   *u* as in *use, fuse*

VI. Learn to tell whether a vowel in a one-syllable word is long or short.

1. If there are two or more vowels in a word of one syllable, the first vowel is usually long and the other vowels in the word are silent. This rule holds good whether two vowels come together, as in *boat* and *float*, or whether they are separated by one consonant, as in *trade*.
Examples: *coat, eat, pie, mine*

2. But if two vowels in a word of one syllable are separated by two or three consonants, the first vowel is usually short.
Examples: *hedge, dodge, fringe*

3. One vowel in a word of one syllable is usually short, unless it comes at the end of the word.
Examples: *tap, hand, get, pin, hot, fun*

4. The vowel *e, o,* or *y* is usually long if it comes at the end of a word and is the only vowel in that word.
Examples: *she, me, go, so, by, try*

VII. Learn the consonants having more than one sound.

1. a. *C* usually has the sound of *k*.
   b. But *c* has the sound of *s* before *e, i,* and *y*.
   Examples: *center, race, city, cycle*

2. a. *D* usually has the sound of *d*, as in *dog*.
   b. But before *i* and *u*, *d* often has the sound of *j* when the *u* is followed by another vowel or the consonant *r*.
   Examples: *soldier, graduate, verdure*

3. a. *G* usually has the sound of *g*, as in *gun*.
   b. Often but not always, when *g* is followed by *e, i,* or *y*, it has the sound of *j*.
   Examples: *gene, ginger*

4. a. *S* usually has the sound of *s*, as in *sit*, (1) when it is at the beginning of a word or syllable, and (2) when it is at the beginning of a group of consonants in the same word or syllable.
   Examples: (1) *send* (2) *nest*
   b. *S* often has the sound of *sh* or *zh* when it comes immediately before *u*.
   Examples: *sure, usual*
   c. *S* at the end of the word usually has the sound of *s* as in *kiss* after *f, k, p,* and *t*.
   Examples: *parts, lips, kicks*
   d. After the vowels and all other consonants, *s* at the end of a word usually has the sound of *z*.
   Examples: *Anna's, beds, goes, purrs*
5. a. *T* usually has the sound of a *t* as in *test*.
   b. But if it is followed by *ure*, it usually has the sound of *ch* (tsh).
   Examples: *nature, creature*
6. a. *X*, at the end of a word or syllable, has the sound of *ks*.
   Examples: *wax, fix*
   b. Sometimes *x* has the sound of *gz* as in *exist*.
   Example: *exact*
   c. At the beginning of a word or syllable, *x* has the sound of *z*.
   Example: *xylophone.*

VIII. Learn the following additional ways of representing single consonant sounds.
   1. Ways of representing *f*
      a. *gh* as in *laugh*
      b. *ph* as in *phone*
   2. Ways of representing *g*
      a. *gh* as in *ghost*
      b. *gu* at the beginning of a word, as in *guard*
   3. Ways of representing *j*
      a. *dge* at the end of a word, as in *ledge*
      b. *ge* at the end of a word, as in *page*
   4. Ways of representing *k*
      a. *ch* as in *chorus*
      b. *ck* at the end of a word, as in *sick, Dick*
      c. *lk* as in *folk*
      d. *qu* as in *conquer*
      e. *q* as in *queen*
   5. Way of representing *m*
      a. *mb* as in *bomb*
   6. Ways of representing *n*
      a. *gn* as in *gnat*

    b. *kn* as in *know*
    c. *pn* as in *pneumonia*
7. Ways of representing *r*
    a. *rh* as in *Rhine*
    b. *wr* as in *wrong*
8. Way of representing *s*
    a. *ps* as in *psychology*
9. Ways of representing *t*
    a. *bt* as in *doubt*
    b. *ght* as in *light*
    c. *pt* as in *ptomaine*

IIX. Learn the following additional consonant sounds.

ch (tch)	as in *church*
ch (sh)	as in *machine*
ng	as in *ring*
ng (ng, eg)	as in *finger*
sh	as in *ship*
th	as in *then*
th	as in *thick*
ci (sh)	as in *special* (Note that *ci* is followed by a vowel.)
si (sh)	as in *pension* (*sh* followed by a vowel)
si (zh)	as in *vision* (*si* followed by a vowel)
ti (sh)	as in *station* (*ti* followed by a vowel)

Index

A, an, 50, 107, 355–362, 376, 382
Abbreviations, punctuation of, 333
Absolute constructions, 116, 117
   ablative absolute, 178
   absolute phrases, 246, 387
   defined, 177, 381
   nominative absolute, 381
   punctuating, 177–178, 335
Abstract nouns, 357
Accept, except, 376
Active verbs, using strong, 43, 63
Active voice, 53, 238, 239, 389
Address, direct, 177, 178, 335
Addresses, punctuating, 278, 335
Adjective clauses, 99, 146, 178, 194, 218,
   247–249
   defined, 381
   subordination by, 22, 23
Adjective-forming suffixes, 375–376
Adjective modifiers, 106–107
Adjective phrase, 261
Adjectives, 43, 47, 49, 98, 106–107, 146, 244
   cutting excess, 211
   defined, 381
   irregular comparatives and superlatives,
   279–280
   participles as, 116
   as transitions, 19, 20
Adler, Mortimer J., 235–236
Advanced Composition, 154, 223, 265
Advanced composition topics, 322–332
Adverb clauses, 146, 178, 194, 200, 212, 218
   defined, 381
   internal, 22, 44
   introductory, 39, 42, 46, 63, 92, 93, 108,
   238, 245, 262
   subordination by, 21–23
Adverb-forming suffixes, 376
Adverb modifiers, 107–108
Adverb phrases, 245
   internal, 21, 22
   subordination by, 22, 32
Adverbs, 43, 52, 98–99, 146, 244
   conjunctive, 383
   defined, 381
   formation of, 107
   irregular comparatives and superlatives
   of, 279–280
   punctuating, 178
   redundant, 212
   subordinating, 72–73
   as transitions, 5
Affect, effect, 376
Agee, James, 176

Agreement
   defined, 381
   of pronoun and antecedent, 112–113
   of relative pronouns, 247–249
   of subject and verb, 114–115
"Alice Falling" (Carroll), 273–274
Alice's Adventures in Wonderland (Car-
   roll), 156–157, 273–274
"All Gold Canyon" (London), 67
All ready, already, 377
All right, alright, 377
All together, altogether, 377
Allen, Robert W., 267–268
Allen, Woody, 258–260
"America: A Woman's Country" (Com-
   mager), 319
American Mind, The (Commager), 316, 319
American Notes (Dickens), 303–304
American Story, The (Catton), 172–174
Among, between, 377
Amount, number, 377
An: see A, an
Analogy, 165, 166, 198, 201, 203
   defined, 163
Anecdote, 291
   concluding with, 240, 241
   in introduction, 204–206
Antecedent, 149
   agreement of pronoun and, 112–113
   defined, 381
Analysis, 134–135
   causal: *see* Cause and effect
   logical: *see* Logical analysis
Apostrophe, 227
   rules for use of, 213–214, 336–337
   showing possession by, 81–83
Appositives, 32, 64, 93, 98, 99, 105, 126,
   177, 178, 194, 218, 246, 263, 276
   beginning sentences with, 38
   defined, 47, 144, 382
   punctuating, 144, 246–247, 278, 334, 336,
   338
   subordination by, 22, 23
Appropriateness, 272, 273
   levels of usage and, 237–238
Arabic numerals
   in outlines, 131
   as transitions, 19
Arabs and the World, The (Creamans), 9
"Are Social Scientists Backward?" (Kenmerer), 163
Argumentation, 95, 134
Arrangement
   of ideas: *see* Thought patterns
   word, 306–307, 311, 312

"Arrow of Time, The" (Layzer), 209
Articles, 81
  with countable nouns, 355–359
  defined, 382
  definite and indefinite, 50–51, 150–151, 281–282, 355–362
  with proper names, 359–362
  with uncountable nouns, 50, 357–359
As, like, 180, 379
"Ascetic, The" (Hesse), 213
Asimov, Isaac, 241
Assembly Language Programming and the IBM 360 and 370 Computers (Rudd), 138–139
"Atlanta Renewal Gives Power to the Communities" (Little), 256
Atlantic Monthly, 153, 204–205, 221, 284, 285, 294, 318
Atlas, 90
Audience, 26, 196, 204, 272
Authority, establishing, 206, 207
Auxiliaries, 76, 387
  defined, 382
  modal, 75–78

Background information in introduction, 204, 208–209
Background of term, 230
Baldwin, James, 263–264, 243, 272–273
Barnett, Lincoln, 137–138
Barzun, Jacques, 43
Basic Carpentry Illustrated, 211
"Battle of Waterloo, The" (Hugo), 66
be verb, 53, 66, 70, 71, 76, 114, 144, 385
  weakness of, 43
"Beatles and Their Beat, The" (Schrag), 68
Because of, due to, 377
Benchley, Robert, 258
Berger, John, 256, 316
Berriault, Gina, 287
Beside, besides, 377
Bettelheim, Bruno, 242
Between, among, 377
'Bore, A" (Nicholson), 232
Borg-Strom, Georg, 255
Boston *Globe,* 84
Boston Review of the Arts, 241
Both . . . and, 182
Bourn, David, 283
Broad reference, 149
Brackets, rules for using, 340
"Building a Sunscope" (*Life*), 34
"Buster Keaton" (Agee), 176
Butler, Nicholas Murray, 296–298, 300, 302

"Cairo, Illinois" (Dickens), 303–304
California Wine Country, 211
Can, 75, 76, 78, 377
"Can We Predict Quakes?" (Canby), 188
Canby, Thomas Y., 188
Can't help, 78

Capitol, capital, 377–378
Capitalization
  in outlines, 131
  rules for, 343–345
Carroll, Lewis, 156–157, 273–274
Carson, Rachel, 2, 5, 19, 20, 164, 268–269, 272
"Case of the Wayward Word, The" (Weaver), 296
Catton, Bruce, 172–175
Cause, defined, 196
Cause and effect, 95, 134, 230, 231
  development of expository composition by, 193–226
Causes, 196–197
"Celestial Navigation by Birds" (Sauer *et al.*), 154
"Censored or Suppressed Works" (Palo Alto City Library), 323–325
"Characteristics of English, The" (Wrenn), 298–300
Chronological arrangement, outline, 133
Chronological development, 4, 18, 32, 34–38, 94, 271
Chronological paragraph, the, 31–62
Churchill, Winston, 306–307
Circular definition, 230
Clarity, 34, 56, 147, 182, 204, 217
Clark, David H., 284
Classification, 230–231; *see also* Logical division
Clause, defined, 44, 382
Clauses
  adjective, 22, 23, 99, 146, 178, 194, 218, 247–249, 381
  adverb, 21–24, 39, 42, 46, 63, 92, 93, 108, 146, 178, 194, 200, 212, 218, 238, 262, 381
  dependent, 44
  elliptical, 180, 215, 216
  if, 76
  independent, 44
  introductory, punctuating, 46–47
  nonrestrictive, 104–105
  noun, 39, 44, 245, 386, 389
  relative, 388
  restrictive, 104–105, 160
  subordinated, 21–22
Cleaver, Eldridge, 188
Climax, 10, 18, 269, 271; *see also* Conclusion
Coherence, 3–5, 7–10, 18, 19, 32–34, 65, 93, 127, 128, 131, 145, 147, 160, 171, 218, 227, 239, 261, 298, 302
  repeating a structural unit for, 293–295
  word repetition for, 263–265
Colloquialisms, 275
Colon, 63, 126, 144, 160, 171, 263, 292, 302
  before appositive, 144
  rules for use of, 336
  and quotation marks, 342

Comma, 32, 64, 74, 85, 105, 126, 127, 142–143, 160, 177–179, 228, 246, 247, 262, 291–293, 302
  in compound sentences, 44–45
  after introductory clauses and phrases, 46–47
  miscellaneous uses of, 278
  and quotation marks, 342, 343
  and restrictive-nonrestrictive elements, 104
  rules for use of, 334–335
  in series, 48–49
  two uses of, 43–45
Comma splice, 72–74, 143, 383
Commager, Henry Steele, 316, 319
Common nouns, 105
Communication, oral versus written, 237
Comparatives and superlatives, irregular, 279–280
Comparison, 66, 95, 134, 175, 177, 182, 295
  of adjectives and adverbs, 106, 107, 279–280
  defined, 382
  see also Figurative language, Inflection
Comparison and contrast, 230, 231, 234
  expository composition development by, 159–192
  transitions for, 161
Comparative pair, 292, 293
Comparatives, 64
  idiomatic, 280
irregular, 279–280
Complement, defined, 382
Complex sentences, 44, 98, 388
Complimentary close, punctuating, 278
Composition, writing a longer, 129–130
Composition, expository
  developed by definition, 227–260
  developed by cause and effect, 193–226
  developed by comparison and contrast, 159–192
  developed by examples, 126–158
  developed by logical division, 261–321
Composition outline, 130–134
Composition topics, advanced, 322–332
Compound-complex sentence, 44, 388
Compound modifier, hyphenation of, 338–339
Compound nouns, hyphenation of, 339
Compound predicate, 31, 55–56, 127, 154, 194, 276
  defined, 44
Compound sentence, 64, 72, 98, 99, 182, 228
  defined, 44
  punctuating, 44–45, 334
Compound words, possessive of, 337
Conclusion, 34, 96, 129, 239–244
Conesford, Lord, 223
"Confessions of a Female Chauvinist Sow" (Roiphe), 240
Conjugation: see Inflection

Conjunctions, 48, 74
  coordinating, 19, 44, 72, 74, 229, 245, 336, 383
  correlative, 26, 126, 181–183, 261, 262, 292, 302, 334, 383
  defined, 383
  subordinating, 22–23, 383
  as transitions, 19, 229
Connectives, 37–38, 143, 177, 271; see also Conjunctions, Transitions
Construction, loose versus periodic, 103
Constructions, absolute: see Absolute constructions
Contact, 378
"Continental Shelf, "The" (Carson), 164
Contractions, 78, 82, 214, 379, 380
Contrary to fact statements, 76
Contrast, 8, 22, 95, 134, 234
Contrast, comparison and
  analytical paragraph development by, 162–175
  expository composition developed by, 159–192
  transitions for, 161
Contrast, vivid, in introduction, 204, 208
Contrasted element, comma and, 335
Controlling idea, 5–10, 18, 21, 22, 67–68, 93, 95, 129–130, 142, 266, 300, 301
Coordinating conjunctions, 44, 72, 74, 245, 336, 383
  as transitions, 19, 229
Correct pronoun reference, 148–149
Correlative conjunctions, 26, 126, 181–183, 261, 262, 292, 302, 334, 383
Cott, Jonathan, 327–329
Could, 75, 77
Countable nouns, articles with, 355–359
"Courtship" (Thurber), 305
Cousins, Norman, 196, 201–203
Cowley, Malcolm, 177
Creamans, Charles D., 9
Credibility in writing, 69
"Crow and the Oriole, The" (Thurber), 330–331
Customs and Cultures (Nida), 8–9, 96

Dangling elements, 215–216
Data, 378
Dash, 159, 171, 179, 302
  and quotation marks, 342–343
  rules for use of, 338
Dates
  plural of, 214
  punctuating, 278, 335
"Day the Bomb Fell, The" (Hersey), 242
Days of the week, capitalizing, 345
Declension: see Inflection
Decline of the WASP, The (Schrag), 68, 166–167, 274–275
Deductive organization, 9, 138
DeFederico, Frank R., 70

Definite and indefinite articles, 50–51, 150–151, 281–282, 355–362
Definition, 95, 134, 268, 301
  development of expository composition by, 227–260
  extended, 230
  logical, 229–230; see also Logical definition
Definition of terms in introduction, 204, 207
DeFrance, J. J., 35
Degree, comparative: see Comparison
Demonstrative adjectives, 381
Dependent clause, defined, 44
Description, brief, in introduction, 204, 205
Descriptive paragraph, 95
Detail, 66, 171, 231
  concrete, 92, 140
  historical, in introduction, 204, 210
  in spatial development, 65
  specific, 69–70, 92, 227, 262, 292
  supporting, 4, 18
Development
  by cause and effect, 193–226
  chronological, 18, 32, 34–38, 94
  circular, 3
  by comparison and contrast, 159–162
  by definition, 227–260
  by examples, 94–97, 137–142
  general to specific, 4
  interrupted by digression, 3
  by logical development, 261–321
  by order of importance of supporting detail, 4, 7
  paired, 162–171
  parallel, 3; see also Parallelism
  in separate sections, 166–168, 172–175
  sequential, 18
  spatial, 65–67, 94
  specific to general, 4
  straight-line, 3, 4, 8
  transitions for, 64–65, 93–94; see also Transitions
Dialogue, punctuation of, 278
Dickens, Charles, 303–304
Diction, 272, 275
Dictionary, 229, 339, 341, 347–350, 386
Differences: see Comparison and contrast
Different from, different than, 378
Digressions in writing, 3
Direct address, punctuating, 177, 335
Direct object: see Object
Direct quotations
  punctuating, 335, 336, 341–342
"Disney and Hefner, Birds of a Feather" (Schrag), 166–167
Distinguishing between ei and ie spellings, 348
Divided reference, 149
Division, logical, 95, 261
  development by, 261–321

Division, word, hyphenation to show, 339
Do, 76
Documents, capitalizing titles of, 345
Doonesbury (Trudeau), 191, 192
Dramatic narrative, concluding with, 240, 242
Drucker, Peter F., 168
Dubos, René, 154, 187–188, 285–286
Due to, because of, 377

Earth Resources (Skinner), 233
"Ecologist Returns to South Asia for Another Look" (Ripley), 222
"Education of U.S.A. Women" (Smuts), 220–221
Effect: see Cause and effect
Effect, affect, 376
Effective Study (Robinson), 36–37
Effective use of participles, 117–118
Either . . . or, 115, 182
Elaboration by logical division: see Expository composition
Electrical Fundamentals (DeFrance), 35
"Electron-Holt Liquid, An" (Thomas), 19–20
Elements out of order, sentence, 178
Elements, restrictive and nonrestrictive, 160, 104–105; see also Parenthetical elements
Eliminating unnecessary words, 100–102
Ellipsis, 383
Elliptical clauses, 180, 228, 382
  dangling, 215, 216
Elliptical phrases, 276
Ells, Michael D., 267–268
Emphatic verb form, 389
Encyclopedia Americana, 96–97
English, British, 142
English Language, The (Wrenn), 298–300
English paragraph, the, 1–30, 129
"English Verb, The" (Fifield), 351
Esquire, 287
Essential Mathematics for College Students (Mueller), 207
Etc., 378
Evidence, 197
Ewen, Dale, 233–234
Examples, 2, 18, 197, 198, 230–232, 234, 240, 271, 295, 301
  expository composition development by, 126–158
  expository paragraph development by, 8, 9, 18, 94–97
Except, accept, 376
Exclamation point, 334, 342–343
Expletives, 54, 294, 383
  defined, 70, 383
  understanding, 70–71
Expository composition
  developed by cause and effect, 193–226

Expository composition(*Continued*)
  developed by comparison and contrast,
    159–192
  developed by definition, 227–260
  developed by examples, 126–158
  developed by logical division, 261–321
  transitions for, 93–94
Expository paragraph, the, 92–125
  development by examples, 94–97
Expository writing, defined, 94–95
Express, L' (Paris), 90
Extended definition, 230
Extended simile, 177

Fables for Our Time (Thurber), 124–125,
    288–289, 330–331
Fact, startling, in introduction, 204, 206–
    207
"Fairly Intelligent Fly, The" (Thurber),
    124–125
Fallaci, Oriana, 327–329
"Familiarity Breeds Regret" (Twain), 242
Farther, further, 378
Fewer, less, 378
Fifield, Merle, 351
Figurative language, 175–177, 199, 303
  concluding with, 240, 244
  in introduction, 204, 211
Figures, plural of, 214, 337
Figures of speech, 175–177; *see also* Figu-
    rative language
Filler words: *see* Expletives
Fine, 378–379
Finite verbs, 84, 116, 117, 382, 383
  defined, 84
  participles as parts of, 117
Finstad, Owen, 259
"Five Evidences of an Education" (Butler),
    296–298
Force in writing, 237–239
  four qualities of, 238–239
"Foreigner Looks at American Writers, A"
    (Gordimer), 171
Foreign words and phrases, italicizing, 341
Forster, E. M. 139–142
Fortune, 168
Fractions, hyphenation of, 338
Fragment, sentence, 84–85
"Friendship" (Adler), 235–236
Frost, Robert, 230
Fuentes, Carlos, 169–170
Fundamentals of Nursing (Murray), 301–
    302
Fused sentence: *see* Run-on sentence

Garrison, Roger H., 231
Gender, 112, 384
Generalization, 95, 138, 139, 232, 267, 300
"Genetic Profiles Will Put Our Health in
    Our Own Hands" (Pines), 277
Genus, 230, 231

Geographical terms
  article with, 360
  capitalizing, 344
  punctuating, 335
Gerund, 245, 386, 389
  dangling, 215, 216
  defined, 384
Gerund phrase, 109, 146, 245, 384, 387
  beginning sentence with, 39
Ghost Towns of the West, 205
"Giant Tortoises Do Almost Too Well on
    Island Reserve" (Bourn), 283
Gifts of Passage (Rau), 8, 22
Gilder, George F., 84
Gill, Brendan, 209, 305–306, 317
Ginsberg, Martin, 243
Glossary of standard usage, 376–380
Good Behavior (Nicholson), 232
Good, well, 379
Gordimer, Nadine, 171–172
Grammar skills, 21–24, 50–56, 75–85, 106–
    118, 145–150, 180–183, 215–218, 247–
    251, 279–281, 311–314
  agreement
    pronoun and antecedent, 112–113; *see
      also* Pronouns
    relative pronoun, 247–249; *see also*
      Pronouns
    subject and verb, 114–116; *see also*
      Subject, Verbs
  articles, definite and indefinite, 50–51,
    81, 150–151, 281–282, 355–362, 382
  comparatives and superlatives, irregular,
    279–281, *see also* Comparison
  compound predicate, 55–57; *see also*
    Predicate
  correlative conjunctions, 181–183; *see
    also* Conjunctions
  dangling elements, 215–217
  elliptical clause, 180–181; *see also* Ellip-
    tical clauses
  modal auxiliaries, 75–81, 250–251; *see
    also* Modal auxiliaries
  modification, principles of, 106–112; *see
    also* Modifiers
    adjective modifiers, 106
    adverb modifiers, 107–108
    noun modifiers, 108–110
  modifiers, misplaced, 311–313; *see also*
    Modifiers
  parallelism, 145–148, 313–314; *see also*
    Parallelism
  participles and participial phrases, 116–
    120; *see also* Participial phrases,
    Participles
  passive voice, controlled use of, 53–55;
    se also Passive voice
  possessive case, 81–84; *see also* Posses-
    sion
  prepositions, choosing correct, 51–53,
    183–184, 251–252, 314–315

pronoun reference, correct, 148–150; *see also* Pronouns

sentence fragment, 84–86

subordination, 21–24, 217–219; *see also* Subordination

Grammar and spelling, 351

Grammatical terms, glossary of, 381–389

"Grant and Lee: A Study in Contrasts" (Catton), 172–174

Great Ideas from the Great Books (Adler), 235–236

Griffith, Thomas, 153, 221, 284, 294

Guide to Creative Writing, A (Garrison), 231

Gwynne, Peter, 255

Had better, 78

Haldane, J. B. S., 269–270, 272

Hardwick, Elizabeth, 243–244

Harris, David, 286–287

Harris, Neil, 159–160, 168–169

Hart, Andrew W., 267–268

Hatsumi, Reiko, 7, 22

Have, 76

Have to, 76

Heilbroner, Robert L., 210

Here at the New Yorker (Gill), 306, 317

Here Is New York (White), 6, 21, 266, 267

Hersey, John, 242

Hesse, Hermann, 273

Hiroshima (Hersey), 242

Historical detail in introduction, 204, 210

Historical events, capitalizing, 342

"Historical Supernovas" (Stephenson and Clark), 284

Holiday, 152, 169–171, 244

Holidays, capitalizing names of, 345

Homonyms, 348–349

"How to Be an Employee" (Drucker), 168

"How to Enlarge a Photograph," 31–32

"How Much Can a Writer Stand?" (Gill), 306

"How the Quechaus Think" (Nida), 8–9

"How to Unclothe an Emperor," 328–329

"How to Write Like a Social Scientist" (Williamson), 206

Hugo, Victor, 66

Humor, 237, 274, 303, 305

in introduction, 204, 205, 210–211

Hyphen, 82

rules for use of, 338–339

"Ice Fish, The" (Ruud), 273

Idea, controlling, 5–10, 18, 21, 22, 67, 68, 93, 95, 129–130, 142, 266, 300–301

Ideas, arrangement of, 3–5; *see also* Thought pattern

Ideas, unequal, 24; *see also* Subordination

Idiom, defined, 384

Idiomatic comparatives, 280

Idiomatic expressions, use of prepositions in, 364–365

Idioms, English, 78

If clauses, 76

"If the Impressionists Had Been Dentists" (Allen), 260

Immediate cause, 196–197

Imperative mood, 383, 385

Importance, arrangement of examples in order of increasing, 95–97

Indefinite articles, 50–51, 150, 355–362, 382

Indefinite pronoun, 82

Independent clauses

and comma splice, 72

defined, 44

punctuating, 334

Indentation, paragraph, 2

"Indian Bazaar, An" (Rau), 8

Indicative mood, 385

Indirect object: *see* Object

Indirect quotations, 341

Individual possession, showing, 337

Inductive organization, 9, 138

Industrial Hygiene (Allen *et al.*), 267–268

Infinitive, 245

beginning sentence with, 228

complementary, 384

dangling, 215, 216

defined, 384

as subject, 216

Infinitive phrases, 98, 146, 147, 182, 193, 218, 245, 387, 389

opening with, 31, 39

Inflection, defined, 384

Ing ending: *see* Gerunds, Participles

Inside Benchley (Benchley), 258

"Intellectual in America, The" (Jarrell), 206, 241

"Intelligence Tangle, The" (Ungar), 284–285, 318

Interjections, 384, 387

defined, 384

punctuating, 178, 335

Interrupters: *see* Parenthetical elements

Intonation, 237

Introduction, 170, 203–211

Introduction to Criminology (Shafer), 195, 200

Irony, 237, 242, 274, 303, 305, 306

Irregular comparatives and superlatives, 279–280

Irregular verbs, principal parts of, 351–355

It (expletive), 70

Italics, 214, 337

rules for use of, 340–341

Its, it's, 82, 379

Jacobson, Michael, 205

"Japan and the U.S.A Different but Alike" (Harris), 159–160

"Japanese Women" (Hatsumi), 7

Jarrell, Randall, 206, 241

Jeans, James, 196–198

"Jenny Lind" (DeFederico), 70

"Joey: A 'Mechanical Boy'" (Bettelheim), 242
Joint possession, showing, 83, 337
Johnson, Dr. Samuel, 230, 274, 276
Johnson, Virginia E., 313, 314
Johnston, Marjorie C., 96–97

Kaplan, Robert B., 3
Kenmerer, Donald L., 163
Key point, concluding with, 240, 242
Key word, repetition of, 135, 263
Krutch, Joseph Wood, 275, 293

Language, figurative, 175–177, 199, 204, 211, 240, 244, 303
Languages, capitalizing names of, 344
"Latin American Universities" (Johnston), 96–97
"Latinos vs. Gringos" (Fuentes), 169–170
Layzer, David, 209
Length, sentence, 40, 272
Less, fewer, 378
Letters
   italicizing, 340
   plural of, 214, 337
"Let's Go to the Movies," 135, 291–293, 295, 301
"Levels for Surveying" (McCormac), 10
Levels of usage and appropriateness, 237–238
Lie, lay, 379
Life, 34
Life on the Mississippi (Twain), 242
Like, as, 379
Lind, Jenny, 70
Linking paragraphs together, 135–136
Linking verbs, 106
   defined, 385
Linking words, pronouns as, 32–33; *see also* Transitions
"Lion Who Wanted to Zoom, The" (Thurber), 288–289
Listings, numerical and alphabetical, as transitions, 19
Lists, spelling, 348–351
Little, Charles E., 256
Logical analysis, 95
Logical arrangement in outlining, 131
Logical definition, 229–230
Logical division, 95
   development of expository composition by, 261–321
Logical progression, 197
London, Jack, 67
Lord, Walter, 164–165
Lot(s), 379
"Love and Radio in the U.S.A." (Schrag), 274–275
Luce, Clare Boothe, 186–187, 264–265, 272
Lucas, F. L., 152, 244

McCormac, Jack C., 10
MacLeish, Archibald, 222
Macroeconomics (Wyckoff), 70
Mademoiselle, 206, 241
Male and Female (Mead), 253–254
"Man to Remember, A," 92–93
"Man and the State" (West), 199
Mannes, Marya, 294–295
Many, much, 379
"Marrakech" (Orwell), 207
"Mars" (Pollack), 69
Mass nouns, 357
Masters, William H., 313, 314
"Mathematics Relation, A" (Ewen and Topper), 233–234
Mathematics for Technical Education (Ewen and Topper), 233–234
May, 75, 76, 377
Mead, Margaret, 253–254
Meaning of Treason, The (West), 199
Mercurial Woman, The (Hatsumi), 7, 22
Metaphor, 64, 175–177, 211
Might, 75, 76, 377
"Military Officer Corps, The" (Creamans), 9
"Miracle of New York, The" (White), 6
Misérables, Les (Hugo), 66
Misplaced modifiers, 311–312
Misreading, punctuating to avoid, 335, 339
Modal auxiliaries, 36, 64, 75–81, 127
   defined, 75
Modern English Usage, 43
Modification, principles of, 106–112
Modifiers, 52, 106–110
   adjective, 106–107
   adverb, 106–108
   beginning sentences with, 38–39
   defined, 44, 385
   hyphenating compound, 338–339
   misplaced, 311–312
   nonrestrictive, 177, 178, 384
   noun, 108–109
   noun compounds in scientific and technical English, 109–110
   restrictive, 388
   subordination by, 22, 23
Modulation: *see* Style, Tone
Monotony, 38, 40–41, 56, 99, 218, 304
   avoiding, 24
Months, capitalizing names of, 345
Mood of verbs, 385
"Mother Sea: The Gray Beginnings" (Carson), 2
Mueller, Francis J., 207
Multiple causes and effects, 197
Murray, Malinda, 301–302
Must, 75, 76
"Myths about Crime" (Shafer), 200
"My Father" (Baldwin), 263–264, 272–273
"Mystique of the Desert, The" (Krutch), 275, 293

My World—and Welcome to It (Thurber), 305

"Naked Nomads" (Gilder), 84
Names
   articles with, 359–362
   comma in, 278
   geographic, italicizing, 340
Names, proper
   capitalizing, 344–345
   reversed, punctuating, 278, 335
   showing possession in, 81–83
Narration, brief, in introduction, 204, 205
Nationality
   article with, 361–362.
   capitalizing, 344
National Geographic, 188, 222
"Nature of Crisis, The" (Murray), 301–302
Negation, defining by, 230, 232–234
Neither . . . nor, 182
"New Lifestyles from Old Philosophies," 126–129, 134
"New Student President, The" (Berriault), 287
"New York I Know, The" (Mannes), 294–295
New Yorker, The, 209, 225, 294–295, 306, 326
New York magazine, 240
New York Times, 243
New York Times Magazine, 210
"Newtonian Relativity Principle, The" (Barnett), 137–138
Nicholson, Harold, 232
Nida, Eugene, A., 8–9, 96
Night to Remember, A (Lord), 164–165
"Nightmare and Ritual in Hemingway" (Cowley), 177
"Noise" (Allen *et al.*), 267–268
Nominative absolute, 381
Nominative case pronouns, 180
"No More a Stranger" (Baldwin), 243
"Nonrenewable Resources" (Skinner), 233
Nonrestrictive elements
   clauses, 104–105
   comma and, 334
   defined, 104
   modifiers, 177, 178, 384
   phrases, 104–105
Nor, 112
North America (Trollope), 263
Notes of a Native Son (Baldwin), 263–264
Not only . . . but also, 115, 182
Nouns, 43
   abstract, 357
   collective, 115
   common, 105
   compound in scientific and technical English, 109–110
   countable, 355–359
   defined, 384

   hyphenating compound, 339
   mass, 357
   modifiers, 108–109
   possessive of, 81, 82
   proper, 105
   uncountable, 50
Noun clauses, 44, 245, 389
   defined, 386
   opening with, 39
Noun-forming suffixes, 374–375
Noun modifiers, 108–109
Nuclear Power (Berger), 256, 316
Number, amount, 377
Number, 112
   apostrophe in, 337
   of articles, 50
   possessive, 81
Numbers
   hyphenating compound, 338
   italicizing, 340
   use of comma in, 278, 335
"Numbers Force Us into a World like None in History, The" (Borg-Strom), 255
Numerals, 19, 131

Object, 53, 382
   defined, 386
   direct, 245
Objective case, 180
Omission, showing, 337; *see also* Contractions, Ellipsis
O'Neill, Eugene, 68
"On the Fascination of Style" (Lucas), 152, 244
Or, 112
Oral and written communication, differences between, 237
Order of importance, organization in, 271
Order, logical, 8
Organization
   in order of importance, 271
   specific to general, 138
Organizations, capitalizing names of, 345
"Originals" (Gill), 209
Orwell, George, 207
Ought (to), 75–77
"Our Diets Have Changed, but Not for the Best" (Jacobson), 205
Outline
   composition, 130–134
   paragraph, 17–18
   topic, 18

"Pacific Northwest, The" (Griffith), 153, 221, 284, 294
Paired development of comparison or contrast, 162–171; *see also* Parallelism
Pairs, ordered, 48, 234

Palo Alto City Library, 323–325
Paragraph
  chronological, 3–4, 31–62
  defined, 2
  descriptive, 95
  English, 1–30, 129
  expository, 92–125
  process, 95, 196
  spatial, 63–91
Paragraph development
  chronological, 4, 31–62
  cultural differences in, 3–4
  expository, by examples, 94–97
  spatial, 4, 63–91
Paragraph outline, 17–18
Paragraphs, linking of, 135–136
Parallelism, 19, 24, 36, 56, 92, 93, 98, 126,
    145–147, 159, 166, 168, 171, 182–183,
    194, 199, 200, 227, 238, 261, 272–276,
    291, 298, 313–314
  faulty, 146–147
Parentheses, 171, 179
  rules for using, 339–340
Parenthetical elements, 104–105, 126, 177–
    179, 291, 302
  defined, 177
  nonrestrictive modifiers and appositives,
    17
  punctuating, 177–179, 335, 338
Parenthetical statement, 64
Park, Edwards, 254
Participial phrases, 23, 98, 127, 146, 147,
    193, 194, 212, 218, 245, 248, 262, 263,
    387
  introductory, 41, 47, 63, 92
  opening with, 41
  using, 116–118
Participles, 76, 85, 146, 212, 245
  dangling, 215, 216
  defined, 386
  effective use of, 117–118
  identifying, 116–117
  introductory, 47
  using, 116–118
Parts of speech, defined, 386; see also in-
    dividual listings
Passive voice, 212, 228, 238, 239, 389
  controlled use of, 53–55
Past participle, 117
Past tense, 146
Pattern, thought, 3–5
Peanuts (Schulz), 157–158
Period, 333
  and comma splice, 72, 73
  and quotation marks, 342
Periodic sentence, 102–103, 228
Person, defined, 386
Person, introduction of a, 204, 209
Personal experience, use of, 95, 138, 206
Personal pronoun, 82
Personification, 175–177

Petrunkevitch, Alexander, 176
Phonetics, using to recognize and pro-
    nounce English words, 390–393
"Photographic Lens, The" (Price), 165–166
Phrasal verbs, 52, 387
Phrases, 21
  defined, 387
  introductory, 46–47, 215–216
  nonrestrictive, 104–105
  punctuating introductory, 46–47
  repetition of, 136
  restrictive, 104–105
  to show possession, 81
  transitional, 19, 136
  unnecessary, 212
  see also individual listings
Pines, Maya, 277
Plural, forming, 214, 347
"Plutonium: 'Free' Fuel or Invitation to a
    Catastrophe?" (Gwynne), 255
Poetry, concluding with, 240, 243–244
Pollack, James R., 69
Pontification, 212
Portable Hemingway, The, 177
Possession, showing, 81–84
  use of apostrophe in, 213, 214
  joint, 82, 83
Possessive case, 336–337
Predicate, 84, 387
  compound, 44, 55–56
  defined, 387
Predicate adjective, 106, 382
Predicate nominative, 114
Predicate noun, 382
"Prediction as a Side Effect" (Asimov), 241
Prefixes, 371–373
  defined, 365, 371
Prepositional phrases, 23, 52, 98, 108, 109,
    146, 182, 193, 212, 218, 228, 244, 248,
    307, 387
  choosing correct, 51–52
  defined, 51, 387
  ending sentence with, 306–307
  in idiomatic expressions, 364–365
  introductory, 31, 39, 41, 47, 334
  review of, 183–184, 251–252
  as transitions, 5
  uses of, 362–365
Present participle, 117
Present perfect tense, 92
Present tense, 387, 389
Price, William H., 165–166
Principal, principle, 380
Principal parts
  defined, 387
  of irregular verbs, 351–355
Principles of modification, 106–110
Process description, 34–35, 138–139, 218,
    231
Process paragraph, 35–38, 95, 196
Progressive verb form, 389

Pronouns, 127, 128, 227
    agreement of antecedent and, 112–113
    agreement of relative, 247–249
    capitalizing, 344
    compound, 112–113
    defined, 387–388
    indefinite, 81–82
    nominative case, 180
    personal, 82
    possessive form of, 81–82, 214
    reference, correct, 148–150
    relative, 113, 180, 247–249
    as transitions, 5, 19, 20, 32–33, 135
Pronunciation, using principles of pho-
    netics for, 390–393
Proper names
    articles with, 359–362
    capitalizing, 344–345
Punctuation
    abbreviations, 333
    absolute elements, 177–178, 335
    addresses, 335
    apostrophe, 213–214, 336–337
    appositives, 246–247, 334, 336, 338
    brackets, 340
    colon, 144, 336
    comma, 43–45, 72–73, 278, 334–335
    comma splice, 72–73
    complex sentences, 44–45
    complimentary close, 278
    compound sentences, 335
    dash, 338
    dates, 335
    direct address, 177, 335
    direct quotation, 335, 336, 340–342
    exclamation point, 334
    geographical names, 335
    hyphen, 338–339
    italics, using, 340–341
    numbers, 335, 338
    parentheses, 339–340
    parenthetical elements, 177–179, 335, 338
    period, 333
    to prevent misreading, 335, 339
    question mark, 333, 342, 343
    quotation marks, 302, 341–343
    restrictive and nonrestrictive elements,
        104–105
    reversed names, 335
    rules for, 333–343
    run-on sentences, 74
    salutation, 144
    semicolon, 142–143, 336
    series, 48–49
    to show possession, 336–337
    time reference, 336
    titles, 336
    variety of, 302
"Purple Membrane of Salt-Loving Bac-
    teria, The" (Stoeckenius), 208–209, 317
Purpose, 2, 5, 131, 134, 272, 303

Question
    concluding with, 241
    modals in, 76
    rhetorical, 276
Question mark, 333
    and quotation marks, 342–343
Quotation, 197, 232
    brackets in, 340
    comma with, 127
    concluding with, 240, 242–243
    direct, 278, 335, 336, 341–342
    indirect, 341
    interrupted, 343
    in introduction, 204, 209–210
Quotation marks, 302
    rules for use of, 341–343

Rau, Santha Rama, 8, 22
Reader's Digest, 313
Reasoning, deductive and inductive, 9
"Recipe for a Breakfast Dish" (Twain), 304
"Recycling Social Man" (Dubos), 154, 187–
    188, 285–286
Redundancy, 101–102, 211–212; see also
    Wordiness
Reference
    broad, 149
    correct pronoun, 148–149
    divided, 149
    weak, 149
Relative clause, defined, 388
Relative pronouns, 113, 180
    correct agreement of, 247–249
"Relays" (DeFrance), 35
Relevance, 2, 19, 95, 197, 266
Religions, capitalizing names of, 344
Remote cause, 196–197
Repetition, 4, 5, 33, 35, 68, 147, 160, 180,
    211, 261
    in developing the English paragraph, 10
    of structural unit for coherence, 293–295
    as transition, 19, 20
    word, 263–265, 272, 273, 275, 291, 293
    unnecessary, 101
Restrictive clauses, 104–105, 160
Restrictive modifier, defined, 388
Restrictive elements, 104–105
Rhetorical patterns, cultural differences in,
    3–4
Rhetorical question, 262, 276, 298, 300
    concluding with, 240–242
    in introduction, 204, 209
    as transition, 19, 20
Rhythm, 130, 147, 275, 294, 303
Ripley, S. Dillon, 222
"Robert Frost and New England" (Mac-
    Leish), 222
Robinson, Francis P., 36–37
Roiphe, Anne, 240
Rolling Stone, The, 327–329
Roman numerals in outlining, 131

Rudd, Walter, G., 138–139
Rules
  for capitalization, 343–345
  for punctuation, 333–343
  for spelling, 345–350
Run-on sentences, 74
Ruud, Juhan T., 273

Sacred terms, capitalizing, 345
Sakharov, Andrei D., 294
Salutation, punctuating, 144, 278, 336
San Francisco *Examiner*, 97, 159–160, 187
Saturday Review, 206
Saturday Review/World, 154, 186–188,
  264–265, 285–286, 294
Sauer, E. G. F., 154
Schrag, Peter, 68, 166–168, 274–275
Schulz, Charles, 157
"Science and the Citizen," 207–208
"Science and Ethics" (Haldane), 269–270,
  272
Science and Human Life (Haldane), 268–
  269
"Science Has Spoiled My Supper" (Wylie),
  265
Scientific American, 19–20, 69, 165–166,
  208, 209, 242, 273, 284, 317
"Scientific Experiment, A," 193–194, 266
Scientific writing: *see* Technical writing
Sea Around Us, The (Carson), 2, 164, 268
Second Sex, The (Beauvoir), 243
Semicolon, 64, 73, 74, 95, 127, 142–143,
  160, 165, 227, 262, 292, 302
  and quotation marks, 342
  rules for using, 336
Sentence
  arrangement of words in, 3
  defined, 2, 388
  redundant, 212
  run-on, 74
  stringy, 117, 118
  topic, 3, 5–10, 67, 68, 129, 134–135, 164
Sentence fragment, 84–85
Sentence length 35, 38, 71, 98, 276, 303
  controlling, 235
  variety in, 40–42, 63, 160, 168, 292, 294,
  298, 302
Sentence openings, variety in, 38–39, 244–
  246
Sentence structure, 272
  complex, 44
  compound, 44–45, 56, 182, 288
  compound-complex, 44
  and length, variety in, 40–42
  periodic, 102–103
  simple, 44, 55, 56, 98–99, 388
Separate comparative or contrastive sections, development in, 166–168, 172–
  175
Separation of subject and predicate, 307
Sequential development, 18

Series, 160, 245, 262, 292, 293, 302
  punctuating, 32, 48–49, 64, 143, 334
Shafer, Stephen, 195, 200
Shall, 75, 77
Should, 36, 75–77
Showing possession, 81–83; *see also* Pos-
  session
Siddhartha (Hesse), 273
Similarities: *see* Comparison and contrast
Simile, 175–177, 193, 244
  extended, 177
Simple sentence, 44, 55, 56
  defined, 388
  variety in the, 98–99
Simplicity in writing, 199, 244
Singular, 81–82; *see also* Number
Sit, set, 380
Skinner, Brian, J., 233
Smithsonian, 70, 153, 205, 254–256, 277,
  283
Smuts, Robert W., 4–5, 20, 21, 220–221
Soul on Ice (Cleaver), 188
Spatial development, 4, 65–67, 94, 271
  transitions for, 64–66
Spatial paragraph, the, 63–91
Species, 230, 231
Specific to general organization, 138
Specific detail, 227, 262, 292
Specific terms, writing in, 69–70
Specifics, 69–70, 92, 95, 140, 171, 227, 238,
  239, 262, 292
Speech, parts of, defined, 386; *see also*
  individual listings
Spelling, 339
  British versus American, 142
  lists, 348–351
  rules for, 345–350
"Spider and the Wasp, The" (Petrun-
  kevitch), 176
Splice, comma, 72–73, 143
Statement, thesis, 126, 129, 134–135, 204–
  205, 240, 241, 243, 302; *see also* Topic
  sentence
Stationary, stationery, 380
Statistics, 69–70, 96–97, 197
  in introduction, 204, 207–208
Stegner, Wallace, 176
Stems, word, 365–371
Stephenson, F. Richard, 284
Stoeckenius, Walter, 208–209, 317
Stranger in the Village (Baldwin), 243
Stress, italics for, 341
Stringy sentence, 117, 118
Strong active verbs, using, 43
Structural unit, repeating for coherence,
  293–295
Structure, sentence, 40–45, 56, 98–99, 102–
  103, 182, 272, 288, 388
Style, 26, 84, 244, 294, 303
  monotonous, 40–41

varied, 41–42
in writing, 271–276
Subdivision, 8
Subject, 38, 39, 53, 70, 84, 215
   agreement of verb and, 114–115
   compound, 114
   defined, 388
   separation of predicate and, 307
"Subjection of Women, The" (Hardwick), 244
Subjunctive mood, 385
Subordinating adverbs, 72–73
Subordinating conjunctions, defined, 383
Subordination, 19, 21–24, 31, 32, 63, 92, 93, 98, 127, 193, 194, 199, 217–218, 238, 261, 262, 276, 302
Substantive, defined, 388–389
Such, Such Were the Joys (Orwell), 207
Suffixes, 346–347, 373–376
   adjective-forming, 375–376
   adverb-forming, 374–375
   common, 350–351
   defined, 365, 373
   noun-forming, 374–375
   verb-forming, 376
Summary, concluding with, 240, 241
Summation, 21
Sunset Books, 205, 208, 211
Superlatives, irregular, 279–280
"Survey Q3R Study Method, The" (Robinson), 36–37
Surveying (McCormack), 10
"Survival" (Cousins), 201–203
Symbols
   as transitions, 19
   plural of, 337
Synonyms as transitions, 19, 195

"Teaspoon, A" (Garrison), 231
Technical English, noun compounds in, 109–110
Technical writing, 19–20, 34–35, 139, 207
   comparison in, 165
   passive voice in, 54
Ten Contemporary Thinkers (Krutch), 275
Tense, 387
   defined, 389
Than, 180
That, 248
The, 50, 107, 150–151, 281–282, 355–362, 382
There (expletive), 70
There, their, they're, 380
Thesis statement, 126, 129, 134–135, 302
   concluding with, 240, 241, 243
   in introduction, 304-205
   see also Topic sentence
"Thinking of Men and Machines, The" (Troll), 204–205

"38 Who Saw Murder Didn't Call the Police" (Gansberg), 243
Thomas, Gordon A., 19–20
Thoreau, Henry David, 176
Thought pattern, 3, 9
"Three New Yorks, The" (White), 266–267, 272
Thurber, James, 124–125, 288–289, 305, 330–331
Time, 191, 210
Time, possessive of, 81
Time reference, punctuating, 336
"Titanic, The" (Lord), 164–165
Titles
   capitalizing, 344, 345
   italicizing, 340
   punctuating, 278, 336, 342
To, too, two, 380
"Tomorrow: The View from Red Square" (Sakharov), 294
Tone, 26, 203–204
   in writing, 303–306
"Tooth, the Whole Tooth, and Nothing but the Tooth, The" (Benchley), 258
Topic outline, 18
Topic sentence, 2, 3, 5–10, 17, 18, 67, 68, 129, 134–135, 164, 270, 300
   placement of, 7–10, 31, 64, 67, 134, 300
   see also Thesis statement
Topper, Michael A., 233–234
"Touching—and Being Touched" (Masters and Johnson), 313
Tramp Abroad, A (Twain), 304
Transitions, 2, 4–5, 19–21, 32, 34–38, 47, 63, 64, 67, 92, 95, 126, 127, 145, 159, 160, 166, 168, 171, 172, 174, 177, 194, 199, 200, 227, 246, 261, 263, 266, 272, 276, 291–296, 298, 301, 302
   for comparison and contrast, 161
   coordinating conjunctions as, 229
   for expository development, 93–94
   between paragraphs, 135–136
   within paragraphs, review of, 277
   pronouns as, 32–33
   for spatial development, 64–66
   synonyms as, 195
Travel Guide to Washington, 208
Troll, John H., 204–205
Trollope, Anthony, 263
Trudeau, Garry B., 191, 192
Twain, Mark, 241–242, 304–305
"21st-Century Woman—Free at Last?, The" (Luce), 186–187, 264–265, 272
Two Cheers for Democracy (Forster), 140–141

Uncountable nouns, articles with 50, 357–359
Understanding restrictive and nonrestrictive elements, 104–105

Ungar, Sanford J., 284–285, 318
Unity, 130, 239
  in English paragraph, 2, 5, 7-10, 18, 19
  see also Coherence
Universe and Dr. Einstein, The (Barnett), 137–138
"University Lore: U.S.A.," 261–263, 266
Unnecessary expletives, 71
"U.S.A.—Many Countries in One, The," 63–64, 67
"U.S.A.'s Bicentennial, The," 97
Usage
  British versus American, 142
  glossary of standard, 376–380
  levels of appropriateness and, 237–238
"Using a Computer" (Rudd), 138–139
Using figurative languauge, 175–177; see also Figurative language
Using participles and participial phrases, 116–118
Using strong active verbs, 43

Variety, sentence, 24, 54, 238
  in sentence length, 40–42, 126, 160, 168, 199, 228, 292, 294, 298, 302
  in sentence openings, 38–39, 244–246
  in sentence structure, 40–42, 199, 292
  in the simple sentence, 98–99
Verb, phrasal, 52, 387
Verb-forming suffixes, 376
Verb phrase, 114, 387
Verbal, 389; see also Gerunds, Infinitives, Participles
Verbosity: see Wordiness
Verbs
  agreement of subject and, 114–115
  colorful, 43
  defined, 389
  finite, 116, 117
  irregular principal parts, 351–355
  linking, 385
  modals, 36, 64, 75–81, 127
  mood, 385
  principal parts, 387
  tense, 387, 389
  using strong active, 43
  voice, 53–55, 389
View of My Own, A (Hardwick), 244
"Violence in America," 153
Vocabulary, 1, 35, 43, 272
"Vocabularies of Aboriginal Languages" (Nida), 96
Voice, 53–55, 389

Walden (Thoreau), 176
Warriner, John E., 154, 223, 265
Weak pronoun reference, 149
Weak verbs, 43

Weaver, Warren, 295–296, 302
Well, good, 379
"We're Different but Alike" (Harris), 159–160
West, Dame Rebecca, 199, 200
"Whales" (Carson), 268, 272
"What Has Posterity Ever Done for Me?" (Heilbroner), 210
"What I Believe" (Forster), 140–141
"What Inflation Means" (Wyckoff), 70
"What Is a Rodeo?," 227–228, 231
"What Will Go on Around the Mall" (Park), 254
Whether . . . or, 182
Which, 248
While, 380
White, E. B., 6, 7, 21, 266–267, 271, 272
Who's, whose, 380
"Why the Sky Looks Blue" (Jeans), 197–198
Will, 75–77
Williamson, Samuel T., 206
Without Feathers (Allen), 258–260
Wolf Willow (Stegner), 176
Word arrangement, 306–307, 311–312
Word choice, 303–305
Word division, hyphenation to show, 339
Word order: see Word arrangement
Word repetition, 262–263, 272, 273, 275, 291, 293
Word stems, 365–371
Wordiness, 70, 71, 100–102, 117, 147
  review of, 211–212
Words
  eliminating unnecessary, 100–102
  italicizing, 340
  plural of, 337
  similar in sound or form, 349–350
  transitional, 19, 20; see also Transitions
"Working Wives and Mothers" (Smuts), 4–5
"Women's Liberation Revisited," 210
Women and Work in America (Smuts), 4–5, 21, 220–221
Would, 75, 77, 78
Would like, 78
Would rather, 78
Wrenn, C. L., 298–302
Writing a conclusion, 239–244
Writing an introduction, 203–211
Writing a longer composition, 129–130
Writing in specific terms, 69–70
Wyckoff, Frank C., 70
Wylie, Philip, 265

"You Americans Are Murdering the Language" (Conesford *et al.*), 223
You're, your, 380